Planting Noah's Garden

BOOKS BY SARA STEIN

My Weeds: A Gardener's Botany

The Body Book

The Evolution Book

The Science Book

Noah's Garden:
Restoring the Ecology of Our Own Back Yards

PLANTING NOAH'S GARDEN

FURTHER ADVENTURES IN BACKYARD ECOLOGY

Sara Stein

A Frances Tenenbaum Book
Houghton Mifflin Company
Boston New York 1997

For information about permission to reproduce selections from this book, write to Permissions, Houghton Mifflin Company, 215 Park Avenue South, New York, New York 10003.

For information about this and other Houghton Mifflin trade and reference books and multimedia products, visit The Bookstore at Houghton Mifflin on the World Wide Web at http://www.hmco.com/trade/.

Book design and composition: Dianne Jaquith Schaefer, Designworks

Aerial photographs on pages x–1 and 268–69 courtesy of Daniel R. Gage / Art of Adventure Photography. Vegetation map on pages 264–65 adapted from map by W. D. Billings, with permission from Cambridge University Press.

Library of Congress Cataloging-in-Publication Data
Stein, Sara Bonnett.
  Planting Noah's garden: further adventures in backyard ecology /
Sara Stein.
    p. cm.
  "A Frances Tenenbaum book."
  Includes index.
  ISBN 0-395-70960-1
1. Garden ecology. 2. Garden ecology — United States.   3. Backyard gardens — United States.   4. Natural gardens, American.   5. Gardening to attract wildlife — United States.   I. Title.
    QH541.5.G37S75 1996
      639.9'2 — dc20 96-32230 CIP

Printed in the United States of America

RMT 10 9 8 7 6 5 4 3 2 1

For Marty

Contents

How to Plant Noah's Garden

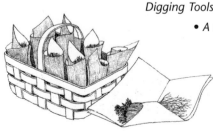

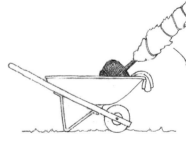

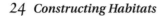

Introduction

Planting Noah's Garden follows its forerunner, *Noah's Garden*, by about three years and by popular demand. Readers clamoring for one's next book is not a phenomenon that happens often—or usually at all—in an author's career. Nor can this author take credit for it. Rather, the book that stimulated such interest relates an experience already shared by many people, though perhaps inarticulately, as a muffled uneasiness or a blurred vision. *Noah's Garden* said what a lot of people had been thinking. The story the book related is simple. My husband, Marty, and I had groomed and shaped our suburban property in the traditional manner and with such energy that in the space of a few years we had transformed the original overgrown farmland into expansive lawns and pretty gardens of which we were quite proud. It hadn't occurred to us that changes in the landscape would affect the land's inhabitants. Quite suddenly, from one spring to the next, great numbers of birds, to whose song we had at first awakened at dawn, deserted us. So, too, was the land abandoned by foxes and weasels, ladybugs and fireflies, black snakes and toads. We had destroyed their cover; we had cleared away their food.

With these changes in the land arose problems that, in our gardening inexperience, we had not anticipated: the cost, the labor, the aphids, the slugs. A well-groomed yard does not work as an ecosystem; it is as helpless as it is barren. We lost by our misdirected effort more than a list of species: we lost our own ease with the landscape.

This realization was, I think, the common experience that found a ready audience. Over the last fifty years of suburban development—and with alarming speed in the last decade—the whole fabric of the natural world in which we once were wrapped has become threadbare: we are lonesome and uncomfortably exposed.

The rest of the story gave solace. Marty and I patched our land back together. That was, of course, not as simple as baring it had been. But as meadows grew and thickets spread and woods filled in, the effect was as dramatic (and as entertaining) as when you drop a napkin on the floor and your cat appropriates it or you open a can and your dog comes running: the animals returned. And, working from the clues our replantings had provided, the very land began to reassemble itself into rich and lively communities as though it, like us, remembered the patterns it had known in earlier times.

So did the book that arose from this experience assemble a readership that flocked to it for shelter and nourishment—and in thirst: *Noah's Garden* was passed around, given as a gift, reread, dog-eared, underlined as though to squeeze the last drop from it. I was asked to speak, at first locally—a reading at a library, a slide show at a garden club—and over the months at more distant places and to larger audiences as the ripples widened from the book's first small splash.

In this way I came to meet the people who fill these pages. For not only was I asked to write another book, I was given the book itself: the cast of characters, the settings and the stories, the plot of how all of us together and all across the country are planting Noah's Garden.

PART ONE

The Further Adventures of a Gardener-Ecologist

America as it was when bison and butterflies roamed free: the Konza Prairie Research Natural Area, a preserve of the Nature Conservancy managed for ecological research by Kansas State University. (James Nedresky)

1 Travels with Butterflies

THE WILD TURKEYS have returned. We hear them gabbling in the red maple swamp below the pond. Now that I've seen them emerge from such hideaways on several occasions—and a friend reports a flock of six practically stationed beneath her birdfeeder all last winter—I wonder if I didn't waste my worry on them during the years I was writing *Noah's Garden*.

But two more years have passed, and I've found plenty to worry about without the turkeys.

Aliens, for instance. Green invaders like the buckthorn that infiltrates our woods. And lying about the buckthorn hedge. I wrote in that book that I had removed it. I hadn't. I intended to remove it; I thought I would have done so by the date of publication. But each time I faced the hedge's healthy growth, its thick foliage and shining berries, the loppers went limp in my hands.

The hedge is gone now, honest. That much is off my mind.

I expended considerable worry on the duck potatoes. I tried to get a good crop going in the pond to feed the ducks, but the muskrats ate them up. That's like eating the seed corn. Dumb muskrats. Then the muskrats disappeared. So I worried about them.

I had butterflies in my stomach all the time. But I know the cause wasn't really muskrats or aliens. It was strangers.

In all my years of writing, I'd been closeted up here in my attic, wielding my computer like the Wizard in his booth. With the publication of *Noah's Garden*, however, the curtain was whisked away and there I was, small and scared, flushed from my attic like a turkey from the woods, traveling with butterflies and gabbling in public.

I became a writer by accident some twenty-five years ago when I was an editor at a book packaging firm, putting together authors and illustrators to create specific books for publishers. I couldn't find a suitable author for a particular series of children's books, so I wrote them. It seemed easy enough: you take a subject you know and dress it becomingly in words so that others, too, will understand. I wrote about the things that frighten and pain young children: I'd been a child; I had four of my own. I wrote about pets (we had nurtured everything from spiders to coyotes) and, expansively and with relish, I wrote about my first love, biology. As my boys grew, I wrote for increasingly older children—the words changing, the sentences lengthening, the concepts becoming more subtle over time—until it came about that the boys were men and I was writing for adults.

How can I explain that change? One doesn't relinquish childhood when writing for children. Rather, one joins the other kids almost in a conspiracy removed from, if not in opposition to, the grownups. We, the children, delight in spiders in part because they disgust our elders, or we light inwardly with transcendence, glow with the sun, and go with the wind in joyful contrast to parents who have forgotten the language of the birds. When I began to write for adults, it was as though I had traded the comfort of the nursery supper table, where I and my sisters had fought and giggled and slopped our food, to join the guests downstairs in sedate and important conversation. Would my parents approve of my behavior? Would my readers?

At least in those early days my feet were firmly on the ground, not dangling, as they were when I first sat with the grownups during dinner: I wrote about what I knew, children and animals and plants. But, as though the child in me stubbornly refused either to behave properly or to leave the table, the words came out edged with subversion—or perhaps I myself was subverted by my subject.

Noah's Garden began in innocence. I had written a book for gardeners on botany, using weeds as my examples, and planned to do the same with zoology—a matching treatise on the habits and adaptations of common backyard animals, snails and toads and starlings. But I looked around our own land—the few acres that my husband and I had cleared and mowed to make a pleasant garden—and found that many of the animals had slipped away without my having noticed. *Noah's Garden* became the story of what has gone wrong with our increasingly inanimate land. The conversation turned to whether we can fix it. The subject shifted from animals and vegetables to the whole body of the land—to ecology.

And with that shift, the solid ground of surety sank away.

When speaking of ecology, one can't surely say that one knows what one is talking about. I know of no ecologist who would claim more than that he or she has a still shot from a movie of unknown plot, without beginning or conclusion, and with a largely anonymous cast of characters. Ecology is seductive, but slippery and certainly subversive, especially as applied to gardening. One forsakes maintaining a static floral display for managing a dynamic floral-faunal-microbial system, and whereas following the rules of horticulture to the letter will yield a perfect pumpkin or a worthy rose, ecology has no rules, and even adhering to its principles doesn't necessarily feed one's pride. One must learn to be satisfied with surprise—and mostly I'm surprised to learn how difficult that is. This was brought home to me one day—for the thousandth time—with the particular sting of fallen pride.

It was October. The warm autumn air was filled with ladybugs, their lifted wings like flecks of gold against the sun. They lit the meadow and, landing, specked with red the leaves and flowers or flew into the house to crowd against the ceiling in search of crannies where they might safely spend the winter. Ladybugs—and their business with aphids, and aphids' business with ants, and both of their goings-on with plants—have been my emblem of how critically the least of creatures is enmeshed in that trackless wilderness of circumstance and relationship we call ecology. The beetle's demise on suburban land has illustrated for me how, by simply mowing lawns or spraying roses, we tinker disastrously with a system that we have neither the intelligence nor the delicacy of perception to ever fully comprehend. What we ought to do, I proclaimed in *Noah's Garden*, is plant a meadow and steer our clumsy feet clear of it while lesser animals, in their vast and cumulative intelligence, run the system for themselves.

And so I did. And here was the result: ten thousand ladybugs—*my* ladybugs—born in my meadow, nourished on my aphids, preparing to winter under my unraked leaves and within my uncut rotting trees and in my screenless window frames. Do as I say, I said to myself—speaking as though to you, my present reader—and you, too, can lavish on the land the gift of ladybugs.

But there was something funny about these ladybugs. They didn't quite look familiar: they had few or many or no spots. I couldn't find such a variety of ladybird beetle in my insect guides.

I went off later in the week to receive an award from a horticultural society—brushed my shaggy hair, wore my pearls, felt momentarily deserving of a silver (plated) medal—and returned to a newspaper article my husband Marty had left for me on the kitchen table. It seems that the ladybugs were the offspring of a more southerly species, released by the USDA to control crop pests, and they were everywhere swarming the neat lawns of suburbia, oblivious of my principles and in numbers equal to those arising well fed from the meadow. My "own" little two-spot was nowhere to be seen.

The episode of the ladybugs happened only recently. I chose the story out of many surprising turnabouts because its drama matches the degree of my abashment at never really being sure that what I advise will have much of an effect or, if it does, what the effect will be, or whether an intended effect will be swamped by others that we can't control.

The Year of the Ladybug is the same year in which I finally gave in to arbicultural advice and had the scale insects on the autumn cherry sprayed to save the tree's sickly life. Where were the lady beetles when I needed them? The summer before, an unpredicted coyote had disposed of a predictable meadowful of rabbits. Even the year before that, as *Noah's Garden* was going to press, this mourner of past turkeys learned of the depredations that growing flocks were wreaking on upstate vineyards and knew there would be grownups laughing at my tears.

Or, worse, sending me back to the attic to consider the coyote that, I heard, had also eaten a neighbor's pussycat.

I lectured for a year in unreality. Face frozen; limbs clumsy. As though the body on the airplane wasn't mine. As though the voice from the podium belonged to someone else. Women will understand what I mean by an "ugly day," when one perceives oneself as numb and lumpish, and no clothes look right. I had a year of those days.

And yet it was the best year of my life.

The bluebonnets of Texas are real! The cow-devoured hills of California look just as they do in pictures. I met a race horse in Kentucky. I spoke with genuine bluestockings at a fabled club in Boston where the carpets were magnificent but worn. I spoke also using a cardboard carton as a lectern, and once in a barn, and often to garden club women who had reason to be insulted by what I said but never were—or never said so.

Do you realize how generous the people of our country are?

And energetic, and resourceful, and loving of the land. In Georgia, a young woman had organized a plant rescue in a forest faced with bulldozers. Before the developer moved in, the group had dug and moved a hundred thousand ferns and wildflowers of some hundred species, several of them rare. I met seed collectors, frog pond diggers, hedgerow planters, bird watchers, and even a woman tagging butterflies in Maine. A youngster at an evening meeting otherwise attended by adults was determined to replace some portion of his parents' lawn with meadow. A grandmother at a workshop had dedicated her retirement years to replanting her whole property as a refuge. In many places, young couples overwhelmed by their first experience of land ownership and bewildered about where to start nevertheless vowed not to repeat the landscapes of the past. I was challenged once about woodchucks, never about turkeys or coyotes. Still, I felt legs awkwardly dangling, feet not anchored to the ground.

My malady was a stew of worry about getting lost and being late, discomfort with strangers and strange places, and stage fright. The butterflies distracted me from writing. (I was supposed to be working on this book.) Letters kept coming. I answered them. A correspondence developed, and in this armchair mode of travel I met more people still, and from more places. Ruth in Arizona cut a metal tank in half to serve water to desert birds. Steve in Omaha watched a stalk of blazingstar in his city yard bobbing under the slight weight of a deer mouse fattening on its seeds. Jo Ann in Arkansas nourished "tree islands" in the lawn. Sabrina in Iowa sent me camassias. My computer shows I wrote 250 letters that year.

All the while I fretted that I wasn't getting any real work done, that there would be no book, that I had lost the thread of it. And all the while the threads were coming together.

You are the fabric of this book. You whom I know but have never met. You whom I've met but never knew by name. You who told the stories, raised the issues, asked the questions that must now be addressed.

You, and your land.

Rising in an airplane higher than the clouds, cities shrink, highways narrow, and the land is unified. There are no lot lines from the sky, no state boundaries, not even clear distinctions among geographical areas whose names—Piedmont, Hill Country, High Sierra—are so distinct on paper. The type of vegetation changes smoothly, the way colors in a pointillist painting shift without hard edges. The land each of you owns is one dot among the millions that compose the painting of our country. Change the tone a bit and the painting changes. Change many dots and the shape of the future is transformed. That much I'm sure about, and I'm sure also of the necessity for change.

I received a report from Steven Rothe, the correspondent whose quarter-acre lot lies in Omaha, on the subject of his New England aster. I hadn't known New England asters grew in Nebraska, but Steven is a stickler for planting species that are native to his region. He is cautious, though; he tries a single specimen before he plants a dozen. So he had, at the time, one aster. Talk about small dots! Yet during the course of the fall migration flock after flock of monarch butterflies had arrived to nectar at it.

The monarchs I know migrate south along the eastern seaboard, which is verdant and interesting from the sky. Others follow the Pacific coast over terrain that is even more distinctive. I hadn't pictured these butterflies slicing straight down the middle of the continent through some of the driest, flattest, most featureless land in America. One doesn't mind having an aisle seat when flying over Nebraska. But these butterflies, from their lesser height and with their different vision, must actually see the landscape as a picnic scene by Georges Seurat, in points of colored light. Twenty monarchs at a time had zeroed in on Steve's one purple beacon.

The hazards of my jittery flights were nothing compared to those faced by these butterflies, the only long-distance fliers of their kind. I was delayed overnight once because of bad weather, and the airline put me up and fed me well. I enjoyed snack flights and dinner flights; the most I could complain about was meals of juice with peanuts. Who is feeding the monarchs as they migrate from our northlands all the way to their wintering grounds south of the border? What happens when they are grounded by a storm?

The southward trip is undertaken by the last generation to hatch as the season turns toward autumn, and this generation is all there is: no eggs are left behind. Only two sites are available for survival into spring. One is in the cloud-bound mountains northwest of Mexico City, at Angangueo. The other is in California, near San Luis Obispo. Populations west of the Rockies winter in California; all the rest fly to Mexico. *The Guinness Book of Records* honors a monarch, tagged in Canada on September 6, 1986, who arrived in Mexico on January 15, 1987, after a journey of 2,133 miles. Tens of millions attempt the migration, but the death rate is appalling. During the months-long trip, each life depends on the late-blooming flowers at which it nectars: dots of yellow and purple, goldenrod and aster.

The return is more hazardous still. This aged generation, the last of its kind, has been preserved through the winter in suspended animation, lulled by the cool air and dewy from the mists of its mountain fastness. It is now nearing the end of its life—and, if it doesn't reproduce, the end of the species as well.

Every schoolchild has been taught that monarch butterflies lay their eggs on just one group of plants—the genus Asclepias, the milkweeds, the only plants their caterpillars can eat. If the butterfly-tagger I met had her way, everybody would be equally aware that the monarchs' northward migration is accomplished by many generations, each of which completes only one short lap of the journey before laying eggs and dying, and everyone would share her concern for the implications of this reproductive relay.

The species requires a virtually continent-wide distribution of milkweeds to see it through its summer odyssey to the final generation, which turns south once more in the fall.

You can't see small roads from an airplane, much less the milkweeds that might grow along their edges. You can't see what people have planted in their gardens. But when you see a monarch traveling through your yard, you have to realize that so far, at least, and in spite of our seemingly disparate biotas, there is an underlying uniformity to this land: we are united in milkweeds; we are bound by flights of butterflies.

No Yankee gardener can write for long about gardening without hearing complaints that information about the Northeast does not apply elsewhere in the country. Californians especially claim that their state is like nowhere else on Earth. And it certainly seemed so to me, delivered to San Francisco from the airport by a mad taxi careening down mountain grades that no god could ever have intended to be city streets. We passed blurred palms, flashes of gold and purple foliage, violently blooming vines, and what appeared by their odd shapes to be

Monarchs nectaring at New England aster during fall migration. (Virginia P. Weinland)

giant bonsai. What is a person used to plain grass and maple trees to make of such exotica? I did not feel at home.

But I was not yet in California.

California has plenty of plain grass and maple trees. Its oaks grow from acorns just like my oaks. Ferns green its woods as they do New England woods. Milkweeds and asters grow along the roadsides. The state's most common gold-enrod is the same species that is most common here. San Francisco's flora looks exotic because it *is* exotic—Australian, African, Mediterranean. Getting out of the city took me back to my native land.

Among my destinations was Larner Seeds, a landscaping and seed supply company in Bolinas that works with native California species. A path took me through a garden of shrubs and grasses representing various coastal and inland communities. The proprietor, Judith Lowry, told me that the garden bloomed with many flowers, too, but they would not germinate until the fall rains began, later in the month. The only vivid color at that time of year was a scarlet Zauschneria called California fuschia; the rest of the garden was pale but not unfamiliar.

The bayberry was unmistakable, although it is a different Myrica species than the one I know and is called wax myrtle in the West. In Judith's yard and later at a botanical garden devoted to California species, I recognized redbud, alder, elder-berry, buckeye, gooseberry, huckleberry, and hazel. Some differences were strik-ing. What easterner familiar with trailing arbutus would have taken the madrone tree to be of the same genus? I can also be excused for not recognizing a six-foot salal as a Gaultheria; our species of that genus is the six-*inch* ground cover called wintergreen.

But back home, perusing the Larner Seeds catalog, I read that salal often grows with western huckleberry. So does our wintergreen often grow with eastern huck-leberry. In fact, the two grow together right outside my kitchen between the stones of a terrace as hot and dry as California's coastal scrub.

I won't belittle that state's diverse and unique flora. New York has 3,022 native species; California has twice that, 6,400, and close to a third of them are found nowhere else. What struck me during that year, though, were similarities.

Everywhere I went, the different landscapes resonated with those I knew well. The Hill Country of Texas, an open and grassy woods of oak and juniper, was like New England fields half grown toward forest, but the Texas landscape was arrest-ed at that point. The ecosystem wasn't strange; it was just too dry to go farther. The western desert echoed with the familiar adaptations of its flora. Glassworts on our sandy coasts look like miniature palo verde trees and similarly depend for both water conservation and photosynthesis on their leafless and succulent green stems. I meet prickly pears here that are as much at home on dry heights above the Hudson as any cactus along the Gila River. If California fuschia dresses Judith's garden in scarlet for late summer, so does the similarly deep-throated flame honeysuckle brighten mine—and her Anna's hummingbird and my ruby-throated one recognize red flowers meant for them wherever they occur. Even the little bulbs and bright annuals that carpet Rocky Mountain meadows in such a hurry during their brief July summer have their occasional counterpart here in pink onion, blue curls, and a tiny yellow starry thing so small that I can't find it in my wildflower guide but I came upon it blooming in the desiccated refuse of an abandoned quarry.

Although such echoes were sometimes mere whispers, I found them as comforting as an old friend in a foreign city. They spoke my language, and it wasn't Gardenese.

If, speaking as a gardener, I say, "Plant a perennial border," you in Arizona ought certainly to object. But if, speaking ecologically, I say, "Plant a grassland," no one anywhere can complain. Your grasses may be different ones; your flowers may be annual or perennial, depending on the length of the growing season and the quantity of rainfall. But there is nowhere on the continent that a meadow system of some sort is not naturally present and therefore can be grown.

Garden writers can't just go on about generic borders without soon dressing them specifically in lilacs or peonies bearing women's names. Ecology is less particular. I can go on for quite a while about systems like wetland thicket, woodland understory, and dryland scrub. I needn't give a rose a name when speaking of a bramble: the term conveys a habitat that may include all sorts of prickly species of wide occurrence and equivalent usefulness to wildlife. This language is so much easier, you see, than Gardenese.

And so very continental!

I came to appreciate how broadly the language of ecology applies when I had completed about a third of my lecture schedule and had traveled about that fraction of the distance across the continent, too. I was walking around the Missouri Botanical Garden with George Yatskievych, the resident expert on the flora of his state, trying to learn what Missouri's "typical" vegetation is.

Right person, dumb question. Missouri, Dr. Yatskievych explained, is one big ecotone, meaning that its vegetation is transitional from one sort to another over the entire state. It is Mississippi floodplain in the southeastern corner, Ozark mountain forest in the middle, and tallgrass prairie as you move northwest. They say of New England that if you don't like the weather, wait a minute;

it will change. In Missouri, if you don't like the ecosystem, drive up the road a piece.

And so I did at other times in other places, coming to realize as the miles passed that while Missouri may be an ecotone on a grand scale, all regions are ecotones at smaller scales. I drove up the Smoky Mountains through forests whose vegetation shifted continually with the altitude. I rode down Long Island through oak woods, past pine barrens, to salt marsh at the shore. A garden writer on Long Island could no more speak for all gardeners on this small glacial dumping ground than a Missourian could speak for prairie, mountain, and riverine gardeners across that great state.

I can, or so I hope.

But there is a snag in the translation. Even at a walking pace, I often had difficulty discerning from the landscape what sort of ecosystem I was in.

Only the black walnut trees along the miles of fences in Kentucky's Bluegrass Country hint that the land was forested before the horses came. Developers of tract housing there or anywhere may leave not a stick or leaf to indicate what might have been the nature of the place. Or the land might have been "corn country," or "rangeland," terms far removed from natural history. Often whatever the land was has been obliterated: the wetland drained, the woodland humus scraped and sold, the desert lichen crust long since destroyed by cattle. My son's suburban lot in California, like the streets of San Francisco, was so bedecked in exotic vegetation that only a little coyote bush sprouting in the vegetable garden reminded me that the land was coastal scrub.

So I worried for some months that even the broadest ecological terms would let slip through the net the majority of homeowners, who, though they may well know they are in Kansas, live on property made strange by the uses and abuses it has survived. My worry was warranted. Ruth Morse in Arizona, who cares for thirsty birds, is a rarity for having discerned in her community of suffering lawns that in fact the land is desert.

But anxiety, as old as life, has an ancient function: it's supposed to make you change your behavior or your attitude; the discomfort is supposed to make you listen to the flutterings in your gut.

What did my butterflies say?

Face reality, and keep your eye on the milkweed.

Ecology's broadest terms, so useful in comprehending theoretical Missouri, are far less useful in describing one's actual lot. Narrower terms apply better. Steven Rothe had bridled at the "city trees" in his yard, alien elms that shade a portion of what once was treeless grassland. But there they are, and that shady corner constitutes "dry woodland" even though Omaha is prairie and the elms are from Siberia.

Your job is to recognize your reality. Mine is to provide you with the means to choose, within that reality, species appropriate to your circumstances, native to your region, commercially available, likely to succeed, but not necessarily resulting in the resurrection on a city lot of grassland that would bury a ranch house to the eaves.

Together, however, we should be able to keep the butterflies fed.

My foolish question in Missouri prompted me to add two items to my library: a pair of wall maps of the coterminous United States and the introductory volume of *Flora of North America*.

The maps resemble satellite photos and are nearly as broad as I am tall. One shows elevation, in a range of shades from mossy bayou to snowy mountain peaks, superimposed on state and county boundaries, major cities, and large towns. St. Louis, where the botanical garden is located, lies at an elevation of 800 feet, whereas the Ozarks reach 2,000 and the northwestern corner of the state levels out to prairie at about 1,000. The second map, in black and white but startlingly three-dimensional, dramatizes landforms and drainage. You can practically feel the water running down the slope of the Midwest to where its three great rivers converge in the Mississippi just above St. Louis.

Volume I of *Flora of North America* is the first offering of a project that will in time expand to twenty volumes describing, from ferns to flowering plants, all the native species from the Mexican border to Alaska and Newfoundland. Since the first volume is an overview, covering such subjects as climate, physiography, soils, and vegetation, I figured that with tome and maps together, I would know better where I was going before I got there.

All went well at first. In the section "Contemporary Vegetation and Phytogeography," a map clearly showed me that Missouri comprises three vegetation types: a prairie province, a coastal plain province, and, cutting between them, the Appalachian province that also includes New York. The characteristic vegetation of each province was described. I was pretty pleased with how well my homework was going.

Then, wouldn't you know it, I ran into Dr. Yatskievych again, this time as coauthor of the chapter "Plant Conservation," and again I was embarrassed. Over most of Missouri, less than 20 percent of the land remains in natural vegetation.

This reality was depicted on a map captioned "Percentage of area potentially covered by natural vegetation for counties in the coterminous United States." The counties colored black had the most natural area—over 80 percent; those with the least remaining were white, and the rest were shown in three shades of gray. The effect was as if a rat had chewed holes in a land that, before there were any counties, would have been solid black. In the western desert and mountain states, the land looks merely nibbled. Central California and the Northwest are definitely gnawed, as are the Gulf states and all of the Southeast. Huge bites have been torn out of the Northeast and Mid-Atlantic states; no rat but a monster seems to have gulped the Central Plains down whole. In nearly a third of the country—including my own county of Westchester—less than 20 percent of the land remains "potentially" natural.

I didn't get the meaning of "potentially" at first. It seemed to mean that such areas are not yet farmed, mined, lumbered, developed, or otherwise too disturbed to support the native vegetation described earlier in the book. But the term, as I read on, became heavy with irony. I was pleased to note that New York doesn't come out half bad on the map—we still have nice black mountain counties in the Catskills and the Adirondacks—but I was appalled to discover that, with the probable exception of Florida (it was not included in the chart), New York has the highest percentage of foreign plant species growing in the wild anywhere on the continent: 36 percent. Amazing. You walk through woods and fields, along roads and waterways, and more than a third of the wild plants you see are immigrants. *Potentially* natural and *actually* natural are not necessarily the same.

California has more aliens altogether—1,160 compared to New York's 1,082—but measured against its native diversity, the proportion is much lower: 18 percent of the total number of species. Among the states for which such figures are available, Arizona has the smallest proportion of exotics, just 7 percent.

The figures don't accurately depict reality, though. Of all the foreign species that have arrived on these shores and successfully naturalized, 60 percent are weeds. A pond I pass on the way into town is circled by purple loosestrife. In that wetland habitat, the vegetation is totally exotic. For all that California has so rich a flora, great stretches of dry hills inland are smothered in Scotch broom. Despite Arizona's relative paucity of exotic species, rangeland there may be infested with grasses imported from Asia, Africa, Europe, and South America.

At the same time that natural areas are shrinking and aliens are spreading, native flora are becoming extinct at an accelerating rate. In the century and a half between 1800 and 1950, 90 native species became extinct. Since 1950 the rate has increased fivefold. *Flora of North America* estimates that by 1998, we will have lost 475 natives in addition to the previous 90—and in a third the time.

Flora's plea for conserving natural areas is understandably passionate and urgent.

But if, in my home state, more than a third of the remaining wild vegetation is alien species, is there really any natural growth at all? And if most naturalized aliens are weeds, does even a pristine patch left undisturbed somewhere in the Adirondacks have a chance of lasting?

No one to whom I spoke during my travels challenged me about the need to preserve and to plant native flora. Had they done so, my sometimes slouching spine of surety would have stiffened as to the sound of prowlers in the night. But I was asked a zillion questions that, simmering in my worry stew, boiled down to what seemed to me a nearly overwhelming responsibility: to show people how to put into effect what they had been inspired to envision.

Few people knew their native plants. Of those who were familiar with their wildflowers, almost none could name the grasses that grow with them. Some had learned that there are native plant nurseries; most bought what was available from local garden centers. Only in the final months of lecturing did I come to realize that the meadows other people mentioned and the meadows I meant were as different from one another as an English hayfield from a Wisconsin prairie.

I bumped hard and often into assumptions that apply to gardening, but not to any garden that I had in mind. Feeding and watering barely enter ecology's lexicon. The careful sculpting of a hole to receive a treasured specimen is not possible when digging for the dozens or even hundreds of plants required for restoration, and rough holes are anyway better for the field-grown, bareroot, mail order stock that I rely on but that most gardeners don't. This sort of work requires economies that aren't written about by horticulturalists, who commonly take pride in the most laborious processes and the most expensive plants. The very goal of horticulture—to grow each individual to perfection—is belied by ecology's communal aspiration: in natural habitats, individuals are subordinate to the system that incorporates them into the body of the land.

As I grasped the fabric of gardening assumptions that this book would have to unravel and the gaps that it would have to mend, I realized that environmentalism also has its snags. Almost everyone was shocked to hear that I don't compost (but neither do I rake) and that I use herbicide (but suffer the little aphids to suck the milkweed). The idea that anyone should kill barberries put birders almost in despair. How could anyone wish to extirpate that popular winter fruit?

The environmentalists I met ranged from the romantic—all plants are embraceable—to the uncompromising—not just native plants, and not just those that occur naturally in one's region, but only genotypes grown from wild seed collected within fifty miles. I scored low on both poetic and purist scales. With all due cringing from the blows this confession will invite, I admit both to planting exotic butterfly bush and to killing (with chemicals!) native goldenrod. I had my reasons. They were misguided or pragmatic. I'm not perfect.

Noah built a wooden boat. He did not deliver it to Eden.

*I*n fact, over the year my worries gradually lessened. If, below the airplane, there remains some trace of biological integrity that has escaped our hand, there remains in us also an underlying ethic toward the land that we have not yet been able to strangle in ourselves.

During the summer, before I retired to my attic to write again, I had an unsettling experience. I had gotten from my conservation department a booklet listing the plant species protected in New York State. Among them were a threatened goldenrod and a declining milkweed that I'd come across at nature preserves, where you'd think protected species would be safe. But a protected species, I read, is merely one that can't be picked or uprooted without the owner's permission. The law doesn't say that the owner must protect a listed species from the weeds that are smothering it (as was the case with the goldenrod, already nearly vanished under honeysuckle vines) or that you must protect it from being mowed before it has had a chance to mature its seed (as had happened to the milkweed, whose pods I found rotting on the ground). So there, on those nature preserves, that goldenrod and milkweed will soon be gone.

The same two species grow on my place. They grow here because I planted them. But I'm free to stand by while they die of neglect or even to kill them outright if I want.

Because they're mine: I own the land.

How strange a notion! The perception of ownership isn't shared by any of the creatures who live on the land, or from it, or cross over it. I own the plants, but not the relationships by which their roots are nourished, or their flowers pollinated, or their seeds dispersed. I own the dirt, but not the living systems that maintain it. Yet ownership gives me license to harm all these things that don't belong to me.

This thought was strange enough in intimate surroundings, touching the goldenrod's velvet leaves, stroking the milkweed's silk. It became more uncanny still as I watched the whole width of the continent, coast to coast, all owned, every acre of it, slide slowly beneath the belly of the airplane bound for California. Conservation departments, nature preserves, the very law of the land, can't protect your lot or mine. It's up to us to do it of our own free will because we understand that the land is not our own but only in our keeping.

So, in California and the next few stops—there were just three to go—that's what I said. And I found that my voice, croaking sometimes from an allergy to speaking, joined a chorus already sure in its conviction. While parents can teach their children table manners, science can't teach us the details of how we should behave in the grownup world of ecology, but grace of manner toward the land, as civility toward people, is a more general and a more enduring state of mind that I had no difficulty conveying. The words had a nice ring to them, but that is because the ethic they expressed is imprinted on our very souls.

So did the Wizard behind his curtain express to those who flushed him out this simple truth: you have the heart, you have the brain, you have the courage. All I have to do is supply the information that will get you back to Kansas, and that, I think, the butterflies have taught me.

Virginia P. Weinland

A buffalograss lawn with wine cups and blue-bonnets near Austin, Texas. The yard is mowed once a summer, after the flowers have gone to seed. (Rosa Finsley)

Planting Noah's Garden

*2 New American Lawn:
First Garden*

I SAW A LOT OF LAWNS as I traveled around the country. I didn't intend to look at lawns; it's just that most places don't offer much else to see. Other arguments aside—noise, pollution, wasted water, too much work—lawns are so boring. What if everybody dressed the same? Why should yards wear uniforms?

A few lawns I remember because they didn't look like everybody else's. One, in the Catskill Mountains, had that dreaded disease . . . *violets!* Blue violets, yellow violets, white ones with purple stripes. I braked the car, backed up, got out, and trespassed in the yard. The woods were filled with violets that spring, and I guess some had escaped onto the lawn and no one had weeded them. I don't weed mine. Floral carpets are prettier than plain green ones.

Out in Texas I saw an *animated* lawn! There it was, rippling in the wind, wave after wave. And it was blue! The species was buffalograss, Buchloe dactyloides, a western native that has a much finer texture than all those alien turfs. (You thought Kentucky bluegrass was American? No way.) Buffalograss is the dominant species on shortgrass prairie, and it loves poor soil almost as much as it hates being watered. It grows only six inches high. You can mow it once a season if you insist, but not until the flowers you've planted with it have set seed. It would be a shame not to let dry grassland express its florid nature.

I met a flowery front yard in California made up of bunchgrasses (they stay in clumps) sowed with dryland annuals like lupines and California poppies, which resow themselves each year. It was late summer: the flowers were seeds and the grasses were golden. Golden, as in "the Golden State," does not refer to precious metal or suntanned blonds; it refers to grass. California grassland is *supposed* to be golden in the summer. The fall rain greens the grass and brings the flowers to life. I saw photographs taken in the spring. Breathtaking. We have no flowered carpets so colorful back East.

We don't even have a lot of short bunchgrasses. We have plenty of short sedges. My favorite, an eight-incher called Pennsylvania sedge, Carex pennsylvanica, grows in tufts that sprout more tufts. With patience, you can establish a turf with it, but I'm not patient, so I planted the sedge with wild strawberries. It's fun to watch the two of them—the sedge with hairy rhizomes and the strawberry with rosy stolons—probe about for openings among the birdsfoot violets, wild petunias, nodding onions, and blue-eyed grass that also grow there. "There" is not a lawn. It's gaps between stones on a very hot and dry terrace, sort of an Eastern scrub. You could kill it with a sprinkler.

I was intrigued in Wisconsin by the latest in the long-hair look: the No Mow No Mo! lawn. The one I visited hadn't been mowed for two years. It belongs to Neil Diboll, who runs Prairie Nursery and developed the seed mix for sale through his catalog. The look is definitely in: floppy, like baggy pants; kind of crumpled; informal and fun to roll around in. His had no flowers, but it gave me an idea.

Here comes a long story.

Down by our pond there was this strip of unfed, unweeded, and generally disgraceful lawn where turfgrass drowned in the spring. So I figured to kill it off for good and sow instead a short sedge meadow mix for wetlands that I'd seen in a catalog. But the catalog said the area had to be wet all season, and this one was baked pottery by August. Better to dig it lower, I surmised, calculating that digging out eight inches or so would be a morning's work. And so it was—for a backhoe. You can't imagine how heavy waterlogged clay can be, and how bulky! Or how hard it is to find a place to put a hillock of soggy soil a backhoe has scooped out.

We were at the same time having a problem with where to put the stone slabs left over from building the terrace. So, putting soil and stone together, we had the backhoe dump the hillock up against a rock outcropping: we ultimately graded it by hand and used the stones for steps to the top of what by then seemed to want to be a woodland glade with that Wisconsin long-hair look, only with flowers. But that wouldn't work because the No Mow lawn is made up of turfgrasses that creep along sideways, trying to stifle any blemishes like flowers.

Neil suggested sheep fescue, Festuca ovina, a short, wispy bunchgrass that's introduced but widely naturalized. Ordinarily sheep fescue grows in sun. Under the oaks in the glade where I sowed it—thinly, so as not to compete with other plants—it grows less stiff, more limpid. Ferns drift through the grass among patches of bloodroot, Solomon plume, columbines, and Dutchman's breeches. The New American *Woodland* Lawn!

I'll let ants plant the violets. That's what they do.

After I saw the Catskills lawn, I looked up violets in the host plant index of my Peterson butterfly guide. It referred me to pages and pages of silvered fritillaries—Diana, Aphrodite, Regal, Atlantis, Coronis, Callipe, Mormon. All the caterpillars of these fritillaries dine on violets and nothing else. The only one I knew was the great spangled fritillary. I'd seen it that summer, feeding ten at a time on butterflyweed in the meadow. The same milkweed hosted monarch larvae later in the summer, but fritillaries lay eggs only on violet plants—and, strangely, while the plants are in summer dormancy, their leaves dry and dead. The eggs hatch in the fall and the little caterpillars spend all winter fasting, each waiting in the dead leaves for its violet to sprout. Really, sometimes it's hard to see why there are any butterflies at all, their lives are so difficult. But there are silvered fritillaries of one sort or another just about everywhere on the continent except in Mexico, so I guess there must be violets just about everywhere, too.

Not usually in lawns, though. The whole point of treating turf with herbicide is to get rid of "broad-leaved weeds," which may mean unkempt growth to some but nectar and fresh greens to others. A habitat, in fact. When the sedge meadow grew up to replace the dug-out lawn, dragonflies arrived. Dragonflies are much more ornamental than the grubs that constitute the wildlife inhabiting my turf.

I got to meet a lot of grubs when we deturfed the piece of lawn that's now the terrace. No wonder the grass had been so scruffy; there must have been fifty or a hundred grubs chewing the roots in each square foot of turf. Beetle larvae have their place, of course; so do the moles that eat them. But unless you do something about one or the other, the lawn dies. You have to be a killer to keep a lawn alive.

People seem willing to do just about anything for their lawn, and not just to keep it living but to keep it changeless, immortality in green. I passed miles and miles of changeless lawn, green when other grass is golden, green when leaves are falling, green again before the violets sprout in the spring. No rest or respite from the sprinkler! And pushed like weary troops to inhospitable outposts: northern lawns and southern lawns and mountain lawns and desert lawns all ache for a leave in the Emerald Isles, where they might lie in drizzle and let sheep tend them. It is unkind to prolong their misery.

The only happy turf I saw was a path. It was a funny little path that wound through a prairie garden in the Midwest and stretched out a bit in back to accommodate a barbecue, then pulled itself in and wandered off, stopping as though surprised at the boundary of the lot where the neighbors' lawn began. I guess the neighbors had felt sorry for the little thing, halted like that with nowhere else to go. So they had begun to guide its progress by cutting away the lawn to either side of it, giving the path a whole new landscape to explore among the beds they were preparing. The path was smiling. I swear it. Anticipating blazingstars to say good morning to, considering a loop around a patch of blueberries, daydreaming of bluets lightly tripping through it come the spring.

*T*his year Good Friday and Passover fell together and probably coincided more or less with the planting festival along the Nile River that I witnessed once and that involves chopped fish, spring greens, and the opening of the land to seed. April is lambing time, the season of scallions and salad herbs, like dandelions in the lawn. To me the month equally means sowing, a resurrection increasingly abstract and mysterious in our concrete world. I'd sown more sedges; I'd done my part.

I was with relatives in New Jersey for the holiday, in about the kind of neighborhood I imagine when I think "suburbia." Nice homes, but not elaborate. Small lots, but adequate. Some gardeners, but mostly people who had a landscape planted some time ago and since then have dutifully maintained it.

Forsythias and azaleas were in bloom. Along the curb sat neat piles of winter leavings, raked from the yards to be picked up by the town. ChemLawn had begun its rounds: the yards were preternaturally green.

I must say that my relatives' yard stood out; it was not up to community standards. The rhododendron foliage was anemic, a condition caused when this woodland species, adapted to acid soil rich in iron, is planted next to a concrete foundation whose leaching lime binds iron like Pepto-Bismol in the bowels. The poor shrub's pale leaves were burned as well: too much sun for a broadleaf evergreen accustomed to the forest. The lawn was bumpy. My relatives, the Zuckers, aren't thorough rakers. Pockets of leaves left through the winter had killed the grass below them: shaded it out, soured it with acid. So there were the usual apologies: we ought to but we don't; we will but we haven't.

Let me state loudly that the Zuckers aren't at fault. As long as horticulture holds out the impossible expectation that rhododendrons and lawns can cohabit—and that their cohabitation is right and proper—ordinary folk are going to feel like failures. I could give them horticultural advice: sun the grass, shade the shrubs; lime the lawn, acidify the rhodies; rake the turf, mulch the foundation planting. But that's unfair. Why should anyone have to do what is laborious, expensive, and unnatural? I'd rather aim a happy path in their direction and hope they'll pick it up.

I heard on television that Americans spend $25.9 billion a year on gardening, but people never say exactly what they mean when they toss out such a figure. Does that amount of money include the lawn service? The water bill? A videocassette about composting informed me that the amount of chemical fertilizer lavished on American home gardens exceeds the amount used in agriculture. That could explain the sum if by "home garden" is meant the whole turfed lot.

Planting Noah's Garden

An article in the *New York Times,* quoting a talking lawnmower at the National Wildflower Research Center's new quarters in Austin, Texas, says there are fifty thousand square miles of lawn in the United States. The same article mentions that "exotic" landscapes—those made up of plants that originated elsewhere—can cost two hundred times as much to maintain as native ones. An incredible figure, I thought—until I mentally compared Martha Stewart's garden to the Little House on the Prairie.

Lately I read also that gardening is the lastest-growing hobby of the baby-boom generation, but I don't see much evidence of it. Certainly the younger double-income couples who are buying property here don't appear in public with dirty fingernails. I wonder if the supposed trend is based on how much they spend, not on how much they do or how interested they are. There's a flurry of new landscaping going on in my neighborhood. It started in the 1980s, when real estate prices soared. Our local nursery seems to have tripled in size. Still, I don't see many people out there gardening. What I see is a lot more landscapers' trucks and landscape maintenance crews. The Zuckers had just hired a mowing crew. Then they joined the ChemLawn club.

One article I read lately really hit my funny bone. It was directed to people who have failed to grow a lawn in shade using "shady lawn" mixtures. "Gardeners who hope to develop lawns in shady spots," it advised, "should consider using a method called continuous seeding instead. Not only does it guarantee a picture-perfect green carpet, it requires using the cheapest grass seed you can buy—annual rye grass . . . Annual rye germinates quickly and will grow in heavy shade for a few weeks before browning off. To maintain a lawn in heavy shade, therefore, all you have to do is sow new seed every three or four weeks throughout the summer."

The National Wildflower Research Center has launched a project to compare the maintenance costs of three model front yards. The first yard is typical of the Austin suburbs, with a lawn of thirsty St. Augustine grass and plantings of exotics. The second is the identical design—and the same lawn—but with regional species substituted for the trees, shrubs, and flowers. The shade tree is a live oak instead of an Arizona ash; the shrubs are Texas sage instead of European euonymous. The third yard dispensed with the lawn. Instead, a winding stone path set among native bunchgrasses leads gently to the door. Who can doubt that maintenance of this no-mow, no-feed, no-spray, no-water yard will prove the cheapest of the three? What can it cost to sweep a path occasionally?

The first path I became fond of was a fictional one I read about as a child in a volume of American tall tales dating from our frontier past. I don't remember the story anymore, just the path—how the wild thing started out all mussed and tangled, how its hair was combed. Seems to me we went a lot too far with combing, got off the path and combed the hills and plains. And far from following its lead, seeing where it went and what it had to show us, we erased the path and lost our way, lost the very land the wild path had wandered through before its hair was combed.

We lost the wetlands: 94 percent of them in Iowa, I read. We lost the old-growth forests and the tallgrass prairie, all but sorry fragments that one may visit like museums. And the lesser ecosystems that are referred to in nature guides but that few paths lead to anymore: thickets, streambanks, meadows, barrens, rocky woods and clearings. It's these modest sorts of gardens that I think we could grow if we put our combs away.

Somewhere along my own path from horticulture to ecology, I lost my original concept of a garden. We had cultivated distinct entities at first—Iris, Rose, Rock, White—all surnamed Garden and each dwelling separately at its address in the lawn. Then Iris married Rock and carried on with sumacs, junipers, and grasses, so now I don't know what to call her (or him). Rose died. White pretty much quit blooming years ago for lack of regular division. Only she and Peony still keep their maiden names. I don't visit the Peony sisters very often. They irritate me. No sooner do I sit down than 'Mrs. FDR' demands to have her corset tightened or 'Sarah Bernhardt' wants me to trim her pods. Names do that, you see: they foster narcissism in plants. The Misses Peony, like spoiled princesses, complain continually of their spots. Plants that enter my premises these days must do so namelessly, stripped to their bare botanicals.

They must settle, not only for generic status, but for a lower-case address. Sanguinaria canadensis inhabits the front woods, which is less assuming even than the Rustic Terrace address at which my relatives live. Other choices—but not for this woodland bloodroot—are upper meadow, lower meadow, wet meadow, bramble. Bramble is a small neighborhood, one that could easily fit the sunny corner of a yard. Only three species are planted there: a grass, a rose, a raspberry. They get along very well and cause me no trouble. And they feed the birds.

That's another thing I ask of plants these days: that they earn their keep. Or at least that they don't interfere with their working neighbors. I don't suppose the named varieties of iris that still survive among the hairgrass and aromatic sumac do anything as useful as feeding birds or mice, but they don't get in the way of others' labors.

I planted a patch of great big sunflowers two springs ago. It was one of those last-minute things. I had sunflower seeds left over from feeding the birds and an empty strip of dirt against a sunny wall of the house, so I poked the seeds into the dirt and let them grow. They were popular with many pollinators, though not those like butterflies, which want long drinks of nectar. Sunflowers are bread and butter plants: protein, starch, and fat with just a dab of honey. When the seeds ripened in the fall, goldfinches came daily for their breakfast.

Titmice finished off the leavings over the winter. I found this amusing because by then the birdfeeder provided a more convenient source of seeds. These heavy-headed flowers turn downward as the season progresses, so by fall the birds must hang upside down to extract the ripened seeds. The titmice reminded me of children who prefer the ingenuity required to get a gumball from a machine than the less interesting procedure of grabbing from a bowl. I noticed the same phenomenon in the meadow where I had planted a woodland species of sunflower in the shade of a hickory tree the year before. There weren't even a lot of them, just what few had come up from a pocketful of seeds collected by the roadside and tossed into the grass. Yet goldfinches sought the dried heads for weeks before they resorted to the tedium of feeders.

Native species are as a rule more entertaining than exotics because of their extraordinarily active social life, but I won't exclude those immigrants that also party. Social butterfly bush is welcome in my garden, although she is Eurasian.

Sunflowers are strictly American. There are about a hundred species of the Helianthus genus—most from North America, some from South America, none at all from the Old World. The ones grown for bird seed are giant domesticated versions of Helianthus annuus, which literally means "annual sunflower." The species was cultivated by the Indians for food; so was the sunflower Jerusalem artichoke, valued for its sugary tubers. I suspect some funny business goes on in the annual sunflower's present commercial breeding because, of the leftover seeds I planted, some grew tall and some grew short, and some flowers were the size of plates while others were no broader than a demitasse saucer. But sunflowers aren't sexually trustworthy anyway: they interbreed promiscuously, especially now that highways have connected their various populations, which range about as broadly across the continent as asters, goldenrods, milkweeds, violets, or I-80. My county agent wasn't able to say for sure which woodland sunflower it was that I scattered in the grass.

It doesn't matter. It worked. A garden is an entertaining patch of plants that earns its living in the real world of birds and bees and butterflies. That precludes, I believe, gladioli.

I'll also claim for this new working garden that it does not require much work. The Zuckers should be relieved to hear that. So should their neighbors. The fact is that only one home on Rustic Terrace has a garden at all, and recalling my days nursing Rose as she sickened and slowly passed away, I don't blame the other neighbors for not putting forth the effort. The wild roses and raspberries in the bramble get nothing from me but an occasional haircut.

The work to get a garden going may certainly be arduous—too much so in the case of the sedge meadow for us to have completed the excavation by hand. So was the grading of the oak glade hard, and the stones heavy, and the sowing and transplanting not exactly easy. I'll have to sweat through weeding it for a few seasons, too. But there will come a time when that garden will attain self-realization and therefore self-sufficiency. Decisions will be out of my hands. Ants will or won't plant violets; Dutchman's breeches may or may not survive; ferns will drift as they wish; wild ginger may mysteriously appear, as it has in another shady place where the gingers that thrive are ones I never planted and those I planted died. I'll weed once a year if I weed at all.

A garden is a place where one accepts and builds on original conditions that are recognizable to a certain community of plants and to the animals that associate with them. If the chosen community is realistic, the garden will, in today's psychobabble, "find itself"—and, as with a well-started child, the parents can pretty much bow out.

In this respect, my strip of annual sunflowers is a failure. The species grows wild here only on disturbed soil—roadsides, waste places. It has no permanent home in the Northeast, where perennials reign. Whether I bought Helianthus annuus in packets, used birdfeeder leftovers, or found some wildlings along the road from which I could collect the seeds, I would have to keep the soil in which I planted them disturbed year after year by hoe and rake—by labor. Weeds also like disturbed soil; there would be no end of them. I should have planted perennial sunflowers, and I will. The woodland sunflowers under the hickory tree have proved their practicality by spreading through the grass from seeds the finches spilled. The flowers recognize their natural habitat; the finches recognize their natural food. I complied with an original condition in a moment's scattering, and I haven't lifted a finger since.

What is the original condition of my relatives' Rustic Terrace, though? Its name suggests dirt roads and hedgerows, but only the developer could say for sure what lies beneath the lawns. Not much, I bet. I'd just gotten back from Georgia and Wisconsin and was soon to go to Arizona. In the Madison suburbs of Wisconsin, developers strip off the two to six feet of black prairie soil down to underlying clay. Those who buy the lots must buy the soil back by the inch. Few buy more than the three or four inches required to sow a lawn. The situation was worse in Georgia. There remain in logged areas of the Piedmont only about nine inches of woodland loam over spent red clay. I saw vast tracts where the loam had been pushed into mountainous heaps scheduled for removal, permanently, to no one knew where. The new yards I saw in completed portions of that development were as raw as wounds; lawns were transfused with chemicals for their survival. So "original conditions" may call for homeowners to begin at the beginning, with pioneers that penetrate and fertilize the soil to prepare it for more refined inhabitants.

That's what grasses do. Not lawn grasses but bunchgrasses, native grasses, those tassle-headed, deep-rooted wild types whose fibrous underpinnings are typically twice the bulk of their aboveground growth. I love their common names: hairgrass, lovegrass, sweetgrass, switchgrass, Junegrass, oatgrass, Indiangrass, buffalograss, needlegrass, and dropseed, moustache, bottlebrush, bluejoint, bluestem, purpletop. Who needs Scott's turf when such romance beckons?

I was astonished to discover how rarely wildflower enthusiasts know even the commonest of their native grasses. On picture postcards, the bluebonnets of Texas had seemed to entirely cover the ground; when I saw them growing at my feet, it was obvious that they shared the ground with grasses. But who knew which ones? Not anyone who was showing me around. Native plant societies that publish lists of wildflowers native to the region omit the grasses in which the flowers grow. Don't they look at their feet? Wildflower seeds sold by the can in garden centers are grassless mixes. Yet wherever the light is bright enough, even under a shady oak or apple tree, flowers grow in grass. Just try to catch a roadside milkweed growing nakedly!

It seems perverse that what in nature is the very matrix of flower gardens entered the horticultural vocabulary as "accent plants" or "ornamental grasses." If a garden is a patch of plants that works without requiring work—that proceeds realistically from original conditions to a self-sustaining system—then gardens must be bedded down with grass. Grass is to meadow flowers as water is to fish: their medium. Even lawn weeds know that.

I collected seeds last fall from woodland asters and goldenrods growing along a shady roadside and scattered them, as I had the sunflower seeds below the hickory tree, among dead leaves and sheep fescue in the upland glade. They haven't germinated yet, but the grass, just one inch high, has already pushed roots six inches into that ungiving clay.

Ruth Morse in Arizona scattered a whole system. She lives in a town on the high desert, where summer heat and drought leave the soil bare for next season's annuals to sprout among the grasses, cacti, and scrub that characterize the natural vegetation. Ruth collected the seeds of wild plants she liked, and tossed

Planting Noah's Garden

Won't somebody give these paths more space to wander?

Only one of these paths, the one running through a prairie yard near Madison, Wisconsin, has been helped across its owner's lot line into a willing neighbor's yard. The other pictures show a stone walk through a wooded yard in a Milwaukee suburb; the dirt path through Ruth Morse's desert garden near Cochise, Arizona; and our mowed path where it curves through switchgrass in New York. They all either make a circuit of the garden or dead-end at a boundary. By extending native plantings and joining paths along rear lot boundaries, we could create generous natural habitat for communities to enjoy. (Clockwise from top right: Rochelle Whiteman, Sara Stein, Molly Fifield Murray, Brad Smith)

them. Friends who collect and sell southwestern species gave her outdated packets of seed to throw around as well. Most of them were eaten by birds. Some survived. Gradually, the native vegetation reestablished itself: cholla, yucca, soapberry, and saltbush on a ground of forbs and grasses.

Is this a garden? Is it a lawn?

My ecological definition can't rightly distinguish between the two. I could call my glade under the oak trees a shady lawn or I could call it a woodland garden. It dresses either name in both grass and flowers. Ruth Morse's yard, our stone terrace, and the short sedge meadow also combine the two. Let's say the difference between a lawn and a garden is one of height. My rib-high meadow is certainly not a lawn: one walks through it, not on it. It does meet my reconstructed definition of a garden: it is wildly entertaining, what with its acrobatic grasshoppers, dancing butterflies, singing bees, and antic finches. It goes about its business without complaint, without a gardener's assistance.

As for the more formal elements of design required by horticulture to define a garden, they have slipped away over the years of my conceptual evolution. What had been the garden wall of junipers that defined the Misses Peony's dressing room grew outward into a thicket of blueberries and dogwoods. As Rock and Iris together grew bigger than the lawn in which they had originally been planted, they lost their architectural identity along with their proper names. We have stone walls and steps—we wouldn't want the paths to lose their way—but snapshots of Ruth's yard show no boundaries at all, nothing to indicate where gardens begin or end. One can't distinguish even types of vegetation: shrub borders, ground covers, foundation plantings, flower beds. As on our stone terrace, Ruth's yard is a scrub community with trees and scattered bushes among the flowers and grasses. Step out of the house and there you are, in the garden. Walk where you wish and you are still there, in the garden.

When I went to visit Ruth, though, double rows of stone had been laid to suggest the ways to wander. I think Ruth should nudge the stones a bit, urge them toward the edge, where they might tempt the neighbors to take up the little path and carry it into their own back yard.

Our path is definitely becoming feral, going back to nature, running wild. It's not even grassy in some places: mossy now, or slicked with pine needles, or pillowed in dead leaves. Down in the front woods you have to wade through ferns as the path winds past the trilliums. Not just violets but shooting stars have erupted in the bend that rounds the patch of bloodroots spreading under the redbud tree. Roots muscle across the path where it loops through the river birch grove, ten years old now and sprouting mushrooms underfoot. We mulched the path in garden style as it entered the darker woods behind the pond, but trout lilies dared to trespass, and the wayward path rudely climbed the crevice in a granite outcrop and then demanded steps to descend again. I gave it a bench at the top of the rock, hoping to pacify it, but it went wild with mayflowers and polyplody ferns. I think the path is beginning to direct our lives.

Can you imagine that it wanted to explore the skunk cabbage swamp below the pond? And that to accommodate it we had to give it stepping-stones to navigate the water? And tussock sedge and flag iris? It wasn't pleased at all with the nasty multiflora roses that barred its way.

No, really, I'm sure of it now that I narrate its progress: the path leads us, we follow.

I'm trying to remember how the path began. To the best of my recollection it was born inauspiciously as a small flight of steps and a short run of turf leading to the Peony Garden—and thence nowhere at all, trapped in the rectangle of a garden room. But it grew fast. These are pushy things, these paths, and they will have their way. When it hit the walls of its cage, it pushed through in three directions and is running still.

And I'm getting to know it, as people once did who ran after wolves when paths were still matted and tousled and hadn't been combed to lawns. The path wants to go on and on, forking and looping, leaping from yard to yard, showing us what it tried to show us before we lost our way: that a garden can be like the First Garden, the whole place where we live.

A cultivated clematis trying to cohabit with a wild bur cucumber vine. (Sara Stein)

Planting Noah's Garden

3 Blueberries, Huh?

Dear Sara,

 Winter is finally here! The seed catalogs have been pouring in. I think the mailman glared at me yesterday. I've thrown in the towel on trying to design my garden other than in vague outlines—I've tried and tried but it defeats me. My goals for this year are:

 Move Syringa microphylla (it needs more sun)

 Move Physocarpus opulus 'Dart's Gold' (it's getting too much sun)

 Enlarge bed around Calycanthus (remove most non-natives)

 Move quince

 Remove forsythia

 Add native azaleas, serviceberries, pawpaws, more plums, hazelnuts, winterberries

 Pleach apples

 Learn about coppicing

 Finish pond & plant around it

 Find local populations of polygalas to collect seed

 Lay down paths and install edging in Four-Square Garden; fence around it

 Well, that will keep me off the streets for '95. I'd also like to take a vacation this year.

 Love, Polly

So went, more or less, Polly Law's New Year's letter to me—except that it also contained a list of species she was raising from seed, observations regarding native plants she'd seen growing along I-80 on her way to visit her family over the winter holidays, a remark that perhaps she ought to know how to lay a hedge as well as how to pleach and coppice, and advice regarding the cultivation of perennial lupines.

Polly, you see, is the genuine article: a *real* gardener.

I met my first real gardener only a few years ago. I know that seems unlikely, but I really am an attic sort of person. Part of my stiffness the year I was so much among gardeners is that I'm not used to their extraordinary vigor. The first real gardener I met—another Ruth, not Ruth in Arizona—is out there daily, rain or shine, trimming this and moving that, watering and feeding. The results are spectacular—a woodland exploding in spring color among soft, mossy paths—but I could never keep up with her. Other gardening friends also work devotedly. One breeds daylilies in yummy colors—tomato, carrot, beet, and eggplant among swirls of cream and butter. Another maintains a perfectly groomed collection of dwarf conifers painstakingly implanted in a cliff. Their gardens are beautiful, of course. Beautiful gardens are what we expect of real gardeners. Their work is public; it is what we see in gardening books and magazines; it is what we visit on garden tours. It is not what most of us can do.

Yet there was an unexpected repercussion from this first acquaintance with real gardeners: they thought my place was a real garden. And so it came about through their kind offices that it has been toured and photographed and published.

At first I felt that I was flying under false colors, hanging out a rag and calling it a banner. But the very first time people came to see this place—and came because Ruth suggested it—the visitors seemed relieved, having first seen Martha Stewart's garden. They said our garden appeared to have grown up by itself; they said they could sit down here and relax and not worry about weeds; they said they didn't want to leave when it came time to board the bus.

So I gradually realized that if a horticultural institution could schedule me and Martha on the same tour, I was not really so far beyond the gate as I thought. If there are similarities among far-flung ecosystems, might there not be similarities among all our gardens?

My friends' gardens do not altogether fly in the face of nature. No matter that the species in Ruth's wooded garden have many nationalities; no matter that their spring explosion is abnormally brilliant. They follow the rules of all temperate forest flowers, blooming before the canopy leafs out, when the air is cool and lit with the woodland butterflies called blues. My woodland glade is not as colorful, but it, too, blooms for blues. One day, walking through what is now a nature preserve, I came upon drifts of snowdrops blooming in the woods. The place had been an estate, and the trail where they bloomed led to the remains of a clay tennis court. I felt disoriented, but the snowdrops, though they hailed from Europe, knew their ecological place.

Riots of daylilies have their counterpart in midsummer meadows; we did not invent the idea. And as I've noticed up in Maine, where I've neglected those daylilies I planted twenty years ago at the house where we vacation, they bloom year after year in the grass that we long ago stopped mowing. So do peonies that predate our occupation, growing there for two score years at least. Daylilies and peonies must be meadow plants. Their memory is long.

We did not make up dwarf conifers. I've seen on exposed rock just such compact and contorted growth as that which characterizes Japanese gardens. The giant bonsai style of San Francisco and the miniature theme of my friend's cliff garden surely originated in the wind-struggled growth of mountains. Gardeners may dramatize, formalize, exaggerate, and edit, but like a caricaturist, who by his art all the more emphatically reveals the human face, gardeners reveal in their creations the underlying landscape that inspires them.

My difference with real gardeners—and my complaint about their gardens—is that esthetic distillations, while well designed to quench our visual thirst, are often neither recognizable nor pleasing to other animals. You have only to compare a perennial border to a meadow to see that pollinating insects don't agree with us on which is the more attractive. Birds don't see our art our way. They don't find topiary as homey as a thicket. Of all the lovely settings that I was shown by garden clubs, few were animated by the songbirds and butterflies that together are the arbiters of ecological taste.

So an uncomfortable question gnawed at me as I garden-hopped about the country: can a real gardener—curator of exotica, sculptor of the grounds, painterly composer of hue and form and texture—allow his or her creation to regress somewhat toward the natural landscape from which it was abstracted?

I'd been on my jittery way for about six months when Polly, just settling into the home she had recently bought, wrote to me the first of many letters that were to set my mind at rest.

"Blueberries, huh?" Polly wrote in that first letter, dated February 1994. "Well, okay."

The second letter mentioned plans for an herb garden, a mixed shrub-perennial border, a woodland walk, a tapestry garden, and flower boxes. Also an order for purple hazel, golden fullmoon maple, and silver weeping pear (no blueberries).

Letter number three, bristling at my query about what influenced her choices, was biographical: Polly is an illustrator who has also been a costume designer, weaver, glassblower, needlepoint designer, and "all-around every-surface dabber and dauber." She has studied native flora and led wildflower walks; she has made numerous trips to the British Isles to study gardens. She is also a birder. And she

*Polly in her tuteur.
(Clare Holland)*

is single, vegetarian, stubborn, dislikes "cant & can't," collects teapots, and once danced with Nelson Rockefeller.

That letter included a long order of species for a hedgerow of berrying shrubs, including blueberries. By December, pawpaws had ascended to the top of her Christmas list.

Some months later there arose in our correspondence the problem of what to plant beneath Polly's lavender gazing globe: big-headed metallic pink alliums? Bronze Iris fulva? A swath of sea oats? And what color to paint the trellised arbor (burnt lime, Polly decided, set off by vines of glaucous foliage: then she changed her mind and painted it pokeberry purple). The *tuteur*—whatever that was; I had to ask—might be planted with golden-leaved hops, clematis, climbing milkweed, flame honeysuckle, wild bur cucumber, or cardinal vine. A hard choice, no? Sometime in the second year of our correspondence arrived a detailed plan for the "New Improved Dark Red Dooryard Garden," listing twenty-four species of shrubs, vines, herbacious perennials, bulbs, and grasses in a space the graph paper told me was smaller than my kitchen.

But by then I had met Polly Law. I knew her for what she is: a real gardener, yes, an embellisher in whose home floors are flowered, stairs sprigged, walls garlanded;

a gardener of Dickensian flamboyance, commodious and exuberant with a smile that could light the sky. A gardener of a new sort: a gardener for the birds.

I'm not a birder myself; they flit too fast for me and I lack the ear to memorize their song. Still, I can tell if there are many birds or few by the cumulative volume of their twittering at dawn and their general business about the place. Years ago, when we cleared our land and mowed most of it to lawn, a sudden absence of birds was my first clue that we were doing something wrong. Their reappearance as we replanted affirmed that we'd found our way again. One day, after the land was pretty well replanted, a birder who wanted help replanting her yard came to visit equipped with her binoculars. What a compliment! She discovered a yellow-throated warbler I didn't know was summering here.

She'd begun to study butterflies as well. She told me she had milkweed growing in her field. When I asked which one, she was surprised. She'd thought there was just one. And this is not the first birder I've met who knows the cedar waxwing but not the red cedar for which it's named.

Bird-watching—or bird awareness, as I'd call the impressionistic form I practice—is a quick way to judge a yard. If, during the nesting period and spring and fall migrations, songbirds are not a loud and lively feature of the landscape, it hasn't met their practical needs or esthetic expectations. It has too few bugs or berries, nothing to drink, and nowhere to hide. For all Polly's pleaching and coppicing and lavender gazing balls, the structure of her garden is four ecosystems—grassland, wetland, woodland, thicket—and the heaped species that express these systems are laid out quite literally as an avian feast.

I went to visit Polly and her garden the first fall of our correspondence, just after I'd given a series of workshops on northeastern ecosystems, and I was carrying that mental scaffolding with me, my ecological version of garden "bones."

I don't see anatomy in color. Woods to me are geometry, thick verticals of canopy trees crisscrossed by the thinner horizontals of a layered understory contrived to catch light descending toward the forest floor: a sieve, or a series of sieves that strain sunlight to shade. Rain falls through the sieve; it is collected below in the sponge of a forest's fibrous roots. These are kitchen analogies; they work for me in monochrome.

I know grassland is made up of myriad separate individuals, both animal and vegetable, but I see it as a tissue in which all are enmeshed. The tint, though vaguely green and dotty, is not important. I see the sweep of the season across the animate expanse, the way the grass lifts with the summer as though the heat were pulling it, the way the flower dots fade and intensify like freckles, crowd now in one place and then another, take to the sky as dragonflies and bees and then settle, solidify, go to seed.

Blueberries, Huh?

The last workshop was on hedgerows—sort of. There is no word for what I meant to convey: untrimmed hedge or woodland edge. Or scrub, shrubbery, brush, thicket. Yet I see this sort of vegetation well enough: prickles and twigs and bloom and bunchiness and berries and bird nests and stout stems and slender stalks laced like seams where systems meet; cowlicks where mice run from glade to garden; sutures where brambles meet the grass. Where our land's anatomy is stitched.

But I see the stitching as it looks in winter, naked.

There was no workshop on wetlands. Wetland flora and fauna may be unique, but their structure isn't. A swamp is a wooded wetland; a marsh is a wet grassland.

Glue these "overlays" on your mind. Comparing the distinctive textures of woods, thickets, and meadows to the vegetation of your yard may help you recognize the complexity that's missing from the typical suburban landscape. (This page, Virginia P. Weinland; page 39, Sara Stein and Virginia P. Weinland [inset])

Either may be sutured with brushy growth, and so may shores of every sort fit one or another of my images.

I carry my ecological scaffolding around with me like three transparent overlays that I can position on a landscape to see how closely it complies. It's become a habit with me, a game I play in other people's yards. Lay the woodland scaffold over a group of trees and see immediately the missing crisscrosses. Lay the grassland image on a lawn and note the shocking blankness. Try the suture on the shrubs and realize they are lumps, not stitchery.

I got to Polly's home at midday after a long drive through mountains, where all roads are sinuous and steep. Polly's acre lot, though, proved to be flat and dull, just as she'd described it: a shoebox lawn hemmed in by huge conifers planted by the previous owners, who had landscaped the property three quarters of a century ago. A path that led straight from the street to the door of the small Dutch Colonial bisected a featureless front lawn. The house was framed in old lilacs and yews, some with trunks as thick as thighs. The rear yard, like the front yard, was lawn. Here and there stood specimens of great age and various origin; Polly reeled their names off like a botanical guide: white pine and Norway spruce, English yew and native holly, Carolina allspice and American cranberrybush with exotic quince, rose, and almond. An introduced magnolia and a giant Chinese chestnut were truly magnificent. A muscled ironwood was as impressive an example of this native understory tree as I had ever seen. Polly had identified them all. But the trees and shrubs stood unrelated, on display, as though waiting for their arboretum labels.

In this boneyard, she was just beginning to assemble the skeleton of her design. It was, to be sure, evidenced at that point by nothing more visually gripping than newly planted saplings and expressive waves of Polly's hand as she painted in the air what was to come. Her strokes, though, were sure and anatomically correct, as though she, too, could see the transparencies through which I viewed her yard. She waved into existence a thickety front hedge, twigged and berried. Against it in the front lawn emerged a meadow garden blowing grassily in the wind. To either side, understory trees stepped forth from beneath the great conifers, trailing at their feet a tapestry of spring bulbs and woodland treasures. These small trees gave way behind the house to sunny arcs of lower shrubbery that embraced more flowers and a keyhole pond, the future home of sea oats and gazing globe. The plan was formal, measured to the straight walk in front, centered on the Four Square Garden in the back, structural both in the gardener's meaning of the term and in my own monochromatic anatomy of landscape.

You can see why I laughed months later, reading Polly's New Year's letter. It seemed to me she already had designed her garden. But Polly, with her Technicolor vision, had only just begun.

This is what real gardeners do: paint in idiosyncratic shades of chartreuse, puce, and purple; filigree in bronze and gold and silver; feather with ferns; dapple with dark foliage; wake the eye with unlikely juxtapositions: three pawpaws and a silver weeping pear. One does not expect a gardener who presides over a collection of two hundred teapots to choose only down-homey types. I am sure, though, that Polly knows her pots as well as she knows her plants.

Polly took to marking with an asterisk the exotic species on her plans and plant lists. Of the two dozen species in the New Improved Dark Red Dooryard Garden, six were of foreign origin, and of these, half were shrubs incorporated from the original landscape. That proportion—about one exotic species to four Americans—is probably the same as in my gardens if I dared to calculate it. The bulk of her choices were ample nectar providers in the carmine shades that hummingbirds prefer. Where I saw a bare frame, she filled in the flesh, flushed the cheeks, and blushed the bosom in a way so forward as almost to embarrass my spare view of propriety. And might she not by such boldness have more hummingbirds than I?

This is the kind of exaggeration that I think real gardeners can do. "Blueberries, huh?" is the right attitude exactly: Polly started her berried hedgerow with a list that ran to four pages on a legal pad; she culled it to those species that are native or naturalized in the Northeast, that would top out at between six and eight feet without trimming, that are highly rated by birds, that together produce fruit over a long season—and that astonish with a burst of yellow berries when you least expect it. Birds don't mind flourishes of that sort. I've seen spring azures sucking nectar at a Leucothoe named 'Scarletta'. Possums will eat pawpaws in the company of a weeping silver pear.

I stayed the afternoon and evening, stuffed myself on tacos, slept upstairs where the "rug" between the beds was painted on the floor, woke up to coffee at the kitchen table where the "oilcloth" was painted too, and drove south with the birds on a brilliant autumn morning elated with surety. Gardening is art, but it hangs well in an ecological frame.

I read in an issue of *American Butterflies* that wherever birders find the most rewarding haunts, there too will searchers of butterflies find their heart's desire. My shelves groan with books and articles telling me how to attract butterflies by planting a garden of their favorite nectar flowers. But in that same issue of the journal, lepidopterists and their protégés tramped along railroad tracks, followed power line rights of way, and explored unkempt meadows edged with brush and woods.

Somehow it is disappointing that these most ornamental insects might prefer the cindered scar of commuter rails to the luscious nectary a real gardener might design. A rail bed, though, is a habitat, and a flower bed is not. A butterfly garden may be a portion of a butterfly's habitat, as a berry bush may be a portion of a bird's habitat, but the spicebush swallowtail nectaring at your sunny marigolds grew up on Lindera benzoin or Sassafras albida in the shady woods, and the songbirds in your garden ate insects, not seeds or fruit, when they were young. *The habitat of spring azures or eastern bluebirds may therefore be several quite different forms of vegetation closely juxtaposed,* as they are along the Amtrak lines where wet ditch, dry bank, thick brush, and trash trees lie like a striped ribbon along 400 miles of coast from Washington, D.C., to Boston.

It is an unacknowleged irony of conservation that land abuse may increase the number and variety of birds and butterflies in areas where cycles of disuse and disturbance maintain disjunct habitat. Waste places, vacant lots, old fields, and roadsides are frequently mentioned in field guides as housing a multitude of pioneers and weeds: common milkweed, stinging nettle, bunchgrasses, mustards, partridge pea, pipe vine, pussy willow, alder, aspen, hackberry, blackberry, sassafras, sumac, tuliptree, wild plums and cherries. All of these are host plants to butterflies that, if they cannot find them for their caterpillars, will no longer be available to nectar in our gardens. Note, too, the bird fruits—and I've only named a few—that are a staple of many birds' diet in every season. These common and scorned sorts are successional species that persist only by nimbly jumping from disturbance to disturbance; they have no place in more permanent ecosystems such as owl forest and prairie chicken grassland. If roadsides, railroads, rights-of-way, and old fields weren't occasionally scalped, scraped, sprayed, burned, or otherwise mistreated, they would lose their unique ecological worth.

Between such sporadic attentions, these places lie neglected. Vines climb and sprawl; trees rot and die; leaves litter the ground; thatch mats the meadow. A mess, we'd say, but this is not how other animals see it. The best-dressed birds that frequent winter feeders—titmice, chickadees, nuthatches, woodpeckers—want heart-rotted snags and punky knots for nesting. Juncoes would rather scratch for their dinner in the dirt than eat seeds nicely served to them. Some butterfly larvae subsist on fallen leaves, not live ones. Many overwinter in unraked litter or the decomposing thatch of meadow grasses. It is simply disgusting that the luna moth—spectacular in size, shaped by a celestial jeweler, and of the glowing pallor for which it is so aptly named—overwinters on the ground in a cocoon that looks like something one should step on. I'm amused to learn the diet of wood nymphs, leafwings, angelwings, and emperors: rotten fruit, bird droppings, dripping sap, dead meat, and dung, not nectar.

Blueberries, huh? Well, okay.

But rotten ones? Unraked leaves? Punky snags?

Nettles, for heaven's sake!

If I were an angelwing—a hop merchant, perhaps —I would not waste my limited resources looking for hops or nettles on which to lay my eggs in a well-groomed subdivision. Perhaps the mental program of an angelwing sends it first on a visual search for a ditch or thicket, there to exercise its olfactory antennae in the habitat where its host plants are most likely to be found. Funny thing is, such a strategy might well bring a hop merchant to Polly's exotic golden-leaved hop vine scrambling up her tuteur.

A tuteur, she explained to me, is a sort of miniature and truncated wood lattice version of the Eiffel Tower, named after the French for "teacher" or "trainer." Its function in a garden might be compared to that of the steel trellis on which high tension wires are strung, or of a railroad trestle, or of a telephone pole: an opportunity for vines. That she chose an exotic hop selection to twine the tuteur was purely esthetic: another yellow eye-shock like the berries in the hedgerow. That the hedge remains untrimmed, however, is an ecological decision. So is Polly's choice not to clean out a wetland thicket that tangles the rear of her lot, where the land dips through a scrap of woods to a remnant marsh. She left standing an old snag between woods and garden, right on the lawn. She neglects what lawn is left and loves the violets, lets leaves lie through the winter in her tapestry beds, and allows the meadow garden to go to seed and stand untouched until the spring.

Naturally, Polly is a land abuser. All gardeners are. Don't think for a minute that the woodland lurking to her rear would not invade her dooryard garden if ever she should stop uprooting the tree seedlings that sneak into her beds. The Four-Square where she grows herbs wouldn't last a season without hocing. This new kind of gardening requires a nice balance of benign neglect and stern abuse: were Polly not to give her hop vine an occasional sharp whack, it would gladly gobble up the trash trees she has planted.

Trash trees!

Yes: chokecherry and wild plum.

The chokecherry happens to be a named variety selected for the rich red-purple of its leaves; Polly chose it to contrast with the golden locust and the silver pear. If I were an angelwing, I would think I had found heaven.

Ruth warned me not to touch the cane cholla, Opuntia spinosior. *It was already too late. (Michael McKeag)*

*I*n the winter of 1994, Ruth Morse became Mrs. James Shilling, and her yard's intimate relations were simultaneously formalized. Where one had stepped out the door into the garden, one now steps onto a wood-railed deck surrounded by a brick patio. The thicket of mesquite bushes is being trained into a grove of mesquite trees. The water trough has been moved aside from its former place of prominence and now is buried to its rim, its identity disguised in clever rockwork. Prominent instead is a second watering place, this one resembling a wishing well where a stream of recirculating water splashes.

Jim Shilling is a man of order who puts the dish drain where it belongs under the sink when not in use and who in principle is opposed to excess bushiness. It is he who had delineated the paths with stones. The new couple is some years past retirement, devoted and seemingly more at ease with compromise than many younger pairs. But I wonder where the line will be drawn between scatterer and pruner.

When I visited Ruth and Jim in May, they had been married only a few months. The funny old round thermometer depicting a roadrunner still hung

Planting Noah's Garden

from the tree where the water trough had been, but its role had been usurped by a high-tech thermometer that records maximum and minimum daily temperatures. The snapshots had shown crude benches for seating here and there in the garden. They were gone; one now sits on the deck, above the garden. I had spent the previous two days walking through the Sonoran Desert, noting a fundamental difference in design from other landscapes: it is scattered, like Ruth's seeds. The shrubs dotting the land are evenly distributed among bulkier or taller cacti. Flowers and grasses appear individually, sporadically, more as tufts than tissue. So, too, in Ruth's yard, cholla, agave, and yucca came up where they came up, never mind the composition of the scene. I wonder if Jim will not wish to group them, to move the larger species like a hedgerow against the wire fence, or arrange them by height and bulk and color as real gardeners do. No fear, though, that he'll ever go exotic: like Ruth, he knows his desert habitat too thoroughly and loves the birds too well.

After I got home, Ruth sent me the list of birds she has spotted in or from her garden, from common robin to beleaguered loggerhead shrike. The list included birds I hadn't seen here since childhood—tanagers, orioles, ravens—and many I never could see in our habitats, like the breathtaking vermilion flycatcher and violet-green swallow, and ones, too, I'd never heard of, like phainopepla and pyrrhuloxia, and owls, hawks, vultures, herons, cranes—and roadrunners, of course. Her astonishing backyard total was a hundred and three species.

Ruth's house is on a residential block of mowed (brown) lawns, around the corner from the post office, barely a stone's throw from the railroad tracks. Across the street is overgrazed range choked with mesquite and supporting little else. Beyond the town are plowed fields and pecan plantations. The only authentic desert is Ruth's two-thirds-acre patch, flocked with birds like filings drawn to the magnet of her yard. I rather preferred the yard as it had been in earlier snapshots. I felt something deeply exciting in the possibility of letting an ecosystem artlessly express itself, shaped only as woods may be shaped by the trails that people travel, by the places where they sit. But who really sits in judgment are the birds, and as between artful and artless, it seems that they are easily fooled by crafty facsimiles of natural habitat.

The week before I left for Arizona, I had gotten a letter from Polly Law in answer to mine regarding the spring holiday in New Jersey, with my complaint that I had been deprived of beer (brewed with yeast and therefore not proper to the matzoh season). The epistle, on handmade paper, was in an envelope of

Sara Stein

Planting Noah's Garden

robin's-egg blue. The first sheet was rust-colored. The second one was as pink as the wild Geranium maculatum. The third sheet was the "burnt lime" of Polly's various trellised works. The contents included another installment in our serial conversation about color.

Dear Sara,

Well, the holidays are over—have a beer. Fortunately, my family's holiday foods are based only on tradition, not mythic significance. The holiday foods that must appear at every feast are Great-Aunt Jean's creamed pearled onions and the Jell-O Ring. It isn't even a real Jell-O Ring anymore. Years ago, as a joke, I had a plastic Jell-O Ring made, complete with fake almonds and celery. Each year we dust it off, put it on a bed of lettuce, and voila! Guests are quite bamboozled.

The population of white-throated and chipping sparrows has increased. My next-door neighbor saw goldfinches for the first time in her life the other day. I figure I've brought them in from the field to my north, and they've expanded since. When they perch on the budding spice bush and the glowing leaves of Physocarpus 'Dart's Gold', they are quite a sight.

I wish I could be as sophisticated about color as you, but I'm just like a kid in a candy store. Eye candy. I figure that after the garden gets established, I'll get tired of playing and settle down to a more reasoned approach.

But for now—whee!

Love, Polly

Biting the dirt, the usual prelude to "developing" residential land. (Sara Stein)

4 *Ellen's Lot*

M Y NIECE ELLEN PUT OUT A FEEDER and no birds came. She won-
dered if it was because the lot was bare, but I didn't believe a lot could be as bare
as she described it. She asked if I would design a landscape for it, but I didn't
suppose she meant more than the usual doorway shrubs. It seemed to me she
had to be exaggerating when she said the soil was too poor for anything but
crabgrass, and I was right: it supported sow thistle and mugwort, too.

I'm of the generation before suburbs. I've never lived in a condo or tract
housing. Ellen has never lived anywhere else. She's used to sights that hurt my
eyes: land that's dirt; landscapes that come by truck. Where Ellen lives, in a new
development on endless acres of former cornfield in New Jersey, the planting is
installed in a day, the way living rooms are furnished. The lawn goes in last,
rolled out like carpeting. That's done here sometimes, too, on model homes; I
wasn't surprised by the method. Nothing, though, had prepared me for the new
chic of suburban style.

I've seen modest developments, but Le Parc is not one of them. The houses
are unabashedly pretentious, faced in stone and brick, arched and pillared,
extended by decks, sunrooms, and gazebos. Each is big enough for a family of
ten. What is modest, compared to the houses, is the amount of land they sit on.
Lots are one-half acre, and on Ellen's cul-de-sac they necessarily narrow toward
the front, where the houses elbow each other uncomfortably across the drive-
ways. The back is ringed by houses glaring at the yard. The effect is unsettling,
like standing in the middle of a portrait gallery where oversize and overdressed
notables stare down from every wall.

When I first stood thus scrutinized in Ellen's yard, the last of the new homes
on her street was still under construction. The outer ranks of houses, though,
had been built six years earlier, time enough for growth to shield or soften the

The view from Ellen's back yard. Her tree is in the foreground to the left; a strip of forest rims the distant background. (Sara Stein)

intrusiveness of those large homes with all their window eyes. Yet the plantings had just the opposite effect. They displayed the houses as a setting displays a gem. Here gold shrubbery puffed up a deck, there twisting trees dramatized an entrance, and in front of almost every house stood a specimen making a statement on the lawn.

In fact, there weren't a lot of lawns: just one.

The entire development was seamless grass, unfenced, unhedged, unbroken by grove or thicket, and merely dotted here and there with young evergreens that, by their tentative placement, seemed to be suffering from agoraphobia, as though they would have pulled together into homier groups if they hadn't been so uncomfortably rooted to the spot.

The only discolored patches in this carpeting were the construction site, still brown dirt, and Ellen's lot. Her ground had been seeded, of course. One doesn't get a certificate of occupancy for a new home in those parts until the lawn's been planted. But for drainage purposes, the natural grade had been elevated with a foot and a half of clay so hard that even the veil of weeds it wore failed to cover it, and black mold grew over it in splotches.

There was one tree: My Tree, Ellen called it, not knowing its proper name. This sole survivor, a decrepit locust, was the only natural feature of the property unless you count the ditch along the rear boundary.

As for manmade features, there was a concrete path from drive to door, two condensers beside the chimney, and, in the front yard, a metal postlike construction that looked vaguely electrical.

Between the obtrusiveness of the surrounding homes and the ugliness of these appurtenances—and the sad tree, the open ditch, the moldy ground—I failed to

Planting Noah's Garden

appreciate the reason Ellen had chosen this particular site. She had to point it out to me: the views.

Sure enough, across the street and beyond that rank of houses was a glimpse of remnant field. And to the rear, beyond more ranks of homes, a strip of forest formed a distant backdrop.

Ellen wanted that field, that forest, in her yard.

*T*he *New York Times* article that described the talking lawnmower also quoted Dr. David Northington, the executive director of the National Wildflower Research Center, as predicting, "In 30 years, the norm will be designing and planting with this goal in mind of resource conservation. You'll see less chemicals, more wildlife enhancement, increased biodiversity. That will be what's expected in yards, businesses, and roadsides. The water-consuming, chemical-intensive landscapes will be rare. They'll be remnants, almost like the native landscape is a remnant now."

I wish I were so sure.

I'm getting on to sixty now, and I must say I've seen some rapid changes during my life. Public spitting was as common as dandelions when I was a child. We've gone from the Marlboro Man to a smoking ban the way a dandelion goes from bloom to blowball. In both cases, the issue involved public health: airborne germs, secondhand smoke. Already, when a tree is sprayed, a yellow placard at my streetfront warns passersby in the same way that a notice warning of contagion was required in cases of typhoid fever in my parents' day. But if I don't spray, my neighbors aren't going to like my dead weeping cherry either, so I'm not sure they'd appreciate that contribution to the public good.

Something is afoot, though.

Horticulture runs one page an issue on a native species that is thought to be worthy of attention. I'd call the feature a baby step in the right direction. Another magazine that ran an article against lawns gave equal space to the lawn industry—a decidedly timid toe in the water, to my mind. A somewhat bolder approach is represented by a spate of books on gardens for dry or shady areas. At least they're the right-plant-for-the-right-place approach, but "xeriscaping" is sometimes hard to tell from rock gardening, and shade gardening leans heavily on hostas.

The most dramatic and widely publicized style swing is toward the "naturalistic" garden: that is, landscapes that look natural but aren't. An example is a new development here, where the roadsides and other common spaces are planted with low-maintenance species—hundreds of ferns, sweeps of ornamental grasses, bold areas of daylilies, sedums, or astilbes interrupted on occasion by drifting shrubs. Or shrubs adrift: most of the species chosen are exotics that aren't at all at home in New England communities, and the flowers, grasses, trees, and bushes support no more wildlife by being placed naturalistically than they would if they were planted with geometric precision.

An almost opposite concept is the National Wildlife Research Center's Rainbow Prairie. It is designed as bands of Texas grasses and wildflowers arranged in order of height, from short to tall, as in traditional borders and with the colors of each band also chosen by an artful gardener. The idea is a just interpretation of a natural habitat: although precisely arranged and segregated by color, the many species nevertheless make up a grassland community—specifically the one that grows on lime soil in Texas Hill Country—and no doubt the birds and butterflies will be as happy there as they are in Polly's garden. The garden won't be low-maintenance, though, not if the plants have their way. Plants just naturally seed themselves about, and they're not going to stay within their color-coded bands unless someone deadheads them in a timely fashion or annually weeds out the mavericks. To me, even the easily managed all-native yard in the center's demonstration gardens falls short of the mark. It is a literal translation—sage instead of euonymous at the house foundation, bunchgrass instead of turf in the front yard. The design deviates no more from the standard suburban form than a 1040 filled out in Navajo.

So Dr. Northington may be right, and I certainly hope he is, but I don't think we're going to get there on tiptoe. Somebody's got to swing that leg over the fence and stride straight out toward the actual natural landscape, which hovers like a mirage beyond the last ranks of houses.

I spent a morning in the Hill Country when I was in Texas. It's a particularly handsome landscape of short oaks and rugged junipers. The junipers, similar to the species easterners call red cedar, grow larger there than they do here and develop as they age a strong shape and muscular branching. Our junipers grow simply conical or columnar; by the time they're old enough to develop the Texas specimens' eccentric sculpture, the forest has moved into their once-open domain and shaded them out. The Hill Country is too rocky, hot, and dry for mixed deciduous forest ever to take over. It remains a permanent parkland studded with trees and carpeted with short grasses and flowers. I took pictures of the hills. Studying them now, imagining them with houses, it seems crazy to truck in a landscape when one is already in place.

I've seen two examples in which the natural vegetation was left intact as homes were added to the landscape. One was a community in the Sonoran Desert, where the developer had carefully maintained a twenty-foot "envelope" around each house as it was built. Outside this minimal space required for construction, the desert remained untouched. Homeowners had to agree not to disturb the desert habitat and, since most had chosen to replant the envelope itself to match the background, it looked as though one had simply painted in the homes on a Sonoran canvas. The same thing had been done in Wisconsin by the owners of a home in the woods, but to even stricter specifications: the construction envelope extended a mere ten feet from the foundation; the house appeared to have been dropped into place among the oaks.

This is what I think should be the goal: houses set within the natural landscape. And if that is the goal, then there is a very different way to approach the design of even a bare lot with no natural features. Instead of thinking centrifugally, outward from the house, one might think centripetally, inward from the surrounding landscape toward its vacant center. Had the worn fields of Ellen's development simply been abandoned, how might the distant forest have reclaimed them over time?

They would not have recovered the vacancy by merely dropping their seed. The soil in such places is too sterile and dry to receive most forest species. The open area would have been reclaimed at its perimeter first by woodland edge species, mostly small fruiting trees and shrubs. Almost all these hedgerow sorts are dispersed by birds; the toughest of them would in this way have gradually repopulated the center. Joining them would be windborne herbacious species— milkweeds, asters, goldenrods, and grasses. The fields, in fact, would for a while be reminiscent of the Texas hills, but this pioneer community differs in detail and is a transient population in our moister region. Although the junipers are a related species, they grow on acid soil, not on lime, and the grass is taller. Oaks, often the first permanent forest species to reseed the evolving woodland, grow among the junipers in Texas; here they eventually replace them. For thirty years or more, though, an old-field succession is among the most beautiful landscapes I know.

In a purely practical sense, a pioneer community was also about the only one that made sense on Ellen's lot.

If you are designing a foundation planting, you can choose greens freely from hundreds of varieties that cover the salad spectrum, from dark spinach to pale endive and purple radicchio, of loose or crinkled texture, matte or glossy finish, and add a touch of flowers if you wish. Never mind that the bowl is made of clay. Soil can

Tuck a few houses into this pleasing landscape for a vision of what a new development could be like. The old field is growing up with pioneers: oak and birch predominate; there are blueberries and bayberries, too. The copper color of the grass identifies it as either broom sedge or little bluestem, both denizens of sterile soil. (Virginia P. Weinland)

Planting Noah's Garden

be dressed to suit—mixed with sand for better drainage, with peat to hold more moisture, or with compost to improve fertility as well as texture. "Good garden loam" is to planting what vinaigrette is to cooking: the basic sauce for greenery.

You can find the recipe for this mix in any gardening primer. Once you have mastered it, you can devote your time to presentation: thus the fancy salad that surrounded Ellen's lot.

Ellen could not, however, amend the soil on a whole half acre.

The reality of her soil turned out to be even worse than what I had initially taken to be her exaggerated evaluation of it. It was the worst dirt I have ever seen.

It contained no earthworms, no organic matter that earthworms could eat. It was as pale as sand, but not crumbly like sandy soil.

We had dug two holes about twenty inches deep, one in the front yard and another in the back, and filled them with water. In "well-drained" soil, the kind demanded by most plants, the water level subsides one inch per hour. Sand drains more quickly; clay, more slowly. A week later, the water in the front hole had finally reached the bottom. The water in the second hole, farther down the slope, was still ten inches deep. The clay the builder had used to grade the lot was nearly impermeable.

We had put trowel-size lumps from various locations in labeled plastic bags—front yard, back yard, left and right—to send to Ellen's county agent for chemical analysis. The fertility report came back in two weeks: only magnesium was present in sufficient supply to support a garden.

The county agent put us in touch with a soil conservationist in another county office who gave us information about the underlying native soil. According to his map, the soil on which the development had been built was a silty loam of fine texture, excellent drainage, and good fertility. Such maps are quite detailed, showing even small pockets of differing soil types. Each type is keyed to a description, called a profile. The soil profile describes, inch by inch, beginning at the surface and to a depth of several feet, the texture, color, and any characteristic streaking or mottling by which each layer can be recognized. We had checked the profile out in the deep end of the ditch, and it matched exactly.

But could plants find that buried wealth? If roots could punch through the clay above, perforating their own drainage holes and reaching the silky soil below, our options would be open. We sent one last lump of fill to a nurseryman for his opinion of its consistency for seed germination and root growth. The surface clay in that respect, as in all others, was as bad as bad can be.

Had I been better traveled at the time, I would have expected this news—or worse: in developments I later saw, the original topsoil had been scraped off entirely to underlying clay or hardpan and removed from the site. So the pioneering strategy that I then thought unique to Ellen's circumstances now seems to have a more general application, and to those of you who may possess such barren land, I refer you to the plant community from which I chose her species: the vegetation on display along Route 1.

*E*veryone must have a Route 1 somewhere nearby. Ours is the old Post Road, which runs from Florida to Canada. I follow that highway to Ellen's house; I follow it also up the coast of Maine to reach the island where we spend vacations. That August, though, as I played with the design of Ellen's lot in the blessed cool of a northern summer, my model was a particular strip on the way to her house where parking lots alternate with vacant lots in various stages of regrowth from farmland that only here and there still has the energy to grow corn.

The shoulder is subsoil pushed aside during excavation or embankments graded with cheap dirt. Some of the vacant lots were once stores or gas stations, with frontage paved in asphalt. From the cracks grow what grew on Ellen's lot: crabgrass, sowthistle, mugwort. There are other weeds—each region has its own barbarian invaders. Most of them are sufficiently horrifying—matted and smothering, tentacled and strangling—that few stop to enjoy their barbs and coils. Still, there can be found exactly what one would look for on a garden tour: a peaceful scene, a comely shape, a striking composition. Or an ornamental species: even in cracked asphalt I spotted two native meadow grasses, switchgrass (Panicum virgatum) and little bluestem (Schizachyrium scoparium).

The vacant lots along Route 1 are in some places populated with wild crabapples, young oaks and birches, and the ubiquitous red cedar, Juniperus virginiana. In the company of the junipers grow brambles—usually blackberries—and sometimes skirts of bayberry (Myrica pennsylvanica) or blueberry (Vaccineum species). Once I saw farther north on a newer highway a stunning combination of junipers and sumac. The sumac proved to be Rhus aromatica, one I hadn't known about before and a species that, with its tripartite leaves and delicate structure, was much prettier than the coarse sumacs I was used to. Although it is more trying to take roadside inventories than to learn the names of the plants on your own property, the procedure is the same. You take a sample. You identify it. Maybe you add it to your want list.

My list at first was made up entirely of intrepid grasses, shrubs, and trees, most of which were classed by genus only: Quercus, Rubus, Malus, not specific nut or berry. The list became specific as I consulted books to see which species were most likely to endure not only the drought to which rugged roadside sorts are usually accustomed but also waterlogged conditions. Sometimes I made substi-

Roadsides just naturally display happy combinations of intrepid plants. This one, shot along a major interstate in Connecticut, is evergreen red cedar, Juniperus virginiana, with aromatic sumac, Rhus aromatica. (Sara Stein)

tutions. Wild roses and raspberries are natural companions in New Jersey; farther north, wild gooseberries join them. I substituted their close relative, red currants. In this way my list grew literally by association.

Meanwhile, as August progressed, there were ditch developments that lengthened this short list. The ditch ran along the rear of Ellen's lot to a culvert in one corner. It was meant to be temporary: the builder was to install drainage tiles before restoring the grade. Runoff from the yard and the cul-de-sac above was thus to be escorted off and away to some distant destination. Such underground streams are as common as lawn in the suburbs, where water is not supposed to be seen or heard, but this one would have involved granting the town an easement through the yard, and Ellen refused to do it. That's how she came to have a swale instead, the only wetland in the neighborhood.

Regrading the bottom of the yard to create the swale involved scooping off some clay, so the good soil there came almost to the surface. I thought it safe to add some woodsy wetland species to the list, but again just common sorts found in soggy roadside sumps and thickets. The excavated dirt could be used to elevate another portion of the lot, giving us at least a hump where the drainage would be good enough for oaks.

What amazed me about the completed list was that all but one species were described in gardening books as ornamentals. (The one exception, raspberries, was included in the same books for obviously edible reasons.) Yet I had gone about assembling the list backward, not from species to enforced cohabitation, as is done when rhododendrons are plunked down in a lawn, but from the community to the species that naturally compose it.

A pioneer community would differ elsewhere in the country, but its role in moderating original conditions would not. Each region has suites of vegetation that can tolerate the most difficult conditions: drought, flood, sand, clay, sun, wind, sterility. Roots penetrate the ground, improving the drainage where the soil is waterlogged, increasing water retention where the soil dries too quickly. Leaves convert soil minerals to organic matter—compost the ground, make it looser, richer, moister. Ultimately, species that could not have thrived in the original harsh conditions begin to grow in the protective shade of this nursery, and gradually a more permanent community replaces the pioneers. I learned in the Southwest that even desert giants may need pioneer species to nurse their start in life: Saguaro cacti, the equivalent of forest trees in the Sonoran Desert, can't survive their early years unless shaded and protected from predation by pioneers like palo verde trees. In time the mightier cactus kills its nurse, but the time is long. Someday beech might grow among Ellen's birches; for now the pioneers will prepare the way.

Ellen, who deals in real estate, told me that the typical young family these days moves, on the average, every five years. She plans to stay on her lot no more than seven. In that brief interval she won't be able to usher in the forest in the distance, but I wouldn't be surprised if by moving day the oaks have had some babies and a tuliptree perhaps has taken root in the birch grove. I couldn't offer Ellen much choice of wildflowers; only a few have a flair for pioneering. Ten years from now, though, the soil will be changed, and the choices will be many. The wetland, rather sparse in species now, will beg elaboration. The land will mature, become more productive and rich in its diversity.

This is not true of unnatural plantings. Merely decorative plants merely grow. In time they grow too big, or they die; then someone takes them out and redecorates with others. Nothing else happens. There is no evolution. There is no profit set aside for the future because, for all the money spent, there has been no investment in the land.

When our concept of land ownership was generational, it must have seemed ordinary to plant a line of sapling sugar maples that someday one's grandchildren would tap for maple syrup. Sugar maples planted along New England roads are well over a century old, some close to twice that age, but hardly anyone is planting young ones. I think this is deeply wrong, or at least inordinately selfish. I know my land will pass into the hands of strangers; even so, I owe them its future. In our present and difficult transition to a wiser suburban landscape, we are all pioneers, preparing the ground for its future occupancy.

So up in Maine I set to work, sitting at the old nursery table where we ate supper as children, watching the fog lower over the cormorants fishing from the rocks beyond the shore. I had snapshots from Ellen to remind me in that contradictory setting of the hard-baked reality of her lot. And I had an agenda of my own. If Ellen wanted to be reunited with the fields and forests that had been pushed so far into the distance by development, I wanted to demonstrate that some approximation of these ecosystems can be coaxed back onto subdivisions, that they can fit on a small lot, that they are affordable, practical, and suitable to fairly conventional families like hers.

The extent of Ellen's and her husband Marshall's rebellion against social norms is that they like lavender carpeting and dislike yellow trees. Their daughter, Rachel, who at five preferred to carpet her own room in shocking purple, requested that the outdoor plan include a plum tree. Perhaps there was a touch of romantic self-imagery in Ellen's wish for a private place where she could retreat into the shade on a summer afternoon to read a book. Nothing more eccentric emerged in discussions about the future landscape. Ellen wanted to have trees, to pick flowers, to grow vegetables, to keep her eye on Rachel, and to keep the eyes of neighbors off herself. She used words like "tailored," "simple," and "natural." As for the details of plans and plant lists, she left the matter entirely to her designing aunt.

However, until then I had never designed another person's lot.

I'd sketched some of our own gardens with enough accuracy to guess the number of plants, but mostly I'd worked on plans outdoors, with hoses to lay the shapes of beds and real plants to fill them in. And I'd developed our landscape gradually, one area at a time, over many years; there had never been a master plan, laid out all at once on a survey, as professional designers do. The only way I can draw is painstakingly and from a photograph. Large sheets of paper frighten me.

So I started small, with thumbnails, working with tiny copies of Ellen's survey on which the house was not much larger than a commemorative stamp and the lot itself could have fit inside a pocket notebook. I sort of doodled; it was fun, like making up a map of an imaginary land in four colors: grove, thicket, meadow, path. I proceeded as though there were nothing more to a landscape than open and closed spaces, tall and short growth, and paths to follow. Eventually I spent amusing hours with these little replicas to see how other plans might meet the needs of other families in different circumstances, but the basic scheme for Ellen's half acre fell into place almost by itself: open front and center, closed along the sides, wooded to the rear. Nothing to it.

But not much information either.

To get from scribbled zones of vegetation to a plan from which to lay out the contours and order the plants, I had to learn from Marty, an architect, something about the representation of real dimensions and from Ellen the measurements themselves. The survey gave major footage—lot lines, house walls, sidewalks—but where exactly was the kitchen door, and where, in relation to it, were the garbage pails? the compost heap? the barbecue? There had to be a meter box to which the meter maid (or man) must find her (or his) monthly way: anti-intuitively, it was at the opposite side of the house from the driveway and garage, where, on my thumbnail sketch, no path led. The apparatus for Rachel's play yard had already been ordered; the safety instructions called for a mulched area extending ten feet beyond the perimeter in all directions. Ellen needed to supervise the play area from the kitchen window; she also wanted a chummy relationship between the play space and the vegetable garden. And more requirements came to light. The sun shone cruelly into the family room during the afternoon; neighbors could see directly into the master bedroom window; Marshall planned to build a patio; Rachel had graduated from plums alone to all sorts of berries.

There was, in short, a little more to this designing business than I had realized.

Marty showed me how to scale up the original survey to a larger size on graph paper and how to position accurately the doors, windows, meter box, mailbox, play set, barbecue, sewer line, electrical service, hose bibbs, paved walks, steps, and other "hard" aspects of the landscape that don't appear on subdivision surveys. I expected to be reduced to tears, but wasn't. I had a little trouble with the play area and patio, so finally I just cut them to scale from another sheet of paper and pushed them about, the way one does with paper chairs and tables to plan a living room.

Marty tried to teach me some fancy stuff, such as how to represent trees correctly, the way real architects do, and something about the arc of the sun that was just too hard to grasp—and that nearly did bring on the tears, convincing me I really didn't need to learn a second profession when muddling along would do.

Also, I returned to Marty the circle template he had loaned me for the accurate scaling of each tree or shrub. I know that's how it's done: one looks up the ultimate width of a species in a horticultural encyclopedia and draws circles to match. I looked up highbush blueberry, Vaccineum corymbosum, just for laughs. The book said eight to twelve feet wide. Such fat cats must have been grown as specimens in botanical gardens. In nature, you can't tell how many blueberries form the thicket in which they normally grow, much less their individual widths. I figured the birch grove was going to be roughly fifty feet square, about a quarter of the back yard. If I had spaced the birches according to their specimen values of forty to sixty feet, the "grove" would have contained one tree.

Plants don't read books, don't grow alone, and seldom in the wild or in our lifetime reach literary dimensions. I treat them as stuff, not things; as mass, not objects. I think of shrubs as crowds and trees as trunks. Even though I eventually had to pin down the number of plants so I could order them, that remained a loose sort of figure because there were no beds in the formal sense, only elastic contours that could shrink or expand depending on how many plants fit into the budget.

I did learn from Marty two trade secrets that gave the drawings a professional look. One is to use nonsmearing Prismacolor pencils for the trees and shrubs. The second is the trick of slipping a piece of rough watercolor paper beneath the drawing to create a foliage texture—the same way that, as children, we used to make a perfect rubbing of a penny. My foliage came out more like cauliflower than leaves, but I couldn't show Ellen anyway what I was really seeing as my mind roamed breezily through those long, lazy August days.

Could anyone draw an actual ecosystem in aerial perspective? One of the reasons suburban landscapes look fussy is that they comprise disparate elements that don't overlap and aren't grounded in the grassy or twiggy matrix that is nature's joinery. I could show shrubs next to trees, but I couldn't depict the way the mound of thicketing dogwood would penetrate the grove of birches or how the roses and raspberries would tangle, or the ferns wander off into the grass, or the huckleberries weave their autumn scarlet among the green bayberries. One can choose the species and put them in their places, but one cannot tell them what to do once the community is assembled.

Ellen, baking on her bare lot in New Jersey, of course wanted more than vegetable texture. She wanted the specifics, the species, the names of the trees whose shade she longed for. I jotted down the actual or possible species in the margins, added notes of explanation, and sent the finished drawing off to Ellen.

And waited.

And felt nervous.

And needn't have.

The measure of success for this drawing was that, from the day it arrived and for weeks thereafter, Ellen and Marshall took it to bed with them at night to wander in their minds through the paper landscape.

And I must admit, it didn't look as if it had been inspired by ditches and fill and vacant lots along that tired section of Route 1.

"Don't offend the neighbors," Marshall had quietly ordered one morning over Rice Krispies with bananas.

As though one should not be offended by yards flashing at one's unshielded eyes every contorted and strangely colored mutant that commerce can provide! Or by the soul-crunching rules that bound these young relatives of mine!

Suburbia has come to signify not only a style of landscape but a cultural style. Front yards are considered the communal possession of everyone on that street, even if an owner can legally plant a private forest right against the sidewalk. One can have street trees—in fact, one often must—but where Ellen lives they must conform to all the others on the street by species and variety. The result on Ellen and Marshall's block is a double row of lollipops. No fences may be erected. The illusion is of no boundaries; the reality is no privacy. In their community, pets must be on leashes; their cat is kept indoors. I remember reading once, in the first sentence of the opening paragraph of regulations for a California condo, that "animals and children" were not allowed.

Well, you can imagine! If I were not subversive by nature, I would in those environs soon become so.

My bow to convention had been a vegetation version of Mom and apple pie: Mom relaxing with her book in the birch grove, familiar to us all from postcards if not in the wild; and apples—not the pie type but crabapples, suitable for jelly—arranged as an orchard in the streetfront meadow of uniform little bluestem grass. I think I was considerate not to march red cedars around the perimeter of the lot (the prohibition is against dead fences, not living ones). I know I don't like it when opaque barriers suggest that my presence in the landscape would spoil the owner's view. Except where the windows had to be screened from prying eyes and the glaring sun, I had left the perimeter somewhat transparent—not walls but drifts of shrubs, not one height but varied, not solid but with openings through which to glimpse the meadow. I'd say that I had done my civic duty, but you might say it was on paper only. For a community accustomed to rolled-out landscapes, what ensued was in fact a pretty messy business.

One fine October day I and my friend Camilla, a practiced gardener and designer, set out in her pickup truck loaded with stakes and hoses to lay out Ellen's lot. It took us and Ellen, too, all day. We couldn't even hammer the stakes in straight to show the locations of the trees; the ground was too hard, and the stakes stood lopsided and wobbly. We ran out of stakes to mark the paths and had to use instead those plastic flags used by lawn companies to lay out irrigation lines; then we ran out of flags as well and had to spray-paint the paths on the ground. The rectangular areas—patio, play space, vegetable garden—were indicated with stakes and strings that looked plain ugly. Day's end displayed a bare lot strewn with crooked sticks, knotted strings, red flags, white paint, and miscellaneous hoses. Even we, armed with the paper plan that made sense of it all, felt shamed by the trashy scene.

But in the following weeks, Ellen and Marshall filled in the makeshift lines with mulch. They raked shredded bark along the edges of areas that would be planted with trees and shrubs, then filled in the contours to the lot lines. They sprayed the paths with herbicide to delineate them clearly against the greenish, weedy ground. The effect was as though a giant, working from the paper plan, had colored it in full size. There, in weed green, the meadow; slicing through it the pale tan path; and there, in bark-brown, the bulge where thickets would billow through the grove that curved below. As on the plan, the eye could sweep the contours all around, grasp the whole, see how that bare ground would grow into a world in three dimensions.

The mulching of the back yard was almost finished when the landscaper delivered the final load of bark. He was stunned. He plied his trade maintaining grounds and putting in new plantings on this development and many others like it. He laid out borders, shaped island beds, lined walks, installed trees, and composed shrubbery along foundations. He said simply, "I didn't know landscapes could be done like this."

So plain a statement from a man whose perceptions had been flipped!

It was not a planar lawn with objects placed on it but a solid geometry cut through by flat paths. It was not a lot with corners but a curvaceous and flowing space whose limits might be perceived from outside, but not from within. We are accustomed to stepping from our doorway into a world without direction, with no place to go and no reason to get there. Who ever visits their blue spruce? Here were routes and places, real destinations. On Ellen's lot, as time goes by, you won't be able to see everything that's there unless you walk to find it.

I saw kids come home from school the day we began to plant. We were trundling stock about, placing shrubs and getting the larger trees into the ground by backhoe. One mother was taking care of five or six young children. Small girls clustered around her on a driveway across the street, mostly talking. Two boys climbed to the top of a dirt heap in front of the unfinished house next door. The mother admonished them repeatedly to get down (it is true, they were throwing clods into the street). A girl in white tights tried to join them, but turned back when warned about dirtying her clothes. Finally the boys broke a bottle against the pavement, and that was the end of their brief adventure.

I felt not just subversion at this way of life but anger. This was not childhood. It was a crime against it.

Except for swing sets and that temporary dirt heap, there was nowhere to go and nothing to do on that suburban landscape. No trees to climb, no piles of leaves to toss or roll in, no woods, no streams, no fields, no paths leading to adventure. Even a clod of dirt is precious when the land has been raked of the treasures children hunt for: pine cones, crow feathers, snail shells, lumps of quartz or mica. No child growing up on that development can make daisy chains or build twig furniture. There's not even a blade of grass long enough to hold between the thumbs to blast a screech from it. Kids there won't search for peepers with a flashlight on spring evenings. They won't chase butterflies, follow fox tracks across the snow, tempt chipmunks with hickory nuts and acorns, or stain their lips with blackberries gathered by the road. They won't have those secret places where children go to escape the eyes of grownups and conduct their private lives. There is no place to hide on that development.

Rachel was also home from school. The giant painting of how her own yard would be planted had meant nothing to her. She was too young to grasp, as the landscaper had immediately, what was to come from the mulch. But the day we were planting, when the crabapple trees were already dug into the front yard, Rachel literally grasped what we were up to. She visited each tree in turn, all seven of them, to touch and pluck their fruit. These were not the sweet dessert she'll one day pick along the berry path, but they were the only fruit around.

By late afternoon, five serviceberries were also in the ground at one end of the swale, and the shrubs for that corner were arrayed beneath them. Incomplete as it was, it looked like woodland. The older children were home by then; more parents had assembled. It was getting dark. Camilla and I were packing up our gear, getting ready to go home. I was vaguely aware of pedestrian traffic through the yard, of talk down in that corner so recently and magically transformed. I didn't hear until later what had happened.

One neighbor decided on the spot to replace her weeping tree with one that would be more natural. Another wanted to replant her whole front yard.

I don't think the people in Ellen's development love their landscape. I don't think they find it comfortable or charming, exciting or beautiful. I think they had a hard time choosing the specimen on their lawn and aren't sure whether their neighbor's choice was better. I think most of them pretty much left the whole business up to the landscaper because they didn't know what else to do. I'm sure their children, as they discover plums and crickets and secret hiding places, will wish they lived on Ellen's lot.

Planting Noah's Garden

5 In Search of Purple Lovegrass

I DON'T KNOW WHY ANYTHING should be as American as apple pie, since apples aren't American. The only native members of the Malus genus are a handful of sour green crabapples, and they hybridized long ago with the zillion immigrants that are now assimilated across the countryside. On the other hand, maybe that makes apples all the more American: I've come upon groups of wild trees, some of which bore red fruit, others yellow or green, ranging in size from peas to dumplings, and growing no farther apart from one another than people at a party. Could Johnny Appleseed have tossed about pits from Siberia and Japan, from every country in Northern Europe, and from China, too? Still, when I think of American fruit, I think of the blueberry and huckleberry tribes, which remain as distinct to their regions of the country and as true to themselves as they were when bears lived in Brooklyn.

I discovered dried blueberries last year—belatedly, I must say. Dried blueberries, along with dried buffalo meat and venison, were an ingredient of pemmican, a concentrated, suet-based, mincemeat-like trail mix carried by Indians on the move. Now they're gourmet nibbles. I think I also discovered why blueberry pie is flavored with spices: it's to make the commercial product taste like its wild cousin, huckleberry. Huckleberries come spicy off the bush. I like to read about these fruits—how wild stands are burned to enliven them, how their berries are harvested with a tined scoop invented for the purpose. Washington County, Maine, is the center of the wild blueberry industry: lowbush blueberries, Vaccinium angustifolium, not the cultivated highbush ones, V. corymbosum, whose large fruit is rather bland. One picks up this information along the way, not looking for it exactly, just tasting, listening, walking, watching, reading along that digressive jaunt called research.

My eastern shrub guide, which covers only half the country, lists twenty-two Vaccinium species, and they're not even all called blueberries. Some are bilberries, deerberries, or farkleberries. Cranberries—what could be more American?—are a Vaccinium species, too. Those Vacciniums called blueberries have added to their common name an adjective that hints at their broad distribution and creative adaptation: early and late; northern, southern, and coastal; high, low, and slender (one is called "black blueberry"). The turn of a page brings me to their close relatives, the huckleberries, Gaylussacia species that again range from dwarf to tall and are distributed in the eastern half of the continent, from the Canadian tundra to the Gulf States. I find even longer lists in a book that sweeps the continent coast to coast along the northern tier: the West is as blessed as we are by blueberries and huckleberries under their confusion of names. I'd love to try a whortleberry pie.

When species have such folksy common names, one suspects that folks must once have been on intimate terms with them. How can it be, then, that when Marty and I planted for an elderly friend at her condominium a specimen of the commonest blueberry, the one whose cultivated varieties of oversize and underflavored fruit we buy in supermarkets, none of the grandparent population strolling by had the foggiest notion what it was?

The bush, grown in the wild and thick with cream bell flowers, did cause comment—it certainly did not look like the yew it was replacing—but it did not light a spark of recognition. Perhaps to these passersby the word "blueberry" applied to a flowering shrub failed to connect to the boxes of fruit they buy. And if berry bushes have no significance to these retirees, I suppose they mean nothing to their children or grandchildren either.

We are entering our third generation of disconnection from the land.

Disconnection is chief among my worries.

All that separated Ellen from her neighbors was a thin veil of nostalgia—not for blueberries, I admit, but for a relict apple orchard where she had once played beyond the confines of her neighborhood. Through this veil she felt the sun-dappled shade, smelled the meadow grass, recalled the stolen fruits of childhood that, once tasted, are longed for ever after.

My own recollection of rural countryside is a richer and stronger brew—pungent with cows, sharp with thistles, running with elderberry jam. The strength of that nostalgia seems to me an accurate measure also of my greater resolution to leave behind me in this world at least a blaze of berries. I don't see how the stranded children of this generation will come to treasure what they have never known.

I don't think the conflagration of the Amazon or the possibility that whales might choke on kids' balloons means much to them beyond that the world is dangerous. I don't believe that glow-in-the-dark firefly handpuppets or save-the-animal cookies will lead them in adulthood to plant meadows or like bats. I'm sure they'd prefer to have the pine tree, where, on a bough level with the dormers, I read Jean Henri Fabre's *Life of the Spider* in aerial enchantment. (Or maybe they'd rather have a huckleberry pie.)

That this disconnection has happened in my lifetime was brought home to me by a book called *Honeysuckle Sipping*, by Jeanné Chesanow. Chesanow was moved by her own recollections to gather childhood plant lore as expressed in such pastimes as petal plucking, burr basketry, and nut games. Among her research tactics was to solicit letters from readers of gardening magazines who might recall how they perceived plants when they were children. Quite a few wrote about hiding places: a perch in a pine tree much like mine, the tunnels of a rabbit warren in a stand of brambles, a space matted down inside a fern glade, an alder thicket, a privet hedge, a boxwood bush, a nest made of grass on a hummock in a swamp.

There was in these recollections a sensual quality, the sort of intimacy or animism by which children endow plants with sentience and affection: milkweed fish, sedum frogs, acorns wearing hats. At the mention of sour sorrel, my tongue curled around long-ago flavors: spruce resin, wintergreen leaves, black birch twigs, the green-flavored sweet of mulberries.

Following these threads of recollection, though, led to their gradual unraveling as farmland turned residential in the years following World War II. The mulberry tree was taken down. Its fruits are messy, says my gardening encyclopedia. The pussy willows that had been my pocket pets were also removed (the same book wastes fewer than twenty words on the species). And the grape arbor: a dark, cool tunnel mingling the incense of cedar posts with the heavy fragrance of ripe grapes and the shreddy touch of bark with softly rolling fruit and springy tendrils. The sweetness of wild grapes is just beneath the skin; the pulp is sour; the seeds are good for spitting. I liked especially the Japanese beetles that skeletonized the leaves, but I guess I was in solo beetlemania. The arbor was torn down. My old pine tree was felled, too. It was brittle and dangerously close to the house.

Still, there were at that time uncurried roadsides where burrs and scouring rushes could be gathered, where I could find touch-me-nots to pop and hawthorn swords to fit into elderberry scabbards. The style now is mowed roadsides, sometimes with daffodils. As a friend in New Hampshire wrote to me recently, a thicket is fast becoming a place you have to drive to see. Certainly Rachel and her friends don't have between them a stalk of timothy to nibble.

I put down Chesanow's book with sadness. The lore that it relates is centuries old, handed down among children through the mnemonics of the natural world, but now dead, severed like brush along the roadside.

We haven't intended to cut these connections any more than some old farmer intended to snare Ellen in the decrepit apple trees he left standing in his field. Now, though, the repair will have to be on purpose—and there is no book on preserving a child's habitat, no field guide to the plants they love. In innumerable books on how to raise a child, I've never seen mention of flowers, acorns, or even hiding places; fruit comes washed, packed with vitamins, pureed: not on the bush, as Rachel wanted it. Sometimes in Maine, when we walk along the granite shore, we see elfin artifacts—cairns of small stones, little winding walls, flat rocks arranged with sticks, bayberries, rose petals, bladderwrack, empty crab claws, and urchin shells. It is important to understand that not all research is carried out in the pages of a book.

My travels began in earnest the fall that Ellen's lot was planted. It soon became clear to me how unraveled is the knit of what I had once thought was "common" knowledge. Much as those who came to listen to my talks were moved to restore connections, few had any clear idea of where to start. Over and over, everywhere and from people of every age, I was asked, in effect, "How do you know what to plant?" Sometimes the question was phrased, "How do you find out what's native?" or "Where can I get a list of species?" Or, more specifically still, "What should I plant to attract birds?" or "Which grass should I choose for a meadow?"

These questions are easy to answer: books, lists, catalogs, government publications, native plant societies, and nature centers provide such information. What is harder to provide is the connective spark—the excitement, the discovery that children experience when they are wild and free and that moves them as Ellen was moved to bring the magic back. What I wish to do is send you off to play, to taste your own wild fruit, to see for yourself what lies at the end of the path.

To follow your purple lovegrass, as I have followed mine.

*W*e traveled to an island off the coast of Maine one summer when our boys were young, went exploring up a humped dirt road past ugly alder thickets, followed the ruts higher still, where huckleberry crowded against the gravel, emerged onto solid rock and into another world: an enchanted garden growing from the granite surface of an abandoned quarry.

I had thought I was too mature to be so stricken. In childhood, wonder was easily aroused by even a grassy glade unexpectedly sunlit in dark sugar maple woods, but what once was magical becomes more plain with age, and glistening days of dew and spiderwebs shine brighter in memory than in the present sun. Yet I was transported.

Pitch pines stood in frozen postures like dancers caught in strobe lights. Cracks overflowed with what I took to be a heather and ran into pools of low blueberries touched with crimson by the chill advance of autumn. Slight depressions—gritty puddles in the spring but bone dry now—were filled with mosses, tiny grasses, miniature asters. It seemed impossible that plants could grow so thickly on so little nourishment or water.

The human past of the island quarries is depicted at the town's historical society. The island was once an important source of granite, and its quarries provided stone for the old U.S. Custom House and the Cathedral of St. John the Divine in New York City, and curbs and cobbles for city streets as well. Old photographs show that the rock surfaces were totally denuded while the industry was active. In some pictures, a rim of spruce forest is evidence of the original cover. One of the quarries was reopened briefly some years ago; the rest have not been worked for most of this century. The largest is filled by springs with icy water so clear that you can see forty feet deep, to where the tracks on which blocks were hauled to the dressing sheds still lie along the bottom. At another, huge blocks of granite, some the size of vans and trucks, lie in mountainous heaps as though dropped in thunder from the sky. But at the quarry we found that day, the uncut surface stretches smooth for acres. Isolated blocks lie here and there like steles recording ancient works, and the garden weaves among them.

The natural history of this bald rock was more elusive. People ask me how much research I do for my writing, and I suppose I do a lot. But not earnestly or with a scholar's sense of purpose. It's more in the way of wandering to see what I might find, and often I discover along even the hard road of textbooks the equivalent of lumps of quartz or mica, gems of information. So, in a book about the Appalachians, I stumbled across the information that what is happening on the abandoned quarry surface is the elemental process of primary succession: the plants are making soil from rock as the first land plants did when the world was new and bare.

The book described how, along bald mountaintops scoured by wind and etched by lichens, unique and rare communities of herbs and grasses make the soil in which later successional stages will take root. Quarry surfaces are not true balds like these, where millennia may pass before erosion and vegetation pulverize

Isle au Haut Mountain, inspiration for the stone terrace. (Sara Stein)

the stone to any depth of dirt. These newer balds support species that can easily be found elsewhere, and the rate at which they create soil is also faster. Yet by comparison with secondary succession, which zips from field to woods in a life-time, time on these stone acres seems to have stood still.

The quarry—called Isle au Haut Mountain (the term is used loosely on the island)—looks to me now just as it did when I first saw it a quarter of a century ago. Only a few tough species root in crevices or survive by grit alone in depressions on the rock. Maybe the crowberry has spread its heathered stems a little farther, mulching its way over the rock on its own litter. The pitch pines that pry into the deeper clefts must have grown some, but the abrasive dirt they grow in is so poor and dry that they are certainly stunted. Here and there, shaggy junipers have rooted among the mats of lowbush blueberry. They may be newcomers. Possibly the rear guard of species that need more soil and moisture—bayberry, lambkill—have advanced somewhat. But the magic of this granite garden is unchanged, and so, for all the years, had been my wish to make a garden like it.

This was sheer fantasy, of course. I don't happen to have a quarry at my dis-

Planting Noah's Garden

posal. But so was Ellen's vision of herself reading in a grove of trees a fantasy, and so was Rachel's odd notion of picking plums. One works from the inside out, from the inner adventure to its outward expression: the discovery of this secret garden, the pleasure that it gave our children, and the many routes by which it led to our present garden are my paradigm for research.

I woke up one sunny morning in July, looked out our bedroom window, and saw the stone garden there below me as though it actually existed. It was a terrace, really, laid in rough and weathered slabs that followed the contours of the ground: they rose gently in the middle, sloped down to the retaining wall, and rose again to meet the bedrock where it breaks into a knob. In its beds grew those dry species that inhabit granite balds, and in the cracks between the fieldstones small flowers glinted among short, tufted grasses that also furred the beds.

I recognized in the image some of the shrubs—the familiar, the actual, the ones I knew the names of. Blueberries, of course—the lowbush ones—with black huckleberry, Gaylussacia baccata. I recognized wild strawberries, too; but what grass was that, which flowers? I can't explain the mystery of this, but it often happens that one creates an image first and then must find the plants to fit it. So began a years-long search to find the plants to fill the picture that, during the next few seasons, we laid the background for in stone.

This research was more complicated than that for Ellen, yet the first plant I found was in fact along a road. Traveling through New England on the way home from the island late that summer, we passed a stretch of highway clouded in lavender bloom. The soft haze, which proved to be the pollen-dusted flowers of a short and sturdy grass, went on for miles along the inhospitably hot and dry median that separated the six lanes of a major interstate. It was just what I was looking for; it fit the picture.

But did it fit the habitat? Although grit and rock were to hone my plant list, the terrace is not a granite bald, and we are not in Maine.

The stone garden I was dreaming of as we sped through the lavender haze was not in any sense a natural environment. It was, at that time, lawn. Because we'd built the house, we knew something of what lay beneath the grass. We'd had to blast the underlying granite to make way for a cellar, and we'd had to install sprinklers to keep this drought-prone back lawn green over the great mass of rock that wasn't blasted and that in places came to within inches of the turf before rising clear of it to form the knob. Despite the similarity of the underlying rock to that of the quarry, and the poverty of the soil that covered it, and the baking heat of this dead south exposure, the natural community here was one of secondary, not primary, succession. Red cedars had grown here before we'd planted lawn; so had birches and young oaks similar to those that now are pioneers on Ellen's lot.

Trees that size, though, weren't in my picture.

Neither were the pitch pines that grow on the quarry. They'd look plain wrong against a landscape of meadow and apple orchard, overlooking a muskrat pond.

There were physical complications, too. Below a kitchen window, a tube spilled condensation water from the air conditioner in summer, creating a sort of wet-land unknown in nature. A third of the expanse fell under the shade of an old white oak, and there the soil was moist, cool, and woodsy. Soil was just dry dirt elsewhere, except where we once had dug and enriched it for a vegetable garden whose exact location and dimension neither of us remembered until the wild strawberries we planted grew to twice their normal height in what was supposed to be a lean, scrubby, undernourished garden.

Then too, the knob was already planted with boxwood and a weeping hemlock. Along the stone retaining wall that created this stretch of lawn ran a line of enclos-ing shrubbery—another collector's hemlock, more box, and a bunch of Japanese hollies. A trumpet vine grew at a corner of the house; a butterfly bush stood next to the garage. The whole area was more or less continuous with an herb garden, of all things. If "natural habitat," like human character, implies some underlying and trustworthy uniformity of traits, then this area was ecologically schizophrenic.

There were animals. A flicker regularly mined the herb garden after a rain for ants extracted from the sand between the paving bricks. A chipmunk had made its burrow on the knob under the weeping hemlock. Butterflies were frequent vis-itors to the bush named for them; hummingbirds enjoyed the trumpet flowers. So, for all that this was not a documented ecosystem, and therefore the flora proper to it was nowhere described, it was a habitat, and its inhabitants had a claim on its future.

Like other people planning natural gardens, I was caught in a web of contra-dictions that nothing so simple as a list of dryland species could have resolved. I had to poke around, cut my own sort of path, and it was only a first taste of the adventure to stop along a highway to see a blooming grass.

We stopped and took a sample of it, our first questionable choice: a grass that grew in sand and in New Hampshire, with not a rock in sight.

I thought I'd finished roadside basics long ago, but until I chanced to pass it in late summer bloom, I'd never noticed that sanded, salted, roadside grass that I hoped would take a central position in a garden almost as inimical to survival as I-495.

But what was that grass?

Grasses are hard to identify; none of my three wildflower guides was of help, although one shows a few grass species whose bloom is striking. Even my county agents, who have given me the names of many plants I've come upon over the years, must send most grass samples to an expert at Cornell for identification. The grasses I feel most secure about are those weeds that occur on our own place and that can usually be found in the Dover reprint *Common Weeds of the United States.* I checked it first: if a plant is in that book, it shouldn't be in one's garden (it wasn't).

No doubt I could have found the grass among the 190 pages of Graminiae

The lawn before it was a terrace. We started to lay out the design by trenching along the curves that were to be paths. Eventually the whole lawn, paths as well as beds, was deturfed by hand (we didn't know you could rent a machine to do it).
(Sara Stein)

microscopically described in *An Illustrated Flora of the Northern United States and Canada,* the three-volume work published by Dover in its second, revised edition of 1913 and known informally by its authors' names, Britton & Brown. But I don't have a microscope. Luckily, a more recent Brown—Lauren Brown—included my quarry in her guide for amateurs: *Grasses: An Identification Guide.* It was Eragrostis spectabilis, purple lovegrass.

Once I have the name of a plant that appeals to me by looks or habitat or both, I can begin to evaluate whether or how to use it. Is it, in the first place, native? Field guides usually give that information, but county agents usually don't. If it is a native, does it also normally grow in my area? At one point in this venture I spotted a striking shrub blooming along a dirt road in a neighboring town and easily identified it in the Peterson Field Guides *Eastern Trees.* It was bottlebrush buckeye, Aesculus parviflora, an American for sure, but not a Yankee: the species occurs naturally over an extremely limited range in the southern Appalachians. The one I saw must have been planted as an ornamental.

How far one wants to pursue such a find depends on how pure one wants to be. My friend and pen pal Mike McKeag never detours beyond species that occur naturally in the Willamette Valley of southwestern Oregon. I like following these loops, though, just to see where they will lead. My decision to get back on the highway will be easier if I find out, for instance, that the bush needs the alkaline soil I can't provide, or is prone to disease, or has invaded and degraded local habitats.

For most finds, the information needed to make a decision is more likely to be found in horticultural encyclopedias than in field guides. I looked up the buckeye in several of these tomes and in other volumes, too: books about woody landscape plants and native ornamentals. Sources never quite agree; authors are biased: I smile to imagine these experts closeted together in buckeye confrontation.

Some mentioned negatives. This buckeye spreads by suckering—which I suppose could be a positive where there's lots of space to fill. In our zone there may not be enough time between flowering and frost for the nuts to ripen. The nuts and all other parts are poisonous anyway (I thought about the chipmunk). And neither the buckeye nor any of its associates grow on dry, rocky, or sandy ground anywhere at all.

Strike that one.

On the other hand, I'd also seen—this time in a garden—Fothergilla gardenii, dwarf fothergilla. It looked like a miniature, refined version of the coarse alder that we pass along the damp ditches of the dirt road leading to the quarry. Unlike the catkinned alder, though, fothergilla breaks into bottlebrush bloom just like the buckeye, and the blooms, I read, are spicily fragrant. Its habit is described as dense, twiggy, mounded, and picturesque; its thick leaves turn every color in the fall—purple, scarlet, gold. It grows in mesic to dry soil in the shade of white oak trees.

But, the map of its natural distribution told me, no farther north than the mountains of northern Tennessee.

I listed it anyway. Brought it home, so to speak. My reading of the Ice Age suggests that many species once at home in northern forests found refuge along the flanks of the Appalachians farther south as the glaciers buried the boundaries of their former range. Their rates of return have depended on their mode of dispersal—wind and birds are rapid transit, mere dropping of the seeds is slow. Or perhaps some species remain trapped at altitudes equivalent in climate to the northern latitudes and haven't been able to hop the intervening valleys. Edwin Way Teale writes in *North with the Spring* of continually losing and refinding spring as he ascended peaks and descended valleys along the mountain spine. As far as I can tell from my never-to-be-repeated drive up Mount Washington—with the children who had insisted on it huddled, crying in terror, on the floor—temperate zone summer never does climb that high, and tundra vegetation stranded at such altitudes will never get back to where it started. The romance of such thoughts eventually moved me to include several southeastern mountain species—especially small flowers common to mountaintops—on the imaginative presumption that, in another ten thousand years, some anyway might regain their former foothold in these parts. (I once read a remark by a geologist that when she gets depressed by the present state of environmental affairs, she reverts to "deep time," in which the smallest unit of measurement is ten million years or so: humans disappear altogether at that resolution.)

Purple lovegrass required no stretch of fantasy. According to Lauren Brown's field guide, the species is native and widespread (Britton & Brown, in which I had no trouble finding it once I knew its name, describes the range of *Eragrostis spectabilis* as "Maine to South Dakota, south to Florida and Texas"). It is a short grass (I had feared it might have been artificially shortened by the summer's mowing). It would indeed appreciate the sand between the stones. And it grows "in little tufts," is perennial, common, and "beautiful." These last attributes were important because they meant that purple lovegrass wouldn't spread by rhizomes into places where it wasn't wanted, would be a permanent planting, had apparently held its own against incursion by alien weeds, and, because it is so showy when in bloom, was probably commercially available.

Purple lovegrass and wild strawberry were the first—and so far only—items on the list of native herbacious species with which I intended to clothe the ground among the bushes on what would be our stone terrace.

*S*o winter came, without much progress. I felt like a vole under the snow, nosing along, sampling this and that without gaining much sense of how one tidbit related to another. I became a member of the National Wildflower Research Center to gain access to its clearinghouse. Through this repository, I sent for lists of native species by state—including shrubs, vines, trees, and ferns as well as wildflowers—and names of native plant associations, commercial sources, and bibliographies. I joined the New England Wild Flower Society and sent for booklets describing various habitats—wetland, woodland, meadow—and listing species for them. The resulting paper snowstorm didn't help.

It was not the fault of these fine organizations. One can't expect the Garden in the Woods, the botanical showplace of the New England Wild Flower Society, to publish plant lists for a dryland terrace trying to look quarryish behind its evergreen front of the boxwood 'Varder Valley'. On the list of meadow plants, species were arranged alphabetically by botanical name, Lupinus following Lobelia. But tracking the species through a field guide (to see pictures of them), one finds the lupine growing in dry, sandy fields, the lobelia mucked in wetland. Like roadside rambles, these short courses in what to plant were very basic: species that have proved successful for the average gardener are visually prominent, and are commonly available. (Wild strawberry was not among them.)

Woody plants were listed apart from wildflowers—and grasses often weren't listed at all—whereas all sorts of plants were to share the beds on the terrace as they do in natural habitats. One runs into the same problem when drawing up plant lists for even the simplest natural garden. I had used a list of New Jersey flora to specify river birch, Betula nigra, for Ellen's grove, and found in a book about plant communities mention of the oaks with which it normally associates, but what ferns might carpet the grove was nowhere stated. The move to champion native species has in general been focused on getting gardeners to substitute natives for exotics, an American birch rather than a Japanese or European. A sense of community is lacking—what goes with what and how the vegetation changes from sun to shade, dry to moist, sand to clay.

To get an overall picture, I sent for a bunch of Sierra Club Naturalist Guides, which cover most areas of the country. The one for southern New England took me on a pleasant journey from the "hilltop community" (where I found most of the species that grow on Isle au Haut Mountain) down through woods and old fields to the "sand plain community" (where I found them again). I began to feel secure about some of the shrubs: Myrica pennsylvanica, the bayberry that had been a member of the terrace's original community, also grows among coastal dunes and on rocky highlands. It spreads at the moister rims of island quarries, too. It was an easy choice.

The volume, though, had little to say about flowers and nothing about grass. And shouldn't dryland mosses be part of this stone-in-sand community?

I can't recall now exactly how my list grew through that academic, trip-interrupted winter. I read other Sierra guides, most of Edwin Way Teale, a book called *Fields & Forests*—what you might call a research meander. I found mention of a plant I hadn't seen for years, pearly everlasting, Anaphalis margaritacea: its beeswax scent came back to me, and with it memories of papery flowers bunched into self-sticking bouquets by their woolly, resinous stems and presented to me by the children one summer. Where had they found them growing, though? Somewhere I came upon rusty woodsia, Woodsia ilvensis, a short, matted fern that grows on exposed rock outcroppings in full sun with dry mosses (Hah! I knew it! But the moss genus was unnamed). I ran across a dwarf goldenrod—gray goldenrod, Solidago nemoralis—that barely reaches a foot high in dry or sandy soil. Some such creature grows also on the quarry balds along with a similarly dwarfed aster. But I'd neglected to sample either and didn't know which they were.

Perhaps I was a spurious traveler, collecting artifacts from this or that stop along the way without understanding much about the cultures that had produced them. Bad enough that I'd never seen a fothergilla except in someone's garden: I'd never seen the goldenrod at all, nor the fern, nor the lovegrass in the company of any of the others. One can see in native plant collections what a wild geranium looks like, but what it looks like sprinkled through the grass is entirely different. Even our nature center began to appear to me suspiciously like a souvenir stand, with its stuffed chipmunks and labeled poison ivy. I longed to strike out over the hills and through the woods as I had dared when I was a child but that now I feared to do alone.

Why didn't I join nature walks led by competent guides? There are many of them, arranged by the Audubon Society and other conservation groups on public lands and private reservations. I'd certainly advise others to avail themselves of this form of education, but my discomfort among strangers prevented me from doing so myself. And where would be the adventure? I don't want to be taught according to a curriculum; I want to discover. If others are to accompany me, that's fine if they can explain what I notice, since knowledgeable people are less cumbersome than even the lightest paperback guides. But I want the leisure to notice, and not even children can spot a robin's egg when they are hustled along by teachers.

But there are groups and groups, and that year I found mine: ALFASAC—the Audubon Ladies Fresh Air and Standing Around Club.

Don't laugh.

*T*he name was tossed with some contempt at the original members twenty years ago by an impatient birder. Taking up the dare, the group, numbering about a dozen now, have been walking together every Monday ever since—minus Audubon. By now their pace is necessarily slow. The youngest are past retirement; a few are well into their eighties. But they were always pokey. Nothing escapes their notice, everything must be examined, and each person's find is shared with all the others.

ALFASAC lunching in the woods years ago, when the women were younger and husbands sometimes joined our Monday walk. (Virginia P. Weinland)

We meet at nine-thirty and hike along the trails of a preserve or public park for about five hours, stopping to eat lunch on the way. I'd say the pace is something like a mile an hour. Some of the trails are as well marked and heavily used as those at nature centers; others, especially on lands open by appointment only, are ones where I would certainly lose my way without guidance. Several members are experienced bushwhackers, who in their younger days laid out some of these very trails themselves. Two have taken wildflower inventories for several of our nearby reservations. Another is a mushroomer; several are still birders. Among them they know ferns and lichens, seeds and pods, buds and bark, tracks and scat. You never saw such a group for knowing things, and saying so. (We still could use a member knowledgeable in geology and a moss aficionado.)

On my inaugural walk with ALFASAC, when I became what I believed to be their mascot, we saw wild turkeys, my first. The next Monday I was shown the difference between a marginal and a spinulose wood fern (the following week I was tested on the subject). We found a yellow fungus called witch's butter and cloud ears I knew only in their dried form at Oriental groceries. We duly noted parallel rows of peckmarks made by a sapsucker around a black birch trunk, squirrel

80

tracks leading back and forth from nest tree to acorn cache, and pods of bladder-nut, winter skeletons of mountain mint still fragrant with summer, stumps of chestnut trees that died before most of us were born, drops of blood on fallen leaves, fox scat of ill-digested bittersweet, and—this pointed out to me under six inches of snow—the exact location of a rare stand of rose pogonia.

There is something of the child in these women's minute observations. When, one day, I was shown through a field lens the curled blue stamens for which blue curls (Trichostema dichotomum) are named, I knew the delight my grandchildren would take on finding it in the stone garden. So, too, might there be pennyroyal for its fragrance—though not for its ugly name, Hedeoma pulegioides—and thimbleweed, Anemone virginiana, for its fluffy cotton seedheads.

None of the areas we walk through is pristine. Follow the tussock marsh a ways and you'll find a bridge, a dam. Climb to the summit of this ravine and you'll come upon a fire tower. Everywhere through the woods run the stone walls that say the land was farmed. Any illusion that you're in the wilderness is shattered by telltale Japanese barberry bushes and glimpses of the homes from which they spread.

Still, these weekly walks have given me both the coherence and the depth of detail that I couldn't get from lists, books, roadsides, or self-consciously educational nature centers. I had read that path rush, Juncus tenuus, grows (as its name suggests) on dry, compacted dirt and had jotted it down beside purple lovegrass as another possible species for the terrace. But to see the little rush actually growing in the traces of a wagon road, along the raised hump where footsteps had created its harsh habitat, told me how to use it appropriately. Sure enough, huckleberries did grow with a dry moss like that I remembered from the island, maybe the same one (or the same genus) that shares dry ground with certain ferns. Yes, here too bayberry and lowbush blueberry are natural companions.

What I hoped for most of all, though, was to see transposed from Maine's northern spruce woods to our more southern oak ones some bald that recreated the magic of Isle au Haut Mountain. I had a firm grasp of how grass gives way to thickets and thickets to woods. How, though, did balds fit in the southern New York landscape? I'd never seen here anything quite like the look of Isle au Haut: that thick, stuffed, stiff, hot, bristling growth that seems rooted in the rock itself.

Then, on a Monday walk when, after eating our lunch midway up the next to hardest climb in ALFASAC's repertoire, we arduously hauled ourselves up the steepest portion of a ravine and emerged onto a bald, there it was (there were the remains of a fire tower, too).

Not exactly the same, not in replica. Cranberry and crowberry (the Empetra nigra I had taken to be a heather) were missing, and stunted oaks grew among the bayberries and pitch pines. But it was similar enough, and the transitions were clear. The small bald, no bigger than the stone garden we were building, slipped easily downward to a dirt road where I saw the taller grass that also grows in our meadow and common highway types of shrub and tree that also form the background. A person who had grown up on island granite would have felt at home there, and kids who had climbed the heights had apparently responded to it in the same way that disconnected youth respond to bald rock expanses everywhere.

Or to asphalt on a subdivision: the place was strewn with broken glass.

*I*f Polly didn't write by hand and on richly colored paper, I'd think her letters were copies of her garden notebook. They contain the same sorts of lists I make in my notebooks, the same scrawled explanations for on-second-thought deletions. Her sketches, while drawn with a surer hand and greater flair, are in content similar to mine (I don't in my own notebooks take the same trouble I took for Ellen). Polly writes reminders—it's hard to tell whether they are from her to herself or from her to me—to collect certain seeds, find a source for a certain plant, move a flower, prune a bush, find out more about a species seen along the road. So do I, home from my walk with ALFASAC, jot down in my notebook a milkweed or a mountain mint on which to conduct whatever further research may be necessary to decide whether to add the plant to my garden.

A recent letter contained a novel and intriguing idea. For the adventure of it, just to see what happened, Polly left the far portion of her back lawn unmowed. Various seedlings appeared. She flagged their locations and inked their names: red oak, ironwood, bitternut, dogwoods (unspecified), viburnums (also unspecified), and a local geranium, Jack-in-the-pulpit, and what she hoped would turn out to be a wild delphinium but that more likely was a related species of Aconitum, a monkshood. So I note along the beaten paths we walk that lovegrass grows with hairgrass as well as pathrush, with sweet everlasting and blue curls as well as with gray goldenrod. In this way, I in my dull spiral notebooks and Polly on her multicolored pages accumulate some concept of the communities of plants that interest us.

Polly intends to harvest her unmowed lawn's would-be woodland in the fall for transplanting among similar company elsewhere in the garden. Once ALFASAC let me pocket a tiny dandelion. For the most part, though, Polly and I both must find commercial sources for the plants we covet. Her letters and my notebooks are peppered with queries: sure, pawpaws, but who sells this strange fruit that once was dispersed by giant ground sloths? Eragrostis spectabilis was nearly moldering on the page, and still the far right column, "Source," stood empty.

The other columns are easy: ordinary information like color, height, and season. The less ordinary the garden, though, the harder it is to find commercial sources. On our Monday walks we commonly see false hellebore, rue anemone, marsh violet, cuckoo-flower, toothwort, and wild leek growing in wet woodland with sphagnum moss and skunk cabbage. Almost this entire community of plants is missing from commerce, although the individuals are neither rare nor difficult to grow. Species that are widely grown are generally recognized as ornamentals, and the criterion of beauty was not much more applicable to the dryland terrace than it would have been to an insectivorous bog.

Nurseries carry what local gardeners buy (the ones in New Jersey look like zoos to me). You can find exotic delphiniums in rare variety, but not the wild one that Polly hoped had sprouted in her lawn. Commerce in natives is conducted almost exclusively by specialty nurseries, often by mail order. A few are widely known because they advertise in national magazines. Most are nearly as hidden as the plants they sell. Finding the growers, and then finding among their offerings the singular grass one covets, is to enter the most unexpected and enchanting of all secret gardens.

I had to buy long johns to keep up with ALFASAC's winter expeditions. I've had to subscribe to more than thirty catalogs to explore the mail-order world of native plants. I gladly think of these expenditures as the cost of my continuing education.

*W*hen I first discovered specialty catalogs, I felt the same excitement as when I was first allowed to sample seminars after chewing through years of lecture courses. Here was the same copious array of choices, each unique and vivid, and conducted with flair, informality, and occasional crankiness: "Forget those weedy, common, not very pretty groundcovers," says one grower. "Try Galax!" A field guide is necessarily like a survey course, impersonal and even-handed. But specialty growers are in the business exactly because they're biased toward the kinds of plants they raise, and their prose often pops with their enthusiasm.

I keep all kinds of catalogs. The plainest is typed on an old portable with clogged letters and is clumsily reproduced on pastel pages—pink, blue, yellow, green—attached with staples. Others are the products of desktop publishing, with text tilted or curved to set off pungent come-ons and a variety of typefaces and line illustrations to match the bouncy prose. Although I found the scrappy crabapple I'd pictured in a rather polished catalog, few small growers can afford the color photographs that are so lavishly provided by Wayside Gardens or White Flower Farm; you can always look the listings up in picture books.

Some catalogs are less educational than others; a few fail to make the grade as texts. They don't give botanical names, so you can't tell which "wild ginger" of the seventy-five species of Asarum is referred to; or, if they offer Asarum arifolium, they don't say where it's from. Sometimes there's plenty of information, but it's so abbreviated that it would try the patience of the most ardent student to figure out that $3.00F+L * \approx MD$ (P) Sp+S–W $1–2^1/_2$ AG 3–8 X DT means that this plant is a new offering, sells for three dollars, is available only in limited quantities and can't be shipped until fall, needs full sun and medium moisture, is a short-lived perennial, blooms in late spring to early summer, has white flowers, grows from twelve to thirty inches tall, wants better than average soil, is hardy from Zones 3 to 8, makes a good cut flower, and is drought tolerant.

Spare me.

Here's a sample, from Eastern Plant Specialties in Georgetown, Maine, of useful information attractively served:

DWARF SANDMYRTLE *Leiophyllum buxifolium*

A tiny leaved, glossy evergreen relative of rhodos with very charming starry white flowers in June. *Native to only a few places in Southern NJ and North Carolina,* this sought after little gem is low & rounded, growing to 1 foot or so with many slender, dense, interweaving stems. This does well here if sited out of wind. Ornamental coppery seed pods dress the plant in fall thru winter. A great rock garden plant for well drained soil!

Or a great stone terrace plant for sand? This homeward portion of the journey is like finding a shopping mall at the end of the trail. Suddenly, having carefully noted the blazes and duly mapped one's course, one comes upon a maze of possibilities, the temptation for a spree. Polly, with her kid-in-a-candy-store expansiveness, can hardly restrain herself. My covetousness had by this point been tempered by experience. Only a few months previously, I might have stretched my conscience to accommodate this rare plant's regionality as I had for fothergilla, but the rough realities of Monday walks now made it seem too precious for my hardscrabble location.

I saved the $3.00F+L * \approx MD$ (P) Sp+S–W $1–2^1/_2$ AG 3–8 X DT catalog; who knows when I might need a wild yam? I almost tossed one that irresponsibly offers water hemlock, Cicuta maculata, without mentioning that Cicuta is the most poisonous genus of the temperate zone, causing death by violent convulsions within fifteen minutes of eating its parsnip-like root. But it offered other unusual wetland plants that I might want one day.

Among a handful of the most informative catalogs, I found dainty asters to go with the dwarf goldenrod already on my list, some of the species identified on Monday walks and jotted in my notebook, and a variety of other drought-tolerant, sand-happy, grass-high wildflowers just like those I had pictured nestling among tufts of purple lovegrass on the terrace.

But I did not find that grass.

Eragrostis spectabilis was not on any of the plant lists I obtained from native plant societies. Nor, for that matter, was it in my encyclopedias. It was not offered in any of the catalogs in my rather large collection. A list of mail order growers published by Andersen Horticultural Library at the University of Minnesota identified one source for seeds. I sent off a query. It wasn't answered.

But I'm not one to accept easily that I have reached a dead end.

There is a final resource that, to trackers of native species, is the equivalent of those unique characters from whom travelers extract the genius of the strange lands they explore. It is the growers themselves. In the larger world of horticulture, growers may be several times removed from retail sellers, but along these smaller byways the growers of native plants and the owners of the nurseries that sell them are usually one and the same. You have only to read their names in the catalog and give them a call. Often, they answer the telephone themselves. Always, they are a mine of information. It is they who have gathered the seeds and cuttings to propagate their stock, who have researched the species in tomes heavier than I care to pore through, who have managed them in cultivation and are intimate with them also in their wild habitats—and who, as it happens, know one another, too.

Thus the final step of tracking down that haze first seen along the highway began with a call to a seed source in Texas, who knew a possible grass source in Connecticut, who suggested another in Vermont, and so on over the wires of America from the Appalachians to the Great Lakes and to the end of the trail in North Lake, Wisconsin.

Prairie Seed Source, if you're interested, carries purple lovegrass.

Now, several years since I plucked that sample of grass for identification, the stone terrace holds some two dozen native species. Many of them were unknown to me on that summer day when the terrace was still a back lawn waiting to be

The stone terrace in its first fall. (Sara Stein)

Planting Noah's Garden

deturfed. They include a prostrate blueberry, Vaccineum crassifolium, as well as familiar lowbush ones; ordinary harebell, Campanula rotundifolia, as well as the extraordinary stiff aster, A. linarifolius. The path rush worked out well. So did the little fothergilla. Huckleberries arrived already growing with their companion moss and also with Gaultheria procumbens, the common wintergreen I chewed on as a child. I found sources for both of those ground covers, too. The bayberries and crabapples came from an ordinary nursery (Sargent's crabapple, which came closest to my picture of a low, eccentric shrub, wasn't offered in a large enough size in the catalog where I originally found it). The terrace holds seven kinds of fruit for children to enjoy as well as wild mints and onions, pods, blowballs, and pepper shaker seedheads and flowers shaped like stars, bells, balls, and hats. One day I discovered the strange goblets of a liverwort that had found its own niche behind a boulder: the Monday walkers were ecstatic. It will be some years more before the beds are as crowded as those cracks and pockets on the quarry—and they will look softer, lusher- -but I've had only one total failure.

I killed, by neglecting to water it, the whole seedling bed of purple lovegrass.

Ripe pods of common milkweed, Asclepias syriaca. (Virginia P. Weinland)

6 *Good-bye, Tomatoes*

A FAVORITE BOOK we used to read to our children was *One Carrot Seed,* by Ruth Krauss. The little boy in the story plants a minute carrot seed. His brother says it won't grow. His father says it won't grow. His mother says it won't grow. But it does grow. In the end, the boy carts off in a wheelbarrow a single, giant carrot.

He watered it, you see.

Sometimes I've forgotten even to plant the seed.

I sent my acorns to the cleaners by mistake. I was really upset about that. They were for the grandchildren to plant here in the woods. I'd collected them myself from a scarlet oak my niece and I had selected at a nursery, so my trees would have been her tree's daughters. You get a little sentimental as you age.

The acorns had been in my jacket pocket for a month before they went to the cleaners, still in the pocket. That same fall I came upon a jar of bottlebrush grass seeds in the refrigerator that had been there for a year. Also a bag of lupine seeds collected one summer in Maine. And one of juniper berries. And another of white fluff with black spots that, had I thought to label it, might not have gone down in anonymity. In all that time, these seeds had moved no closer to the earth than the dill and coriander on the spice shelf.

Most of the time, my plans to gather seeds from some plant I admire are foiled by inattention to the seasons, and I remember the seeds the next time I see the plant in bloom. I remember purple lovegrass when it's purple.

That's why I thought it would be wise to buy seeds instead—in packets that reminded me what to do with them; in spring, when peas and corn could join them on the kitchen table with labels and a marking pen to focus my attention. I figured if I thought of wild seeds as vegetables, at least I might get them in the ground.

That decision turned out to be the first of three experiments in as many years that taught me enough about planting seeds that I'm almost ready to try carrots.

*T*he catalog had plenty to choose from. Robert Ahrenhoerster, the owner of Prairie Seed Source, listed at the time seeds of 169 species that he had collected from the wild and from prairie restorations. All were available in packets. I had bought grass and flower seed in bulk to plant our meadow and had sowed it in much the same way one sows a lawn; the results had been as random as they ought to be in such a planting. For the terrace, where I wanted to realize the more planned and particular image that had formed in my mind, I intended to raise the seeds in nursery beds in the vegetable garden, then transplant them to permanent locations when they'd grown large enough to move. This is what Ahrenhoerster intended. Each packet provided enough seeds for a bed of ten square feet, which would yield in most cases fifty or more transplants to move eventually from nursery to permanent location. The price per packet was a dollar.

Just for fun, I figured out the area that the mature plants would cover if I planted one packet of every species offered, and each seedbed yielded fifty transplants, and they were eventually set into a garden at one-foot intervals. The result—for an investment of $169—turned out to be a garden roughly 85 by 100, or 8,450 square feet, something like a quarter acre.

Tempting, no?

But figuring the area of the seedbeds, I'd need a nursery plot about forty feet square, bigger than any vegetable garden I know of except Nancy Ross's. Nancy Ross is a Master Gardener whose specialty is heirloom vegetables and who, when I first saw her garden, was growing oats, peas, beans, and barley, not to mention wheat and potatoes, a dozen kinds of summer squash, thirteen varieties of pepper, seventeen tomato types, and a mystery miscellany that included hon tsai tai, tyfon, scorzonera, malabar, amaranth, and edible lupine in an area larger than the average front yard. It was the apparent ease with which Nancy raised so many kinds of plants from seed that inspired me to try, but her participation in my project followed by a year this first order from Prairie Seed Source, the one that included the ill-fated purple lovegrass.

It was modest as seed orders go: two grasses, an onion, and five other wildflowers. Even with so small an order, the area of their seedbeds erased the lettuce patch, my favorite fiery hot Thai peppers, half the corn, and any possibility of Kirby cucumbers.

After the soil had warmed in May, I marked out the eight beds, each measuring two by five feet, along the front of our sloping vegetable patch. Nancy mulches with salt hay between rows or beds in her exquisite garden, and I did the same. The hay keeps down the weeds and improves the soil as it rots. In my case, the hay also assured that I'd know where the beds were: I already knew from sowing the meadow that these wild species don't leap up as fast as lettuces, and I feared being unable to distinguish the beds from the surrounding dirt if they weren't framed in hay.

Following the catalog instructions, I prepared the beds carefully, loosening the soil with a garden fork and grooming it smooth with a rake. The smallest of these seeds are individually barely visible to the naked eye: they are sown on the surface and merely patted in. Their beds must therefore be exceptionally fine; mine, I'm proud to say, were velvet.

When all was ready, I sowed the seeds into their perfect beds and retired from the garden in the expectation that, given an extra week or so, they would behave like vegetables.

Hah!

No wild species behaves like a vegetable.

By the time the corn was knee high and most of my carefully penned labels had been broken off and scattered by the dog, the velvet beds still showed no signs of life. Tomatoes were already forming on the vines when the first seeds sprouted—in a heap against the low side of their bed, where a thunderstorm had washed them. The Prairie Seed Source catalog hadn't said anything about beds being *level*. I guess people from prairie country automatically think flat.

That first sprouter was the purple lovegrass.

I think.

It could have been the onions. That's another thing about these wildlings. They throw their early energy down to their roots; the tops may be so small at first as to defy identification.

They dried to death at pinky height anyway. So did the sprouts in two other beds that might have been grass—or onion. I had sown these smallest seeds mixed with sand for their even distribution, and I knew the paling sand was supposed to remind me when to water. I'm sure it was signaling its moisture to me daily, but I wasn't watching.

Nothing else germinated.

My only success was a packet of path rush, the Juncus tenuus that I'd seen growing on Monday walks along the trodden paths from which it gets its common name. The seeds had arrived as a bonus with another order; I found space for them next to a bed of dill. When I planted the dustlike seeds, I stamped them hard into their bed. That explains why, unlike the grass, they didn't wash downhill. Path rush's aptitude for thriving in dry dirt explains why even I could grow it.

By September, when flopped tomatoes lay rotting on the ground and I'd harvested all two meals' worth of 'Rosa Bianca' eggplant, the path rush bed boasted at least a hundred pretty little plants, mature at six inches high and already flowering. The dill had equally thrived on my neglect. I harvested its seed heads, purchased the Kirby cukes there had been no room for, put up some quarts of pickles, and moved the darling rushes to the stone terrace where, had the other plants survived, I might have had hundreds for only pennies each.

So you can appreciate my distress that September, torn between greed for cheap plants and guilt at my ineptitude for growing any but that one from seed to transplant size. It was then that I turned for help to Master Gardener Ross.

Master Gardener is a program offered through the County Agricultural Extension Service and taught by both county agents and volunteers. The courses one takes to be certified are free; in return, one gives that knowledge back to the community. Some graduates help with community plantings, such as those at libraries or school campuses, or do volunteer work for parks and reservations. Others give talks and slide shows. Nancy Ross does that as well as teaching propagation and vegetable gardening to aspiring Master Gardeners. She is a good deal shorter than a cornstalk, and though she must sweat and smear like other gardeners, she is elegant in repose, as when entertaining guests at the dinner party where she introduced me to her all-organic, flabbergasting garden. One would be hard put to decide which was better groomed.

All I asked for was advice. It seemed that it had been a mistake for someone like me to plant wild seeds directly into beds too far from the house to note their desiccation. Perhaps I should have started them in flats, under lights, and indoors, where I couldn't help but see them. Then, as I do with eggplants and tomatoes, I could have put the flats outdoors beneath the kitchen window, where I could continue to keep tabs on them over my morning coffee, and only when they toughened up a bit plant them in the garden.

What did Nancy think? When should I start seeds that might take months to sprout? How did she arrange space for so many seedlings? I was like my own uncaged tomatoes, flopping abjectly for want of support. I suppose that's why Nancy, who gives every tomato plant much more than it expects, decided to stake me up.

In short, she asked her Master Gardener class if anyone would be interested in growing for me, from seed to a size that could be moved into a bed, these wild and recalcitrant species. Eleven students signed on.

The new catalog arrived in February, my month of self-indulgence. I was understandably more lavish with this second order than with the first. The care of these seeds was not, after all, going to be my responsibility. All of the species were to be ones adapted to the unwatered habitat of the stone terrace. I chose purple lovegrass, for the second time, and wild strawberry, birdsfoot violet, hawkweed, harebell, snakeroot, a lupine, a baptisia, a coneflower and—who could resist them?—kitten tails and pussy toes. I ended the list with a valentine from me to me of sweet everlasting.

Gradually I realized what I was getting myself into.

Supposing that each of the eleven propagators would want to try her hand with more than one species, the order should be for something like two dozen packets. But, supposing also that they were successful, the sprouted plants would have to be moved from flats or pots into nursery beds to grow on to transplant size. Many of these slow starters wouldn't be big enough to move to permanent locations until the following spring. So for a year, at least, the vegetable garden was going to be a nursery.

So long, sweet corn.

Farewell, dear rosy eggplants.

Good-bye, tomatoes.

*T*his time around, I asked Robert Ahrenhoerster about relative ease of germination before I sent the order. Our consultation scratched the most obdurate species from my list—the baptisia, for example. To test its germination rate, Robert had planted a hundred seeds in a wooden flat outdoors. The first summer, twenty germinated and were transplanted to a bed. In the second summer, another eighteen seeds germinated; in the third summer, twelve more. By the fourth summer, the flat had rotted out and he ended the test.

I didn't think the Master's apprentices had figured on a four-year project. I knew I hadn't. The edited order included no species that were notoriously difficult.

The packets arrived in March, some with special instructions. Except for wild strawberries, which came as dried fruit that proved to be an icky job to tease apart to separate the seeds, the most that was needed was a soaking in warm water. Of course, four hours in warm water required a certain attention to detail. But Nancy Ross's crew was accustomed to—even avid for—horticultural fuss.

Perhaps that explains the spectacular failure of that year's experiment.

One day in mid-July they all arrived with notes recounting their experience. Some carried flats and pots; others came with empty hands—or their flats and

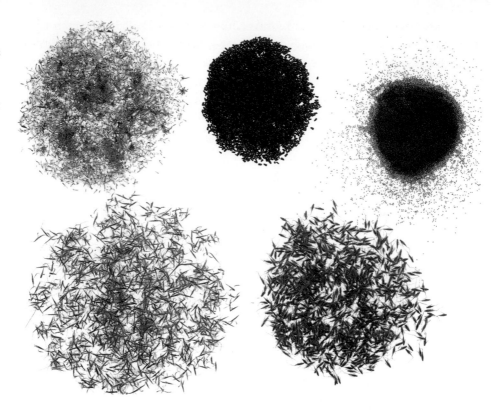

The seeds of wild natives may range from powder that a sneeze would blow away to stuff that might fill a lumpy mattress. Only some growers and collectors can afford the labor and equipment needed to remove attachments and debris from wild seeds. Clockwise from upper left: cardinal flower, Lobelia cardinalis; Indian grass, Sorghastrum nutans; little bluestem grass, Schizachyrium scaparius; showy goldenrod, Solidago speciosa; yellow coneflower, Ratibida pinnata. (Bill Pellgorsch)

pots were empty. The flats of wild strawberries were full and lovely; those of sweet everlasting were full of caterpillars. The surprisingly rapid and successful germination of another species was explained only in the following spring, when, transplanted to the garden, the plants turned out to be forget-me-nots, mislabeled. Of the six species that sprouted, the total yield filled one row in my vegetable garden. Fourteen species had failed to germinate at all. Three seeds of another had germinated, only to die of damping off. All the sprouted purple lovegrass had died of heat over the grower's one-week vacation.

Understand that these women were experienced gardeners. Some had been raising plants from seed for decades. They did as they had always done. Their professional soil mixes were moist and spongy. Some had wrapped the flats in plastic; others misted daily. If seedlings appeared, soluble fertilizer was added to the watering regime. Seeds of cultivated flowers and vegetables that they were growing at the same time and with the same treatment flourished (as did the long-cultivated wetland forget-me-nots). I can't blame the growers for being discouraged. When trays of wild seeds did nothing for two months, most spilled them out to make room for something more promising, like lettuce.

It may have been that treating these dryland types like lettuce did many of them in. Seeds might have drowned; seedlings might have choked on fertilizer. But I think that even if the soil and moisture had been better matched to their natural habitat, wild seeds' slow and staggered germination precludes raising them this way for home gardeners. One can't check trays of dirt day after day, month after month, with joy and concentration. One resents the space they take and the thankless inaction of the seeds. Sooner or later, the effort is abandoned.

Nancy Ross offered to try again. The experiment was about to enter its third year.

*T*he funny thing is that all the while, during both my trial outdoors in nursery beds and theirs indoors in flats and pots, the answer to how to keep seeds under suitable conditions for very long periods—and in the space of a shoebox and even over vacations—was sitting both in Nancy's library and mine.

At that dinner party when I had first seen her garden, Nancy showed me a book she had just bought. The spine was black, without a title. The title itself was dry: *Seed Germination Theory and Practice.* The design was crude, the printing primitive, the text rife with abbreviations meant to keep the number of pages within the author's home publishing budget. Still, I ordered it. I guess I looked at it when it arrived; I can't say I read it. Nancy, too, had put the book aside: it didn't pertain to vegetables. Both of us had forgotten about it.

Then, after the second failure, a novice gardener in my workshop told me about his own success using a method of germinating seeds described in detail for twenty-five hundred species in a book by a retired chemistry professor named Norman Deno. I ordered it (so now I have two copies).

Briefly, the method described in *Seed Germination Theory and Practice* involves germinating seeds inside folded, moistened pads of paper towel stored in sandwich bags. Five hundred such pads, each holding the number of seeds in an average packet, take up one cubic foot of space. The pads need remoistening every two or three months. As the seeds germinate, they are moved into pots under artificial light. The pots, too, are kept in polyethylene bags. The seedlings need watering about once a *year.*

The opportunity for neglect appealed to me enormously. So did the possibility of actually seeing germination taking place. So did the kind of fussing. As a former bug collector who used to raise to adulthood any sort of insect that spun a cocoon, I liked the idea of peeking into pads for emerging radicals—embryonic roots—that announce when germination has begun, perhaps examining them through a field lens, and planting the sprouts with forceps in rows in pots like tiny gardens.

What appealed to me even more was the science. Horticulture has always annoyed me by saying what to do without explaining why. I may not treat plants tenderly, but I want to understand them.

Take the horticultural instruction to "stratify" the seeds one has collected. The term comes from the way growers originally stored seeds over the winter: they spread them in flats between layers—strata—of sand or peat and stacked the flats in a cool place until spring planting time. Picture Mr. MacGregor in his Wellingtons, stacking flats stratified with cowslip seeds in the shed where Peter Rabbit hid beneath a flower pot. Mr. MacGregor was probably the last person to overwinter seeds in quite this way, but the term lives on.

When seeds are "moist stratified," the storage material is damp; when "dry stratified," the material is dry. Horticultural recipes also require that seeds be dry stratified or moist stratified (or one followed by the other) for specific periods of time, depending on the species. The reason given is to "overcome dormancy."

But what is dormancy? And in what way does being cold overcome it? And why should seeds differ in whether their "sleep" is better overcome in dryness or in damp? And how can it be that the only species that require awakening are woody ones? The book says that seeds of herbaceous species, once they are ripe and dry, can simply be planted: warmth and moisture are all they need for germination. The seeds both Nancy's crew and I had planted obviously disagreed.

So does Deno. The seeds of *all* species, he insists, have some way to delay germination at least until they are dispersed from the parent plant. Most also have a way to delay sprouting until conditions are at least possible, if not optimal, for the seedlings' growth. Dormancy is hardly a time of sleep: it is a period when the seed is actively engaged with its environment, experiencing the passage of time and the changes in temperature and moisture that will prepare it to sprout when the circumstances are suitable for its survival. Even a brief period of drying may tell the seed that it has left its parent.

Deno explains that the experience is fundamentally chemical. Substances that prevent germination are destroyed during dormancy, a period he calls by the more active term "conditioning." Molecular biology has elucidated some of the chemical mechanisms. They are readily understandable, crudely analogous to pulling plugs and breaking locks and letting clocks run down. And they relate with remarkable intelligence to the natural history of the plant.

Imagine a desert annual whose seed ripens at the onset of summer's drought and germinates during the cool winter rain in time to repeat the act before the following drought. For "drought" read a period of dry storage (alias dry stratification), when chemical reactions in the seed run down its summer clock. Then, and only then, is the seed ready to recognize "winter rain"—a period in a moist paper towel pad kept in the refrigerator (alias moist stratification). When that cycle of chemistry is complete, the seed is free to germinate—but still at 40 degrees F, refrigerator temperature. If, before germination, the seed is brought from winter to summer—moved to a room temperature of 70 degrees F—it simply dies. The seedling sprouted in the refrigerator, however, can immediately be moved out of the cold into a nice warm pot.

It is both convenient and interesting that the plant definition of "winter" is 40 degrees F, for that is not only the temperature of our refrigerators but also a fair average for North Temperate Zone winters. Similarly, our normal room temperature of 70 degrees F is average for North Temperate Zone summers. These two temperatures are the only ones that Deno used in his germination experiments, and these two seasons are the only ones that most plants need to know. (A few recognize spring or fall by chemistry requiring temperatures that oscillate often and unpredictably between 40 and 70 degrees; these he kept in padded Baggies in the equivalent of Mr. MacGregor's shed.)

A "season" as measured by seed clocks varies in length according to the species (you'd expect a northern hickory to require a longer winter than a southern pecan), but with rare exception seeds are agreeable to Deno's simplification: three months for summer, three months for winter. Germination that ordinarily would take years of calendar time is therefore cut in half: three months at 40 degrees, then three months at 70 degrees, equals a year in chemical terms, yet only half a year has passed. Taking the baptisia whose staggered germination tried even Robert Ahrenhoerster's patience, the seeds might have been cycled between refrigerator and cupboard at three-month intervals for twice the yield per calendar year without the aggravation.

Most grassland types, including those Nancy's volunteers and I had tried, turned out to be naïve as wild species go. Following their winter dry storage at the nursery, all or a high percentage of the seeds should have germinated during one three-month summer cycle. They were not like wetland plants, which, by including in their chemical repertoire a final cascade of reactions energized by light, insist on knowing that they are in a sunny position before they'll deign to sprout. Nor were they as canny as cacti, which won't proceed unless signaled by gibberellin, a plant hormone produced by desert soil fungi only in microhabitats moist and rich enough to support a cactus seedling in the scorching heat. Certainly they were not delicate, like woodland wildflowers whose seeds, accustomed to being harvested by ants who eat their fruity flesh and leave the pits to germinate in humid chambers underground, die immediately on drying. Compared to the difficulties of raising these more worldly types, there was no excuse for failing to germinate the meadow simpletons that I—I can't resist it—was still collecting.

By the time I studied Norman Deno's book, the fall after the Master Gardener fiasco, I had become more careful. I had collected a dozen kinds of seeds over the summer in packets, not pockets. Each packet was labeled with the species, the location where I found it, and the date. The packets were stored in a cardboard box on a kitchen shelf, a conditioning regime that Deno would abbreviate DS70 (dry stored at 70 degrees F). Liatris spicata seeds were dated August; it was now December, four months later (DS70 4m in Deno's shorthand). I looked up the results of his experiments with this eastern meadow species commonly known as dense blazingstar:

> *L. spicata* germ. 70(100%), ind. t 7d, 5%/d) and 40(100% in 3rd m) using seeds DS 6m at 70 and 70(100% ind. t 7d, 2.5%/d) and 40 (60%)–70(40%) using fresh seed.

With some pain at first—the abbreviations became easier with practice—I translated thus: Deno used two batches of seed, one fresh, the other stored dry at room temperature for six months. He used several regimes with both batches and they all worked; that is, the seeds of both fresh and stored batches, no matter how they were treated, all germinated. The differences were a matter of how long it took. Comparing fresh to dry seeds, for example, both began to germinate within a week (ind. t 7d = induction time seven days) when put in moist pads at room temperature. However, the batch of dried seeds germinated at the rate of 5 percent a day (5%/d), while the fresh seed sprouted at only half that rate. Many of the fresh seeds had apparently not finished their summer preparations and needed extra time to wrap things up in their moist condition. From my point of view, the results meant I'd have to wait just a month for dried seeds to sprout but nearly two months for fresh seed to complete germination.

However promptly the dry seeds, once moistened, were prepared to sprout at summer temperature, they were reluctant to do so at winter temperature, 40 degrees F. In fact, it took them an entire three-month "winter" to sprout (100% in 3rd m). The fresh seed was even more reluctant: 60 percent at last sprouted at winter temperature; the remainder sprouted only when "summer" arrived—when they were moved, still in their moist pads, to 70 degrees F. Clearly, dense blazingstar seeds can't do their chemistry as fast when they're cold, and this pokiness keeps them from sprouting until, having gotten through the dead of winter, odds are that spring is just around the corner.

How smart! How understandable!

You can see from this density of information why Nancy and I had managed to lose this book in our respective libraries. But you can also see why, when I tucked the blazingstar seeds into their moistened pad, I felt for the first time that I had a language to use with them.

"The winter of your drying is over now," I said. "It is warm, moist summer."

And "Yes," they said, "Yes!" and germinated.

December is a stupid time to start seeds that, because you think they will die, you have made no further preparations for. I had no pots, no soil, no lights, no stand. Neither, at that time of year, were these items stocked by hardware stores featuring salt for icy walks or garden centers holding sales on poinsettias.

I did manage to get a bag of brown stuff dotted with white foam blobs and several plastic pots in an exceptionally vile shade of green. The fluorescent fixture I had used previously for raising vegetables from seed might still have worked, but it lay blotched with rust in our leaky basement, and I didn't want to see it. The blazingstars limped along on a kitchen windowsill, but I knew that I would fail again unless raising plants from seed proved attractive as well as easy.

So I invested in a stunning setup: a sturdy plant stand made of square aluminum tubing that supports four shelves, each lit by a pair of fluorescent fixtures and holding five trays filled with fifteen pots apiece. I decided for no good reason that each pot could hold nine seedlings (Deno hadn't specified a number). The stand could therefore potentially hold twenty-seven hundred plants. Had I done this arithmetic before my rash purchase, I would have ordered a smaller setup, but I must say that my commitment to my seedlings was increased in the same measure that my bank account was depleted.

When the impressive apparatus arrived, I started the germination of all the other seeds I had collected. I also duplicated the previous year's order from Prairie Seed Source, and these seeds, too, went into pads stacked in the refrigerator or cupboard. With a new and strange reluctance, I set aside for Nancy some Turk's cap lily seeds that I had gathered and that she particularly wanted to try.

Then, in Wisconsin, I saw a display of more seed packets holding still other species, and bought some, and discovered, too, that my ALFASAC friends had stashed away still more seeds for me. Altogether, there were forty-seven species for this hen to hatch that spring.

Thirty-nine species germinated. Some—fat seeds like milkweeds—hatched into robust seedlings the size of bean sprouts. Others I had to bring forth from their pads with surgical forceps for delivery to their pots. Each immediately revealed its character. A coneflower lay a pair of thick leaves upon the soil and left them there unchanged for months while it worked below ground on its roots. A wetland milkweed, less concerned about the future of its water supply, concentrated on pushing up toward the light as though expecting at any moment to be overshadowed. Harebell, the most delicate of infants and of seeds so small that I had to mix them with sand and sow them in a tray to sprout, proved on transplanting to have complex root systems five inches long below their teensy tops. A mountain mint had no babyhood at all: from the beginning its leaves were leathery, its stem stiff, its scent hearty, its proportions quite grownup. A thistle made prickles right away. Other species remained so slim and tender for many weeks that I feared for their survival.

The thistle germinated while still in the refrigerator and I felt chagrined: had I left it in the chill too long? But no, the seeds turned sullen in the kitchen summer, and I had to put them back beside the butter. I was not an obedient disciple: I didn't do as Deno does—wait patiently for the end of each three-month season before switching to the next. Some seeds got one-month winters or two-month summers and still sprouted, but the seedlings may have been stronger had their hurried nurse not interrupted their gestation.

Another of my deviations from standard practice was to grow the seedlings in a mix of mostly sand. What soil I did use was not sterile, contained no peat, and was not meant for potting. The bag was labeled Topsoil; it was supposed to be dumped in an outdoor bed or barrel, complete with its sticks and stones. Nothing dire happened.

The really precarious period, I found, was weaning the seedlings from their incubator. Deno assumes that we fellow gardeners know all about "hardening off," but "we" isn't me, and anyway, gardeners don't usually raise tomatoes in pots swathed in plastic bags at a hundred percent humidity. As my son who is a plant molecular biologist explained to me after the first seedlings I removed from their Baggies withered to death in a day, plants accustomed to a saturated atmosphere don't produce the waxes that normally protect their leaves from drying. You have to poke a few holes in the bag, then wait, then in a few days poke more, and only after the air in this gradual way reaches ambient humidity, expose the seedlings fully. Also, the term "daylight" applied to fluorescent tubes does not mean "sunlight." The very milkweeds that had so avidly sought closeness to the tubes got a bad case of sunburn on their first trip outdoors.

They didn't die of it.

I wish some had. I wish I'd given Nancy half the seeds at least. A friend adopted some of the milkweed seeds after they had germinated. Two weeks later I offered her half a dozen other species of excess foundlings, and she wouldn't take them in. She'd realized how much space they take, even at nine per pot. I hadn't imagined how many seeds come in those modest packets. I tried to feel no guilt about those that rotted in their pads—no guilt at my relief.

I like to think they died on purpose, as a quirk in the plot of their species' ultimate survival. Species whose seeds are particularly popular as food may produce more empty husks than embryos in the hope that a bird or mouse, annoyed at being cheated, will leave the rest alone. I do hope that explains the peculiar failure of the sunflower seeds—the western one, the woodland one, and the Jerusalem artichoke. They were supposed to go in the bed where the annual sunflowers had been, the ones the goldfinches had eaten upside down. Perhaps I just should have tossed the seed over the ground, as I had those under the nut tree in the meadow. Maybe their chemistry proceeds in fits and starts in an atmosphere of fluctuation and unpredictability. I hope I was, like the Master Gardeners before me, merely too kind a nurse.

I am ashamed that of my half of the Turk's cap lily seeds, only two pots' worth germinated. Nancy's did no better, though.

Nothing comes to mind to explain the odd behavior of the grassy plants I tried. A sedge (unidentified) that I had collected in Maine the previous summer did fine. So did a nice little grass called Danthona spicata. Two others—a dropseed that I already have plenty of and another, called sweetgrass, Hierchloe odorata, that I particularly wanted—did not germinate. Well, two sweetgrass seeds did sprout. They're somewhere in the vegetable garden now, where I may never find them. I got one miserable purple lovegrass for all my effort. I wasn't surprised. It's my nemesis.

But never mind; it's too late now anyway.

I threw sheep fescue seed at the stone terrace beds last fall, and it immediately sprouted. The vegetable garden is overfilled with other babies, and more still wait in refrigerator winter, on the summer shelf, or in the basement under lights. If there is to be room for them to grow up outdoors, I probably will have to dig out those healthy purple lovegrass plants that, finding a source for well-grown one-year-olds at last, I naturally rushed to order.

Neil Diboll in his field of queen of the prairie, Filipendula rubra, at Prairie Nursery in Westfield, Wisconsin. These hefty, healthy plants will be shipped bareroot when they are dormant. (Susan A. Roth)

Planting Noah's Garden

7 *Speak Roughly to Your Little Plant*

I USED TO BUY POTTED PLANTS to dig into my garden. Big fat bushy ones; overfed, in fact. The soil, or whatever it is growers put in these pots, holds water like either a sponge or a sieve. There seems to be no middle ground. Sometimes in the garden I run into an old pot-shaped lump of whatever-it-is. Or whatever it was: the plant has long since died and rotted; only the ghost of its rootball is revealed in those nasty bits of white foam that "lighten" soilless mixes and don't decay.

My friend the gardener who grows dwarf conifers in a cliff says that she expects only 50 percent of the plants she buys to survive to their second summer. Perhaps that's because she pushes the limits of what's possible for the plant or in our climate. But just as often, and even with native plants suited to one's site, the fault is in the canning.

The roots of canned plants have never felt real dirt. They have not had to push past so much as a pebble, have not reached deep for water or fought for nutrients, have met few microbes—have met instead the walls of their container and vainly circled it. Such roots continue to circle when transplanted, never finding new nourishment and eventually starving the foliage above. Starvation is all the more likely because customers insist on bushy specimens. To achieve that plump look, the grower must pinch the plant back repeatedly, and the excess foliage that results taxes the ability of its roots to feed it all the more. Customers also insist that their plants be in active growth, preferably in flower, and early: by Mother's Day, for instance. To present plants in that precocious flush of leaf or bloom weeks before what's normal in the region, nurseries often buy their potted plants from warmer places. Thus a canned winterberry I bought some years back expired over the winter. The species grows wild in New England, but not the strains of it accustomed to the Piedmont in Virginia.

The winterberry very likely was a clone. The maple lollipops on Ellen's street are clones; I'd guess from their uniforms that they are Acer rubrum 'Autumn Glory'. Horticulture calls them "cultivars"; botanically they're clones. A clone is a plant that has been vegetatively reproduced from a "mother" plant by division, stem cutting, graft, or tissue culture. Each clone is identical to the mother plant and to all her other clones. Most of the container plants sold at nurseries are clones of a single parent chosen for her looks. The last clone I bought was a Carolina allspice—a lovely one, full-figured and dressed in flashy foliage. But where was the scent? The grower, enchanted by her beauty, had neglected to sniff the mother and so brought into the world the Carolina nospice.

The aroma that this plant ordinarily wafts about repels herbivorous insects. Should any insects find my deodorized specimen, I might have to dispatch them with a sprayer. It is not unusual for such plants to have been routinely sprayed during their raising.

The pampering and primping that ill prepare a pot-grown plant to hit reality also inflate its cost. You're paying for the dirt and for the cost to ship it. You're paying for the individual attention that a canned plant requires—its several repottings from seedling to retail size, the feeding that has speeded its growth, the grooming that has kept it full, the daily waterings, the necessary sprayings, and the cost to bring it to that peak of false promise when it is presented at the nursery in full bloom.

Cost becomes a critical issue in ecological gardening: so many plants are needed to achieve a fitting density of hedgerow, a proper layering of woods. Even a small meadow garden eats up a lot of plants. Whereas in a traditional border you might give a flower a whole square yard in which to reach its full potential, you give meadow plants a square foot or two. You want them to be crowded; you want no open ground. That means you want perhaps three times as many plants per area planted than gardeners usually figure. I, for one, am not three times richer than the gardeners I know.

And I am not half so kind. I make no beds for plants, nor do I feed or water. I'm tough on roots and lazy with the sprayer. I want plants I can speak roughly to, and they don't come in cans.

I get most plants the old-fashioned way: dug up, shaken off, and shipped to me bareroot. You can buy native grasses, flowers, shrubs, and even trees this way—and not in skimpy sizes, either. They are shipped in spring or fall, when the plants are dormant. The survival rate is close to 100 percent, and the cost is about a third that of plants the same age grown in containers. My cost per area planted is therefore about the same as that for other gardeners; my cost per year is less, since few plants need replacement.

Bareroot plants are grown in fields in real dirt nourished naturally, with fungi to feed their roots and birds to eat their pests, without clench of pot or pinch of pruner or daily inundation, in every sort of climate, and from the seed of parents left to manage their own affairs in full possession of their genes. Each plant is handled three times: when planted, when dug, and when shipped. So they are cheap. So they are tough.

For all these reasons, bareroot plants are the ecological gardener's best choice. But for these same reasons, bareroot plants don't look like your average chrysanthemum, either.

Most people have never seen a plant undressed. The experience can be shocking. Especially if you have ordered thirty woodland wildflowers that all fit neatly into the palm of your hand. I was at first dismayed by ferns that looked like last year's birds' nests, embarrassed to show my husband the bundle of sticks that was to be a wetland thicket, panicked to open a carton stuffed with roots.

Dormant plants tend to look dead. Plants, we think, are green, but these are not. We know the tops of plants, not their bottoms. At least a bareroot shrub has both: a dormant flower is a topless bottom.

Ferns are too primitive even to have that elaborated underpinning botanists call root. The hairy underground portion is a stem, a rhizome, although it does the same job roots do: absorbing minerals and water. Leaves grow from buds on the rhizome. Their fancy shape earns them the special name frond, but if there is any sign of foliage in the dormant plant other than an occasional residue of dead stuff, it will most likely look like a bump.

Some fern rhizomes are shaped like knobs. This year I got cartons of cinnamon and ostrich ferns for the wetland where turkeys have been gabbling. The rhizomes were supposed to be planted with their buds at the soil surface, but, confusingly, the water-absorbing fibers stuck up, not down. I had to go by the frond bumps to tell which way to put them. Or I could have planted the knobs sideways. That's a good compromise, don't you think?

My niece Ellen planted a hundred hayscented ferns under the birch trees. I advised it (and hope she doesn't get mad at me when she sees how fast they spread). When she was finished, she wasn't sure that she had actually planted them. They come as flat mats, maybe the size of your hand but thinner. The top surface appears more closely knit than the bottom—sometimes. Or there may be a greenish sign of foliage to come. Or there may not. I told Ellen to rake the mulch off a patch of soil, scratch the surface to loosen it, lay the mats out like pancakes on a griddle, and rake the mulch back over them. That's not a convincing act of planting, but that's how these ferns grow. I bet I've planted plenty of hayscented ferns upside down, and I bet they've never noticed.

I happen to like another invasive fern that is generally unpopular: bracken. The grower who carries bracken doesn't list it in his catalog, not because he doesn't like it but because customers have complained that it didn't survive transplanting. It doesn't look as if it would grow—it comes as sticks about as thick as pencils with a bud here and there. But, like the carrot seed, it does grow. It's just slow to get started. Then you can't stop it. Bracken has grown clear across the continent in nearly every climate. At least it's impossible to plant this kind of rhizome upside down. You dig a shallow ditch for it and lay it on its side.

If you've pictured these fern endeavors accurately, you will have noted a problem: once the lump, the mat, or the stick is planted, it's gone. Nothing shows for all your work. And it won't for weeks—and it may never if you trample on the planted area, breaking off the tender fronds as they unfurl beneath the mulch. This difficulty is not exclusive to dormant ferns. It's the same with woodland flowers. You can see what you're doing while you're doing it. Then the planting disappears. I once showed Marty a whole day's work and he said, "Where?"

Most native woodland flowers are ephemerals: they sprout, bloom, and ripen seed in the sun of early spring and are done with their work by the time trees shade them. Then they enter a very long period of dormancy. Their leaves wither and drop. No trace of them remains above the ground. For the rest of the year—a good nine months—ephemerals live modestly on the energy stored in their underground parts, banking their reserves for their reemergence in spring. There are exceptions—woodland asters and goldenrods behave like their meadow relatives; the Galax! touted in my liveliest catalog is evergreen (some ferns are evergreen, too). These and some of the ephemerals may be shipped as whole, dormant plants with real roots emanating from a crown to which a few of last season's dead leaves may cling. New buds may be visible at the crown, but don't expect to be impressed. These buds, if you can find them, should be at or barely below the soil surface when planted.

Usually what you get when you send for woodland types is not the whole plant but a part of it. The parts are rarely roots. What may look like a thick, meaty root is more likely a storage stem, a rhizome like a fern's, and not a whole rhizome, either, but a chunk of one perhaps no longer than a thumbnail. Sometimes I've gotten giant rhizomes, pinky size. They're smart, though, despite their size. I've laid fragments of bloodroot and wild ginger rhizomes on their sides just below the soil, and they've understood perfectly well which way to go: the leaves grow up, the roots grow down, the rhizomes grow out in all directions, and pretty soon the pieces form a patch.

I got a whole lot of Dutchman's breeches to plant in the shady lawn/oak glade this spring. I could hardly get them in before they fell apart and skittered off. They were tubers—plump outgrowths of a rhizome—which for some reason tend to be round and roll like marbles or miniature potatoes. These were actually clusters of tubers the size of popcorn kernels that were flimsily attached to one another. I didn't see a sign of any roots or dormant buds, or any directional clues to their whereabouts, but I have faith: I stuck them in just deep enough to cover them, and they came up. It's wonderful how a plant's own sense of direction is unaffected by the planter's lack of it.

Corms and bulbs are less confusing; sometimes they're even big enough to weight the palm somewhat. A corm is a swollen section of underground stem from which both roots and leaves sprout. Short roots are usually visible; leaf buds may be too small to notice. A bulb consists of fleshy storage leaves similar to a garlic clove; it is pointed at the leaf end, with roots sometimes showing at the blunt end. One is supposed to plant corms at a depth twice their thickness, bulbs at a depth twice their length, and both right side up. As if it mattered: it doesn't. What mattered to me was that the Jack-in-the-pulpit corms and the Camassia bulbs I planted in the oak grove were as big as pearl onions. The Dutchman's breeches had tried my trifocal eyes.

All the woodland things together took only a couple of mornings to bury. Then came a two-week respite. Then came the prairie plants.

A prairie plant is a reward, a relief, something you can grab hold of. Although some grassland perennials come in little bits—bulbs of mountain meadow species, tubers of blazingstars, rhizomes of the spreading heath aster, Aster ericoides—most are big, robust roots topped with a crown of buds that you can plainly see. In general, meadow and prairie perennials are drought-adapted plants. Their deep roots have a trencherman's capacity for food and water, and their hairy, leathery, or narrow leaves resist desiccation. But, as I said, they are not like chrysanthemums.

Whereas a chrysanthemum grows from snip to bush in a single summer, a prairie plant at that age may have grown two leaves. A chrysanthemum breaks

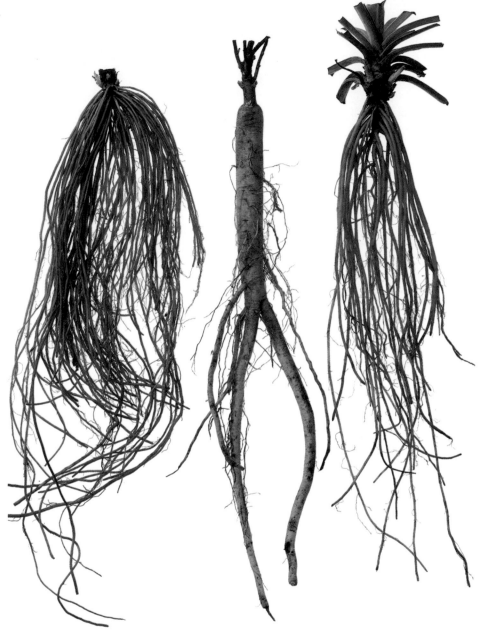

Bareroot forbs. The dancing taproot is butterfly-weed, Asclepias tuberosa; to its left is mop-bottomed showy goldenrod, Solidago speciosa, and to its right a whopping mop of beardtongue, Penstemon grandiflorus. (Bill Pellgorsch)

into bloom in its first season; prairie plants may spend two years against the ground before branching out and may not venture into bloom for another year or more. You're not paying for the tops when you buy these wild types. You're paying for their underground investment.

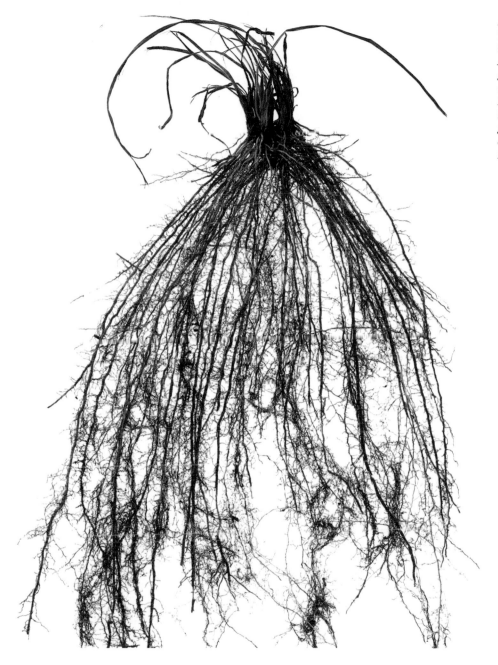

None has the tender or coiled root mass typical of pot-grown ornamentals. The earthy, fleshy bottoms of most species extend straight down, some like mops and others like carrots. Milkweeds, silphiums, lupines, and baptisias are the carrot type. Their sturdy taproots may be single or forking and up to a foot long at the time of shipping. Since taproots frequently grow to six feet or more and must be dug out whole if the plant is to survive transplanting, these species are sold young, at one or two years, rarely older. The crown is at the broader, top end of the taproot, marked by dry leaf stalks in fall, by swollen or sprouting buds in spring.

Aster and goldenrod roots are fleshy, too, but spread thickly from the crown like the strings of a mop. The strands are long but branch little or not at all. The crown of mop-rooted species is likely to be broader than that of taprooted ones, with buds around the perimeter. Because they're easier to dig up, I've usually been able to get at least two-year-olds, sometimes three-year-olds. I order the biggest size I can get. Marty, to whom dormant ferns are dead and bits of woodland flowers beneath notice, helps me plant items that measure up to his shovel. Big roots impress him.

Last October, I ordered fifty bluejoint grass plants for the wet meadow, to be delivered in the spring. Come January I ordered fifty bluejoint grass plants for the wet meadow, to be delivered in the spring. Guess what. The grower thought I wanted a hundred plants. What could be wrong with him? Can't he recognize senility when he sees it?

This wetland grass, Calamagrostis canadensis, wasn't like any prairie sort I'd seen before. The plants were long skinny rhizomes with sparse thready roots here and there. I assumed they wanted to be planted sideways. I assumed Marty would not be interested. I was right on both scores.

Most prairie grasses have deeply satisfying roots that hang like beards from the crown, richly branched and fibrous and with a total surface area much greater than that of the more simply structured roots of prairie forbs. The synergy among native bunchgrasses and the grassland flowers associated with them is partly due to their contrasting root systems. Grass roots may not penetrate the soil as deeply as the deepest-digging forbs, but their fancy root systems mine the top several feet of soil with great efficiency while flowers growing between the clumps mine the soil below. The root system of a lawn may extend a few inches below the surface; the root mass of a grassland may fill a depth of several yards. The efficiency of grass roots results in lush top growth—typically of greater bulk than that of meadow flowers. The decay of this annual accumulation of thatch adds organic matter to the soil, recycling nutrients rather than allowing them to leach away, enriching soil rather than impoverishing it.

There is thus a certain majesty inherent in a carton of prairie grass. But some imagination is needed: the plants come trimmed of their hay for shipping purposes. I doubt that Marty would stoop to dig for them were it not for their great beards.

Our apple orchard arrived in a standard UPS box. Our wetland thicket came with a rubber band around it. They had tops, at least: in woody species grown naturally, the stem is about as high as the root is long. Of course, this equivalence is not what one is used to in top-heavy container-grown stock, whose root length is limited by the depth of the can. Also, the dividing line between crown and root is not so obvious. Theoretically, the crown is just above the point where the first root branches from the stem. Actually, the root may not branch at that point. One can only hope the grower hasn't washed away the dirt line left when the plant was dug up.

Unlike herbaceous plants, which can be purchased bareroot in small quantities, shrubs and young trees are usually sold by the bundle, in quantities of no fewer than ten. Larger trees may be bought singly or in groups of three or five. The vocabulary of size is confusing, for it arose among wholesale growers uninterested in conveying a visual impression to the gardeners from whom they ordinarily are several steps removed.

I have bought—and briefly raised, and since sworn off—"seedlings." Seedlings are what rabbits eat for breakfast. The thicket-in-a-rubber-band was whips, young plants several feet tall but unbranched. Young branched stock is "transplant size." The apple trees for the orchard were transplants. What the term actually means, I figure, is the smallest size at which a common roadside nursery might pot up a plant and stand a chance of selling it (in some catalogs, a synonym is "retail size"). The apple trees certainly were as old as the container stock sold in gallon or larger cans—and, like them, were clones grafted onto dwarfing roots. They bore strong names like Freedom and Enterprise, but they had not been groomed for bushiness. In fact, for their own good and to fit them into a regulation carton, their branches had been lopped to stubs. They arrived, in short, well prepared for what awaited them.

I got a call last winter from a magazine editor who was interviewing gardeners about what they most look forward to in spring. I knew what was expected of me—forced forsythia, six-packs of lettuce, fat nasturtium seeds, that first fragrant mowing of the lawn, or the sensuous dispersal of black compost mined from the heaped harvest of last autumn's leaves. Or the arrival of a celebrated rhododendron plumped with buds. Or the joy of dirty fingernails, at least.

I drew a blank. My idea of spring is checking out the skunk cabbage, not digging the cold earth. Bareroot plants are not the sort of thing you can't wait to unpack and admire. Those I order begin to arrive in chilly April.

Of course I'm pleased when the UPS man drops the knocker and the dog barks at the carton on the welcome mat. Naturally I open it. PLANT IMMEDIATELY, the carton says. They all say that. I close the carton and store it in the refrigerator. That's about the same temperature as it is outdoors.

Nurseries that handle bareroot stock try to ship at the beginning of the week so that orders arrive in time for weekend planting. But if Friday is frosty, Saturday is rainy, and Sunday is someone's wedding, what can I do? I make them wait.

Growers have various packaging techniques. The cleverest I've seen is a zipper-locking food storage bag inflated with a breath of air before sealing. The humid air keeps the washed plants in perfect condition and acts as a cushion to keep them from injury during shipment. Flowers have also come to me packed like blintzes—laid on thick white paper lined with damp sphagnum moss, then folded and rolled up. Other growers use foil or plastic wrap but leave the stem end of the package open: plants need air as well as moisture. The grower from whom I buy grasses packs the plants in layers of damp peat in a carton lined with barely moistened newspaper. Other dampeners are coarse sawdust and shredded newsprint. I got a six-to-eight-foot oak tree that made the journey in spritzed excelsior. It waited in the garage, not the refrigerator.

I respect the care the grower has put into the packaging and seldom tamper with it. The packing material is intended as a humidifier, not a wetting agent. It feels like clothing on a foggy day. The roots are merely damp, like those of scallions kept fresh by a good greengrocer. Usually it's a mistake to remoisten: wetness encourages rot and mold. Think of keeping salad greens in good condition for a week; bareroot plants need the same cool temperature and humidity. I've kept orders cool in their original packaging for as long as two weeks, the outer limit for a head of lettuce, too. I know that complaints to the grower about the condition of the plants may not be honored if I haven't followed instructions to PLANT IMMEDIATELY. But like those roots that will not leave their seed to try the soil until the temperature rises, my hands stay firmly in their pockets until the calendar says May. The real rush is not to unpack the lopped stems and topless bottoms but, once they are unwrapped, to get them quickly into the ground.

I read somewhere a serious discussion about planting meadow gardens. The writer said to dig all the holes first, each as big as a bucket and spaced at one-foot intervals.

Take a moment.

Picture it.

Laugh.

Ha-ha is my response to quite a few horticultural instructions. They remind me of the course my sister-in-law, Ellen's mother, took during her first pregnancy to learn how to diaper a baby. She became quite expert at the technique using a life-size doll. The actual Ellen, though, kicked and squirmed, and her mother found that elbows also were necessary to the job.

Real plants don't float motionless over holes, suspended lightly between thumb and finger, perfectly centered and at the proper level, as they seem to in illustrations. Whether the hand shakes or the plant jerks or the earth moves, the operation requires more muscularity, an emphatic elbow. I perfected a diapering technique that involved placing the baby belly down over my knees, holding him there with an elbow implanted firmly in his spine, and getting on with the business without apology. That's how I treat plants. I have to. What if I'd had triplets that came with the instruction DIAPER IMMEDIATELY? In these, my most fertile years, I often have three hundred plants damply waiting with equivalent instructions.

That's why I find the advice to dig a hole comical when prying a slot will do. Digging a hole requires multiple jabs with a shovel and leaves a messy pile of dirt. A slot requires one push only: the dirt is opened, not removed. The plant is pressed against one side of the slot, held firmly in place with a thumb against its neck, and stamped in with a heel.

I chortle at cautions to handle roots gingerly. What is one supposed to do when the grower raises grass in soil so soft that the plants arrive with roots twelve inches long and one's shovel hits hardpan at eight inches? Why, cut the roots to fit, of course, with kitchen scissors. I shudder at gruesome tales of amputation to fit the Procrustean bed or Cinderella's slipper, but plant parts aren't comparable to body parts: they are replaceable. Lop a limb and another grows, cut a root and it proliferates. Under natural conditions, the light-absorbing leaf surface is balanced by the water-absorbing root surface. One manufactures carbohydrates, the other contributes minerals, and between them they form the substance of the growing plant. Balance between top and bottom is maintained through normal trials and tribulations. Should grubs chew on an oak tree's roots, leaves fall or twigs die back. Should caterpillars eat its leaves, root tips degenerate in proportion. In dormant plants, the stored wealth of the previous summer is all in the roots. Naturally, if you cut them, you will retard top growth somewhat. An aster with its mop trimmed may grow less over this first season than it would have otherwise, but it will remain in balance.

I'm not as keen on shortening taprooted species such as dock or milkweed. Although carrots grow new tops from even a stub, these wild species seem less resilient than garden vegetables. Sometimes I do snip them short a bit. Usually, if they don't fit their slot in a vertical position, I plant them diagonally. Why don't illustrations ever show a slanted plant?

One wouldn't want to slant a woody plant. It would grow up bowed. Nor do I trust a shrub or tree to compensate quickly for root damage due to the grower's digging or the planter's Procrustean inclinations. Thus I treat it to an equal trim on top.

I once received a double amputee that I must say appalled me. It was the oak tree, six to eight feet tall, shipped bareroot in excelsior. The grower had called to say that UPS wouldn't accept packages that long; to move the tree by other means would double its cost. Should he lop it? Why, sure. Why not? I thought he meant the root alone; then I would trim the branches. He meant both root and stem. I got the log between.

It is a tribute to plant resilience that nevertheless it lived, though its brave attempt to regrow from the base shamed this plant abuser. I would have picked the tree up whole had the grower not been far away in Ohio. The sizes in such catalogs leap from vague "transplant" to full dimension: inches of trunk thickness, feet of stem height. One can get bareroot trees two inches in diameter or over ten feet tall. Ellen could have had her birch grove bareroot from a nearby grower if she'd dared to try.

Now, I think, she might. She lost a lot of potted shrubs that first ferocious winter. The bareroot ones did fine. But perhaps the spoiled plants would have done better had she done as I do: spank them soundly as she pulled off their pots.

*T*he buckthorn hedge that I said I had removed (but hadn't) was grown from bare whips. We didn't plant it ourselves. In those days, twenty years ago, we thought that such a planting could be done only by professionals, so we had a landscaper do it. So, too, the potentilla hedge (also bareroot), the four balled and burlapped sugar maples that frame the hedged parking area, and the pair of canned boxwoods that used to guard the walk. All were professionally planted by a landscaper from the nursery—at double the ticket price.

This colossal waste of money went on for several years. I thought the role of gardeners was to fill in the blanks from flats and six-packs, from three-inch pots to possibly the daring size of gallon cans. And this I did gingerly, cradling the plants, fearful of disturbing their tender roots. I should have recalled that bumpy roads and loud vacuum cleaners soothe babies better than stillness does; I should have realized that TLC is not always the best preparation for stress and competition. But when one spends money on others' expertise, one doesn't want to think the money is misspent. Then the boys started college, and their tuition left us without the cash that earlier had deceived us.

We learned to handle bareroot plants. We learned to plant balled and burlapped stock. We learned even how to move those fat boxwoods that first had guarded but ultimately barred the way to the front door. Certainly we learned the roughness appropriate to pampered and potbound stock. But last fall, more prosperous now that our children have almost finished their seemingly interminable education, we slipped back into that complacency that only money can buy. We have to show for our backsliding a miserable summersweet hedge to replace the vigorously invasive buckthorn I had lied about removing.

We bought the new shrubs at the end of the season, when they had spent all summer spiraling their confining pots. The tops looked okay, which is to say that the plants had been dutifully fed and watered. I didn't check the roots; I was in a hurry. My calendar was clogged with weekend trips, and having caught myself in a lie about the hedge and knowing that I couldn't face this new book without the lie corrected, I just wanted the job done, no matter how or with what quality of stock.

We hired experienced men to grub out the old hedge and plant the new one. I was coming through the mountains, dropping in on Polly Law, and driving south with the birds while the old hedge was exchanged for the new. And it did look fine when I got home that Monday and Marty showed me how he, with a little help, could get along without me.

By mid-May the following year, when other Clethra alnifolia we'd planted elsewhere had lush foliage, the summersweet hedge was still alarmingly bare. I scratched upper twigs to check whether they were green beneath the bark to find that whole branches were dead. I searched the main stems at the bottom of one sorry plant for incipient leaves. There were some; the base was still alive. Around it the perfect circle of the pot-formed roots was visible at the soil surface: I could have grasped the plant by its stems and pulled it out. It was in the ground but not attached to it. It had not actually been planted.

One must sometimes buy plants in cans. Public enthusiasm for plants whose dress is visible—and whose private parts are not—has forced many growers of native plants to supply them packaged. A little wild rose I love comes no other way. Junipers are easily grown in fields, but their scant and sprawling roots don't survive transplanting unless forced to compactness by containment. Or one is in a hurry, as I was for the hedge, or at a loss to compose a planting without some bushy plants to fill out the vision. The bayberries on the stone terrace were potted.

I whacked them hard against a rock. That's what should have been done to the summersweet. It knocks the dirt out of them; it makes them bareroot. It reveals their true anatomy. The bottom of a bayberry is not shaped like a pot.

Uncoiled and untangled, the roots proved to be three times as long as the pot was deep. Those at the perimeter had been trying to escape; new stems had sprouted through the drainage holes. This is how bayberries grow—outward, spreading new shoots as they travel. The central roots were older, woodier, the structural anchor that holds the plant in the ground. Nutritional work is done by feeder roots. These always are new—paler, more elaborate, and more tender than the woody anchors from which they branch. They function only at their tips, where root hairs sprout daily, drink thirstily, and die. From one day to the next a plant mines a different area of soil, exhausting each microscopically local resource and probing for the next. Cutting an old root forces it to grow new branches, and these exploratory newcomers increase the feeding surface of the plant.

So, judiciously with pruners, I trimmed the anchors and cut off the stem-sprouting roots entirely. I thought it unwise for the bushes to be so rambunctious at this point, when they were about to be weaned from the blue tablets that had fed them in their pots.

Other species have different root systems. A whack alone may not free the roots of a blueberry potted for too long. Its fibrous mass, grown thick as a loofah against the walls of its container, can't be untangled into individual roots, can't be rejuvenated by judicious pruning. It needs a proper slashing. I bought a special knife for this purpose, one with a hooked blade on a substantial handle. I slash vertically at intervals all around and hook out the bottom, too, until the mass hangs open and in shreds. If matted roots are more succulent, I scratch them loose with fingernails instead. New feeder roots will sprout along the slash or scratch lines and, not meeting the pot walls that had forced them into a down-ward spiral, they will grow outward into unexplored ground. They will dig in, grip the soil, suck it dry, grow on, reach the edge of their hole, and push on past it. Only then, when a plant has pushed beyond its excavation, when a stiff wind can't top-ple it and a strong arm can't uproot it, can one fairly claim that a potted plant is planted.

The summersweet merely had been moved to those larger pots known to horticulture as "perfect" holes: straight-sided, flat-bottomed, smooth all over, and greater in volume than the root ball in about the ratio of a three- to a one-gallon can.

Having seen early on such masterpieces dug under the supervision of profes-sionals by their well-trained crews, I used to rail at Marty for his messy digs. His holes were bowl-shaped. Their sides were rough. There was little more extra space than was necessary to replace the soil around the positioned plant.

Now I find that horticultural wisdom is moving toward Marty's untutored dig-ging and my educated meanness. Knives and rocks and scrabbling fingernails are coming into fashion. One is cautioned lately that smooth sides present a barrier to root penetration; one is told to rough them up. The pot shape is out and the bowl shape is in. I think the pros already jam the hose nozzle through the roots to settle the plant in a slurry instead of ineffectually dribbling at the surface. Soon they may get meaner in the matter of fertilizing. At any moment now, they might reach the ultimate conclusion: bareroot is better.

Part of a planting of 2,500 mountain laurels installed by one of the Naturals, Elaine Matto, in the midst of a middle-class suburban community. Such ambitious plantings aren't possible for most people unless they can buy stock at wholesale. (Elaine Matto)

8 *The Naturals*

THE LAST WORKSHOP I GAVE expired at two-thirty on a Wednesday afternoon in October. At two-forty it was reborn as the Naturals. We were the same people; we occupied the same chairs. But we had become a different group. I didn't do it, but I couldn't stop it. It's just that no one got up to leave when it was time to go.

We had spent the hours since lunch listening to everybody describe their property and their plans for it. I should have thought of doing this much earlier. I should at least have inquired at the beginning what sort of background these people had and why they had enrolled in the workshops. I should have noticed as I led them single file along the paths, identifying, explaining, babbling wisdom like water in a brook, that they were learning things from one another behind my back. Or maybe, had I known what they knew, I would have been too intimidated to teach them anything at all.

Three were professional landscape designers; of these, one was also an expert in moss identification and an illustrator with a sideline in botanicals. Three were retired: one a former librarian of a state university arboretum, another a former science teacher, and the third the student Master Gardener and experienced propagator who had been responsible for my buying the second copy of Dr. Deno's book. The group also had an amateur ornithologist who nets and tags migrating birds at a nearby sanctuary, a woman who maintains a large property as a wildlife refuge—the one where a flock of turkeys attended the feeders over the winter—and a self-described "maniac gardener" who displayed eight-by-ten glossies showing, against snowy woods, a portion of her planting of twenty-five hundred mountain laurels.

Only one woman fit at all my preconception of what my students would be like: at that verge when one's devotion to traditional gardening weakens, at that moment when a touch of ecological nourishment might bring a ready bud to flower. But tough Alma, challenging my bias in her raspy smoker's voice, could hardly be described as a bud.

These things they knew of one another; I was the only outsider in the group. Even my belated awareness of their professionalism was off the mark, for the other knowledge they shared was that this venture in fact was intimidating to each as an individual. They had come to appreciate one another's support. They had come to realize that their endeavor was communal and, in a deeper sense, an effort in which each person's action affected the way all of us live on the land.

So they wouldn't leave, refused to disperse until they had found reason to meet again and keep on meeting.

They hoped I would join them.

Within ten minutes the group decision was to visit each property in turn: walk the land, identify the species, and help one another decide what to plant and where. It was the logical thing to do.

The workshops, given at my home (I didn't have to worry about being late or getting lost), had concerned the basics of local ecology. In May, when spring ephemerals were in bloom, we discussed woodland, its structure and its role in recycling, erosion control, and water conservation—its environmental impact, so to speak. In July, when the meadow was in full performance, we dealt with relationships among animals and plants—the who-eats-whom of grasslands, the social economics of the system. The October workshop, when dogwoods were in fruit, was about birds and berries, migration and dispersal, the wheel of the seasons and the exchanges of energy that bring the flora and fauna through the year. I gave a lecture; I showed slides; we ate lunch; we walked along the paths. For each workshop, participants received course notes, instructional sheets, and lists of species for the habitat.

The course sounds dry to me, abbreviated this way, but I feel passionate about such subjects and—as I gather now from the group's teasing—I gesticulate extravagantly while discussing strawberries that hug the ground so mice will find them or dogwoods that display their fruit for flocks of birds to see. The result, apparently, was inspiring: the Naturals hoped to make what I described come true. But inspiration accompanied by species lists is like the Christmas spirit accompanied by shopping lists. One needs something more to keep the spirits high: the company, the jollity, the *oohs* and *ahhs* of admiration.

We met every few weeks through the remainder of the autumn. In some ways these visits were like my walks with ALFASAC—adventures in scrutiny. But on our

Monday walks, when we saw a wetland endangered by invasive species, or woods too young to have much of interest in them, or a dry field where heath aster ought to grow but didn't, we could only remark on it and walk on. The Naturals found not only species that members didn't know they had but opportunities they hadn't realized: a grassy opening in woods that could be dappled meadow, a hard-to-mow embankment that could be a splendid hedgerow, a wetland rich in native sedges where lilies, too, might grow.

The choice of plants was easy: we had our lists. Sources weren't a problem: all the species on the lists were in my catalogs. The spirit was with us. People who had previously chosen one plant at a time were cheerfully contemplating replant-ings in abundance. We were approaching Christmas when, having combated the loneliness that might otherwise have dampened our separate enthusiasms, we recognized that other despoiler of the season: the monetary cost of generosity.

I believe I was the one who suggested a novel sort of shopping spree: we would break for the holidays and hit the New Year with group orders large enough that we could buy at wholesale.

Unlike the furniture business, where the line between retail and wholesale is clear, there often is no such strict distinction in the mall-order nursery business. The descriptions of quite a few of the companies listed in *Gardening by Mail* are fol-lowed by the designation "R&W"—retail and wholesale. In many cases, retail and wholesale price lists turn out to be the same. The difference is only in the quantity: the price for three plants is retail; the price for a hundred is wholesale. In other cases, there are two separate price lists. The retail list allows one to buy plants indi-vidually and requires only a modest minimum order. The wholesale list offers price breaks in larger quantities and may set the minimum order at a higher dollar value.

There also are strictly wholesale mail-order growers whose clientele is largely other nurseries. The buyers may be another layer of wholesalers that buy stock bareroot, grow it for several years in the field or in containers, and sell the plants to retail garden centers when they have reached commercial size. Or they may be the roadside retailers themselves, who merely pot up bareroot plants and charge you for the service, or mail-order houses that buy in bulk, repackage in smaller quantities, and sell the same bareroot, dormant stock to retail customers. The same principle applies to plants in containers at the outset: six-packs, flats, and pots offered by retailers usually represent a change of hands—and not necessari-ly even a change in the size of the containers.

Each move has a drastic effect on the price. A fern that I might buy for a few coins at the original wholesaler might be sold to me for three dollars by another mail-order house, for six dollars potted up by a roadside garden center, or for twelve dollars as a groomed plant on display at my upscale nursery.

I learned all this over a period of years, first from a friend and grower who explained the basics of the nursery business to me, then through my own perusal of catalogs, and finally through an experiment in group buying with friends and relatives the previous spring.

The experiment had not been particularly successful. The people for whom I ordered were not a group. They didn't know one another; they had no common cause. They were like gardeners who go to plant sales in hope of finding bargains, but the bargains were modest: price breaks in quantities of three or six, discounts available for placing orders early in the season, specials on overstocked plants, and savings achieved by upping the total dollar value of the order to bring down the percentage charged for shipping and handling. While gratifying in its way, this sort of finagling did not turn out to be worth the time and trouble. I could have gotten bareroot native shrubs, four feet tall and costing less per plant than a can of beer, if I could have found a home for fifty of them. Or, had my order been able to meet a minimum value of $500, I could have supplied large bareroot trees in quantities of five per species. Only ferns and some wetland herbs and shrubs in containers had been ordered in sufficient quantity to buy at wholesale. Those ordering wanted too few of too many kinds of plants to put together anything like the feast of greenery with which, as the first snow fell, I hoped to celebrate the new year for the Naturals.

Those of you who have experience with groups rightly blush at my naïveté. My total history as a member was with ALFASAC, which has no dues, no offices, no responsibilities, and no communal pursuit beyond the fresh air and standing around that its acronym implies. The Naturals was as loose a group, and though they called me "Chief" sometimes, they said it with a smile, for my organizational skills extend no farther than the distance between me and my computer.

My preparation for the first meeting in January was to spread thirty catalogs enticingly on the dining room table. The other members brought pencils and wish lists with the species listed alphabetically by botanical name (I had that much foresight; growers list species in the same order). No one had considered what might happen when twelve excited people met thirty exhilarating catalogs and one pocket calculator with no rules of order.

We found, for example, that although people had to plan habitat by habitat and order catalog by catalog, habitat and catalog did not neatly correspond. A prairie grower also carried woodland species. A wetlands listing gave as much space to drought-resistant plants as to flood-tolerant ones. Also, the group had based its lists on those I had prepared for the workshops, whereas the catalogs offered a wealth of goods no one had imagined. I had an excellent wholesale source for ferns, and everybody wanted them—but often for no better reason than that ferns are likable and these were cheap. Some catalog copy, too, was overwrought, and color photographs often were too rich by far for the spare diet of essentials I had in mind. Chris, the moss expert, held the calculator. As each species description was read aloud, people called out the number they wanted in the manner of the stock exchange on a bullish day.

By the third meeting we had found our way through the kaleidoscopic confusion of that first session and had laid out the protocol we have followed since. We withdrew the delicatessen of catalogs and cut the menu to four: a wetlands specialist, a prairie grower, a source for woodland forbs and ferns, and a general list of bareroot shrubs and trees. We then limited the choice further by drawing up our own blanks listing those species that could be ordered from each catalog. Our order blanks named only plants that are native to the region, easy to grow, and basic to their habitat: flowering but not Chinese dogwood, Christmas but not maidenhair fern, little but not big bluestem grass.

The lists were drawn up by study groups of members working on similar habitats. For instance, I was working on a sunny opening in a red maple swamp, another was developing a pond shore, and a third was improving a wet meadow; we all could consider using woolgrass, cattail, and flag iris. Because we'd visited one another's properties, we also knew members who were working on wet but shady woodlands; understory shrubs such as spicebush and summersweet might be added to our list. Ferns weren't in the wetlands mitigation catalog, yet several species are basic to these moist habitats. The study group working on the fern and wildflower catalog needed to know which ones. Each study group also wrote a brief description of the chosen species on the order blank so that when they were distributed, everyone would have the information needed to buy intelligently.

Intelligence, we found, does not flourish in haste. Wave a full-color catalog depiction of Turk's cap lily at an eager group that has not had time to absorb its habitat requirements, and those who have no place for it will want it anyway. Then you must tell this person that it won't grow in his dark woods and that person that it will fail on her dry bank, and soon the time is up and the orders not complete.

In September, three months before we ordered, we distributed a packet of planning materials to each member of the Naturals. It included a copy of each catalog and its limited order blank and Habitat Sheets, which group the species by community. That way, if a member was planning a hedgerow, he or she might choose both this viburnum and that grass even though each appears on a different order blank. The three-month lead time also gave us the leisure to look up the offerings in field guides and books on horticulture or to see them growing in gardens or in the wild (and to study the catalogs for species not on our limited list; members were free to order privately whatever they wanted). By mid-December, each person's order blank was to be completed in pencil.

The reason for this precaution was that when we added up the numbers at the order meeting, we might find that the total for a species was just under the number needed for a major price break. Perhaps we needed another twelve plants to reach a quantity of fifty or another two plants to reach a price break for ten. Then, in a group spirit, one or several members would increase their order to reach the goal.

The Naturals' first group wholesale order amounted to 2,139 plants—including hundreds of trees and shrubs—at a total cost of $3,415.06, about a fifth of what equivalent stock would have cost at a retail nursery.

I was at about this point in this chapter when my computer died, descended over the space of a morning into idiocy, leaving me finally with that equivalent of the flat line on a heartbeat monitor, a blinking question mark on the screen.

I had not backed up "New Book." Not the recent portions anyway. I had to remove the CPU's brain-dead hard drive, encase it in an antistatic bag, and ship it off to California, where possibly the magnetic trace of my manuscript could be recovered. I was lost in ignorance of how the system worked, anxious at its disassembly, dubious of its reconstruction. Plain scared, in fact. My hands shook. I cried.

I called Carm. Carm called Chris and Alma. Alma called Dianne. The next day they all came over to work in the garden with me: to weed, to talk, to dig, to joke, to prune, to laugh. To finally get it: how had I failed to grasp before the group support the Naturals had relied on from the outset?

As usual, I lagged behind what they long since had discovered. Moss Lady was helping Turkey Feeder lay out her shrubs. Propagator was moving stones for Retired Librarian. Ex–Science Teacher was hatching schemes for a local arboretum's plant sale with at least three other members, one of whom—our only Computer Literate—was creating the graphics for the display. They had left me alone to write, but I had lost that grip on solitude, and there they were to catch me in this net they had been tying.

The extent to which the net had already grown took me by surprise. Chris of the mosses had come upon a man who raises luna moths and distributes their cocoons for others to raise in turn. She and Sondra of the turkeys were both releasing the adults they had cared for into their proper habitats. All three landscape designers had sought with new fervor clients interested in habitat restoration, and their success was growing. Alice, who had taught ecology to youngsters for twenty years, had convinced our (decidedly ornamental) arboretum not only to allow the Naturals to set up a table at the plant sale, where advice would be offered on native species, but also to arrange for the following spring sale a special section of native plants that the staff and she and Elliot—now a graduate Master Gardener—together would propagate. To this end also, Carm, the retired librarian whom I had known mostly for her oft-repeated "I'm overwhelmed; I don't know where to start!" was selecting species for propagation that would compose several small habitat gardens to get beginners going. Grown sons and daughters had become involved in various endeavors; friends and neighbors wished to know how they might join us. The net was spreading, yet we were bursting at the seams.

The week after my digital documents arrived safely home, the crew showed up again, this time to plant a moss garden around a birdhouse beside the pond. The morning work was hard and dull—hacking grass, breaking clods, grading soil. And it was baffling: only Chris, who calls her business Mossaics, had a mental picture of what this pondside clearing was to be. We worked, in a sense, to no purpose and without organization. Someone gathered stones, someone hacked the dirt, someone raked the mulch, and someone lopped the roots: we moved from job to job, lay down this tool and picked up another, directed less by any sense to be made of the landscape than by snatches of conversation, bursts of laughter, a sort of flowing chumminess that was new to me.

It had been the same the week before; the work got done, but strangely beyond any awareness of the effort. I had thought that to complete a job, you had to say "Do this; do that," assign a task, designate a person, at least lay out the steps of the project. The pencil-and-paper work of group ordering certainly had required discipline and planning. Yet from this day of physical labor I have no memory of any procedure at all. My images are non sequiturs: the places they had traveled—Madagascar, New Zealand, Antarctica, Tibet. The way the stepping-stones should go—"one foot" stones to indicate direction, "two feet" stones to indicate arrival. Brand names of bicycles; botanical names of mosses. A wonderful farmer's market; a troubled granddaughter. Tree roots. Arthritis. Dianne said to me, "Say 'All those delphiniums!' again," so she could catch in her camera my arm-tossed dismissal of English gardens.

That's what I remember: the colors of fond teasing and good humor, scraps of these women's lives, bits of their knowledge. Someone mentioned the novel *How to Make an American Quilt*. I remember that.

By lunch the clearing was smoothly raked and subtly graded. Bushes had been moved, the shore cleared of vegetation. Stones were placed. Steps led to the water. What had been severed roots scavenged from dead trees seemed now, half buried, to emanate from living trees. The place had been transformed at full conversation—by a work *party*.

The afternoon was mud and mosses, the muck and goo of primitive sensuousness watered to a quiver, squished between the fingers, smoothed and patted and pressed with dripping sheets and spongy pillows of moss whose names all rhyme with rhythm: Hypnum, Triticum, Atricum, Climacium, and Dicranum. There is both art and science in moss placement. One that grows at the base of trees set off by its jeweled brightness the partially excavated roots as though they had been molded in platinum. A tougher moss that can be better stepped on "popped" the small indicator stones that showed which way to go. Pale apple-green rounds and ovals of Leucobryum emphasized the high points of slight rises, and these drier spots are also where this genus naturally occurs. Smaller emerald bits—"sparklers," "brights," Chris called them—drew attention to a lichen-covered stone, a fern-sprouted log. A dark and curly moss filled a hollow where the clearing is wettest. At last I learned the genus of the moss that grows on dry heights and, by then, also on the stone terrace: Polytrichum. It looks close up like a forest of tiny pines. Chris placed it to fur the sunny bank where three steps descend to the water.

A moss garden is not of great ecological moment. We found millipedes and centipedes among the sheets and pillows, a huge mole cricket and some little pill-bugs, but the important role of moss is as a bed for tree seedlings in the forest, and if you let a moss garden be a bed for trees, it will not remain a garden very long. Also, the surface must be watered, weeded of grass, swept of fallen leaves, and protected from romping dogs and children. You must walk barefoot on a moss garden if you walk on it at all. Such a planting is, I must add, rather precious, with its false roots, chosen stones, tastefully positioned strips of lichened bark, and odd spots of liverworts.

So although I had planned before the computer broke to put in such a garden in that dank spot where patches of moss already outnumbered those of grass, and had arranged for Chris to design it, and had been eager to learn the names and ways of these ancient and peculiar plants (their sperm is secreted in upright cups from which rain splashes the squirming liquid over the female parts), I had not intended to write about the project. The book was proceeding logically. I was in the middle of the most practical part of it, the very center and fulcrum: the economies of group buying. I was speaking roughly: do this, do that, whack the plant and run the group, lay the facts out plain and flat the way the 800-number tech person told me to take apart the computer. The mention of *How to Make an American Quilt,* and our striking parallel in piecing together our mosses and ourselves, made me change my mind and speak gently of this subject I was given.

One does not want merely to be told what to do and how to do it, what to buy and where to get it. What I needed at the time of my electronic loss was a human presence, someone working there with me to reconstruct the missing data. It was not enough that someone in California reassured me that 90 percent of lost documents are recovered. I needed the reassurance given with an arm around the shoulder or, as Alma does most brilliantly, with that belittlement that punches one's perspective back in place. I had expected the Naturals, when they were my "students," to work in isolation recovering ecosystems more complicated by far than my computer. Even the first step—pulling out the cables, herbiciding the turf—really was too radical for me or for them to do alone.

The fulcrum therefore shifted, although this chapter still lies at about dead center of the book. I can explain how to organize group buying. I can tell you that the purpose of the Naturals is to help one another start as many new replantings as there are members. I can attest that we use methods described in the instructional portion of this book—taking inventories of our properties, using surveys to lay out plans. I can add that what we really want, but don't yet know how to do, is to seed other groups, to help other people, to piece together by patches, however small and sparsely laid at first, the quilt that binds us to one another and our land.

What I can't explain but wish most ardently to express is the affection with which we itch and sweat our way through a hot summer day's attack on Carm's infesting weeds or why, when we are done, we are not even tired.

I said that my year of talk and travel at last came to an end in the fall, but there was one exception. I was asked to speak the following spring at the University of Wisconsin's Madison Arboretum, the site of the first tallgrass prairie restoration, and, on the same weekend, at a dinner in Milwaukee in honor of Lorrie Otto, the founder of the Wild Ones, a group that has carried the practice of prairie planting into midwestern yards. This was not an invitation I could turn down, and for it I broke the silent moratorium I had promised myself.

The visit started with lunch at Lorrie's. Her home is reached through a determinedly suburban neighborhood—more neat, more clean, more conscious of propriety than any I know of in the East—and her wild corner in its midst is therefore all the more startling. One sees first a patch of tallgrass prairie. It has been much photographed, usually with Lorrie posed among its towering flowers. But it is only as big as the field of a snapshot camera held at medium distance.

Around the bend comes the driveway, paved with blocks that form an open grid so that grass grows up and rain drains through. I noted birdhouses everywhere, and birdseed too, and then a peculiarity about the windows. They were covered with chicken wire so that birds in full flight during migration would not, deceived by their transparency, dash themselves against the glass. Then Lorrie emerged from the doorway, flamboyant in bright red, arms open to hug this perfect stranger.

We had not met before nor even corresponded. Simply, we are part of the same bee, although at the time I had no sense of it. We had soup and salad and Lorrie's homemade bread for lunch. The other guests included a grower, a teacher, a volunteer at a public garden, and a Wild One or two—as various as the prairie in their personalities but in that same sort of unison by which communities grow. Wine was served; snapshots were taken. I was scheduled to stay overnight with the Wildest One (Rochelle Whiteman won't mind the appellation), who on the way home from Lorrie's managed to talk without breathing as she screwballed through the side streets, pointing out every prairie yard in the whole city of Milwaukee.

Planting Noah's Garden

The next morning Lorrie and I were driven by Richard Barloga, a field biologist, to the home, halfway between Milwaukee and Madison, of that previously faceless Robert Ahrenhoerster from whom I had bought dollar packets but who now appeared to me, small inside a buffalo coat, a reborn Johnny Appleseed. Bob does not grow seed crops; he is a wild collector. The day was cold; the wind was biting. Pasque flowers were in bloom on Bob's own home prairie among the other hundred-something species that he has cataloged.

We drove here and there to grassland remnants. Alumroot, a plant of dry wood-

The moss garden the morning after it was completed. (Sara Stein)

land here, grew there on "goat prairie" along with an Opuntia—the prickly pear cactus that grows in the East on coastal dunes—and a hairgrass that in New England, too, is a sign of worn-out ground. Or was that in Madison, where we ended this mythic afternoon with a blessed beer?

Certainly it was in Madison that I met the little path, so cunningly inviting in its continuation into the neighboring yard. I know for sure because the path was in a prairie garden designed by Molly Murray, the landscape architect and educator who had seduced my appearance at the podium.

Molly is a more stolid sort than the tall-tale, red-cloaked, bison-robed figures to whom I had so quickly and so warmly become accustomed during the previous day. I didn't know what to make of her at first. She said little but knew much: geology, archaeology, ecology; ancient mounds and Indian trails and pioneer history as well as how the hills and fens of Madison were cut and filled to build the flat city; and the technicalities of restoring tallgrass prairie and Wisconsin oak savanna. I'd ask a question and get an answer as if I had pressed the button at a drinking fountain to enjoy a spurt of water. But gradually Molly sprang leaks, and by the time I flew off on Sunday, I was as saturated as moss in a rainstorm.

Since that astonishing trip, I've tried to untangle the threads by which it came to be. I knew Robert Ahrenhoerster only as a source, but Neil Diboll, on whose consultation and Prairie Nursery catalog I had relied to sow our meadow, had since become a friend, and he and Bob had trekked and collected in the wild, as had Bob and the field biologist who drove us to his home. Neil, educated at the same university where Molly teaches, had been closely involved with her in landscaping projects and has been a favorite speaker at the Madison Arboretum and for the Wild Ones in Milwaukee. Molly Murray is a friend of my editor's daughter, Jane, and it was she who suggested my name as speaker. My editor herself, Frances Tenenbaum, had sent Lorrie Otto bound galleys of *Noah's Garden* to review in the Wild Ones' newsletter. I had recognized Lorrie immediately from a photo of her, dwarfed by her prairie patch, that I had first seen in *The Natural Habitat Garden*, by Ken Druse, who also photographed our meadow for his book. And I could trace any one of these threads—photographer, biologist, editor, educator, advocate, designer, grower—to their connections with others I have met or corresponded with in Oregon, California, Arizona, Texas, Missouri, Kentucky, Georgia, North Carolina, Virginia, Delaware, Massachusetts, Connecticut, and New York.

I had been slurped unknowingly into some amorphous substance of which the word "network" gives too flat a concept. "Moss" perhaps is closer, "fungus" still better, implying as it does multiple and tender threads that nourish themselves invisibly underground and only when the time is ripe suddenly fruit into mushrooms.

Sometimes we get discouraged, our little group of twelve groping for the means to make ourselves visible, to offer our fruits. But like the fungus discovered in the West that proved to be the largest plant on earth, centuries old and covering in an uninterrupted mesh some two and a half square miles of land, we belong to the body of an organism wonderfully large and lively. We can order as a group because growers propagate the plants. We can give advice because ecologists uncover the information we disseminate. We can act locally, but elsewhere across the continent, along these mycelia by which we're all connected, other fruiting bodies make visible the work.

I wouldn't have thought that gentler meant more voices. Or that gentler might be louder, too.

These dark alumroots seem a sinister reminder of the evils of collecting, but in fact they are among the numerous offspring of wild parents that, had they not been propagated by collectors, would not be growing in my garden. (Sara Stein)

Planting Noah's Garden

9 Questions of Collection

W HAT A TEDIOUS MORNING this has been! I've been counting the number of species offered by native seed catalogs: the winner definitely is Southwestern Native Seeds of Tucson, Arizona. I counted 350 species altogether from Arizona, New Mexico, Colorado, Utah, Idaho, Montana, Wyoming, Texas, Mexico, and California, plus two, unexpectedly, from Ohio. The typeface was tiny; I counted twice to be sure. When I finished, I saw that the owners, Sally and Tim Walker, had conveniently printed the total number of species in the upper-right-hand corner of the last page. There are many ways to waste a morning.

Of course the number seems meager compared to the twenty-five hundred species with which Dr. Deno has performed his germination experiments, but he works with seeds sent to him from all over the world. In fact, Sally Walker has been one of his important suppliers. She also supplied Ruth Shilling in Arizona with seeds to scatter in her desert garden. One of the snapshots Ruth sent me shows a gorgeous scarlet penstemon. The Walkers list forty-three penstemons in their catalog. They truly are walkers: they spend five months of the year collecting seeds in the wild.

This couple also photographs each species and maintains a herbarium of pressed specimens with records of where and when the plant was found. From them southwesterners can buy seeds collected not only in their own state, but in their own county. Other collectors are equally careful. Bob Ahrenhoerster collects seed for Prairie Seed Source in southeastern Wisconsin—not in neighboring Minnesota, Illinois, or Iowa; not even in more western or northern portions of Wisconsin. He won't mix grass seed collected from the dry top of a moraine with seed of the same species collected in the moist dip below. He refuses to confuse their genes.

He refuses to *select* genes either. He is against collecting wild seed by machine, the way grain is harvested, all at once and all at the same height on the stalk. What about seeds that ripen later? What about plants that grow shorter? He hand-picks each species high and low and over and over to be sure his collection represents the entire gene pool of that stand. He will not sell in bulk outside his own area for fear that a large new population of a species could genetically swamp a rare or remnant population whose unique adaptations would then be lost.

This attention to preserving the local integrity of genetic information is one form of the collector's obsession. There are others. Some collectors gather seed from many locations expressly to broaden the spectrum of genetic information in their stock. Some are hooked on rarities regardless of geographic origin or ultimate distribution. Others would as soon take seed from a rare plant as bludgeon their grandmother.

These points of view, seemingly at odds and often expressed with considerable crankiness, are all born from the same passion: to preserve the diversity of our native flora. Collectors of rarities are expert propagators whose mission is to cultivate vulnerable species as insurance against the present threat of their extinction in the wild. Those who preserve a specific gene pool wish to bank unique traits that may save a species from disaster in the future. Those who maintain a broad genetic spectrum hope to arm a species to repopulate locations where it had been extirpated in the past.

I take no sides in the matter. I'm from the East. I buy what seeds I can without guilt, knowing that none of them originated hereabouts.

My total count this morning, including Southwestern's listing and ones from California, Wisconsin, Missouri, Minnesota, and Oklahoma, came close to a thousand native species. I didn't have to count eastern meadow listings because there are none. One excuse is that, in contrast to prairie, desert, and mountain grassland species, whose seeds can be stored dry, most of our native flora are woodland sorts, whose seeds must be planted fresh. Another reason, though, is that there's hardly a scrap of native grassland left to pick from.

One notable exception in the Northeast is an endangered ecosystem called the Hempstead Plains, situated behind a chain-link fence in the suburbs of Long Island. We have coastal grasslands, too—salt marshes. Otherwise, the "meadows" that owners may proudly point to are alien forage crops, escaped ornamentals, household herbs, and agricultural weeds with a smattering of the most indomitable Americans, like common milkweed and Canada goldenrod. The category Eastern Prairie is an empty one: the Indians once kept it full by burning; the Europeans cleaned it out with plow and scythe and cattle. Even those few natives

Planting Noah's Garden

that linger in old fields are routinely mowed before their seeds can ripen. Sometimes tufts of this and that are left—around rock outcrops, along thickets, at the base of road signs. But the idea of easterners arguing the genetic pitfalls of mechanized collection is absurd.

So we can't be purists. The wild strawberries that came from Bob Ahrenhoerster were presumably pure southeast Wisconsin, but if there is a remnant on my land that they could swamp, I haven't found it. The blazingstar seeds I germinated using Deno's method are from a broad-based midwestern stock, and the broader the better, I say. The species, theoretically an eastern one, no longer has representatives that might retain a local flavor. Among the most successful meadow flowers I've planted is stiff goldenrod, Solidago rigida, purchased from the same midwestern source—Neil Diboll's Prairie Nursery—but here it is an officially endangered species whose extant sites are guarded like state secrets. My ideology out of necessity favors something over nothing.

Even what that "something" ought to be is in doubt. Records of species that once grew here are "historical," meaning that they date from farming times. "Prehistorical," as far as eastern grasslands are concerned, means prior to four hundred years ago, when the European colonists arrived. There is no inventory to suggest what meadows looked like then.

Yet I am haunted by that ghost of meadow past. I got a glimpse of it on the island in Maine at a spot where there had been a blowdown some years before. Neil was visiting. We went walking among the uprooted spruces, just curious: maybe the raspberries would be ripe. I thought I pretty much knew the kinds of growth on the island—old hayfield and sheep pasture, spruce woods, cranberry bogs, blueberry flats, scrub growth on old quarries, tidal communities around the shore. But here was something new: a sedge and grass meadow made up almost entirely of native species that had been waiting half a century for those spruces to blow down.

It was not lush (and the raspberries weren't ripe), but this poor sprouting of hairgrass and angelica instead of quackgrass and sow thistle was like a wraith from the past, and I reached to catch it before it vanished. Thus the sedge seeds that went home with me that fall and the beginning of that addiction which must drive all seed collectors of whatever stripe. Neil predicted what would happen once I got a taste of it, and he was right.

Back home I began to collect with increasing seriousness: a woodland goldenrod found on a rocky bank, an anise-scented goldenrod discovered near the dismantled fire tower, the annual called blue curls that grows in sandy places, and an unusual milkweed that grows with it.

These species, like a northern blazingstar that I've heard still exists on New

England barrens and now hunger for, are not offered either as seeds or plants in any catalog. They are the genuine article: not only species that must have grown in native meadows four centuries ago, but direct descendents of that northeastern genetic stock. We will never see the ghost full-face, unshadowed by the death that long ago befell it. But some portion of that natural heritage is in the seeds that can still be found, and I never go walking anymore without packets to collect them.

Chris, though, whose obsession with mosses is on a larger scale, never drives anywhere without shopping bags. No one sells moss spores; collecting is a job for elves, not people. (When moss is grown from spores, the whole fruiting clump is pulverized in a blender with buttermilk to spread it.) The one source of moss plants I know sells them in six-packs—half a dozen tufts, each about the size of the half-dollar it costs. That's okay for the Polytrichum plugs one might scrunch into cracks between terrace stones. It's not okay for planting a whole moss garden, and that's another reason I hadn't intended to write about it.

The mosses in that garden were all collected.

Native plant societies and conservation groups warn never to collect in the wild. Native plant nurseries are expected to state that they never do so; if they do, we are expected to boycott them. Among the groups of plants whose choicest species have been locally collected to extinction for their curious behavior or sheer rarity are sundews and pitcher plants, orchids, ferns, alpines, and cacti. Princess pine, a clubmoss of the Lycopodium genus, has been pulled to the brink to make Christmas ropes and wreaths. Sea lavender, Limonium nashii, is used in dried arrangements and seems likely to follow. Ginseng has been collected to near oblivion for its roots' reputed medicinal properties. The latest panacea is Echinacea, the genus of coneflowers disappearing now from roadsides; collectors believe its roots cure even the common cold. Commercial mushroom hunters in the northwestern forests pluck every salable one they find, leaving none to waft its spores to new locations; gourmet groups here pluck just as carelessly for their own delectation.

The consequences of unscrupulous greed and ignorant consumption have stained all plant collectors with moral opprobrium, and ALFASAC, for one, does not allow the taking of anything but small amounts of seed. However, it's hard to see offhand a clear relationship between collection and protection. Ginseng is not protected in my state. Mountain laurel, which clothes oak woods for miles in many places, is protected as an Exploitably Vulnerable species, meaning that it could be collected to extinction if only people would stop buying those canned types so easily available at their nursery. Nobody protects mushrooms: they're fungi, not plants.

Such seeming irrationality does not sit easy with me, and I set out a winter ago to find some reason in it.

One morning when snow lay heavy on the ground, a hungry kestrel diving into a red cedar near the feeder caused an explosion of juncoes, finches, wrens, and sparrows. The effect was similar when I, driven by moral hunger, dove into the thicket of bureaucracy to rouse the information I knew must be hiding there. I wanted to understand how protected species are chosen and by what laws they are spared. But, like the kestrel, I emerged from the thicket as hungry as I had been before, despite the flurry of information I had roused.

A spur of guilt caused me to take the dive: thirty-five of the species we grow on our property are on the list of protected plants in New York State. Three of them are accorded the direst classification, Endangered. Some we grew from seed; some we bought as seedlings of plants collected in the wild; some are the wild-collected plants themselves; some we ourselves collected in the wild.

I had received the list of New York's protected species during the summer I collected the sedge seeds from the ghost meadow in Maine. The new booklet had arrived five years out of date. The first step in understanding this business of protection, it seemed to me, was to get the updated version of that list as well as the latest list of federally endangered and threatened species.

The federal list turned out to be easier to extricate. I roused "John" at the Fish and Wildlife Publication Unit of the Department of the Interior somewhere in area code 703, Virginia. His speech was slurred like kestrel wings, and he was reluctant to repeat his name lest that common syllable reveal his identity. Still, there arrived one week later a list called *Endangered and Threatened Wildlife and Plants: 50 CFR 17.11 & 17.12.* Good enough. We don't expect perfect clarity from the feds.

To get an updated state list, I was referred by the New York State Department of Environmental Conservation to Doug Schmid, senior forester, Division of Lands and Forests. Schmid was perfectly articulate but unable to help. The revised list had indeed been prepared through the joint effort of himself at DEC, the state botanist, Dr. Richard Mitchell, who described his role as that of plant explorer, and Steve Young, who maintains an inventory of rare species and habitats for the Natural Heritage Program, an arm of the Nature Conservancy under contract to DEC (I hadn't expected bureaucratic simplicity, either). The only trouble was that DEC didn't have the budget to print the new list.

So, affecting the innocence of an ordinary citizen tempted to pocket a seed but alarmed at the possible ecological and legal repercussions, I dealt with what I had at hand.

Ten federally endangered or threatened species were listed as naturally occurring in New York, according to historical records. Only three of them were also listed by the state. That might reflect the age of the list, or it might mean that the other seven species were already extinct in New York. None of the ten species was in my field guides. I guess there's no sense describing what one isn't apt to find.

There was no hint in either the state or federal publication of what sorts of habitats extant populations might occupy. The Natural Heritage (or Natural Areas) Program, which maintains a database of rare species and communities in every state of the Union and all the provinces of Canada, does not make its detailed location maps available to the public: they are "sensitive information." I heartily agree with that policy; tell people where the last remaining stand of prairie smoke exists in New York State and some fool will rush to dig it. But shouldn't novices be warned about how, in general, to recognize a rare community?

Rarity itself turned out to be a slippery concept. Each species has a natural distribution in the wild. At the outer limits of that distribution, the species is ordinarily rare—and may always have been so. Anemone canadensis is not protected in New York but is protected in neighboring Massachusetts. When the New England Wild Flower Society included the species in a meadow planting some years ago, it seemed a good deed, but within a few years the society had taken to calling Canada anemone "Canada enemy": it had overrun the meadow. The entire planting had to be destroyed to get rid of what turned out to be a common and invasive species elsewhere.

The three endangered species growing on our property are side oats grama (Bouteloua curtipendula), prairie smoke (Geum triflorum), and the stiff goldenrod (Solidago rigida) that has been so successful in our meadow. Traveling west toward the Ohio River, all three become increasingly common until, at their homeland on the plains, plants can be purchased by the hundred or seed by the pound. I happen to know of a remnant natural stand of stiff goldenrod at a preserve nearby, but who needs to steal a plant that's cheap and can be charged on VISA?

Both lists, by naming many sedges, sent a flutter through me. The plants I'd collected for the terrace and the seeds I'd collected in Maine were both of species that my county agent had not been able to identify. The New York list, published as a booklet, is intended to educate citizens about species they should have special respect for. Presumably, such knowledge would at least prevent foolishness like that of the woman whom I came upon years ago picking a bouquet of pink ladyslippers in the woods. But how is such a woman, who had no idea that they were orchids, to learn anything from a booklet that lists species by botanical and common name but offers no clue about how to identify them? The only illustration was one on the cover, a ladyslipper. Even had the woman learned from that picture that the flowers she had found were orchids, she still would not have known that she was not allowed to pick them on someone else's property (mine, as it happened). The booklet did not even state the law.

I thought I knew the law. I thought it was as Norman Deno presents it in his book: "The United States Government and State Governments have published lists of endangered species. It is illegal to distribute these plants or seeds of these plants."

There's an example of clarity!

However, there is no such law in New York State. It is perfectly legal to distribute both plants and seeds of even the most endangered species. And not just "distribute," as in giving a friend a fern; one may also sell them. What the law says is that one may do so from one's own land or from others' land only with the permission of the owner. Property rights, not plants, are what matter.

This I learned during my telephone conversation with our senior forester at DEC in Albany. Doug Schmid explained to me a fundamental difference in the legal status of plants and animals. Animals move freely across state boundaries and therefore are under the aegis of the federal government. Plants are rooted in the ground and therefore are private property. Though other states may have more stringent regulations, in ours property owners can dig protected plants for sale or even herbicide them, or they can allow anyone else to do so. Even rare plant communities, such as those that grow on limestone outcrops in this otherwise granite state, can't be protected if they are on private land. The only real protection is through purchase as public parkland or by conservation groups. The Nature Conservancy, for example, buys and manages whole habitats.

Even on lands set aside as preserves, though, no law requires that active measures be taken to save diminishing species. For all its potential genetic uniqueness here at the edge of its natural range, that remnant stand of stiff goldenrod that I found at a local nature preserve is rapidly dying under a blanket of alien vines.

Hoping still that federal regulations would prove to be more stringent, I put in a call to the Department of the Interior, Division of Fish and Wildlife, Publications Unit Law Library, to see what birds might be hiding in that thicket. But funding, I was informed after beating the bush with some vehemence, no longer covered the dissemination of such information. It was suggested that I might be able to flush it out from local "depositories," meaning university libraries, where such stuff hibernates.

Eventually I discovered that the federal government, while according animals special treatment because they are mobile, denies mobility to plants: one cannot transport endangered or threatened plants or seeds across state lines.* Otherwise, the federal law is the same as it is in New York. One can distribute plants and seeds of federally protected species in one's own state as long as they are taken from private property with the permission of the owner. So, on one's own property, one can destroy at will any federally protected species that grow there.

Like the disappointed kestrel, I emerged from the thicket with a sense of emptiness. The law forbids me to collect the common ostrich fern, allows me to collect the rare morel, and gives me no guidance at all on how to revitalize this ghost-ridden land.

At the dark end of our terrace, below a birdbath and in the shade of the oak, grows a collection of alumroots, Heuchera species. The picotee leaves of one are royal purple underneath. Another has pale, almost papery leaves, more starry in shape. The foliage of a third is meat red. A few are mottled; on others, only the veins are picked out in color. They all come from the Smoky Mountains of North Carolina, where their parents were collected.

When I was traveling in the South, I went to visit We-Du Nurseries, where the alumroots were grown. The nursery's name is constructed from those of its owners, Dick Weaver and René Duval. Weaver and Duval explore the mountains that surround them, searching for the variegated leaf, the uncommon color, the dwarf, the sport, and the species that seldom are offered by other growers. Their catalog spills jewels: a copper-red iris, a bell-flowered clematis, and marsh pink, hoary skullcap, starry campion. The mountains where these men hunt are rich in rarities; the Appalachians are said to contain a greater diversity of forest species than exist anywhere outside the tropics. I listened to their tales of discovery with wonder but, like a child living the Arabian Nights, in full knowledge that my world has no such magic. The Heuchera americana that grows on my terrace—those alumroots of the mottled and vein-struck leaves—is native here. Yet I could search our forested hills and rocky gorges for years and never spot a glint of red or purple, or even the plain green foliage of the common sort. The ladies of ALFASAC last saw an alumroot growing in the wild in 1986.

The plight of that last alumroot is indicative of what really is threatening our native species. The county park where it had been sighted is Marshland, a nature

* A permit to transport federally protected species across state lines is available to commercial growers, who may then sell the plants they propagate across state lines as well. A notice must accompany the order, requesting that the customer not introduce the species into "natural habitats outside its original or historical range." They are to be garden plants, not wild ones.

preserve bounded by Long Island Sound on one side and by highway, shopping malls, and residential neighborhoods on the others. A lone persimmon grows there at the limit of its northern distribution. The woods are a disjunct community of sweetgums, separated from similar sweetgum woodlands farther south by many miles of city streets and suburbs. The blazingstar I grow here was once recorded there, but that was twenty years ago. Marshland is a "preserve" in the sense that it is a fossilized habitat that is slowly eroding, immobilized by the matrix of inhospitable land around it.

Regardless of the government's insistence that plants are rooted and therefore permanent attributes of "property," mobility is critical to plant survival. This need for mobility explains the astonishing ingenuity by which plants have arranged for their seeds' dispersal by wind and water, by ants, mice, birds, and bison. No plant community is forever. Conditions change—hepaticas are overshadowed by hemlocks, wood lilies overgrazed by deer, trilliums overrun by the wild and aggressive leek called ramps—and the species must move on to the next opportunity. Whatever grassland species were historically recorded, whatever woodland species were recorded even twenty years ago, their survival depended on both the mobility of their seeds and the movable feast of new habitat to occupy. Potential mobility is still intact. It's just that there's no place to go.

The annotation of the 1986 sighting of the alumroot at Marshland is penciled in the margin of a wildflower guide. The marking is its memorial; its actual existence in the wild has become theoretical here. This is true of most of the species I've purchased from We-Du Nurseries and other sources of woodland plants. I look catalog offerings up in Britton & Brown's *Illustrated Flora of the Northern United States and Canada,* last updated in 1913. Its venerable age combined with the twenty-year history of ALFASAC notations gives me strong clues: if the natural distribution of Heuchera americana extended to southern New York fourscore years ago and the ladies have found it in just one location—a decade ago—chances are it's sequestered too far up the mountains to return except via UPS.

But the morality of moving woodland plants around makes me more uneasy than trucking meadow species. Commercial collection can't be blamed for the scarcity of native grasses or goldenrods; no one much notices that they're missing; no one covets them so no one collects them; anyway, anyone can raise them from seed. Of our state-protected Exploitably Vulnerable species, the majority are woodland plants—including all clubmosses, all orchids, all trilliums, and all but two ferns. These coveted groups are notoriously difficult to raise from seed or spore or to grow to salable size in cultivation—or, in the case of orchids, to propagate at all. One result has been that most commercial offerings are of plants collected in the wild, the ones you're morally prohibited from buying because they can't be certified "nursery propagated."

This prohibition did not arise in genera like Heuchera, which is easily raised from seed and as easily cloned by division. If the last alumroot at Marshland had been collected, a hundred plants could soon have been returned. This is the service that collectors like Weaver and Duval provide.

They don't even try though to raise trilliums from seed. Norman Deno writes about the tribulations encountered by those who do. The seed must be fresh; drying is fatal. Germination outdoors in flats takes four years or more. Few seeds sprout at all. Those that do behave in the most desultory manner, each year putting out a single leaflet until, by the third year at a minimum, the plant has stored enough nutrition in its root to produce the typical three-part trillium leaf. The time from germination to flowering is at least four years and often six, making the total from seed to salable plant a minimum of ten years.

Deno had a similar experience at first. Experimenting with Trillium grandiflorum, a large-flowered white trillium that colonizes my woods, he got radicals to emerge from fresh seed during a prolonged series of three-month cycles: first at 70 degrees, then 40 degrees, then 70 degrees, 40 degrees, 70 degrees, and again at 40 degrees—a total of eighteen months. But no cotyledons—embryonic leaves— ever developed, and the seedlings died. Guessing, though, that this ant-planted species might require the growth hormone produced by fungi in woodland soil, he tried again using gibberellin. With this treatment, 74 percent of the fresh seeds germinated at 70 degrees before the end of the first three-month cycle. Cotyledons followed at the shift to 40 degrees, and the first true leaflet developed within six months of gathering the seed. With that hastened germination, Deno managed to cut in half the time needed to raise a salable plant. But a plant that has been tended for five years costs five times as much as one collected in the wild, and it is still not a feasible proposition for growers whose plants usually require no more than one year from seed to shipment.

Weaver and Duval take a middle road. They grow collected trilliums in their natural woodland setting. The oldest plants, which develop several buds at the crown, can be cloned by careful dissection of the rootstock. As these older plants are harvested for propagation, young seedlings fill the excavated gaps, and eventually the open-pollinated youngsters also reach salable size.

The step from this semicultivated technique to wild-collected stock is not as great as dire warnings imply. All the trilliums that now grow in my woods, and most of their woodland companions, were shipped from growers who can't state in their catalogs that their stock is "nursery propagated." The plants propagate

themselves by seed or rhizome in woodland owned and managed by the grower. The grower crops the stands—digs individual plants or plugs of spreading species—and lets the gaps refill before cropping the same stand again. The land is often managed to encourage stock: growers may reseed gaps, flood marshes, burn clearings, thin trees, cull deer, weed ramps. Certainly they do not let vines smother their flowers or mow their income down before the seed is ripe. Wild-cultivated collection is perfectly legal: all applicable state or federal permits and inspections are duly noted on the plants' shipping cartons.

One New England source I use has been cropping his forty-acre woodland for three decades now. I questioned him about trilliums, the wild collecting of which arouses particular opposition among conservationists because the whole genus has indeed been decimated by unscrupulous diggers. This grower thins and sells the oldest specimens from his trillium colonies at intervals of several years. The gaps meanwhile fill with seedlings that would otherwise not have found space to germinate. Germination and growth are better than in cultivation because the woodland soil naturally harbors the necessary fungi: the seedlings mature to salable flowering plants in about four years. The method may seem unconventional to those who think of "growing" as something done in pots or beds, but this "collector" is propagating trilliums much as We-Du does, although on a larger scale and thus at a lower cost.

Of course, there are still those who rape the wilderness, who deserve whatever shunning we dish out. But my suggestion to conservation moralists is to hone their language. The woodland plants I buy from this source are properly described as wild-cultivated. The person who grows them is properly described as a plant disperser.

I asked Chris about moss collection in just the way I might ask an unfamiliar commercial source. In my experience, the more closely you question unscrupulous suppliers, the quieter they become, whereas it is hard to shut up those who love their work and do it wisely. My conclusion was that Chris collects mosses correctly and that I could, too, if I were willing to give up all else and devote myself entirely to their study.

Mosses are so common, abundant, and durable that, as Chris says, the authorities seem not to have considered protecting them—or even to have noted their existence. Like algae and lichens, mosses strike people as an aggregate—a stuff, a crust, a fuzz. Yet some seven hundred moss species have been identified in the Northeast alone; perhaps ten thousand worldwide. The distribution of a species may be vast: moss spores, like the finest dust, can travel two thousand miles with the wind. Their durability is uncanny: specimens of dried moss in herbarium collections have been known to resume growth when moistened even after fifty years of storage. I watched with disbelief as Chris crunched dry Leucobryum alba between her palms, let the fragments fall to the ground like bread crumbs, pressed them in where they had fallen, and watered them. Sure enough, they grew.

On the other hand, and regardless of their windborne potential, other species grow only under the most particular conditions—on lime rocks or in the constant

Chris, a moral mosser. (Dianne Rosenthal)

mist of waterfalls. Some never have been successfully transplanted under any conditions and are as rare as similarly uncultivable orchids.

Chris collects with exquisite care. She digs no moss whose species she can't name; she doesn't take even the most common sort if it is not common at that site. Of pillowing mosses, she harvests pieces no bigger than her hand; of sheeting ones, no more than one quarter of the sheet—and from the middle of a patch so it can fill in from the sides, or from the bottom of a rock so it can grow back from the top. Recovery takes about two years. Chris photographs and notes the location of each collecting spot and does not harvest again until it has entirely regrown. All the species she collects must meet two ecological criteria as well: they must occur naturally in the vicinity to which they will be transplanted and they must transplant successfully on the specific site.

Think, then, of what one has to know to be a moral mosser! At the time I questioned her, Chris had studied moss identification and ecology for four years under the guidance of a mentor and had learned to identify reliably to the species level forty northeastern mosses of the hundreds that have been named. Only half of those she could identify grow in our area; and of these, she collected only those ten species that could be expected to thrive in our clearing. I once had moved an emerald cushioning moss that grows over marble chips on our balcony to the granite birdbath on the terrace two stories below. That was ignorant, if not unethical, collecting.

And there is more to moss collection than expertise. Chris, coming upon a scene of rare loveliness, will not mar it with a trowel. No, *cannot* mar it. Her hands are stayed; she is transfixed.

Awe is out of fashion. Few plead for nature based only on its beauty. But in a paradox of conjunction, both those who collect with passion and those who are as passionately against it will be found, if you question them closely, to have come to their positions through some experience akin to that transcendence Chris feels in the presence of a natural mosaic so beautiful as to make its disturbance sacrilege.

I flew south three times over our skinned land. I flew west across the continent too—over the Central Plains and the deserts and mountains beyond the Continental Divide—but that was not as painful as flying south over the eastern forests. One knows, of course, that the prairies were peeled away by plows, but Nebraska, Iowa, and Kansas look simply green from such a height, and one can't tell whether the uniformity of color is grain or grass. The western mountains and deserts may appear ravaged from the ground, but from an airplane they look like a geophysical map, suitably green, tan, gray, or white according to their elevation. In the East the land looks flayed.

It was my misfortune, I suppose, to survey this side of the continent first from the air in late winter, when plowland is bare dirt and the pale membrane of grass over fields and lawns seems flimsy compared to the thick forest hide that once covered the East and is now cut to pieces. The pieces, richly textured even from the air but oddly shaped, reflect the luck of their topography. Rounded fragments are tops of hills too steep to cultivate or live on; sinuous strips run along rocky ridges. The largest pieces—whole mountains dark with conifers among the hardwoods—are skirted by square fields cut into their easier slopes or irregularly notched and gouged as though whittled by a child feeling for the soft spots. I felt in my own skin the scalping of the land as though I were a burn victim, aware that what remained of my hide might never stretch to cover the thin, bare expanse of my terrible injury.

On the second of these trips I met Jeane Reeves, a surgeon of sorts who was involved in a grafting operation. The work sounds ghoulish: Jeane had collected in the wild some 100,000 native plants of 104 species, including just about every eastern rarity a woodland gardener might covet. She had, in fact, cleaned out acre after acre of unspoiled forest, taking ferns, orchids, clubmosses, even flowering shrubs, chestnut trees, and the aquatic green dragon that I long to find someday growing in a wild and forgotten marsh. She did so morally, legally, wisely, and successfully—though the operation was futile in a way.

Jeane collected from an expanse of five thousand acres in the foothills of the Smoky Mountains: densely wooded, strewn with mossy slabs of granite, washed by creeks, cut by deep ravines—and about to be peeled for development.

The land had belonged to a county in Georgia within commuting distance of

A bit of Towne Park before development . . .

. . . and the fate of such wood-lands. The trees are burned; the soil is sold. (Jane Rosenberg-Coombs)

Atlanta. The county sold the forest tract to a large corpora-tion, which in turn parceled out to smaller development com-panies those portions planned as subdivisions. The hills have since been graded to fill ravines; the creeks run underground in pipes; the valleys are paved roads; the forest soil is scraped to clay. The entire area—which I'll call Towne Park—is now a planned community of shopping centers, municipal build-ings, schools, and churches that serve vast residential tracts of large houses on small lots.

The same thing is happening here—is happening everywhere, I guess—and it had never occurred to me that one could do anything about it but get mad, write letters to county officials, vent steam at zoning board meetings—and learn how little one's feelings matter to commerce. I had never imagined that one could just pick up the telephone, as Jeane did, and assemble crews of volunteer diggers that eventually included grounds crews from colleges, nature centers, and botanical gardens, Master Gardeners, garden clubs, horticulture students, conservation organizations, schoolchildren, and even the unlikely North Georgia Bonsai Study Group. Nor had I realized that a plant rescue project on such a scale could be activated by a common citizen without official sanction, under no auspices, belonging to no group, and lacking any training in botany, ecology, conservation, or law.

The law was as simple as I've said: Jeane had only to get the developers' permission to dig all the species that grew on the property they owned regardless of the plants' state or federal status. She was able to get permission to collect on about 1,250 acres. She scouted each area to be dug ahead of time (in order not to lose diggers in the forest). Digs were scheduled at the rate of two or three a week in the preferred transplanting seasons of spring and fall, less often and only under the threat of bulldozers during the summer drought. The crews comprised a core of botanically experienced diggers who supervised less knowledgeable volunteers. Plants were collected in the morning and transplanted the same afternoon into habitats similar to those where they had grown. Survival was excellent: the grafts took well in other woodlands. The rescue operation was successful, though of course the patient from which the grafts were taken died.

I traveled south again on my own to see the dead development and a woods that had received many of its rescued plants. In the meantime, I had sent for and received an interesting document: a master's thesis written by a graduate student in landscape architecture at the University of Georgia who had attempted to measure in monetary terms the loss of forest to development. Calculating at current retail prices the replacement cost of canopy trees, understory species, and a sample of ferns and wildflowers, she had come up with a figure just short of a quarter of a million dollars per quarter acre. This figure is wildly underestimated, and not just for the obvious reason that large canopy trees aren't replaceable at any price. Dollars can't be assigned to unknown quantities and qualities of soil, seed, pollinators, dispersers, diversity, or age. The value of an ecosystem is inestimable. The master's student knew that; so does Jeane Reeves and so do I. We are all groping for a guiding ethic.

On this second visit, a good deal of my surveying of the countryside was by car, and I found it difficult to recapture the pain one feels viewing the flayed forest from the air. Things are bigger at ground level—or one can imagine that they are. The wooded ridges that appear as slivers of flesh from an airplane seem from the road to be the edge of a forest that might extend beyond the horizon and all the way to grassland on the plains. Surely the little woodlot that I visited would not have been visible from the air. Driving by it on the road could not have revealed its singularity. Even a morning's moseying around barely hinted at the richness of a woodland ecology in which children can be counted among the indigenous fauna.

The site was a Montessori school on a narrow lot, "landscaped" (if that's the right word) by Jeane's fellow collector Paula Refi. It didn't look landscaped; it didn't look like a school. Azaleas were in bloom when I arrived. Seedlings of beech, tuliptree, and maple leafing out in the little woodland showed that here, in this suburban oasis, the forest ecosystem was renewing itself as it is failing to do on less loved and nurtured tracts. Above the brook, which had once been a drainage ditch, phantom crane flies appeared like bits of lace in spots of sunlight and as quickly disappeared in shade. The children came and went in much the same way, first weeding among young vegetables, then climbing on a rock, or down on hands and knees searching a pool for tadpoles.

The children were neither excited nor subdued as they explored but somewhere in between: engrossed, but easy; not indifferent to the woods—not awed, either—but rather awaiting the small adventures that came their way. I thought of the boys on the dirt mound in New Jersey, tossing clods and getting nothing for it but a scolding, and of how quickly and how pointlessly their activity had escalated to breaking bottles. Their scrabbling in the dirt should have yielded something wonderful, an emerald beetle, maybe, or even just an earthworm. This is what is missing in most children's lives, this lifting of stones and poking at soil to see what goes on in the real and living world. The children of the Montessori woods will not lay waste the land. Andrew, cradling a baby cornsnake in his open palms, will not grow up to bash it with a shovel.

Yet the half-acre woods had barely escaped demolition. The area had been cordoned off for years while school and town battled over the raw ditch whose roaring floods and crumbling banks were hazardous to children. The town wanted the waterway contained within a buried culvert, no matter that the trees would have to be removed in the regrading. It had taken the school and Paula years to convince the town that natural woodland vegetation had held waterways against erosion in the past and could do so again. When permission to restore was finally granted, it had taken plenty of rocks and rescues, too, and months of the parents' work.

Or, should I say, that's all it took: no powerful machines, no grandiose engineering—nothing approaching the half-million-dollar price tag the graduate stu-

Children of the Arbor Montessori School in their natural habitat. (Paula Refi)

Planting Noah's Garden

dent had placed on such an ecosystem—to bring back frogs and phantom crane flies, to have bellworts and mayflowers bloom, to open the doors and let the children out into their natural habitat.

I can't find as many answers to questions of collection as I can raise. But between the two perspectives, the brutal aerial view and the ground-hugged intimacy of the Montessori woods, I sense an ethic growing.

I like my Smoky Mountain alumroot; I like my New England trillium and my Wisconsin goldenrod. I think it is both important and moral to rescue, collect, propagate, distribute, transplant, and in every other way possible give back to our native vegetation the mobility that has been lost on this skinned and butchered land. But I think the purpose of these endeavors ought to be to reassemble plant communities, not to collect plants.

Main Street on the terrace in late summer. The path is wide enough to accommodate a garden cart. Others entering to either side are narrow footpaths among the planted beds. (Sara Stein)

10 *Lunch with Animals*

STONE TERRACE IS A PLANNED COMMUNITY of 0.07 acre in Westchester County, New York. The residential facilities include an underground complex for ants, bird-sheltering outskirts of dense shrubbery as well as a downtown bird apartment tower, and chipmunk quarters in a retaining wall along the periphery. Appropriate zoning, notably the shady side of town and a wetland preserve under the air conditioner drip, provides also for toads and crickets.

A major feature is the public bath, where residents and guests come for drinking water. It overlooks a central village square primarily intended for large mammals such as humans and dogs, but in all other respects this is a decentralized town plan. Unlike the planned community of Towne Park, where commercial and residential districts are distinct, Stone Terrace offers a market garden that extends throughout the village. Neighborhoods may specialize in particular foods; thus one could refer to Strawberry Path, Blueberry Flats, Milkweed Circle, and so on, just as in other developments there may be Elm Court, Chestnut Street, Palo Verde Boulevard—except that the references in this case are to actual vegetation.

The town runs east-west against the white cliff of a stucco house and faces due south. Its major artery is a service road that accommodates wheelbarrow traffic. Alleys and plazas—meandering or irregularly shaped in keeping with the informality of the plan—are paved with fieldstone slabs laid in sand. A unique system of parks and greenways connects the paved areas. The smaller parks are planted with low grass and flowers; the larger ones, wooded with fruit trees and shrubs. Greenways connect these open beds via planted cracks and gaps between the paving stones, providing another mode of transportation for inhabitants who prefer not to cross bare rock.

A tiger swallowtail nectaring at Joe Pye weed . . . and the black and yellow argiope spider that ultimately snared it. (Sara Stein)

In addition to availing themselves of the gardens provided by the Terrace Planning Board, the citizens have shown remarkable ingenuity in provisioning themselves. Thus one might observe a monarch caterpillar dining at Milkweed Circle abruptly skewered by a soldier beetle. Or, later, the caterpillar's empty skin being transported across town by a cleanup crew of ants. Indeed, the community as a whole is to be commended for its economic efficiency. Recycling is the rule: used spider web is incorporated into hummingbird nests; dead grass is collected by wrens; composting is performed by soil microorganisms. A generally high standard of living is maintained by intensive industry and avid consumerism such that birdseed produced by pollinating bumblebees is sought after by finches and ants produced by that industry's indefatigable reproduction are picked over by flickers. A sideline of many citizens, chipmunks as well as birds, is planting fruit pits as they do their business.

In summation, we feel that we have created an exemplary community that might well be replicated by others who, like us, enjoy having lunch with animals.

Once the Monday walkers allowed me to collect a native dwarf dandelion, *Krigia virginica*, from a rocky summit along the Hudson Highlands. The reason they gave for this lapse in guardianship was that the hill is not a nature preserve, merely a park, and the dandelion is certainly not protected.

The plant was tiny; I stowed it in my empty sandwich bag. I had never seen a native dandelion—nor known that there was such a thing. I don't know if it has any particular wildlife value. I doubt it. It just seemed to me that it belonged on the stone terrace.

The dandelion joined quite a few other plants dug from scruffy places like dirt roads, gravel pits, and quarries. Usually there was no other way to get them. They're not handsome enough to make it to a nursery. A few are included in horticultural encyclopedias with the withering comment "of little ornamental value." Certainly the dwarf dandelion fits that description, but in fact it's too insignificant to be described in gardening books at all.

I wasn't after beauty; I was looking for community. It doesn't matter that the bristly dewberry "has little value" to horticulture. It suits its terrace niche. Such unimpressive shrubs as black huckleberry fit in very well. So well that no visitor has ever asked the name of that skinny species; so well that no one has noticed it at all.

No one notices the creeping potentilla dug from a quarry, the clumps of sheep fescue cropped from a pasture, the shaggy dryland moss pried from sterile ground. Sharp eyes might find delicacies—blueberry, crowberry, cranberry, strawberry, wintergreen—but birds and chipmunks are better at finding them than humans, so mingled are their stems, so blurred their shapes among the grasses.

The cranberries came from a friend in Maine, where the species grows wild in his fields. He dug us shallow squares of turf containing both the cranberries and whatever grass poked through them. You couldn't give these unkempt squares away at a retail garden center. Cranberries sold through other channels are cloned, commercial varieties raised in flooded bogs and more at ease saucing turkeys than spreading through dry grass.

I wanted the grass as much as I wanted the cranberries. I'm glad that the lowbush blueberries were contaminated with wintergreen. A wild rose arrived aboard a huckleberry sod. Hawkweed came in fescue clumps. The dewberry hitchhiked with the moss.

I wonder in what sods the grasshoppers arrived.

Or if they did. Perhaps they merely recognized the habitat as I recognized their rightness when they moved in.

We have plenty of grasshoppers in the meadow, but they are not the kind I most loved when I was little. The ones I loved lived on a barren portion of my parents' "farm," as we still called it long after Roosevelt the horse was dead and so was the farmer who had named the horse after Teddy, not FDR. The barren place was a hump of granite thinly and only partly turfed with hawkweed, strawberry, dewberry, and grass that burnt crisp in August. The grasshoppers were stone gray; it was hard to make them out against the rock. But walk however quietly across their territory, and up they flew on noisy wings fanned black and yellow in the August sun. I can't summon any element of this memory without the others barging in: bare feet, hot rock, hairy hawkweed, crunchy turf, soft strawberries, gray grasshoppers startling through the summer air.

The next time I encountered the grasshoppers was when we first visited the Maine island for vacation. They live there on the baked quarries that became the exemplar for our dry terrace planting. I suppose we might have brought them home as eggs in dirt with the Potentilla tridentata that we collected or maybe with the dryland Polytrichum mosses that I was finally able to identify by genus at least. But, like my own memory, a habitat partially assembled summons the missing components to complete the picture, and that may explain the stone-gray grasshoppers of my childhood rattling before me as I walk across the sunburnt terrace.

There, also, black and yellow argiopes, to me the handsomest of our large spiders, snare color-matched tiger swallowtails appropriately in the butterflybush still remaining from the days when the terrace was a lawn. Toads prefer the moister end in the shade of the white oak, against the cellar wall among the Smoky Mountain alumroots. A family of chipmunks has burrowed new rooms below the birdbath made of granite from one of the quarries where the grasshoppers might or might not have originated. Bluebirds nest in an antique house of unlikely design and unknown history. The terrace stones themselves were hauled here from Pennsylvania. The plants frankly are from anywhere I could get them— retail nurseries, wholesale growers, raised by hand or collected in the wild, and from north and south of here and west to Oregon. Three beach plums, which fit into this community by the skin of their teeth, were a gift from the Easthampton Garden Club on Long Island.

So while it is true that the stone terrace looks too natural to arouse visitors' curiosity about individual species, that animals seem not to question its authenticity, that natural models inspired it, and that research suggested many of the plant species, this habitat has been put together "by gosh and by golly," as my Utah aunts might have said. It is arch, disingenuous, contrived, bastard. And the whole idea started, actually, with the stones.

I grew up with rocks and crowbars, with stone steps, stone paving, stone walls, stone cellars. And with traditional techniques for handling stone: raising boulders from the ground on smaller stones; drilling holes to let the ice in winter crack the biggest ones; moving stones across the snow on wooden sledges; dressing stones with a mason's hammer to fit them into walls; chinking the cracks between them with the chips. Our Connecticut town was populated by Italian stonemasons who scorned cement.

Marty, too, has stones in his past. His mother explained to me quite seriously that his love of rocks, and especially ones of monumental size, was inherited from Great-Uncle Fritz, the tombstone cutter.

The first rock that I recall in our married life was a gigantic one on a granite ridge above our first house when we were young and poor, had four children, one bathroom, and no interior doors. No front steps, either. The house was entered up a dirt ramp. The rock was to be the base of a flight of steps rising to a stone-paved entry. The one Marty had his eye on was perhaps half the size of a coffin.

We moved it down the granite ridge, across the top of the ramp, and into position at its base one Christmas afternoon. There had been a snowfall, then a thaw and sun so warm that we shucked our jackets. The day still shines to me. It isn't often in those early years of marriage, so beset with bills and diapers and cornflakes on the floor, that one's husband suddenly appears to be a brilliant man. I had not seen rocks moved his way before, rolled into place on logs along a plank. I thought he had invented it. In fact, the method is as old as all the others and requires no particular talent. The talent is in the placement of the rocks, and I am still impressed by my husband's ability to see how stones will fit.

That first house was in such rocky terrain that it had never been farmed and therefore lacked the rubble walls so characteristic here of any acreage that has ever been fields. The land we bought next and live on still was more open, cut through and bounded by stone walls of the rubble sort. Over the years, Marty rebuilt one wall after the other, remarkably turning what had merely been some farmer's dumping edge into straight and steady lines. But he had used the best slabs as top-stones or for steps and paths, so few flat stones remained, and the terrace might not have sprung to mind if we hadn't stumbled on the fact that rocks are sold.

I didn't know one could buy rocks. Flagstone, yes. Slate too. Belgian block and other forms of dressed stone cut from quarries. But not these shards of American crust wrenched free by weather and strewn about by gravity and glaciers. Yet there the rock sat to the left of the entrance as we drove into the masonry yard one day to buy some bricks. It was thigh-high and long enough to lie on, as rectilinear as rocks come, and it was still wearing the lichens and mosses of its origin somewhere in the Pennsylvania woods.

Marty, in all our many married years, had never yielded to any buying impulse whatsoever until he found rocks for sale. Here is this man who irritates us all by having no idea of what he wants for Christmas who suddenly wants a rock; a man who can walk through a department store without touching anything, not even silk or fur, but who strokes the rock; a man whose peace of mind requires knowing nothing about expenditures, who asks the price, inquires about delivery, rationalizes this monumental stele as a garden bench, and only gives it up because delivery is to the driveway only and no coveting could make a two-ton stone in that location a reasonable purchase.

But a good masonry yard is like a department store. Along the aisles were stacked wood palettes holding stones of all sorts and sizes, from the rip-rap used on eroded banks to smallish pavers, larger stepping-stones, and huge fieldstone slabs. Marty stroked the slabs with obvious longing.

The yard also could order rocks to any dimension, square or oblong, flat or round. Their man in Pennsylvania, who combs the countryside in this unique endeavor, could find whatever Marty wanted. The ultimate rationalization was that I myself had long wanted something solid to discourage the garbage truck from backing over the front meadow twice a week, and so I received from my husband a pair of smaller, squarish rocks for my birthday that October.

That was the October when, one sunny morning, my mind's eye saw the stone garden laid out as though complete below our bedroom window. And thus began the custom by which, for birthdays, holidays, and anniversaries, Marty and I gave each other rocks.

It was a mad idea. Marty was by then past sixty. As he puts it, rocks had grown heavier than they were when he was young. And whereas the paved entry that he laid at that first house was maybe ten feet square, the terrace I had in mind measured forty by eighty feet.

We gave each other rocks for three years.

The round wooden table where we eat our lunch is in the shade of the oak tree near the stone basin on the terrace. There we sip our beer while the chipmunk laps her water. Sometimes we have our morning coffee at the table. If it has rained overnight, a flicker is likely to join us. Sometimes we eat supper there; as the sun goes down the toads come out. Lepidoptera are always fluttering about, butterflies by day and moths by night. Hummingbirds prefer early morning and late afternoon for nectaring—and prefer us to behave like garden statuary. Bluebirds, far from being disturbed by our presence at any time of day, move their activities closer. I think they're waiting for us to finish our meal and get to work again stirring up insect meals for them. They like us; they follow us around. But most of all they like the terrace.

I had not anticipated the extraordinary popularity of this place, its magnetic pull that draws so many animals from the surrounding landscape. Today, late in February, the largest flock of bluebirds I have ever seen—there must be more than forty—have spent the morning winging about the terrace with a pair of cardinals, who sit with them like Christmas baubles along the branches of the Sargent crabapples. There is constant traffic in chipmunks; I can't see what they're so busy with this time of year. A squirrel, who heaven knows could store food anywhere, brought nuts fifty yards from a hickory tree to bury them in the terrace last fall. Today it is digging them up.

It's not as though these animals have no other place to be. All the species except the stone-gray grasshoppers were already supported elsewhere when we began to lay the stones. The meadows, woods, and pond accommodate them all and are more authentic in their vegetation, less devised in their construction. There are as many berries in outlying hedgerows as ripen on the terrace, but less frequent visitors. There are as many milkweeds in the meadow as there are here, but fewer butterflies. And how is it that here, of all places, a praying mantis landed on my shoulder one day as I was weeding?

In the case of some species, the special attraction of the terrace is readily apparent. Ants immigrated in quantity because of the sand, which to them is stones, a good construction material. They have multiplied into a vast underground colony and in the process improved the original conditions. The terrace, when it was lawn, was clay over hardpan over rock. Rain filled it as a bowl is filled, leaving no space for air. Since we added only a few inches of sand at the surface and ants need more like four feet for their comfortable rest, they had no choice but to tunnel through the underlying layers when building their elaborate quarters. The bowl is now a sieve, and the dryland vegetation is the better for the ants' aeration.

The ants, in turn, explain the visiting flickers, who show up reliably after a rainfall on the correct assumption that their prey will be out in force and preoccupied with hill rebuilding. But ants are everywhere, after all, and the flickers are not.

Naturally, birds come to drink and bathe in the basin: that was its purpose. But why juncoes in winter should forage in plant litter on the terrace rather than around the corner in the white garden or down the steps among the Misses Peony remains a mystery. I understand the sheltering attraction to wrens and sparrows of the boxwoods, hollies, and dwarf hemlocks that still rim the terrace. However, that shrubbery rims the terrace because we never moved it, and it did not burst with birds when the terrace was a lawn.

It could be that mere crowdedness is the draw. The surrounding landscape is diluted; the terrace is concentrated like cream from the milk of a more thinly spread and less richly nourishing substance. Trees, shrubs, flowers, and grass; fruit, pollen, nectar, and grain—even nuts if you count the oak tree—here are heaped on the same platter, and each kind of animal that eats its share may become the meat of others. Many pollinating insects are attracted to the flowers; many birds swoop after them. Sheer activity tends to have a concentrating effect; as anyone who has put out a feeder knows, the bustle of the first few birds arriving soon attracts a larger crowd. A brush of the hand across the meadow, though, tells me that many more insects inhabit each square yard of it than inhabit an equivalent area of terrace, so it is hard to see why the bluebirds spend an inordinate amount of time here.

So do human animals, and not just the two of us, and not just when lunch is on the table.

In the years since *Noah's Garden* appeared, quite a few people have toured the grounds. At first there was no terrace, and groups tended to disperse around the property much as the other animals did. We would note a thin trail of visitors along the path through the woods behind the pond, a cluster investigating the meadow, a few walking among the birches, or a couple pausing to chat in the peony garden. When the terrace was completed, the pattern changed. People still dispersed here and there, examined this and that, yet their separate routes converged on the terrace. There they gathered, there they crowded, there they sat, and there they stayed. Seating in the white garden is cooler. Seating in the peony garden is more traditional. Seating on the bench above the pond offers a better view. Sitting rocks in the woodsy birch grove and on the ferny mound are really more comfortable than the hotseat rocks of the sun-baked, ant-crawled terrace, where there are chairs for only six.

I realized that it was not the horticultural interest of this garden that drew them, for this is where the dwarf dandelion goes unnoticed, where no one asks to know the huckleberry. And surely it could not be the wildlife, for even the follow-me bluebirds forsake the terrace when ladies of the club arrive.

I have come to think that the animal magnetism of this place has to do with the complexity of its design and its construction. I suspect that we are drawn to the terrace for the same reason that other animals are, for the same reason that I was inspired by natural granite gardens, for the same reason that Marty gladly took on a task that would take so long to complete.

Biologists dryly call the phenomenon "edge effect." Animals are attracted to abrupt contrasts in the landscape: shorelines, outcrops, hedgerows interrupting fields, trails slicing through woods. The logic is that the greatest diversity of species—the most kinds of food—is to be found where one ecosystem abuts another and plants of both systems intermingle. The attractor is not the food itself but the contrast that indicates its likelihood. The charm of the terrace is its edginess.

This helps to explain our visitors' relative indifference to the species growing there. Their eyes are less arrested by any mass of vegetation than they are drawn to wander the paths, peruse the openings, follow the edges. It explains the strange behavior of the juncoes. Like children in a toy store, their attention is pulled now to one display and then to another, and the more aisles there are, the more tempted they are to explore them. Just as I first imagined the terrace looking down on it, so do birds spy it from above. They sit on the branches of the oak and can't seem to stop themselves from repeatedly descending to scratch or poke about as though this really were a market square, with wares laid out enticingly, set off against the paving. As for a toad's-eye, edge-on view, I can tell you something about that as Official Weeder: it has seemed to me (on hands and knees) that there must be a mile of cracks between the stones, each like a miniature hedgerow rising from the rock.

All this was merely an accident of design. My plan, of course, was to provide food, shelter, and water for the animals. The paving, however, was for our own convenience: a clean, low-maintenance surface; a way to have a garden to sit in and stroll through instead of merely walking past it; a patio right against the house, within our living space. Yet the effect far exceeds my expectations. The stone terrace is like a double exposure, patio superimposed on habitat, and it is impossible to tell which snapshot overlays the other, the humans eating lunch or the bluebirds watching them.

*T*he bluebirds had been breeding here for years in their made-to-Audubon-specification boxes in their genuine northeastern little bluestem meadow when, done with buying rocks at last, Marty presented me with an absurd antique birdhouse for Christmas.

I had seriously studied birdbox design. Each cavity-nesting species has its requirements: a certain size of hole drilled a certain number of inches above a floor of a certain dimension surrounded by walls of a certain height—and the completed box, with drainage and ventilation holes, mounted the correct distance above the ground in the proper habitat. Since the bluebirds, apparently literate in Audubon specifications, had immediately recognized and occupied their box, I launched Marty on a project of making boxes for other species and was adamant that they be built to spec. So Marty, grumbling, constructed hairy woodpecker boxes and downy woodpecker boxes; wood duck, tree swallow, and screech owl boxes; ledges for swallows and shelves for phoebes. He remarked later that the problem must have been that we had neglected to put nameplates over the doors, for no species moved into the box built for it.

Except the bluebirds. Year after year, the male and his two wives faithfully returned to their pair of perfect boxes in the meadow—until we erected the absurd house on the terrace.

The house was obviously not designed for any known bird except perhaps the ubiquitous house sparrow, for whom no one in his right mind would wish to provide housing. It has three peak-roofed towers of different height. Each tower contains two apartments stacked one above the other and entered by a private hole. There are six apartments altogether, but the holes are too small for communally nesting species, such as purple martins, which anyway prefer plain white, not the outrageous combination of rose and turquoise preferred by this antique birdhouse's fantastical creator. The entrance holes face in all four compass directions, so the north wind doth blow into some apartments, and the south sun doth shine on others, and there are no drainage holes or vents to protect the inhabitants from driving rain or broiling heat.

The bluebirds loved the house from the moment they laid eyes on it. They spent day after day in ecstasy, popping in and out of holes to investigate upstairs, downstairs, tall rooms and short ones, north, south, east, and west exposures. The impression we had, sitting in the spring sunshine lunching on the terrace, was of a cuckoo clock gone mad. The birds never so much as sat on their unpainted boxes.

The polygamous family raised four broods in two batches in the fancy house that summer. For the first time, we got to see the fledglings up close as, under their parents' supervision from the branches of the overhanging oak, they took their first splash in the basin. This is the charming difference between a meadow in the background and a habitat on a terrace. We had never before witnessed the fledging of young bluebirds, when their wing feathers sustain them in their first clumsy flight. Nor had we known that, like robins at that awkward age, their breasts are still childishly freckled.

One morning in late winter, at about the time when bluebirds begin to assess the real estate, I was looking out over the terrace and saw a mouse scurry into the

alumroots below the window. I had already suspected that mice frequented the terrace because a cellar window, left open a crack for ventilation in the winter, was their probable route to the dog chow kept under the kitchen sink. So I stood there watching, hoping the mouse was foraging for something more outdoorsy, when it flew away.

This surprising and tiny creature, mouse size, mouse color, and similarly scurrying, turned out to be a winter wren. I saw it (or them; the sexes look alike) only a few more times until July, when a pair of these flying mice took to sitting on the roof of the bird apartment house, much to the annoyance of its azure occupants. The wrens could hardly wait. As soon as the last bluebird had fledged, they moved into the rose and turquoise tower.

One inconvenience of this ill-designed antique is that it has no provision for cleaning. Birdboxes are ordinarily designed with a hinged front or removable roof so that one can annually empty out the old nest and its accompanying debris, which may harbor overwintering parasites that would jeopardize the health of the coming summer's nestlings. The only way this house can be cleaned is by hooking out the old nests with a bent wire hanger. The bluebird nests came out in pieces; made of twigs, they are not well constructed. The winter wren nests, tiny and tidily woven of the finest dried grass, came out whole. The tally was four blue-bird nests, two wren nests. All six apartments had been occupied.

Was the reason the classy neighborhood? Was it the house's fruity color? Was it the stimulus of so many holes? For whatever reason, the box was Superhouse, and its attractiveness both to us and to the birds spelled an end to the dreary business of building to dull specs.

No doubt Audubon is quite correct in its designs, but so may an engineer be correct but choose to build a charming covered bridge instead of a tarred overpass. The numerous birdhouses there used to be, when people built them for amusement, included log cabins, windmills, churches, schoolhouses, outhouses, and mansions. And had porches, balconies, cupolas, cornices, chimneys, flagpoles, and shutters. And were made of shingles, thatch, bark, logs, coconuts, grapevines, and nail kegs; or had once been codfish, cigar, salt, or herring boxes. The truth is that cavity-nesting birds have certain physical requirements; the whole truth is that their requirements can be met well enough by a house that also tickles us.

Marty, freed of specifications and no longer grumbling, spent that August building for the birds. He made six houses, all different. In the fall we erected them on posts in the meadow that sweeps along the driveway. In the spring birds moved into all of them—regardless of their architectural style, in spite of their proximity to one another and the road, and even though they were painted Art Deco shades of turquoise, rose, and yellow.

So why do people buy cut-out ducks and plastic pink flamingoes? What is this traffic in bronze toad faucet handles and cast stone rabbits? It seems to me they represent a sad misunderstanding. Surely we have an urge to both animate and ornament our garden, but we fail to see that animals and artifice are compatible. Where we might realize double exposures, we perceive instead separate photographs: there the kestrel in the wilderness, here the stone bird perched on a fountain.

The kestrel that flushed a flurry of birds from the red cedar tree was real enough; the feeder that caused such a concentration of its prey was artificial. Of all the double exposures possible in our yards, only feeders are commonly applied. The wit that used to be expressed in bird shelters and drinking fountains is captured well in a squirrel feeder I saw in the hardware store the other day: a wooden table at each end of which was a spike for a corncob and a chair for a squirrel. Silly, for sure. Ornamental, maybe. Not even necessary except to spare the bird seed. But closer to the bone of our humanity than squirrel-handled hose bibbs and morally superior to Polly's lavender gazing globe that reflects the human face, distorted.

Many summers ago in Maine we came upon a sculptor chiseling a rotund bird from a granite egg ground smooth by the tide. He worked outdoors, at a wooden table that held sand to steady and support the stone as he chipped the gentle contours. He took us into his studio where there were many granite birds, all charming and each uniquely expressing the subtle curves of the original stone. I would have bought them all if I could have. I would have put them everywhere in the garden to come upon surprisingly, like doves in bushes. In those days to buy even one would have meant macaroni for a month.

But Marty's rapt attention to this way of working stone, the annual frustration of finding a gift for a man who can't say what he wants, and my own desire for rock birds in the garden led me to give him that year a set of chisels and an egg-shaped granite cobble. So do wives hope to get what they want through thoughtful generosity.

It didn't work. The stone disappeared; maybe it will turn up under a bush someday. The chisels are missing, too, except for one that inexplicably wound up in a toolbox under the stairs in Maine, where it reappeared a couple of summers ago just as I was hatching a new bird idea, the granite basin.

The gardens had changed over the years, and so had I. There was no place left in them or me for stone birds. The terrace was nearly finished. A few large boulders that we had pried from the woods above it were waiting to be tumbled into place as sitting rocks, and that seemed artifice enough. A commercial bath of any sort would have looked as wrong as a cast rabbit among the real ones that graze there in the morning. But animals must drink.

A card in the ferry office advertised granite cut to size for steps and hearths. There had once been stone-dressing sheds on the island; one still finds here and there pieces of round pillars or carved cornices, broken, unfinished, or never sold. Except for the bird sculptor, though, no one had worked in stone for decades, and no piece even as simple as a step had been available in all the years we had been going to the island. So this ad for cut stone was something new; the advertiser was a young man, a handsome islander named Joe Reynolds, who considered making a granite basin for the birds barely a challenge to his skill.

In fact, it was astonishingly easy. We scouted a couple of quarries to find the right slab—a squarish one, rough, like the other stones on the terrace, and about six inches deep. It took two strong men to lift it into Joe's pickup and, back at his house, onto a sand-heaped platform similar to those used by sculptors to absorb blows that otherwise might break the stone. Joe used a diamond-coated blade in his circular saw to shape the contour of the bowl by cutting kerfs, shallow parallel incisions that begin at the edge of the bowl, dip smoothly toward the center, then curve back up again to the opposite rim. Marty chipped out the ridges between the kerfs with a hammer and the stone chisel and also chipped away at the corners and edges to round them out a bit. He would have spent happy hours pulverizing with a hammer what remained of the kerf lines in the bowl if Joe hadn't cut him short with a grinder mounted on an ordinary electric drill. We left the bowl pretty rough; Audubon says that birds slip on polished surfaces. At the end, Joe drilled a hole through one corner to accommodate a dripper, a copper tube and valve apparatus that was made for us (Marty's not a plumbing person). The plumber cost more than the stone and stonework. Even so, the total came to just two weeks of macaroni.

The granite basin. Mother Chipmunk lives beneath the bush behind it, but she's camera-shy. (Sara Stein)

The very day the birdbath was installed, the mother chipmunk who lives among the rocks behind it hopped to the rim of the bowl and summoned her youngsters for a drink. It became her official lookout as well as the table on which the family eats acorns collected from the terrace oak. In time the basin was discovered by a flock of song sparrows, then by the wrens, bluebirds, and mourning doves, juncoes, finches, and chickadees: each uniquely shaped, nicely contoured, smoothly finished, neatly textured, plump, sleek, streaked, flecked, grained, slate blue, shale red, lime white, granite gray, and all alive.

So much for garden statuary. We have the real thing.

*T*wo images play in my mind. One is a Persian miniature of a garden depicted on a trading card I had when I was a girl. The other is back yards I used to see from the train when I commuted to the city.

These back yards always interested me more than the front yards ever did. There was laundry hung to dry, wading pools for children, sometimes a playhouse, too, or a doghouse or toolshed, and vegetables—tomatoes, squash, pole beans—and peach trees, grapevines, the climbing rose 'Paul's Scarlet', and beds of dahlias or zinnias contained by white-painted rocks, wire wickets, or bricks set diagonally to form a fancy edge. Nearly every yard had a patio, a charcoal grill, a table with an umbrella. And sometimes plastic butterflies on sticks, a whirligig, a family of fake ducks, and things saved that might be of use one day, like scrap lumber or drainage tiles or a stack of asphalt shingles. Men watered with hoses in the summer evenings; children played. I saw smoke rising from the grills in these small worlds behind the railroad's chain-link fence, worlds self-contained and intimate, made comfortable and close, not planned like other gardens but much attended and enjoyed, most vividly inhabited.

The Persian garden on the trading card was tiny, like the yards along the commuter line. It, too, was enclosed, though by walls, not rusty fences. And if elegance was evident in its spare geometry and subtle ornament, the elements were similar: fruit trees and flowers, paving and seating, a pool fed by a fountain, bright birds and butterflies, a pet gazelle. You wouldn't hang your laundry in such a garden or stack your kindling there, and the occupants looked to be a prince and princess, not Joe Blow and his wife grilling hamburgers as the five-fifteen roared by. But these are differences of wealth and style, of formal garden design as opposed to the more haphazard accretion by which back yards grow along the railroad tracks. It seems to me the urge behind them is the same: to create an animated intimacy where one can take one's ease in some semblance of the natural world, where fruit grows on trees and water shimmers in the sun, where there is shelter in the shade and children playing. Where there are animals, gazelle or mutt, stiff semblances or real and lively flying.

Wandering the aisles of such recollections, I come upon more recent ones. Again, there are two. The first is a computer simulation game in which one creates a small world—shapes its topography of plains, mountains, and waterways, vegetates it with species of one's choice; populates it with all sorts of animals—and, with the click of a button, lets the ecosystem run in animation. I bought it out of curiosity; these simulations have become very popular with children. I wasn't clever at it, however. Mostly my carefully devised worlds became overrun with roaches or died out altogether. But the animation was engrossing, and I replanted and repopulated world after world before I gave it up.

The second image is recorded in a snapshot taken at about the same time of a nearby development in a middle-class neighborhood on a brilliant Sunday afternoon. The shot is remarkable for its emptiness: there wasn't a soul outdoors. I wondered where the children were, but I'm afraid I know. They were indoors exploring in simulation a world more lively than the fifty-acre lawn that constituted their planned, inanimate communal yard.

Asian bittersweet, Celastrus orbiculatus,
dressed in Halloween orange and chartreuse.
(Sara Stein)

Planting Noah's Garden

11 *The Weeds of Halloween*

I DROVE ALONG the country roads one Halloween morning toward a nearby reservation and my regular Monday walk. The autumn air was balmy, but a line of thin clouds to the northwest rode a stiff breeze that scuttered the last of the sugar maple leaves along the tar. The day would darken, the wind would rise, the rain would hit by evening. Already the goblins of the plant world were materializing throughout the countryside.

I watch this phenomenon each year with mounting dread. The goblins, known to conservationists as invasive aliens, are rapidly increasing in number and in geographic spread. They are not mere nuisances like brambles in a hedge: they do real harm. Like ghosts, they are invisible during bright summer days, when their forms are lost in the general greenery. Then, in one dark autumn storm that strips the woodland bare, they materialize in the lurid colors of their unseasonably clinging leaves.

By the morning after Halloween, the extent to which these aliens had penetrated the woodland was clearly visible. Yellow-green tatters of Asian bittersweet shrouded the skeletons of our native trees. Huge splotches of that same strange yellow-green were Norway maples growing from pools of their own black shade. Clots and mats of honeysuckle bushes and vines greened woodland floor that should have been plain brown. The colors altogether reminded me of cheap masks sold in drugstores or discount chains: poisonous chartreuse combined with the bittersweet's orange berries and the Day-Glo pink leaves of winged euonymous.

These aliens obey a rhythm out of time with that of the surrounding natives. They come from other places, whose seasons don't coincide with ours; they leaf out earlier in the spring or hold their foliage later in the fall. They're not set to the

Farmer's Almanac. And their syncopation is apparent all across the continent.

I had been in Wisconsin the previous Monday. The season there was more advanced: temperature in the thirties; bur oaks and hickories already stripped of leaves. There, the ominous green that penetrated deep into the wind-whipped woods was a buckthorn of European descent.

The week before I'd been in California. The hills were at their driest; the temperature in the Bay Area still climbed past seventy by noon, and there had been no rain since March. The grower at the nursery I visited there called autumn "the tan season," though to me the scrap of native coastal scrub she tends seemed more a mosaic of silvery greens and grays among tufts of dry grasses tinged pale olive at their base. Atrocious splotches of bright green interrupting the subtle coloration were Senecio mikanioides, a creeper from South Africa that covers everything in its path much as kudzu does in the Southeast.

Kudzu was still blanketing roadsides in green when I passed through Virginia on my looping route back home. That evil has buried seven million acres of the South. I look in vain for a word better than mere "weed" to convey the threat of such invaders.

I thought it wise during that year of travel to pretty much keep my mouth shut about weeds. They have too many defenders. But now, without fear that mention of barberry will arouse a flock of birders, I assert my right and obligation to clear the invaders out with the certitude of any good homeowner cleaning up the streaks of toilet paper and shaving cream that litter the yard the morning after Halloween.

Weeds have been variously defined, but invariably from the human point of view. A weed may be unsightly to the cultivated eye, like rank growth along the railroad tracks; or it may arouse our prejudice because it irritates us like poison ivy; or it may harm us financially, like thistles where we graze our cows or grass where we grow our beans; or, as one of Webster's definitions puts it, a weed may be "a tree or shrub of low economic value that tends to grow freely and by its presence to exclude or retard more valuable plants." I could almost go along with that definition if it weren't for the accompanying example: "Gray birch is a common [weed] species in much of New England."

I am not talking about birches.

The definition of a weed that I champion is more restrictive and less subjective than those arising in agriculture, attempted by gardeners, or acknowledged in dictionaries. It arises from the less anthropocentric vantage of conservation.

Conservation recognizes weeds by this mark: they degrade habitat. They kill ecosystems. They alter water tables and soil chemistry. They drastically reduce diversity. They abort succession. They cause animals to abandon the site. They leave their habitats biologically moribund.

These habitats include any that you might own or hope to nourish, from a bit of high desert to a bur oak grove to a patch of northern meadow or a corner of southern bog. There is hardly a project I have been involved with or learned about that did not begin with weeds and continue with weeds and end, if it ended successfully, with weed capitulation. Yet, with rare exception, the species to be feared instead are treasured: show me the family that dreads its privet hedge.

When I was growing up in New York City, I looked forward every spring to the budding out of privet. The first green of the year, it meant that it was time to oil roller skates and forage through the junk drawer for a stick of sidewalk chalk. I can still smell the tender foliage unfurling as I skated through the thin sun of April past greening privet thickets already then escaped to Central Park.

Privets, honeysuckles, buckthorns, barberries, and winged euonymous all invade and destroy a woodland habitat, and they all do it in the same way. As birders have often pointed out, their berries are popular with birds. That's how they escape cultivation. As gardeners remark, they are easy to grow under all sorts of conditions, even in the shade. That's why, wherever birds plant them, they thrive and spread, even into woods. As everyone agrees, these plants are attractive. That's why they are so widely grown; that's why there are so many sources for their spread. If part of their attraction is their lingering color late into the fall, so too are we pleased with their precocious leafing out so early in the spring.

And that, their early greening, is these plants' particular evil.

I've walked through April woods infested with Japanese barberry, Berberis thunbergii. Maples aren't in flower yet; a month will pass before the oak trees swell their leaves. The sun warms my shoulders and sets the barberry foliage sparkling. The effect is pretty. But beneath the bushes the maple wing, the bloodroot seed, the coiled fiddlehead, are already in their shade, and I know better than to bother looking for these springtime gifts in such a woods.

That period of precocious shade, roughly from mid-April to mid-May here but earlier in mellower climates, is just when the forest floor relies critically on sunlight. During this briefly lit spring window, wildflowers bloom, tree seeds sprout, ferns unroll their fronds before the shade is pulled back down. In woods infested with early-greening aliens, the shade is lowered before the forest floor has even woken up, and the innocents die unmercifully in their sleep.

I used to look at shrubs with a gardener's eye and plant them with a gardener's ignorance of their behavior. What did I know of Scotch broom when I planted it

It is only May; the sun shines through leafless trees. But Japanese barberry, already in full foliage, completely shades the ground. (Sara Stein)

in my garden? Nothing but how wonderfully it bloomed and in how buttery a yellow. It didn't seem possible to me that this treasure, killed by the cold one winter years ago but still recalled with fondness, was the same beastly weed that I ran across this year in an article in *Sierra* magazine called "Botanical Barbarians." There my former ornamental was shown slobbering up a hillside in San Bernardino National Park in Southern California, burying in yellow all the native vegetation. The same species, Cytisus scoparius, has escaped from cultivation on the eastern shore, where it drowns the dunes in butter.

I had planted autumn olive in equal innocence and enjoyed enormously the sight of its red berries hung in silver leaves. The nursery label didn't say that Eleagnus umbellata and its Russian olive relative, E. angustifolia, have spread their silver gleam over meadows and prairies from the East Coast through the Midwest, destroying grassland as though beneath a permanent rime of frost. In fact, I had thought that planting these fruitful shrubs was environmentally correct: they were at the time—a mere ten years ago—widely recommended and lavishly planted to feed the birds.

Sorry, birders: I must now hit this nerve. The fact that a plant feeds birds does not vindicate its use. It is true that without the northward spread of multiflora roses, we

Planting Noah's Garden

Yankees would not enjoy the song of mockingbirds on moonlit nights. But if those rose hips enable that one bird to make it through our northern winters, the meadows that might otherwise flourish where multifloras have invaded would support many more bird species on the myriad insects they provide in spring and summer, the variety of grains and flower seeds they offer in the winter, and the rodent diet they serve up all through the year. One slaps the label "weed" on a species, not because it is without virtue, but because whatever virtues that plant may have cannot outweigh the countless virtues of the entire habitat it displaces.

It makes no sense to measure a broom, a rose, a buckthorn, or a barberry against its own absence—an ounce of nectar or a pound of fruit or a yard of cover versus nothing. You must weigh the broom against Sierran chapparal, the rose against Pennsylvania meadow, the buckthorn against Michigan oak savanna, the barberry against Connecticut sugar maple forest. Conservationists now estimate that in the last ten years, invasive aliens have destroyed more habitat than development has.

*B*eside our veterinarian's office, in dank shade and poor ground insulted often by his canine patients' watering, grows an extraordinary vine. It rises in a bed of English Ivy from which it climbs some twenty feet to the top of a vertical rock face. In contrast to the smallish lobed foliage of the ivy in the bed below, this vine's evergreen leaves are oval to almost heart-shaped, and each is easily the size of a Saint Bernard's paw. The stems are stout; where they overtop the rock, they reach out branches devoid of the holdfasts typical of ivies. Branches display clusters of small flowers in the spring; by summer they are hung with bunches of black fruit.

Few recognize this vine and many ask about it. Not even the doctor, who knows that the upper, unfamiliar fruiting portion is merely the mature extension of the familiar juvenile English ivy he planted many years ago, realizes the threat this stunning plant poses to the surrounding woods. If you are from the Pacific Northwest—or from any of many other local spots where this goblin has run wild—you will not be so naïve.

The first site I visited in California was our son's home in El Cerrito. He and his wife, young gardeners just learning that parsley is not a perennial herb, were somewhat curious and mildly concerned about the greenery that clothed the entire frontage, climbed the canyon rise along the driveway, clothed the shrubs, topped the trees, and obliterated any shorter plants that might have grown there. I was baffled myself at first: English ivy is extraordinarily variable, and this big-leafed, blunt-lobed cover didn't look like the potted types I see for sale in the East. I learned soon enough to recognize its invariably dark and gloomy color, unsuitable to the "tan season" and frighteningly ubiquitous. From the neat yards of suburbia it ran like ink along rural roadsides, stained grooved canyons, and bled deep into woodlands of coast redwood, bay laurel, and live oak. In areas of high rainfall farther north, English ivy has spread through forests like the black plague.

We have nothing quite like this northwestern vine infection in northeastern woods, but give us time. The first thing I did when I got home was pull out the wintercreeper, Euonymous fortunei, that I'd sentimentally planted years before. You know how these things are: sprigs of the vine had been part of a floral arrangement for a family wedding, and I thought it would please the young couple in years to come to see how large and comely their bouquet had grown. It took five minutes to plant; I just stuck the sprigs into the ground, where they promptly rooted. Days of work were needed to dig them from the shockingly large area where they had rooted over the rich humus, shot through mountain laurels, crept up oaks and hickories nearly to the sunlight that vines need to fruit. In another year or so nothing could have prevented the wintercreeeper's bird-dropped seeds from spreading unchecked through the neighborhood.

But let's not bird bash. We plant this stuff. Over and over, as I traveled around the country, people eager to demonstrate their correct abhorrence of the suburban lawn told me how they had replaced it with ground covers. Sometimes I managed a crooked smile, as when someone commending goutweed, Aegopodium podagraria, was interrupted by someone else who was struggling to get rid of the goutweed invading her equally invasive pachysandra. Just when I thought I'd learned the worst of all our follies, I heard of a miraculous vine that in a single summer had completely clothed the chain-link fence surrounding a tennis court on the coast of Massachusetts. The owners couldn't sing its praises loud enough. The vine was kudzu.

Really, it is time we shed our innocence. How can it be that my own Extension Service, in *A List of Ornamental Plants for New York Seashores*, still recommends Hall's honeysuckle, the twining, strangling Japanese honeysuckle that overcomes woodland edges here, the Lonicera japonica that has become a plague of monstrous proportion farther south? And how is it that our local nurseries still display in the full regalia of its brilliant turquoise berries the notorious porcelain vine, Ampelopsis brevipedunculata, which already blankets vast acreage and hardly needs to be further distributed in gallon cans?

In 1934, in answer to "many requests for information," *Horticulture* ran a brief article describing how to grow Asian bittersweet. The concluding paragraph read, "The production of bittersweet on a commercial basis is considered a possibility and apparently a number of growers have this fact in mind, in the East as well as in the West." You'd think the sixty years since that first spark of interest would have been long enough for us to see that growing this thug had not been a great idea.

174

Planting Noah's Garden

Yet Andersen Horticultural Library's *Source List of Plants and Seeds* lists fourteen nurseries that offer Asian bittersweet, Celastrus orbiculatus—among them several of our most popular mail-order houses and no fewer than eight wholesalers. Can you believe it?

I'd like to round up everyone who promotes or propagates or sells these smotherers and set them down by a roadside for a while to see how quickly they are buried alive.

*I*n California, at a conservation forum attended largely by people who have come to be called "tree huggers," a sweet-faced young woman reproached me for my prejudice toward aliens. "After all," she said, "all plants grow from the same earth."

No, they do not. They grow in different portions of the earth, in differing conditions and as members of distinct communities within which, biologically speaking, they know their place. Move them from that place, release them from their competitors, free them from their predators, give them license to behave without the external disciplines that have controlled their behavior in their homeland, and they may grow up barbarians.

It's never popular to speak against trees; too many of us have wept over *A Tree Grows in Brooklyn.* I don't believe Betty Smith knew when she used the tree of heaven as a metaphor of hope and fortitude that Ailanthus altissima is a poisonous species whose success rides on its ability to kill its neighbors. There may not be much to mourn in the species an Ailanthus might kill in a littered vacant lot, but neither is the tree one to let loose along country roads, where dogwoods, hawthorns, crabapples, viburnums, and all the other fruitful growth of woodland edges ordinarily hold sway. At least the tree does not, like Norway maple, march straight into the forest.

Of all the invasive aliens that haunt our woods, none frightens me more than Norway maple. I see it multiplying along the roadsides, trunk after trunk of the dark mother trees, their young poles crowding the rubble walls, their seedlings littering the ground. Lost among the gloomy horde are the last survivors of what this species is replacing: a row of fine old sugar maples planted by farmers more than a century ago.

The sugar maples will die without issue. The soil where their seeds might have sprouted has been poisoned by the Norway maple roots. What I am witnessing, year after year, is the sugar maple's gradual extinction. In fact, I have seen the extinction of whole woods. No tupelos, no oaks, no hickories, no ash: just Norway maples growing in their own toxic earth. Not even ferns grow in these poisonous groves.

The ability to inhibit other species by chemically suppressing their germination or their growth is known technically as allelopathy, and it is common among plants. Goldenrods, for example, are also allelopathic to sugar maples. A field of goldenrod can therefore delay the succession of a sugar maple forest, but the fact hardly sends chills up my spine. Quite a few ranks of pioneers normally intervene between meadow and maple woods, and the maples will succeed as the field is shaded out. Presumably the Norway maple hails from some community of species immune to its particular poison, as sumac and red cedar are immune to goldenrod.

For months I cringed when people rebutted my objection to toxic aliens with a reminder of our notoriously poisonous black walnut. One day with ALFASAC we stumbled on this native's unmistakable nuts strewn across our path and proceeded only with great difficulty to discern the parent tree from the surrounding butternuts, mockernuts, pignuts, and varieties of oak. It's true that you'd be a fool to plant alien apples beneath black walnut boughs, but do try the tree's old understory pal, the native Asimina triloba, fondly known as pawpaw.

I suppose within a million years or so, some California oak will evolve a tolerance for eucalyptus, too; some form of scrub will move in among the alien acacias. For now, consider with what smugness I was informed that hostas grow perfectly well with Norway maples—and picture that future forest populated by the slugs that hostas attract in vast numbers.

I'm reminded of an old hackberry I know, one of only a few left on a nearby reservation. The last I saw the tree, its leaves were pimpled by a gall. Somebody once studied the ecology of that gall—who made it, who used it, what place it held in its microhabitat. It turned out that the gall, formed by an insect that preys exclusively on hackberry leaves, supports by its own flesh or the flesh of those that eat it a fauna of no fewer than sixty species. When you lose native flora, you lose native fauna too. Nor do you regain an equivalent fauna by the addition of an alien: these species arrive with little if any animal baggage.

"Paperbark forests," wrote Robert Devine in *Sierra* about an Australian tree invading Florida, "are eerily quiet; virtually no insects, birds, or other animals can be heard." The species Melaleuca quinquenervia infests the Everglades Conservation Area, which is supposed to act as a protective buffer around our national wetlands treasure. Where there had been sixty to eighty native plant species before its arrival, only three or four remain. Each floral loss is accompanied by faunal losses. Ecologists generally figure that the number of animal species associated with each native species is about twenty, but, counting galls and all, the number is probably much higher.

Paperbark has devoured half a million acres of the Everglades Conservation Area and is "swallowing an additional 50 acres of wet prairie a day." Brazilian pepper, another invasive alien tree in subtropical ecosystems, has reached Everglades National Park itself, where it has consumed a hundred thousand acres in just

Some vines are good vines . . . Poison ivy, Rhus radicans, produces in the fall large clusters of translucent white fruit that is ranked among the ten most important foods to wildlife. The young plant here won't mature until it reaches the sunlight at the top of its host tree. There it will display its fruit to migrating birds against a background of vivid orange or scarlet leaves. Unlike the many alien vines that strangle their host, smother it in shade, or topple it under their weight, poison ivy does no harm at all to the trees it climbs.

Unfortunately, about 70% of the population gets an itchy rash from the oil in the plant's leaves and stems. For that reason, homeowners single out this vine for total eradication —regardless of its ornamental and nutritional value and whether it grows where people are apt to touch it.

My plea is this. If you have poison ivy growing in an out-of-the-way place, let it be. I also have a terrific idea for highway departments plagued by graffiti artists: plant poison ivy against bridge abutments and sound barriers for the dual purposes of decoration and deterrent. And, of course, to feed the birds. (Virginia P. Weinland)

three decades. One can carry a metaphor too far, but "devouring," "swallowing," and "consuming" are in these cases too literal for comfort. The tamarisk trees introduced to southwestern wetlands have drunk them dry; the ground is now too desiccated to support the native flora and fauna that used to thrive there.

Funny thing is, none of these invasive species except paperbark is targeted by the Noxious Weed Act, passed by Congress in 1974 to control commerce in our most destructive species. It is ironic, too, that many of them were introduced by the Department of Agriculture in the first place. What is truly tragic is that every one of them is still for sale.

*I*n preparing this chapter, I culled from native plant society and conservation publications a list of the scariest alien vines, shrubs, and trees. Comparing that list to the species index in *Source List of Plants and Seeds*, I found a perfect match.

Every single one is offered for sale in this country. Even kudzu is sold, crazily enough, by a seed supplier in California. (Perhaps with equally crazy optimism I assume it is available for research only—on the means to kill it.)

I'm getting cranky, no doubt about it. No season seems suitable to me anymore. I look for scented violets in what's become a garlic mustard spring, for bright roses when pallid honeysuckles bloom, for blackberries along bittersweet roads.

I've grown unaccustomed to this place.

And it's getting stranger all the time. A vine that tried to take our land this summer looked as if it might have slithered from a flying saucer.

The alien Polygonum perfoliatum was described in the *New York Times* one August while we were on vacation. The drawing resembled no plant I had ever seen. The leaves are equilateral triangles that clasp their petioles. Round goblets encircle the stem at the leaf axils, as though the plant could gather liquid from the atmosphere or exuded some potion of its own. The species climbs by clawing over other plants with reverse barbs that cover stems, petioles, and even the veins on the undersides of leaves and along leaf margins. The common name of the plant is mile-a-minute. That's an exaggeration: it grows only six inches a day. The article warned that this new invader, which had arrived not by UFO but in a mundane shipment of Asian rhododendrons to Pennsylvania, was rapidly moving south.

Well, let me tell you, mile-a-minute is rapidly moving north as well.

I know because no sooner had I gotten home than one came at me through the blueberries. Its barbs clung to my bare skin. Another caught my ankle at the mailbox. They were in the meadow. And among the birches. One had prowled deep into the shade below an elm tree. By the time I found the last patch late that September, it had formed a thick blanket of strands over twenty feet long. We had been away only a month.

The article had not described the color of the leaves. They were pale, pale green. Like luminescence. The creamy flowers, too, were pale as wax and lit up when the sun shone through them. The sweet and fleshy fruit hung in clusters of iridescent sky-blue berries more beautiful than any I have ever seen. When fully ripe, the blue deepens to rich purple.

You know what I wish?

I wish the fruit raised blisters. I wish the leaves caused a rash. I wish the plant were slimy and ugly and stank of rotting flesh. I wish all the weeds of Halloween inspired such nausea that no one could abide them on one's property.

I suspect, though, that most people get about as exercised about such weeds as our new neighbor, who, when warned that we had spotted mile-a-minute in his yard, shrugged and said, "I'm a city boy, what do I know?" and left it there to spread.

The local source of the weed was at that time a mystery. Typically, a new species spreads radially outward from a center of concentration. Because P. perfoliatum is spread by birds, though, and the fruit ripens in late summer, the pattern of its distribution more likely was eccentric, skewed in a southerly direction along the route of the autumn bird migration. In fact, I later found out that our state Department of Environmental Conservation had been expecting the weed's New York debut along the Delaware Water Gap, close to its point of origin in Pennsylvania, and had been monitoring that area for some years

In the spring following our scattered sightings, the property up the hill from the pond was vacated, placed in receivership, and thus made available to snooping. We entered through a gate to an old farm road bounded on both sides by rubble walls but long since grown back to woods.

When we had bought our portion of the original farm, the hillside and the wet meadow where the land leveled out along our boundary had been mowed every summer, but to one side of the farm road a large portion had since been let go wild, and it was here that we emerged over the rubble wall into a scene from Hell.

The former meadow, about two acres, was heaped with vicious multiflora roses coiled by snakes of bittersweet. The ground was laid with snares of honeysuckle vines, leafless and like wire early in the spring. We saw no living mile a minute. We saw the lingering nightmare of the previous season: straw-colored thatch covering nearly the whole abandoned acreage, six inches thick in places, stacked even over grapevines, vying with the bittersweet, heaped over what remained of native

Mile-a-minute looking as wicked as it is. (M. Tashiro/ EarthBase)

dogwood and pussy willow, and covering the ground as well in its barbed hay.

Later, Dick Mitchell, our state botanist whom I had consulted on protected species, called it a "monster." Ted Kozlowski, our county forester, said it reminded him of when he was vacationing in the South with his seven-year-old son, who, tucked into bed one evening after watching a scary movie, had been reduced to terror by a tendril of kudzu coiling through his open window. It was like that, this weed. But wouldn't you think, therefore, that someone besides me in our presumably threatened county had heard of it?

When the field of horror began to resprout in May, I called my county agents. They'd never heard of it. They referred me to Ted the county forester, who hadn't heard of it, either. These people get hysterical calls daily about fire ants and killer bees, which here are figments of overwrought imagination: I understand their skepticism toward this citizen's report. What I don't understand is why the state DEC, whose naturalists had been alerted to a possible invasion years before, had not communicated its concern to the counties, or why Cornell University's College of Agriculture, from which emanate our county agents and the information they proffer, also had not seen fit to warn their minions of the weed. And don't our county employees read the *New York Times*?

Ted promised to check my story with Albany and call back. The phone rang ten minutes later. Within a half-hour he was collecting samples for "positive identification" by the state botanist, Dick Mitchell. The weed was ankle-high.

Positive ID was made one week later: the weed scratched my shins.

It took another week to file a report with the state Department of Agriculture and Markets, whose commissioner is the only person authorized to order the eradication of a noxious weed on private property. The weed tugged at my knees.

Albany arrived in force to survey the damage and devise a strategy one month after the samples had been taken. The weed by then was ripping at their shirts.

At that visit, a strategy was outlined: all properties within a one-mile radius of the central infestation would be surveyed by naturalists. The location of each plant or the extent of each patch of it found would be flagged with fluorescent orange plastic streamers. For the mumblingly explained to me reason of "avoiding excessive use of herbicides"—but I think more for fear of political repercussions—the method to be tried was one that had never been tried before. They would bring in a generator, hook it up to a steam cleaner—the kind used on sooty buildings—and kill the weed with heat. Then, to prevent further germination and hopefully also to destroy the seed stock in the soil, they would cover the steamed areas with black plastic.

We were invited to a neighbor's barbecue, the "What do I know?" one. Mile-a-minute was rising not between but *through* head-high multifloras. How do you lay black plastic over that terrain?

I found another patch of the barbed menace in our meadow. It was in bloom.

There was a problem about the one-mile survey: not enough naturalists were available to do the job. There was not enough money, either. Why did I think the county owned steam-cleaning equipment? It didn't. The equipment had to be rented; the nozzle was the wrong one; a different nozzle was ordered.

All residents within the surveyed area were to be mailed a bulletin describing the weed, its danger to private property and the public good, and a photograph that happily, because the federal government was suitably concerned, had already been issued in full color by the USDA to state forestry departments in Pennsylvania, New Jersey, Delaware, and Maryland (not New York). I was given a copy. Damned if I could have recognized Polygonum perfoliatum from that Most Wanted poster, which failed even to show its weird triangular wrap-around leaves, its odd pale color, its waxworks blossoms, or its purpling fruit.

By the last week in July, the weed had topped the tallest growth in the nightmare landscape up the hill, and fruit was forming.

I'd like to say that the men came with steam cleaners and black plastic as in a science fiction film and that the scary movie ended with a father tucking his son safely into bed. That's not what happened. Steam cleaning didn't work. Herbicide was used. And though there is a moral to the story, there is no conclusion.

*I*f the odds of an amateur botanist living next door to the first infestation of mile-a-minute in New York was like winning the state lottery, the chance that that really was the first and only infestation is much slimmer. There are undoubtedly other infestations unnoticed and spreading fast. The patches here are discouraged, that's all. They'll come back. It takes four or five years of repeated killing to eradicate the vine—if everyone in the community is aware of it, reports it, and does his or her own part in uprooting it or poisoning it wherever it is found.

I wish this genie of invasive aliens were not too big to cram back into the bottle, but I know that can't be done. Containment, diminishment, vigilance—the sum total of aroused community response: that much I can ask.

I can ask it because, when people take it into their heads to loathe prairie dogs or gray wolves or timber rattlesnakes, or when they perceive that wetlands, woodlands, or grasslands interfere with their livelihood—or with their developments or golf courses—they tenaciously and sometimes with considerable moral satisfaction put forth the effort to destroy them. If property owners were to attack destructive alien weeds with the same venom that they now mistakenly direct toward poison ivy, the weeds of Halloween would shrink as meekly from their rage.

Three of the nineteen frogs that inhabit Polly Townsend's small and improbable pond. (Polly Townsend)

Planting Noah's Garden

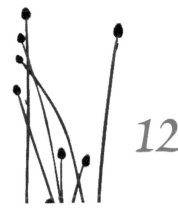

12 *Just Add Water*

"*H*OW TO BUILD A BOG?" wrote Mike McKeag, reminding me of the question I had asked him. "Dig a hole, line it with rubber elastomer, loop a length of Netafin subsurface irrigation line along the bottom, and fill the thing to the brim with bog fill."

The bog fill, and not the construction, Mike proclaimed to this elastomer-innocent, Netafin-naïve correspondent, is the real problem. He "made do," as he put it, with commercial compost, local clay, and enough lime to sweeten the mix somewhat. He is far from satisfied. It preys on his mind that his Oregon backyard bog, a fern and skunk cabbage community, might be less than authentic in its particulate and microbial composition. He fantasizes about being in the mail-order bogsoil business. His catalog would include soil mixes for as many bog types as there are Ben & Jerry's ice cream flavors, each cleverly named and illustrated with a color photograph of the community of vegetation suitable to it. Shipped dry, of course: just add water.

Mike has a way of making things sound easy.

I myself think that everything to do with water is technical and complex. The stuff is hard to handle. It runs. It leaks. It evaporates. Does anyone out there have a truly controllable hose?

For a while I thought I'd waxed too eloquent on the subject of water in my last book. Just about everywhere I went, people wanted to tell me about their plans for a frog pond, and I was afraid they'd blame me if it didn't work. It's not that I don't believe my own words, but I've never built a frog pond. I sure didn't believe that the first one I saw actually in progress was going to work.

It was in Garrison, New York, and I apologize now to its owner, Polly Townsend, for my lack of faith. (I must also explain that several of the gardeners I mention happen to have the same first name. It is their parents' fault.) This Polly lives, first of all, on an unpromising site, a steep hillside where the nearest pooling water

that frogs might breed in must be way down somewhere. The pond itself was just a hole in the hill, dug with a shovel. The liner was not elastomer but a weathered piece of swimming pool cover scavenged from a trash heap, and it leaked. The liner was uncovered at its edges, held casually in place with a few stones. There was no planting. There was no plumbing. The pond was kept filled (somewhat) by hose. The water was green with algae. A plank floated in the middle. I figured the great big bullfrog sitting on the plank was a freak of nature.

The next thing I knew, Polly had replaced the swimming pool cover with a proper liner, installed a sloped stone coping around the edge, sunk pots of rushes and arrowheads in the water, planted mistflower along the bank, and provided photographic evidence of the result: nineteen frogs were in residence.

I eat my words. It's what Mike said. Just add water.

*T*hrough four years of correspondence and a memorable visit, I can't recall Mike McKeag's ever mentioning frogs. He speaks often of water. To me, frogs and water go together like chicken soup and noodles, but he likes the clear broth itself. Or is his passion more in the flow than in the stuff? His waterway meanders over stones, cascades into a pool, and seeps into the shady bog below his wooden deck.

No, that's wrong. It only seems that waterway and bog are connected because both are wet. The water to the bog, I recall now, is fed separately into the Netafin subsurface irrigation line loop. I remember because Mike explained to me about adjusting the water flow to compensate for evaporation. So he doesn't "just add" water: he controls it. With a faucet.

The other water, the water that meanders and cascades across the yard, comes from a buried three-hundred-gallon tank: the "headwaters" of the stream that flows into the pool. Somewhere down in the pool is a filter, like the ones hidden in watering cans that get clogged with leaves so the water dribbles on your feet instead of the flowers. A submerged pump pushes the water back uphill to its beginning through two-inch plastic piping. I know all about that piping: it has a magnetic attraction for garden forks.

The stream runs for fifty feet downslope across the back yard of an eighth-acre lot that measures only sixty feet wide. It was not dug by hand. A Bobcat (not the animal, the machine) and a trencher excavated the bed. A landscaper and a stream and pond specialist supervised the construction. Their men laid the stones: authentic native basalt sporting real moss. "All this didn't happen in a day," wrote Mike in *Pacific Horticulture*, describing his native yard. "It took a few weeks."

I was awfully glad to hear that someone had had the good sense not to take on a rock-hauling project without professional help. Especially one that involved pipes and electrical wiring. It's important to know exactly where the buried wire is so you don't hit it with a shovel. I know where mine is. I hit it with a shovel when we were building the terrace.

Mike, with the help of a strong grown son, did build the bog. Except that it's filled to the brim with bogsoil and watered from underneath instead of from above and that the plants are planted in the soil instead of in pots, there really isn't much difference between a bog and a frog pond. In construction, that is. Frogs prefer ponds.

And now I find I've been wrong again. Mike *has* mentioned frogs. At the end of his *Pacific Horticulture* article, he describes "the Anna's hummingbird sipping nectar from the honeysuckle, the flock of pine siskins working the hedgerow, and the frog calling for a mate from the pond." He wonders whether these animals are fooled by the illusion of his yard—by its planted meadows and aspen grove and thimbleberry bramble—or perhaps have really found a home.

Yes, Mike, they have found a home.

But it is not so simple as just adding water.

I recall with great fondness the "invisible paint" books we used to have as children. The pages were outline drawings that, like magic, became splashed with gaudy color at the touch of a wet brush.

I was reminded of this activity when, some years ago, business with a publisher in San Diego took me by air across the southwest desert for the first time. Astonishingly, there appeared below giant green polka dots against the tan ground. Someone said that they were crops being raised under the long arm of a

Mike McKeag washing silt from his artificial stream. Silting is minimal now that the surrounding meadow of red fescue, Festuca rubra, has filled in. (Michael McKeag)

slowly sweeping circular irrigation system. I hadn't known you could turn dirt green by just adding water.

The same phenomenon struck me as, on wheels now, I approached the San Diego suburbs. There I was, driving through chapparal country, enchanted with the soft, blurred colors, seeming almost to hear the scuttle of lizards and breathe what I imagined would be the resinous fragrance of the scrub, when the ridges on the ocean side turned green. Green and bougainvillea magenta, green and jacaranda blue. I could see the sprinklers sparkling in the arid air.

Such gaudy stripes are also appearing now around Phoenix, Arizona, where desert is being "developed" at the rate of an acre an hour. The *New York Times* showed photographs of the development in progress. The bulldozers had cleared away century-old saguaros and irreparably chewed up the desert crust to make way for homes on lawns. I saw a color photograph somewhere else of a similar but completed development, also in the desert. It was all green lawn. Of course, what else? And what could be worse? The central feature of the community was a lake! Manmade, need I add. Big enough to sail on.

I've said that if we each add our little dot to the landscape, a new painting will gradually emerge from our pointillist endeavor, but these splashes of color are not what I meant. In fact, I realize that if flying over the Tucson suburbs one could see the dot of Ruth Shilling's seed-strewn desert garden from the air, it would be like an invisible painting because she has *not* added water. Not to the desert soil, anyway.

She does keep that water trough for birds, the one that's just the inner tank of an old hot water heater with a portion of one side cut out. It lies on the ground; she fills it with a hose. The water trough is more the size of dot I have in mind.

Ruth tells me that water is to birds in the desert what boxes are to bluebirds here: the scarce resource that limits their population. The concept of a limiting resource is a classic of population biology. In the desert, bird populations rise or fall with the number of drinking spots because water is the scarcest of the resources they need to reproduce. Here, we may have plenty of water and food, but natural cavities are rare; we will have no more breeding bluebirds than we provide with boxes.

The concept is neatly logical, and it holds true in natural habitats. But its application to extensive suburban development is dubious. When Towne Park in Georgia is completed, it will cover nearly eight square miles. Some residents will surely put out feeders, but they may be as disappointed as my niece Ellen was when no birds came to her treeless cul-de-sac. If there is a scarcity of food on so vast a housing tract, so is there a scarcity of water and shelter—a scarcity of habitat of any sort, contrived or natural. Our stone terrace couldn't be a Great Attractor if there were no surrounding landscape from which animals could be

Ruth Shilling's water trough was cut from the inner tank of a hot water heater. There's a perching rock at one end, and the bottom is lined with stones to give birds secure footing while they drink and bathe. (Brad Smith)

attracted. Mike's frog may well live on his eighth-acre oasis, but it did not spontaneously generate in bogsoil.

At the rate the Phoenix suburbs are spreading—an acre an hour grows to 8,760 acres per year, or more than thirteen square miles annually—there won't be any habitat for long from which anyone might come. Subdivisions are spreading as quickly up the Sierras, down the western rivers, and around every boom town to the eastern shore. The real desert is not undeveloped arid land where lizards scurry and peccaries run free. The American desert is the well-watered greensward of our endless tract developments, and it is spreading from coast to coast faster than the sands of the Sahara.

We are like impatient children, spilling water over an invisible picture to make it appear all at once instead of tediously, bit by bit. The image has splotched and run; we are ruining it. We are spilling water when what we need is its pointillist provision.

Geography was my favorite subject in elementary school. We got to color maps and print the place names in our finest hand. We molded continents in clay and attached to them small artifacts—a splinter of wood, a chip of coal, a fluff of wool—to indicate natural resources. On tests, we were required to draw from memory the country we were studying or a whole continent with its isthmuses, peninsulas, islands, mountains, lakes, and rivers. Atlases were my favorite kind of book; I lingered lovingly over the globe in our school library. An early photograph shows me in kindergarten putting together a wooden puzzle of the United States of America. I'm holding California in my hand; I recall that it was yellow.

Now that I have on my attic wall two huge maps of the United States to improve my orientation, I realize how crude my previous geographic images had been. The maps measure three by five feet—too large to hang separately in this little room. With one over the other, I must lift the colored one, which indicates elevation, to see the black and white one, which shows landforms and drainage systems in stunning relief and exquisite detail. The image is a far cry from the pointy peaks we drew to indicate the Rockies and the blue squiggle that served us as the Mississippi. It is even a far cry from the best relief maps of that day, when it was still possible for a young geography student to miss the intimate relation-ship between topography and drainage. On this map, based on both ground survey and satellite image, water seems actually to run, drip down slopes, trickle into valleys, form streams, flow into rivers, spread into ponds and lakes, sink finally into desert playas, or wash out to sea.

I purchased the two maps when I had become lost in Sierra Club Naturalist Guides. The guides present an overall description of, for example, the Piedmont, the southern Rockies, the North Woods, the southwest deserts. Each volume includes the area's geological history and present soil formations, the major ecosystems, and sketches of the flora and fauna that characterize them. I had hoped to give myself a sort of armchair tour of the country by reading all the guides, but even in southern New England, my own familiar portion, I soon became disoriented. It's one thing to have driven along the Connecticut River many times; it's another to picture the river valley's width and course, slopes and feeders. Why should the range of the tuliptree halt abruptly at the Connecticut-Massachusetts border as though it respected political boundaries? Or finger north along Massachusetts's border with New York as though following something not shown in the guide's simple drawings?

So when the maps arrived, I took to reading the books in their constant presence, poking into swamps and fingering mountain balds as once I had traced out the routes of the great explorers on the globe at school. I happened to be studying that yellow piece of wooden puzzle, California.

California, said the map, has a zillion streams! No, said the guide to the Sierra Nevada, it does not. The Central Valley has none left at all; its streambeds are empty, the water spilled to irrigate celery and lettuce. The author could not even describe the valley's riparian vegetation, since, unlike our tuliptrees, it had not been studied before it was destroyed.

The tuliptree's respect for state boundaries turned out to be topographical, based on moisture gradients. Its range ends abruptly at the drier foothills of the Berkshire Mountains but follows the Hudson north along the river's moist valley. The many lakes shown on the map in flatter portions of southern New England accorded well with the guide's descriptions of the grass pinks, ladies' tresses, fringed gentians, meadow lilies, and rose pogonias typical of our wet meadow ecosystems. But here my intimacy with the area belied both book and map. What remains of such wetlands is mostly to be found on preserves; elsewhere they have been drained. The truth of the riparian woodlands so well described in nature guides is that most have been cut down and cultivated as lawn and field. The reality of the countless little rills that lace New England on the map is that they are ravaged by spring floods, glutted with silt, and dry up in summer. The soil is no longer root-matted, spongy, deep-down damp and trickling: rain spills off the land too fast.

The maps don't show and the guides don't describe what lies below the surface: the country's largest water system, the aquifers that feed our springs and wells. This is fossil water, as oil is fossil fuel. It has percolated through soil and stone for thousands or tens of thousands of years and is a finite cache. Or it is at our time scale. Theoretically, aquifers are a renewable resource, recharged continually by rain. But each molecule of water raining on the land's surface may take a hundred years to reach the underground reservoir that traps its further flow, and we are emptying the tank faster than it is refilling.

Ruth Shilling had to lower her well pump to reach the water, which had fallen twenty-six feet in a decade and a half. When I was a child summering in Connecticut, people got their water from shallow wells that filled with groundwater or from natural springs. Artesian wells that tap to the aquifer from which such springs arise were not common then. My family was among the first to drill this modern sort of well on the old farm where we had previously hauled water from a spring. The spring sank; it's gone, its deep source spilt and squandered.

A picture of my country has been building, layer by layer: from the microcosmic washout of an anthill, to the foot-deep scours in the many rivulets that used to trickle gently among the skunk cabbage and ostrich fern of our red maple swamp, to pale silt fanning from our rivers as the airplane rises over the sound, to that cloud-high altitude from which the land looks peeled, to an arresting and appalling image: the raw surface oozing the moisture of America's lifeblood.

I met Katrina Thomas by chance in a bookstore one July and went to see her wetland garden. Sheep grazed the green pastures. A brook ran lazily between steep banks. Very steep; we climbed down a full flight of stone steps to reach the level of her garden, where pickerel weed bloomed on a sandbar against a flood-borne snag and blue flag and bottle gentian grew where the channel broadened and water lay limpid at our feet. The steps are a measure of how deeply the streambed has been scoured. The soil was gnawed and scarred with runnels. The brook is a rip-tearing monster in the spring, and it had bitten the banks away. The water must once have run through Katrina's yard, not below it. But that may have been a century ago or more.

Violent spring floods and aggressive erosion date from the clearing of land for agriculture. Spongy woodland soils earlier had been natural irrigation systems, metering out the water, feeding it slowly and steadily through the season. Where the land was fairly flat, tame spring floods deposited a yearly film of fine sand and silt beyond the banks, and this is where wet meadows, with their orchids and their gentians, were once to be found. Katrina's brook runs for miles through residential tracts and rural countryside plowed for crops or hayed for fodder. The sheep that graze the land to either side are the very animal that by its close-cropping of Old World pastures created the creeping turfgrasses that are now our lawns. Water runs off this shallow-rooted land as from a roof or road, and nothing now will slow it except replanting the ravished valley it has carved.

Katrina had bought the farmhouse on this plot of land in anticipation of her eventual retirement—which age, according to others' less exacting standards, she had already reached. I found this new acquaintance unnerving: sharp-boned and beautiful, strong-willed and single, not the sort of person to invite a stranger over to flatter either the visitor or herself. Yet a person who raises around her such a blizzard of apparent non sequiturs that it took me an hour to realize that I had not been summoned to admire iris but to consult on crown vetch.

My gardening encyclopedia describes the pretty pink and white pea-flowered crown vetch, Cornilla varia, with amusing ambivalence: "Although native to Europe, this has become widely naturalized in the northeastern U.S. and can become a vicious weed in any garden. . . . Crown Vetch increases rapidly by sending out underground stems in all directions and also the shoots may root where they touch moist soil. It is excellent for planting on steep, rocky banks and growing at will, but should not be planted in a well-kept garden, for even though the above-ground shoots may be pulled up where they are not wanted, roots will be broken off and remain in the soil and continue to act as invading weeds for years. It is also a fine plant for preventing soil erosion on banks."

Spring flood along Katrina Thomas's stream. You can see how thin the turf is: the torrent has torn out huge chunks of it. Farther along the stream, below Katrina's house, is her deeply gullied garden. (© Katrina Thomas)

In fact—and on the advice of her county agent—Katrina had planted crown vetch to hold her bank against erosion, and just as the encyclopedia warns, it had become a vicious weed. The distinction between her "well-kept garden" and her erosion-controlled bank had disappeared. The weed had spread along the brook through the wetland garden and into a bed of daylilies many yards from where it had been planted. It had crept over the rim of the bank and was prowling through the lawn toward new horizons. How to get rid of it and what to put in its place were the questions on Katrina's mind.

In this circuitous way I entered a world as new to me as the Landforms and Drainage map had been: the world of mitigation. The very term was new to me; I had just obtained the catalog of a nursery specializing in "wetland mitigation." Like other bookish travelers in strange lands, I looked up the dictionary meaning: mitigation is "to cause to become more gentle or less hostile; to make less severe,

192   *Planting Noah's Garden*

violent, cruel, intense, painful." It is in the nature of flowing water to carve and reshape the land, cutting into one bank and piling silt along another. Rivers change course; hills erode to plains; lakes shallow to marshes. These changes are inevitable over time. My understanding was that the purpose of wetland mitigation is merely to slow the hectic pace, to gentle the waters.

I had misunderstood. Wetland mitigation is to make less painful the destruction caused *to* wetlands, not by them, and the purpose is to protect the water—its cleanliness and plentiful supply—not the integrity of its habitat. Thus property owners may be permitted to drain a marsh if, in mitigation, they create an equivalent wet area; or they may be allowed to deforest a bank if, in mitigation, they replant the new erosional surface with something else. What that something is— and whether the rare green dragon that grew in the original marsh can grow in its replacement, or whether wood frogs will breed there or wood ducks find food to eat—is often beneath the notice of the law.

As we two foolishly bootless ladies drove past miles of crown vetch to Pinelands Nursery one cold November day, we were, ironically, out to mitigate a previous and wrongful mitigation.

We had made an appointment with Don Knezick, who with his wife, Suzanne, owns Pinelands Nursery, but he was delayed by an emergency soil test for a client. His one autumn employee didn't know who we were or why we'd come, so we wandered around. It was hard to walk among the half-barrel polyhouses, on the scant boards and strewn branches that were the only route through thick and slippery mud. There wasn't much to see at that time of year. The plants, started from seed or cuttings late the previous winter, were mostly sold out. Discarded pots and plug trays lay heaped about. Katrina, a professional photographer, had brought her camera, but she did not take any pictures. There really was nothing to see.

Don Knezick arrived, immaculately dressed as though for a tour of display gardens. He was tall, dark, handsome, committed, and totally professional.

Don does not deal in crown vetch. With one exception—a willow introduced by the Soil Service and for that reason suspect—Pinelands deals in species native to New Jersey and the surrounding area. The Knezicks grow wetland plants like tussock sedge and soft rush and dryland ones like bear oak, pitch pine, and lowbush blueberry. Quite a few of them are equally at home drowned or desiccated, making them a good choice for seasonal wetlands such as sumps, which puddle in the spring and dry up in the summer, or episodic ones like ditches, which carry runoff during storms. Mitigation also involves salt-tolerant species to hold dunes along the shore, carpeting or thicketing ones to hold steep banks, and species that can grow on sterile dirt where all the topsoil has eroded. The nursery grows all of these through sophisticated technologies in quantities then incredible to me.

I was transfixed. In some of the polyhouses water flowed through long, shallow tanks along a central aisle. In these grow emergent aquatics like pickerel weed, Pontederia cordata, and woolgrass, Scirpus cyperinus. The salinity of the water is adjusted for salt marsh species; spartina is grown first in fresh water, then gradually accustomed to its ultimate habitat by measured additions of salt. Smaller plants are grown in plug trays from which they are popped like ice cubes at planting time. One can, I learned, "contract" for these or larger plants—arrange for them to be grown to order—in quantities of five hundred or five thousand, or even by the tens of thousands.

Don demonstrated the use of erosion control products—fiber mats, biologs, fascines. I had never heard of these things. In one polyhouse, a late contract for an aquatic rush was growing in two-inch-thick coconut-fiber bog mat submerged in water. He lifted one corner to show us the roots spread throughout the fiber. The plants were only a few weeks old. The mat can be rolled up, plants and all, then rolled out over the bed of a watercourse as turf is rolled out over a golf course—the difference being only in the quality of mitigation.

I had almost forgotten Katrina, left with her camera dangling. Don suggested that the best choice for both erosion control and wildlife habitat would be switchgrass, Panicum virgatum, a rhizomotous species that with its spreading roots would quickly hold the soil on her shaley bank. The bank measured seventy by twenty feet. At the rate of one plant per square foot, fourteen hundred plants would be needed to replace the crown vetch. We could contract for them. Erosion control mats would be worthless on her bank because they could not be laid smoothly over the numerous shale projections. Katrina did not need arrowhead, fox sedge, duck potato. She did not want fascines, bog mats, biologs.

Something came over me. The excitement of technology? The self-importance that comes from plants grown specially to order?

Or impatience with Katrina for attending to the near bank, where her garden grew, but not to the far one, where erosion was more severe and a wetland thicket to hold the soil might also slow the water eating other people's land downstream. Or simply curiosity, experiment, the gathering of new material for a book.

The upshot of our visit that November day was an order for the following spring that Marty and I rented a van to haul and then distributed more or less equally among my niece's ditch, our pond, and Katrina's eroded bank.

*I*he muskrats were gone. For the first spring since we had dredged the pond and planted its meadowed shore, no brown babies played hide-and-seek under the little rowboat, no mother muskrat steered bouquets of meadowrue across the water with what had come to seem feigned innocence. Don Knezick, whose nursery lies among farm ditches heavily populated with muskrats, had been unable to advise me on how to establish a muskrat habitat in spite of the presence of its occupants. I was glad they were gone.

I sat on the terrace ripping holes in bog mat, pushing into them plugs of various aquatics to replace those the muskrats had consumed before their desertion or demise. Eighty miles south, my niece Ellen was planting fourteen hundred plugs of woolgrass and soft rush in fiber matting rolled out along her ditch. Eighty miles north, Katrina was valiantly inserting an equal number of switchgrass plugs among the herbicided crown vetch on her bank.

Summer came. Our bogmat plantings flourished and began to fill in the pond shore as I had hoped and as would be needed to support muskrats when a new family moved in. Ellen's Juncus effusus and Scirpus cyperinus began to hold their own—to slow the water, to hold the soil rushing from cul-de-sac to culvert. Katrina's switchgrass rooted in and grasped the crumbling bank. I wished I had tried more, tried everything: fiber biologs that looked like giant luffa sponges stuffed with marshy herbage, thick ropes called fascines made of silky dogwood or pussy willow sticks.

The fascines particularly intrigued me because they are the living material itself, fresh-cut, cord-bound wands that sprout into instant thickets. I had found, among the Monday walkers, a potential customer for fascines of red osier dogwood, Cornus stolonifera, for a ferociously steep storm channel that cuts her lot almost vertically, but I hadn't realized that they must be planted a month earlier in the season than I had thought to order them.

Then, picking up the *New York Times* one morning, I saw an article by Anne Raver. This wry and adventurous gardening writer had been involved in the shady business of rosenapping in cemeteries. It seems that grieving families over the centuries of European settlement have often planted Old World roses as memorials and that these genuine antiques are easily cloned from cuttings. I'm not much interested in Old World aristocrats, but a native shining rose, Rosa nitida, that I had often admired along the roadside had been buried in bittersweet over the years, and I knew also of a native Carolina rose smothered in honeysuckle at the verge of a condominium. Each had become a rare example of its once abundant kind, so I ventured forth with pruners and, following the can't-fail boxed directions in Anne Raver's article, started cuttings in Ziploc sandwich bags.

Every one took root.

So why not homemade fascines? If I can bag, so can I bundle.

Down by the pond, between an old boulder and the young sedge meadow, grow five red osier dogwoods. Excusing the fact that they are a dwarf selection of the species and that in general I disapprove of cloning cultivars, their knee-high scarlet stems look mighty nice in winter among buffy skeletons of wool-grass against the frozen pond. Marty was at it with the stones again, rebuilding rubble walls down by the lower wetland, planning steps, choosing rocks to bridge the waters, envisioning this wet wonderland as I had envisioned the dry terrace three years before. We had found tussuck sedge, flag iris, swamp milk-weed, marsh fern. But the extent of erosion was shocking. What ten years before had been a watery lacework playing over the surface was now ugly ruts gouged by spring torrents originating in new development upstream. I'd never heard of woodland wetland mitigation. But, again, why not? I imagined mitigating thick-ets of dwarf dogwood woven among lush green skunk cabbages under red-blos-somed maples like swamp Christmastime in spring. Or one patch, anyway, just to see.

Toward midspring the year after that first Pinelands order, when the marsh marigolds were blooming and the dogwood buds had swelled, I snipped a batch of wands, bundled them inexpertly with butcher's twine, lay them down in grooves along a trial channel, and lovingly buried them.

That, too, worked.

Could it be that water is not so hard to deal with after all?

I began to feel—how shall I put it?—more *manly* about controlling water, more akin to Mike with his elastomer and Netafin. But it was not waterway construc-tion that I was dealing with: it was the gentling of plants.

"*I* wonder if we will notice an increase in our electric bill, running this pump day and night?" Mike McKeag wrote to me the day he turned on his watercourse for the first time. He had considered a solar panel; using solar energy to lift the water back to its source upstream would be a "proper hydrologic cycle," he remarked. But then, Mike considered, the electricity that drives his pump is gen-erated by turbines at Bonneville Dam on the Columbia River, and he proceeded to give me a brief course in solar-driven hydrology—ocean surface evaporation, cloud formation, precipitation, drainage, the eventual recycling of water through the river system and its turbines back into the ocean whence it came. He seemed satisfied that his waterworks are part of the solar-powered natural cycle after all. "My stream is a little wheel driven by the big wheel of the Columbia River," he concluded.

Our pond in fall. Although a pair of Canada geese breeds here in the spring, the broad band of vegetation planted along the shore keeps flocks from congregating. The species loves a lawn, but won't walk through tall grass. (Sara Stein)

It sounded good to me. That was in July 1992.

In March 1995 a letter from Mike arrived containing a spreadsheet entitled "Electrical Power Cost Before and After Stream Installation." The increase was more than noticeable: his bill had nearly doubled. Further, he had learned the lifespan of a pump: two years, four months, eleven days. He had just bought a new one.

Then came more figurings. Factoring in the cost of the pump over its lifetime, plus the increase in electrical consumption, his total monthly expenditure for running the stream came to about one dinner for two at a moderately priced restaurant (my own figuring tells me electricity must be cheap in Oregon). He wasn't worried about that minor sacrifice; the pleasure of flowing water was well worth it.

But he had a new concern: the consequent increase in household power consumption, which had doubled to a total of 6,800 kilowatt-hours per year. "How many Columbia River salmon has it cost to create habitat for the frogs, birds, and insects that use our stream?" he wondered.

He was considering a windmill. I'd been considering salmon.

When Mike's letter came, I'd just finished a book called *Our Natural History* by Daniel B. Botkin, an ecologist who has been directing a study of salmon in northern California and western Oregon. In one chapter, "Down the Columbia," Botkin discusses multiple reasons for the drastic decline in this stream-spawned, ocean-going genus: chinook, coho, chum, sockeye, and pink salmon, and their close kin, steelhead and cutthroat trout.

When the Columbia River ran free, salmon had been reported in "almost inconceivable" numbers in the journals of Lewis and Clark, the first Europeans to venture down that western river. The extent of salmon spawning grounds was also astonishing. Botkin found evidence that salmon were staple fare for Indians along the tributaries of the Columbia River system for many hundreds of miles inland.

There is no single reason for their present decline: there are many. Overfishing. Irrigation. Dams. Reservoirs. Channelization. Clear-cutting. Erosion. But Botkin's point is that if there is no single reason, there is also no single solution: no right answer, no rigid management policy that practiced uniformly over time would mitigate this fish's precarious existence.

Salmon need landslides in the mountains because that gravelly debris is the source of the clean pebbled beds in which they spawn. They need fluctuating water levels that at times aid returning adults, at other times help their seabound fry. They need floods to carve new meanders and marshes where the young seek shelter from predators. They need storms to fell forest trees, to dam the stream, to form quiet pools and splashy ripples. They need fires to clear the banks, to let alders sprouting in the new, bright light replenish the soil's nitrogen for the next generation of great forest conifers. They need the regrowing forest as well, for only in its shade is the population of diatoms, young salmons' primary food, sufficient to feed their growing appetite. The survival of salmon depends on numerous small catastrophes; stasis, says the Salmon Law of Nature, kills.

Botkin's hope in writing *Our Natural History* is to bring us toward a new understanding of the environment, to realize that the natural world never has existed in a static state such as we imagine the "primeval forest" or the Columbia River to have been before human interference. He asks us to be flexible, experimental, to allow change, admit error—and avoid in the future monolithic controls such as those that have curbed the freedom of 4,600 miles of waterway in the Columbia and Snake River basins, a third of the 14,700 miles of river that salmon traveled at the time of the Lewis and Clark Expedition.

I had not read Botkin's work before, but Mike had. I suspect that Botkin's insistence that there is no such thing as a "climax" community—that nature is always in flux and cannot be predictably contained—had something to do with Mike's research into bog communities, his conclusion that there are as many kinds of bog as there are biologists reporting on them, and his fantasy of many-flavored bogsoils.

We speak at different scales: Botkin of great ecosystems, I of small properties, Mike of miniature bogs. But I think we three are part of a new environmental harmony in which no single voice declares the right solution. Mike's solution to providing wetland habitat would be the wrong one if it were the only one, if we were all to pump three hundred gallons of water uphill continually through our yards. His bog, Katrina's brook, Ellen's ditch, my pond, Ruth's trough, and Polly's hole in the hill are other solutions—soft, in harmony, and equally mitigating in our otherwise water-squandering suburban desert.

I am sometimes impatient with how slowly pictures emerge from small dots and worried by how quickly the canvas is being painted green. I'm mad at the developers of Towne Park for razing the very watershed by which the aquifer now bleeding onto lawns could be replenished. I'm annoyed that the owners of Rock Rim Ponds in my own "towne" seem unaware that their mowed-back style silts my pond and runs the soil from my swamp. But mostly I'm relieved to consider the advantages of this particular suburban scale I work with and write about: small enough in Mike's case that a frog pond makes a difference; big enough on our place that natural wetlands can be restored to diversity and muskrats.

Our suburbs are populated with so many kinds of people in such varied circumstances that if we can break out of the monolithic uniformity of lawns, we will be free to find our ways as variously and flexibly as streams once found the sea.

By the shelter and nourishment they provide, dead trees support more life by far than living ones. Here a red maple, which needs light to germinate, grows from what ecologists call a nurse log. (Virginia P. Weinland)

13 And Through the Woods

*T*HE TUNE HAS BEEN STUCK in my head for a week now: "Over the river and through the woods, to Grandmother's house we go." I'm not sure I have the words right. Maybe it's through the "trees," not woods. Or "into" the woods, not through them. I think the words are from a poem; I'll go to the library and look it up, but not yet.* The differences interest me.

If Grandmother lives over the river and through the *trees*, the sleigh ride to get there doesn't sound like a long enough journey to wax poetical about. You could just about see her house on the other side of the trees, and it wouldn't matter whether the horse knew the way or not. If you have to go *into* the woods to visit her, the poem takes on a sinister cast. To the best of my recollection, the granny *in* the woods is a witch—or a wolf.

I have mixed feelings about woods. I can recite their environmental value like a mantra: water conservation, climate moderation, soil maintenance, pollution control. I spent considerable time in the woods as a child—indeed, in what I believed to be the forest, which is older and darker, with no openings in the canopy and no sunlight on the ground. And bigger: I can call the strip along our pond "woods"; it would be laughable to call it "forest." Woods is what you walk through to get to the other side. You walk into a forest and hope like crazy you'll get out again.

Woods are where foxes and coyotes hang out when they're not trotting down the road or looking for mice in the cornfield. Lions and bears and wolves live in the forest. That's why there aren't a lot of wild beasts to frighten little children anymore;

* The poem turns out to be by Lydia Maria Child. It is "Grandfather's house," not Grandmother's (she appears later, "in her cap"). But to get there, one does indeed go "through the woods."

there's not a lot of forest. Wherever you poke streets into a forest, it turns into woods, even if the old trees are left standing. The edge grows up in undignified stuff like blackberries, and serious forest birds withdraw as if they had a phobia toward light.

To be honest, I'm not sure that where I went as a kid was a forest; I never went far enough to find out. It was too scary. I found my way up the hemlocked hill like a little mammal, by memorized landmarks—a stricken tree, a rock seamed with quartz, that sort of thing. I looked for snails and salamanders; once I found a copperhead. But I never went over the ridge to see the other side. Back downhill led to the stream, and the stream led out to the meadow, and I wonder now if I ever went farther than a hundred yards from the sound of water. Probably the hemlocks were just woods.

A survey recently reported that people's commonest fear of the outdoors is getting lost in the woods—more frightening than snakes, more dreaded than spiders, more awful to consider than stumbling off a cliff. It doesn't seem to matter if they are used to the woods or have never even seen them: they're scared either way. When we of ALFASAC go walking in the woods, we exercise strict rules. No one may wander out of sight. The first person to reach a turn or fork in the path must wait for the others, and heads are counted before we proceed. To these women, some of whom blazed the trails themselves, their tales of losing their way are vividly relived, the shock of disorientation still disturbing to them and palpable to the listener.

I have my own story, from the time I was a young mother living in the woods. Snow had lightly fallen overnight, and the children were restless. I put the baby in his crib for a morning nap and set off with the other boys and the dog up the wagon road that ran beside our land. This was our hundred-times-taken path, broad and clear, marked by double ruts, running straight through beech trees, then chestnut oaks along laurel ledges, bending only once to accommodate the foundation of a former barn. We left the road to mount a ridge to see the other side and suddenly were nowhere. The road disappeared. We lost our footprints. Snow lay in patches like camouflage among brown leaves. Ledge followed ledge; trees followed trees; time rang with panic in space without direction.

The dog, fed up with our foolishness, led us on the five-minute walk back home to the baby, still sleeping in his crib.

I have also noted, on our Monday walks, that though we often stop in the woods to examine this or that or hear the latest story, we do not take a rest until we reach an opening. It may be where a stream broadens over flat rocks, at the verge of a meadow, or at a height where we can see beyond the trees and over the countryside. We have a need, I think, for clarity of view, for woodland before or behind us, paradoxically unobstructed by trees. If we enter the forest with exhilaration and wonder—feet slowed, voices lowered—we emerge from the shadow with a sensation of relief, and our pace quickens and our voices rise. We are more surely human out in the open, where our race began.

The home I visited in Wisconsin that was built within a ten-foot envelope in order to protect the surrounding trees was not really a house in the woods. It was a house in a clearing in the woods. Grass and brambles grew in sunshine to one side; you could see through the trees to the prairie and a pond below. I heard of a development in North Carolina that's been built according to the same principle, like the one I saw in the Sonoran Desert but in the woods. The tract includes substantial wetland donated to the Nature Conservancy, and 10 percent of the home sales figure goes into a wetland management fund. I guess I could take living in the woods if I could get out to watch the turtles basking in sunshine at the marsh. But it sure was a relief to move out of the woods and into the open when we built the home we live in now.

So I understand why, when culling unwanted brush from woods, it is so difficult to stop before the space is overcleared and all that's left is trees. I understand why woodland gardens, lovely as they are, will never be as popular or published as open, sunny ones. And I understand in the deepest, biological sense why the suburban savanna is the landscape that feels right and safe to us.

*T*here was an outbreak of chipmunks this year, a real epidemic. My friend the woodland gardener live-trapped nineteen on her acre lot in an attempt to save her lilies before every one of them was eaten in the bud. The population density of these charming ground squirrels ranges somewhere between five and ten per hectare or a peak of about four per acre. Such measurements are taken by field biologists, tagging their subjects in natural environments. My friend's garden is even more edible; she has always been overstocked with chipmunks. Never before, though, *five times* the normal peak.

The phenomenon was general in southern Connecticut and nearby New York. Other gardening friends reported it. The Naturals noticed it, too. I saw chipmunks on the stone terrace climb the cherry tree to eat its blossoms. They took the wild strawberries in the pink, not waiting for their full ripening.

This was a year, too, of sprouting oaks. They sprouted from buried acorns in the herb garden. They came up among blueberries on our stone terrace, in the vegetable garden, and in the peony beds. Hickories, too, sprouted through the woods. Most years you don't see this many seedlings; usually squirrels and chipmunks eat all the nuts they store.

A quarterly journal from Cornell Plantations in Ithaca, New York, reported the results of a study just conducted in that upstate region of an invasion of second-growth woodland by young beech trees. It seems the woods that spring were popping with beeches just out of their nuts. Our beech also had produced an astounding nut crop the previous fall. So the phenomenon, called "a mast year" after a German word for forest food, was not merely local. The article didn't mention chipmunks.

By fall, though, squirrels were in the news. Gray squirrels were being killed by the hundreds crossing highways through the Catskills and all the way to Albany. In one case, 280 carcasses had been picked up by a road crew along a three-mile stretch. Droves of squirrels were not only risking thruways but swimming rivers and reservoirs in what appears to have been an urge similar to that which drives lemmings to migrate when their numbers grow too high. The reason, biologists guessed, was the nuts.

The connection is the flip side of the rule that population is limited by the scarcest resource. Populations increase as resources increase, peak at densities higher than the habitat can reliably support, then decline to build again when the opportunity arises. (The article dryly commented that the highway toll may be "nature's way of correcting the problem.") Trees also vary in their reproductive rate. Some oaks produce acorns only in alternate years; all nut species tend to produce bonanza crops in years of maximum sunlight. The population snapshot that develops, though, depends also on predation—the number of nuts eaten by the chipmunks, the number of chipmunks eaten by the cat. The repopulation of a woodland by beech or oak or hickory occurs when the ebb and flow of nuts and squirrels don't coincide. A swell of nuts must meet an ebb of squirrels if there are to be enough left over to sprout. Since it frequently happens that the squirrel survival and birth rate rise in the spring following the bonanza crop, the necessary syncopation is built into the system: every so often, perhaps once or twice a decade, nut trees produce a surplus that regenerates the forest.

My friend's woodland garden, though, is not regenerating. She has no cat, no foxes or coyotes. Her overfed chipmunks are nearly twice the size of mine, plump enough to produce two annual litters instead of the usual one, satisfied to live closer to one another than is normal for the breed, and loath in adolescence to leave their birthland as other young chipmunks do. I'd be surprised if there's ever a nut left to sprout, but even if there were, my friend would pull the seedling up. She's not managing a woodland, after all. She's maintaining a garden.

Her community is old as suburbs go—the modest homes on acre lots were built more than thirty years ago. The developer left the back yards intact: typical

Red oak acorns sprouting in spring from a cache overlooked by squirrels and other animals that in years of high population consume all the available nuts. (Virginia P. Weinland)

oak and hickory woodland with an understory of dogwoods. Owners thinned the growth, selected larger trees and culled the small ones, formed clearings, raked the ground and planted lawn, added ornamentals. Some of the dogwoods are now magnificent specimens; the oaks are splendid shade trees. Realtors would call the landscaping "mature," by which they mean that future owners need do nothing but maintain what is already there.

But young nuts aren't growing there: they're raked and tossed in the fall or chopped up by the mower in the spring. The neighbors aren't managing woodland; they're maintaining grounds. As though trees were permanent, as though oaks live forever.

The oak trees Ellen planted on her New Jersey lot died in their first summer and had to be replaced. The Quercus genus is in general slow to grow and hard to move. The rugged root runs deep and is damaged in the digging unless the tree is very young. Few nurseries carry much of a selection—mostly just the more tractable lowland species whose roots run closer to the surface, like those of pin and willow oak. We managed to find scarlet oak, but what I really wanted for Ellen was a species of greater substance and eccentricity, like the bur oaks that are the mainstay of midwestern oak savanna. It was a case of imagination outrunning research. Bur oaks don't occur where Ellen lives and aren't carried by her nurseries. My more shockingly incorrect assumption was that bur oaks are pioneers on disturbed land. I found out later that they are better compared to tribal elders confined to reservations.

I saw bur oak savanna in Wisconsin. It might have been devised by Capability Brown as an example of the classic landscape school of design. The great trees grow scattered, singly and in groves. The ground beneath their broad arms is sun-dappled. One grove that I remember on a rise in rolling countryside was carpeted with birdsfoot violets. Where such sites have been restored, prairie sweeps among and through the groups of trees—like bluegrass through stands of walnut in Kentucky's horse country, like pasture under elms left at fence lines to shade New England cows, like golden grass through coastal live oaks on California hills, like Frederick Law Olmsted's design for Central Park, like college quadrangles and grand estates. Like the very breath of our nostalgia, the suburb of our dreams.

Suburbs have been built on midwestern oak savanna. Some of the trees easily date back to when prairie swept from tree to tree and grove to grove across the gentle billows of the land, but the ground was plowed a century ago and now is lawn, and these old trees are the last ones of their kind that will ever grow naturally in such places. They may live to be five hundred; they may drop brave crops of nuts; they may feed the squirrels that plant them for ten human generations. But bur oak acorns can't sprout among field weeds or in lawns. They are like elephants: most enduring as individuals, most likely as a species to become extinct.

This possible fate is sad enough, but short of the general sadness I feel for the future of suburban land. It breaks my heart that oaks are hard to transplant. Their taproots make them the perfect yard tree, not needing extra water, not too competitive with other plants. Their foliage doesn't sourly spoil the soil like needled evergreens or densely shade like those other denizens of suburbs, the maples.

Open, grassy woodland or savanna is the natural prototype for parks and suburban land-scapes. This scene is of blue oak, Quercus douglasii, savanna in the foothills of the Sacramento Valley, California. (Sonia Cook)

I like maples a lot until I try to get other plants to grow among their thirsty surface roots, in their heavy shade, and through the ton of leaves they shed that crust to cardboard by the spring. Oak leaves make the perfect mulch: porous and richly rotting to soft forest soil. We needn't worry about maple reproduction. Their wings fly everywhere and sprout carelessly, wherever, no chipmunks needed.

Four maple species are native in my region: silver, red, striped, and sugar. We have more than a dozen species of oak. The eastern edition of my tree guide lists thirty-four altogether; the western edition adds an even more impressive fifty-two. Oaks range in habitat from wet swamps to dry sand barrens. (A couple of species grow even in that tough slice of continent through the Dakotas and Nebraska.) Some turn red or wine in the fall before they drop their leaves; others turn brown but hold their leaves for months; the live oaks of the southern tier are evergreen. I can always tell a maple when I see one: the foliage is generic. The "generic" oakleaf shape, which you'll find, for example, to the right of the torch on a dime, is the non-native English oak, Quercus robor, an odd choice of a symbol for the motto *E pluribus unum* in this land of many oaks—some resembling magnolias, willows, chestnuts, or hollies. They are like us, each species lending local color in its area of greatest concentration, but each also adaptable, widespread, and—to the consternation of plant genealogists—apt to interbreed. ALFASAC is often baffled as to the parentage of acorns.

Acorns are the form in which most oaks are sold—by the pound. I splurged on a pound of scarlet oak acorns to replace the ones I sent to the cleaner's and kept them in their box on the kitchen shelf all winter. That's why they didn't germinate when I planted them in the spring. They needed to spend the winter damply buried in the woods.

This I found out from M. Nigel Wright, who grows nuts and oaks at Windrose, his nursery in Pennsylvania. I had called him out of embarrassment—not so much for my acorns as for my prose: I had written myself into a corner. Here I was, recommending the perfect genus by which we could create the drifts and groves of an ideal savanna landscape, then having to admit that oak growth and reproduction are more troublesome by far than Johnny's apple seeds. I was boasting that, of all the woody plants in these United States, oaks rate the highest in food value to wildlife—ahead of pines, blackberries, cherries, dogwoods, grapes, and junipers (maples are in tenth place, trailing poison ivy), only to be forced to admit that popularity with wildlife is part of the oak's problem.

Mr. Wright set me straight. Oaks are easy to grow. You just stick the acorns in damp peat over the winter in your rodentless refrigerator. Then, when a radical sprouts from each acorn in the spring, you break that would-be taproot in half. That makes the acorns grow a whole bunch of roots, not one. Then you plant the sprouted nuts in bottomless pots: when the roots hit the air, the tips stop growing, and a fibrous root system grows in compensation. Then you take your nice little fibrous-rooted six-inch oak seedling and grow it on in a browserproof, hothouse sort of commercially available translucent plastic tube called a tree shelter. By the end of the summer, your acorn has grown into a four-foot oak. In three years, you've got yourself the equivalent of a ten- to twelve-foot, $300 specimen of balled-and-burlapped stock.

Well, I was amazed. And Mr. Wright was pleased. He quite naturally agrees that oaks are the trees to buy.

So I escaped embarrassment along this scaffold of snipped radicals and bottomless pots, but the problem remains of our old oaks' sadly curtailed fertility. No one has to be convinced of their nobility, but magnificence can be a tree's undoing, too. The Bedford Oak, a landmark here more than four hundred years old, spreads its mighty branches in grand and wrongful isolation at a crossroad.

Oaks belong to woodland and savanna, not on ground locked by tar and turfgrass to their seeds' germination, but in soils kept soft and fertile for their acorns by native forest and savanna vegetation. These are the ecosystems where trees cohabit, and trees removed from them only seem to stand alone because they live so long. My plea is that we stop seeing them as street trees, shade trees, specimens, or ornamentals; stop revering trees singly as though they were heroes to be worshiped by locking them out of the general society and preventing their reproduction.

But, I admit, I had no idea how to bring oaks back together on common ground in suburbia's small yards until a letter arrived from Jo Ann Teas, a most determined and outlandish correspondent who tends tree islands in the suburbs of Arkansas.

$$\text{``} \frac{ta}{tb} = \sqrt{1 - V^2/R^2}, \; E = MC^2, \; PR^2, \; MC = \pi, \frac{2d}{c}, \; Me\sqrt{(1 - (vic)^2}, \; \Delta E = \Delta mc^2 \, (Y_2 \, VT)^2 \, ! \text{''}$$

said the lady bear meant to be Jo Ann on the Valentine's Day card her husband sent her; "o," said the gentleman bear meant to be her husband.

Jo Ann, at the age when grandmothers are supposed to be baking cookies, is earning a degree in earth sciences with electives in astronomy and quantum mechanics. "Quiet and unassuming," she described herself in one letter enclosing a newspaper article about her battle with the highway department over the mowing of wildflowers on the median strip that faces her home. The next letter held a pressed specimen of Queen Anne's lace, the flower perfect but less than nickel size, a lesson in what drastic action a plant may take to bloom in spite of mowers.

Jo Ann finds the septic tank. (John C. Teas)

Sometimes there are snapshots: baby raccoons climbing up the carport, Jo Ann herself in a hole up to her shoulders, triumphant in her archaeological discovery of the septic tank.

Thirty years ago, when the Teas family bought the house, the land in what is now the suburbs of Fayetteville was heavily wooded. The view was of the Ozarks with their oak-clad hide intact. Now the hills are scraped and turfed, and the area is pretty much like anywhere else. One snapshot taken through the strip of woods that lines the Teas place shows an adjoining house and yard on a development called Park Place. I could have mistaken the site for Le Parc, New Jersey.

A mistake like that happened while I was in Arizona. I had gone with Mike McKeag to meet Ruth Shilling and see her desert yard. Hers was one of four home landscapes that had recently been videotaped by *CBS This Morning* for a series on gardening. The other three landscapes were mine, Mike's, and the Arbor Montessori School in Georgia, where many of Jeane Reeves's rescued ferns and flowers had found a second home. Naturally, when the piece was aired that Friday morning, we all were watching—Mike and I in a Tucson hotel, Ruth at a friend's house, and Jeane at home in Georgia.

In one scene, the camera panned a series of anonymous front yards while my voiceover remarked on "instant landscapes," "green deserts," and so on. I thought

Planting Noah's Garden

the footage was from stock. Ruth assumed the neighborhood was mine. Jeane recognized it as Towne Park, the development where she had collected plants. She was upset. She feared the publicity might sour her relationships with developers, on whom her continuing rescue efforts depend. A close-to-tears message on the answering machine awaited me at home.

In fact, the yards were along Mike's street in Oregon. His own distinctively northwestern frontage had been cut off the end of the shot, leaving the scene stranded in Anywhere, U.S.A. Even in Arizona, about halfway between Ruth's house in high desert scrub and the Dragoon Mountains wooded with piñon pine, blackjack oak, and juniper, we passed through a retirement community that was indistinguishable from developments elsewhere—or, for that matter, from land-scaped parking lots.

I can't say that I'd know exactly where Jo Ann's yard is by identifying the trees, but I'd know I wasn't in New England. The Shumard oaks that grow there remind me of our scarlet oaks, but their heavy foliage looks exotic to my Yankee eye. The leaves are bigger than my hands; their points spread wide like startled fingers. The trees strike me even in snapshots as southerners, like magnolias—and so they are: a bottomland species, says the guide, not like the scarlet oak, which sticks to high-er ground and stops just short of Arkansas. I wouldn't expect the casual visitor to notice leaves or look them up, but the style of Jo Ann's yard must surely arrest the passing eye: the oaks grow on wild islands in the grass.

Crammed in among geological expositions on Arkansas bedrock (accompanied by hand-drawn profiles), red-hot recipes from her Thai daughter-in-law ("mash and smush the carrots"), and the tragicomic tale of the stopped-up sewer pipe and long-lost septic tank emerges, letter by letter in our three-year correspondence, the continuing saga of Jo Ann's tree islands. I can't quite capture her idiosyncratic voice, much less the leaps by which her thoughts progress, but—to abbreviate the story—it occurred to Jo Ann one day some years ago to let nature take its course among what had been the separated oak trees on the lawn and see what happened.

She let the grass grow, leaves fall, seeds sprout. At first each tree stood on its own island, defined by the mower, but over a period of about five years Jo Ann joined them to each other like an archipelago risen from the sea. "Wandering gar-dens," she called them, a term that describes the meandering design but also sug-gests the many species that wandered in, as turfgrass gave way to leaf mulch and the soil grew soft and rich: pioneering edges of wild cherry, red cedar, Virginia creeper, and wild brier rose; a future canopy of shagbark hickory, mockernut, and walnut; an understory of redbud and flowering dogwood; a floor of ferns, mosses, trout lily, spiderwort, and violets. The older oaks are reproducing—post, red, black, and chinkapin. Some species wander in and wander off again: False indigo put in a splendid appearance, displayed itself in pendulous, fragrant, buttery flowers, and withdrew.

Also, a tomato came up. This was because, to join the original islands, Jo Ann bridged them with compost over the intervening lawn. And not all the seedlings are those that dropped in by natural vehicle. She planted the connecting links with species offered by the state Forestry Commission, thus the Shumard oaks that suggest a southern yard—and that have grown to fifteen feet in four years. Other than such additions to hasten island growth, her attitude has been "wait and see": wait and see how the wind blows, what the birds drop, the chipmunks bury, the ants drag in. She hopes in this way to see the oaks and hickories take back what is rightfully theirs, to let the land reveal its true nature.

The notion is romantic. Tree islands, like islands in the sea, are populated by the accident of what grows upwind or nearby. In any suburban community, what grows upwind or nearby is overwhelmingly exotic. I asked Jo Ann about exotics. Wintercreeper has stolen the central island and is spreading up the oaks. The honeysuckle is Russian; the privet Japanese. The only other natural source of revegetation is whatever memories the soil holds in its seeds. Throughout the continent, soil remembers best its recent history, its days of plows and mowers, its fresh heritage of weeds. Jo Ann's islands bloom with bedstraw, buttercups, and daisies. I asked about trilliums: none has arrived.

The memory of woodland wildflowers is brief. Their seeds are commonly those dispersed by ants, like olives chewed, their pits dumped in the trash. I wouldn't expect that ants would drag them very far across a lawn. These are the seeds that die when they are dried. Cultivating the soil, even to the shallow depth of lawn, dries up all recollection of trilliums.

I was taken aback to realize how advanced a case of wildflower amnesia is suffered by my own northeastern woods even when they appear, by their healthy trees and richly scented humus, to be quite normal. I had gone in April to see the woods still remaining—still to be "developed"—at Towne Park in Georgia. One reads of woodland "carpeted" with flowers, but I had always thought of the term as poetic license. Here it was a literal description. Jeane and her rescue crews had already removed thousands of plants, yet where my Monday walkers might rejoice to find six hepaticas, here were hundreds. And while we must often go to one preserve to see one species and to a different one to see another, here dozens of species grew in the space of a ten-minute stroll:

This is an extraordinary picture—not because it's unnatural for spring ephemerals to carpet the forest floor, but because these Dutchman's breeches, Dicentra cucullaria, were doing so in Armonk, New York, in a small patch of second-growth woods surrounded by suburban homes. Maybe someone planted them? Maybe you could too! (Virginia P. Weinland)

trillium, toothwort, bellwort, spring beauty, Solomon's seal, anemone, violet, columbine, trout lily, geranium, and more orchids than we could see in a year of Mondays. We are careful never to step on wildflowers, but one can't avoid it where there's no bare floor.

This Georgia woods was not virgin forest but, like ours, just second growth. The largest trees measured perhaps twenty inches in diameter; they were the same age and some were the same species as our own, although there the trees grow taller. With a few exceptions, the wildflowers, too, were ones that we can find in the North if we search with diligence. But this southern woodland's memory was intact, and ours is not.

The woods we Monday walkers know were farms until about World War II, when farmland was released from agriculture. By then, what remained of its forest database lay sparsely banked in hedgerows or in woodlots culled for firewood. Fifty years has not been nearly long enough for its recovery. The Georgia woods had not been farmed; the disturbance from which it was recovering had been an episode of logging, also during the war. Despite that seeming devastation, the forest seedbank remained in the soil, and the system had been able to recover.

We left Towne Park past newly bulldozed areas. The forest loam lay heaped, awaiting transport and processing for sale elsewhere as screened topsoil. It was the forest memory, soon to be erased.

And weren't there ants in those heaps? Eggs of worms and beetles? Spores of ferns and fungi? What if the soil is sterilized and sold in bags for houseplants? Where have all the chipmunks gone that burrowed in that earth?

When my computer lost its memory, I spent anxious days wondering what sources I could use to reconstruct what had been lost—old address books and letters, earlier copies of the manuscript, fragmented memories. It turned out that the documents themselves had not been lost, just any way of reaching them. This is the predicament of tree islands. Data once made available through the ecosystem still exist in remnant woods, but access to much of that information has been lost. The common ground Jo Ann has created for her oaks and hickories is detached from the circuitry by which intelligence was once conducted. The system is corrupted.

I hadn't realized until just now, when I was locating Fayetteville in the Ozarks, that my handsome wall map shows the highway system of our land. I guess I was too involved in blue rivers to notice the thin red lines that connect us clear across the mountains and the plains. I could get in my car right now and drive to Arkansas, maybe take Jo Ann a gift of seeds or rhizomes or maybe plants of white wood aster for her archipelago. This is the responsibility that has devolved on us. We're the connections now among isolated trees and groves, the dispersers of forest species.

The sod may have a short memory, but not Jo Ann and I. Why, we go back some sixty years! And we haven't lost our trilliums.

The first birch grove I remember was in a field where my father had planted seedling pines and spruces that even in those days were offered by the government for reforestation. Dad fancied them for Christmas trees and groomed them accordingly. The gray birches, though, came up by themselves. By the time the curried

Christmas trees had grown to cutting size, the birches were grown up and repro-ducing. I suppose by now their fallen trunks lie rotting in oak woods, or maybe the old field is a new development. Trees that grow fast rarely live long, and it's doubt-ful that the birch grove of anybody's childhood can be revisited in old age.

Our Monday walks often take us through acres of black birch, a common species in early woodland succession here. You'd think its botanical name would be Betula nigra, but in the sometimes abstruse parlance of botanical nomencla-ture, that name is reserved for river birch, whose bark is the color of peach ice cream. Black birch is B. lenta, which means "slow" or "tenacious," depending on which botanical word root dictionary you read. No birch is slow, but this one cer-tainly is tenacious in tough places. The bark is actually a rich mahogany, smooth and shiny like the bark of a young cherry. We used to call it sweet birch for its sap, from which Indians made syrup. The twigs taste like wintergreen.

I suggested black birch to Ellen for her grove; it's about as authentic a pioneer as gray birch in New Jersey, but less troubled by pests. She chose river birch instead; she'd seen our own grove of that species. The bark peels in pastel tatters that glow when the sun shines through them like fingers held before a candle.

My favorite of the genus, though, is paper birch, Betula papyrifera. In one grove I know in Maine, the trees' snowy trunks stand knee deep in ferns, and it was this I had in mind when, for our second grove, I bedded birch in bracken. A definite progression of pioneering partners is evident as one travels north. Our usual old-field combo in southern New England and New York is gray birch, B. populifolia (its foliage resembles that of poplars), with red cedar, Juniperus virginiana. Somewhat farther north, gray birch is replaced by paper birch, and its companion is white pine. More northward still, its pioneering partner is red spruce or either of two low, shaggy junipers, J. horizontalis or J. communis.

We didn't set out, as Jo Ann did, to group our trees in islands. We were making gar-dens, and as they grew we joined them. It was practical to connect them with pio-neer communities: they are cheap to plant, easy to establish, and fast to grow. Iris was an island once; now it's linked to the wooded rise we call the mound by an isth-mus of juniper, birch, and sumac bedded in hairgrass, lovegrass, and white flower-ing spurge. The birch and bracken grove was planted to extend the woods, to give the path another turn and destination, but now I see that it could link the grove with a red oak stranded on the lawn and push on past the oak to link the iris garden, too.

We're connecting the dots.

A pattern emerges that is like those optical illusions in which a figure shifts from one object to another. Were I to draw a map of our place, it could be seen two ways: as the openings, the paths we follow, or as the planted ground, the

The smaller of these pictures was taken the day we planted the river birch grove. The larger was taken seven years later, in 1994. (Sara Stein)

Planting Noah's Garden

path the vegetation travels. In Gary Hightshoe's *Native Trees, Shrubs, and Vines for Urban and Rural America,* the whole country is mapped in vegetation paths by figures that show the natural distribution of each species by county across the continent. The biggest continuous gray swath is the path blazed by Populus tremuloides, quaking aspen. The aspens in our woods here loop along that path north into Canada, thence west and south to the aspens in Mike McKeag's Oregon yard, pausing on the way to dip through the Rockies all the way to Arizona. To reach Arkansas, I'd have to take the red cedar or red oak route, or the Sassafras Express. Sassafras would get me to Maine, Georgia, and Michigan, too, and past Arkansas into Oklahoma and Texas. These are trail-blazing species.

I look through a magnifying lens at the gray swaths on Hightshoe's maps: they resolve into printed dots. I count about forty sassafras dots in Jo Ann's county. The entry under "Species; associate" tells me that sassafras moves also with persimmon, pawpaw, hornbeam, hop-hornbeam, sweetgum, sourwood, flowering dogwood, American elm, red cedar, white ash, black locust, hickories, and oaks.

I can't believe now that I had planned to lop the flock of young sassafras cavorting downslope from the oak glade. How could I have been so inhumane? It would have been like mowing down gray squirrels crossing the highway.

*W*e were sitting in the treehouse when the snarling began, on safari with a cocktail above the swimming pool as night fell in the jungle and the beasts came out to prowl. Marty and I had been invited to dinner at Sondra Peterson's wildlife preserve.

When someone claims their property is a wildlife preserve, I am properly skeptical. I have a neighbor who says that of her place, and all she means is that she has a good-size chunk of woodland that isn't managed, never mind that barberry is despoiling the habitat. Anyone in our parts who owns acreage has the wildlife that comes with it: squirrels, chipmunks, skunks, woodchucks, raccoons, possums, rabbits, muskrats, mice, moles, voles, and shrews, along with common woodland birds and far too many deer. Sondra has some twenty wooded acres. Of course she has animals, too.

Yet something in the quiet certainty of her claim caught my attention. It was at the end of that last workshop, when the group that was about to become the Naturals refused to leave. If I didn't then know much about these people, neither did they nor do they now know much about Sondra. She has money, but we don't know where it comes from. She was married once, but we don't know to whom. She has beauty; the rumor is she used to be a model. She is gracious and socially at ease but so reticent on the subject of herself that one leans to believe her words as though they were a secret in a whisper. Still I was a doubter until we walked with her that summer evening in her woods.

We might have been strolling with Saint Francis. "Mrow," she says, and her cat runs up to follow her. "Dee dee," she calls, and chickadees call back. Sondra mimics the calls of many woodland species with such accuracy that, unable to contain their curiosity about this long-legged, brown-clad bird in their territory, they approach to investigate. We passed the vernal pool where wood frogs mate; I'd have liked to hear Sondra converse with them in their one-word banjo tongue, but the pool was dry by then. We saw dead trees where woodpeckers bed, and the swamp where, also in natural hollows, a pair of wood ducks hatch their eggs each spring. Emerging from the woods at the far end of a pond, we saw a large patch of rough-stemmed goldenrod and common milkweed, weedy species that I was about to suggest removing when Sondra proclaimed the place a feeding station for bees and butterflies. At the woodland edge farther along the shore was the deer feeding station, a raised wooden tray replenished with deer chow daily.

This degree of softheartedness toward deer in our overrun area would have seemed to me eccentric, if not downright foolish, were it not that feeding deer was part of a management strategy that in fact had seemed to work out well. The other so-called preserve I know is in bad shape. About the only thing the deer have not eaten is the barberry; they bite off seedling trees as though with loppers; there are no new oaks to replace the old ones when they die. Sondra's woodland was not only clear of invasive aliens but fully clad with lowbush blueberry, mapleleaf viburnum, swamp and pinxter azalea, mountain laurel, and flowering dogwood among tree sprouts and saplings in every stage of growth beneath the rich canopy of parent trees. I shut my mouth.

We continued back toward the house past a planting of dead trees. Red cedars, specifically. To hold native trumpet creeper and honeysuckle vines for hummingbirds. New plantings were everywhere, the result of our group wholesale order the spring before: young dogwoods, viburnums, blueberries, and serviceberries to edge the woods and feed the birds. I was pleased to note that these, at least, were fenced against the deer. Even saints don't wish to tempt the devil.

The swimming pool wasn't chlorinated; the bullfrogs that sometimes share it and the swallows that dip to drink there might be harmed by the chemical. A biological filter system is used instead. Wild turkeys come to the terrace that surrounds this pool for corn during the winter, and it is here that we ended our tour with a climb up to the treehouse with drinks and (vegetarian) canapés.

The treehouse, screened against mosquitoes and comfortable with mats and cushions, overlooks a ledge behind the pool where, beside a pan of fresh water,

A sampling from Sondra's kitchen gallery of animal snapshots, all taken through the windows of her house. Clockwise, from upper left, raccoon, red-bellied woodpecker, deer and turkey, and bullfrog. (Sondra Peterson)

the day's table scraps are put out every evening for the animals. The snarlers that night were a litter of young raccoons squabbling over the tastiest bits. Each year the mother brings the babies here as soon as they are weaned. Once Sondra saw a fox eating from the pan alongside the raccoons. The skunk family didn't appear the night we were there; our scent and voice were unfamiliar to them.

Deer appeared as usual, quite tame, needless to say.

We had supper by candlelight on a small rear terrace that overlooks the pond. Sondra's son Craig and his friend Nadine joined us—shining with idealism, crazy about animals, Bambi lovers, animal rights folks, the sort that couldn't harm a fly. We had found a bluebird dead below the trumpet vine. The just-hatched nestlings, too, would die with only one parent to feed them. They would have to be raised by hand. The local naturalist who collects luna moth cocoons for the pupas' safekeeping (they otherwise are eaten by woodpeckers) had judged Sondra's woodland a suitable habitat for their ultimate release. The first arrival was completing its metamorphosis clothed in netting on a windowsill.

The table was cleared; the plates were scraped.

The snarling subsided. The animals had finished eating and the night was dark as we pulled out of the wildlife preserve and headed home.

We awoke the next morning to a most peculiar sight. A crow was standing on the rim of the granite basin holding in its beak some object that it was repeatedly dipping in the water. It turned out to be a potato chip, from a bowl we'd left out by mistake at lunch the day before. Was it too salty for the crow? Or was it soaking the chip to soften it? Is this behavior common in a crow's repertoire or were we witnessing a remarkable event that could not have occurred in the bird's natural habitat? What is the natural habitat of crows, now that they have lived in fields and parks and yards for so long?

We left our dinner scraps in a pan on the terrace table that night. They all were gone by dawn, before the crows were up. The terrace must be even more inhabited than I had thought. Raccoons or possums would have to be added to my terrace wildlife list. But is this degree of intimacy with wild animals wise?

A week later the dog of another member of the Naturals was bitten by a rabid raccoon. The dog had to be quarantined (and kept incommunicado) at a kennel for the next six months; the owner, splattered with blood and spit, had to undergo a $2,200 series of inoculations. In the same period of time the media reported that deer ticks, whose population increases in proportion to that of deer—and which carry the Lyme disease that had put still another of us out of commission for two years—are now infected with ehrlichiosis, a disease that can cause death.

We don't live in the forest. Even if we wanted to, we couldn't, since by moving into forests we destroy them. Our manner of habitation is compatible with groves of trees patched by prairie like those of oak savanna, with small woods like Sondra's, and with islands and isthmuses by which we may keep routes open among remaining woodland ecosystems. Animals will move along these routes; it is they who will carry the forest seeds—cherries in their bellies and acorns in their cheeks. We have a choice regarding the mammals that have adapted to this suburban compromise. We can either eradicate them—as was recently suggested for raccoons on Long Island and has long been practiced with coyotes—or we can accommodate them.

To the extent that eradication has been successful, it has been ecologically disastrous. Kill the coyotes and suffer the ground squirrels; exterminate the ground squirrels and lose the oaks. The seemingly middle road of live-trapping and moving chipmunks to other woods is not an answer. My friend's woodland garden will soon be replenished by her neighbor's broods; those she moved to other chipmunks' territory will be harassed to a merely slower death. Accommodation is really the only tenable option we have.

But I have become sly like a fox in the wisdom of my age. How better to control the deer population than by slipping birth control hormones into the does' morning chow? How better to administer oral rabies vaccine to raccoons than in their nightly scraps? These are not my private fantasies. Field tests are under way; humane solutions are moving toward our own back yards.

I think Saint Francis would approve.

*T*he last of the Norway maples was taken down last year. We had the branches chipped and used the chips to mulch the bracken in the birch grove. I knew not even poisoned chips could discourage that aggressive fern. Now I know better.

I know so much by now that words would ooze from my ears if I didn't spill them onto paper. But I have an awful time recalling when sagacity started or how it came about. Wisdom is like trees: it grows, but imperceptibly.

Can it be that we carried the beech tree to its present site in a wheelbarrow? That was, I think, during our youngest son's junior year in high school; now he and his wife have just had their first baby and the tree is having nuts. If it weren't for before and after snapshots of our first pioneer planting, I wouldn't believe how small the birch trees were the day we planted them; the saplings have grown to nearly thirty feet in these seven years. Sugar maples once the size of bean poles now amply shade the courtyard where we park the car. They were the last trees we had planted for us when we built the house, eighteen years ago. Since then we've planted by ourselves a whole woods, every layer of it, trees to ferns. That's in a corner behind the pond, over the bridge to the left, past the wet meadow, beyond the blueberries.

In the days when Rose and Iris lived apart from one another and each was surnamed Garden, Marty might say, "The roses have aphids," and I knew just where to look. Now, if he says, "The roses are blooming," I have to ask whether he means the ones in the swamp, or along the pond shore to the right below the switchgrass, or on the rise to the left before the inlet bridge, or the ones raised from cuttings and still waiting to be moved from the former vegetable garden. Confusion has grown like the bushes we planted to edge the woods, has spread with the meadows we sowed for the land's reunification. This blending of the varied habitats that now defies articulate nomenclature was a project we began to work on ten years ago. I was fifty then; Marty was fifty-five.

That seems late to start something so ambitious, but one has more time in middle age, with the children grown and gone. One's sense of responsibility has developed a fine patina. It wouldn't have occurred to me as a young wife fretting in the woods to plant a white oak as a near-immortal legacy to the twenty-sixth century, five hundred years from now.

I was thinking of doing that next spring. A big tree, I was thinking: Quercus alba, maybe fifteen feet, three-inch caliper, balled and burlapped, to accompany the other white oak on the mound and replace the Norway maple. The rootball on a tree that size is very heavy. No problem. We are so accomplished now, so learned and efficient. I pictured us driving to the rewholesale yard in our new black pickup, to be delivered this Thanksgiving. I'd ride the maw of the front-end loader like real landscapers do, select the white oak from its block with stunning expertise. And, home again, I and Marty, now of the sixties generation, would urge it up the mound on planks and logs with prybars—cleverly, knowingly—to plant as a reminder to coming generations of what they ought to do.

I can't remember how I became fluent enough in the language of size and species to buy like landscapers, who travel in trucks loaded with instant yards. I know I used to feel uncomfortable buying without a business card at my rewholesale yard. But I used to feel uncomfortable, too, if my hem hung crooked or my children had a tantrum on the street. It wasn't so long ago that I felt uncomfortable when people took me for a gardener. It's only six months ago that I shucked my nervous butterflies on the calm and friendly prairies of Wisconsin. What you do, if you learn to do it well, you eventually become, and I'm as much a landscaper now as any pro. Or I will be when I get the truck.

Or so I was thinking as I preened the fantasy of the marvelous white oak.

Planting Noah's Garden

Of course my elders at ALFASAC had the ill grace to inform me that the white oak already growing on the mound was, in fact, a swamp oak.

There is no end to one's continuing education. No degree is offered. One never graduates. My own course of study reminds me of a story tough Alma of the Naturals teases me with when she thinks me boastful. It's one her ancient father used to tell again and again. The punch line is, "and humble, too."

But neither Alma nor her father can remember any longer what the story was.

Our little blue-stem meadow in June. The grass is less than a foot high, and the only flower blooming this early in the season is foxglove penstemon, Penstemon digitalis. (Sara Stein)

Planting Noah's Garden

14 *Little Bluestem Meadow*

W E SET OUT FOR MAINE at dawn on the last day of July with our new dog, Girl, and our old cat, William, left behind our little bluestem meadow, green and flowery; passed fields of grass gone to hay, cut or baled; arrived that afternoon to find the front lawn abloom with opium.

I didn't know what the flowers were, just that they were poppies and had not been there before. A curtain drain had been installed over the winter, and the lawn was a wreck. The poppies grew from the wreckage, among the chunks of granite churned up by the backhoe.

I had brought with me Anne Raver's book *Deep in the Green*, a compilation of her articles for *Newsweek* and the *New York Times*. I read two chapters that night, another two over coffee in the morning. You can't read this book fast; it jerks the heart too much. You have to stop either laughing or crying to turn the page. I didn't get to Chapter Ten, "Forbidden Poppies," until another day had passed.

"Pale lavender," writes Raver, and "deep wine." Smooth leaves, drooped buds that unbend at night to open suddenly when no one is watching them. I'd thought opium poppies were red, like the poppy field in Oz. These were the color of Easter eggs. It occurred to me that on this island, seafarers lie rooted in every family tree.

I called a leading member of our island garden club. She couldn't confirm my suspicion but referred me to two other experienced gardeners. One had had poppies of this description in her garden for thirty-seven years, all offspring of a few seeds once given her by a neighbor. The other recalled them from her mother's garden; she placed the date at least sixty years earlier. Neither knew their full name. They just called them poppies.

I called Polly Law. I thought that if there were a flower of wine and lavender with pods as pale as milk glass, she'd be the one to know about it.

Polly knew; she grows the poppies, opium poppies, Papaver somnifera.

It's no mystery to me that the 'Fiesta Brava' peonies that I tried for years to mow to death on that front lawn survived on their fat rootstocks, which must now be as big as legs underground. But that poppy seeds outlive people's recollection of the flower's identity, that they reappear in disturbed ground as fresh as the first ones brought home, perhaps, by a sea captain in the days of sailing ships, seems both exciting and perverse. One can't know, looking at a lawn or field, what resurrection might be waiting there. But how disappointing that this most familiar dirt recalled an exotic and not its natural heritage. Nothing but garden annuals came up in the backhoe's trace.

A friend told me that an acquaintance of his, a Britisher, had been awarded the stewardship of an English field that is part of the National Trust. It is his responsibility to see that it is mowed properly and on schedule, as it has been for a thousand years.

A thousand years.

My friend has seen the field. He says it blooms twice—early, before the haying season, and again with different species before it is mowed a second time, later in the summer. I suppose the early flowers include the European Shirley poppy, P. rhoeas, which turns English fields bright red in June and also proliferates in our island gardens. I imagine the later crop of bloom includes those flowers so common along Maine roadsides in August that islanders think of them as native: chicory, cheeses, yarrow, tansy. Give our flowers a millennium of such regimentation and perhaps they, too, will adapt their timing to the mowing schedule. Or perhaps the history of English hayfields is the opposite: mowing customs for all that time accommodated the wild habits of the plants.

Or, again, it might be that unaccommodating grassland species that grew in England's green and pleasant land a thousand years ago became extinct.

The Nature Conservancy has one mission: to preserve vanishing species. It is this organization that, through its Natural Heritage Program and with the cooperation of state conservation departments, locates and maps rare plant populations and prepares lists of protected species. Much of its effort is aimed toward buying whole habitats where the endangered system itself may be protected. The rare northern blazingstar, Liatris borealis—the one I want that no one sells the seed for—grows in Maine on the Kennebec Plains under the protection of the Nature Conservancy. The Federally Endangered sandplain gerardia, Agalina acuta, is known to exist still in only eleven locations worldwide. Six of these sites are on Long Island; one is the remnant Hempstead Plains.

I had imagined the Hempstead Plains all wrong. "Plains" is such a big word, so flat and broad, so open and expansive. I knew it was just a scrap of eastern prairie in sandy soil on Long Island that originally had measured four miles wide by sixteen miles long—sixty thousand acres compared to today's forty-acre parcel. I'd also been told that the remnant is in two pieces: one a public park belonging to Nassau County, the other the private preserve managed by the Nature Conservancy. The Nassau County Department of Parks and Recreation warned me that its half was overgrown with shrubs and trees. Marilyn Jordan, the stewardship ecologist for the Nature Conservancy portion, mentioned that the disturbed periphery on its half is invaded by weeds, though the center is still fairly well preserved. I was trying to arrange a visit to this better half. Although the first possible date was a month away, Dr. Jordan sent me a map. It floored me.

Hempstead Plains, the last remaining indigenous tallgrass prairie east of the Alleghenies, is squeezed between a golf course and a sports arena on a community college campus surrounded by city streets for miles in all directions.

I can't think why I expected otherwise, except for the knee-jerk imagory of "plains." Even on the Central Plains, where a four-mile-wide strip of grassland would amount to less than a snail trail on a freeway, remnant prairie is a patch along a railroad right-of-way or a back corner of a cemetery. It may be that cultural and natural history were in concord in Old England; they were certainly out of whack around here.

The colonists first used the Hempstead Plains as a common upon which, according to one Daniel Denton in 1670, "grows very fine grass, that makes exceeding good Hay, and is very good pasture for sheep or other Cattel." It's the natural history of American grasslands to be grazed, but before the European settlement, the grazers of the Hempstead Plains were bison, not cows. There's a big difference. Bison don't chew in the same place all summer like cows in the pasture; they don't crop the grass to the ground like sheep. European pasture grasses survive intensive grazing by growing sideways, just as their lawn descendants do. Our bunchgrasses never learned evasion.

But it was cultural, not natural, history that dictated how the settlers conceived the eastern prairie. The bias is deeply rooted in the English language: grass, according to the dictionary, is "green herbage that affords food for grazing animals." The Old English word is "græs"; one may "grass" as well as graze a cow, says Webster.

The dictionary says to see more at "grow"—apparently its root and that of "grass" are related. "Grow" means "to spring up and come to maturity." Grass may do that in the thirsty desert when at last it rains, but as for our native bluestem meadow, it sleepily disagrees. No tallgrass type can be described as "springing up." American prairie is slow even to peek out of the covers. My friend who knows the British steward raises cows. They have been out to pasture for a month before our meadow lifts a blade. As for "coming to maturity," prairie grasses take from May to November to finish their reproductive business, and that's just counting their seasonal cycle, not the three years it took them to mature from seed. Our mother tongue seems to speak of racier phenomena than the lazy pace of prairie.

I turned next to "spring" and learned something really startling: the American spring is the months of March, April, and May. In England it's February, March, and April. By that calendar, prairie species spring in summer.

That the English were astonished to note that a cow lying down was lost to view suggests their innocence of tallgrass prairie. People got lost on the Hempstead Plains; they couldn't see where they were going over the grass. The remnant is not that tall; presumably big bluestem and Indian grass, which top five feet at least, were once a much larger component than they are now. One can only guess at how such a shift might have come about, but a shift in cultural history seems likely.

The Indians regularly burned tallgrass prairie—evidently with even greater frequency than lightning naturally sets dry grass afire—and for a while the settlers followed their example. But they seem not to have fully appreciated the different risks involved for moving Indians and settled townspeople. In 1658 a large fire threatened the Town of Hempstead, and thereafter legislation was enacted to prevent farmers from "wantonly" burning. Later documents record fees paid for fighting fires, fines levied for setting illegal fires, and procedures to be followed for legal burning to increase the hay crop.

Haying, of course, was not in the natural history of the Hempstead Plains. The town set a date after which grass could be cut for hay: July 25.

Native tallgrass species on the Hempstead Plains are little bluestem, big bluestem, switchgrass, and Indian grass. They all grow in our meadows, too, and I can tell you that in late July they are just beginning to stalk out, and not at all prepared to go to hay. The alien grasses that now contaminate the Hempstead Plains are redtop and bluegrass, two of the many pasture sorts that arrived here both accidentally and on purpose with the European settlers. Could it be that these were what was meant by "hay"?

Pasture grasses differ from prairie grasses as fundamentally as cows differ from bison. The European species that usually inhabit what homeowners refer to as their field or meadow evolved in a reliably moist and moderate climate and at higher latitudes than our prairie ones; their natural history accords well with what to Americans is England's off-season calendar.

I never had understood the Shakespearean Midsummer Night, which falls on June 21, the summer solstice and, to my astronomical mind, the *first* day of the season. But if the English summer begins on May Day and extends for a quarter of the year, then summer ends on August 1, and the solstice is about as middling a summer date as the heavens will allow.

The immigrant sheep fescue on our terrace goes along with this schedule. Like other cool-season grasses of European origin, it springs up in the English spring, matures come the English summer, and by two weeks after Midsummer Night has gone to seed. Thereafter, and in preparation for the English autumn on the first of August, the seeds harden on the stalk, and the plant is prepared to suffer the reaper if it must.

On the terrace the whole plant, blades as well as stalks, shuts down like an unwatered lawn for the remainder of the summer: *our* summer, under our stronger and more constant sunlight, our harsher drought, our heat waves that leave cool-season species gasping for air through gaping pores, dehydrating through sweating leaves, dying that brief death called dormancy. The brown fields we pass on the way to Maine in August are dormant.

The grasses in our meadows, though, are green, and the flowers have just begun to bloom. These prairie plants are warm-season species. Their natural history is different, and so is the chemistry and physiology they evolved in coping with their difficult home climate. They don't suffocate in bright light; they don't gasp; they don't dehydrate. They squint their pores against the heat and keep on growing. If I wanted to hay our little bluestem meadow after all the species had ripened their seed and prepared for winter dormancy, I'd have to wait 'til Halloween.

Halloween—All Hallow's Eve—marked the New Year on Old England's agricultural calendar. Refreshed meadows were green and growing then, like turfgrass in October.

No doubt disharmony between cultural and natural history would have doomed the Hempstead Plains even if it had not been so dangerously close to New York City, so attractive to commerce as potential truck garden and then as commercial district and residential suburb. In time, what with the cows and the scythes and the firefighters, the Hempstead Plains would have become what most eastern meadows are—Old World pastureland and hayfield, not New World prairie.

In the event, progress was much faster. "If the whole of this open waste was disposed of and inclosed in separate fields," predicted *Thompson's History of Long Island* in 1843, "the agricultural products of this portion of the island would be nearly doubled. A stupid policy, consequent upon old prejudice, has hitherto prevented any other disposition of it, than as a common pasturage. It is hoped the time is not far distant, when this extensive tract shall abound in waving fields of grain, yielding not only support, but profit, to thousands of hardy and industrious citizens."

Thompson's hope was soon realized. "Two yokes of cattle or a team of three horses are required to break it up," wrote Winslow Watson to describe the plowing of the thick prairie sod in 1860, when sixty thousand acres of the plains were thus arduously reduced to twelve thousand. Garden City, the utopian prototype for early suburbia, took ninety-five hundred more acres nine years later. Early in this century, other huge tracts of this "open waste" were "disposed of" in the Cradle of Aviation: Hempstead, Mineola, Garden City, Hazelhurst, Curtiss, Roosevelt, and Mitchel fields all lie on the Plains (the preserve is entered from Charles Lindbergh Boulevard). Much of the rest became not grain but potato fields, and they were gobbled up by Levittown, the suburb that in 1947 became the model for postwar tract housing. Now there remains just that one scrap of sod in the maze of commercial and residential development that crushes it to near oblivion on the map.

I saw the Plains on a drizzly day in fall with its keeper, Dr. Jordan, and her young daughter Claire. It is a melancholy place. Marilyn opened a padlock to let us through the chain-link fence and along a path through thirty feet of that rank growth of ragweed and mugwort that chain fences everywhere seem to attract. The interior was more open, sandy, sparse, slightly rolling, crusted with patches of moss and lichens, nowhere lush, beautiful but sad in buff and copper, laced with pale skeletons of wild indigo, and here and there a milkweed pod spilling its damp silk. We found the sandplain gerardia.

It was growing in a protective cage of chicken wire on the high side of the enclosure, with a view across the sand to an old air field, which explains why there still is any Plains at all, for this nineteen acres was just a neglected edge that no

Our "meadow" in Maine, about mid-July. The grass has already ripened seed and is well on its way to summer dormancy. The few flowers are agricultural weeds at the end of their blooming period. The grass will be hay for the rest of the summer, and no other flowers will bloom. (Fred Pillsbury)

one needed. One precious Agalina was in bloom. Six inches high, the flower was minute, magenta, and rather intricate in shape. Marilyn had to pick it. The Conservatory herbarium lacked a specimen. Soon a squadron of police cars began to roar and screech over the landing field. It's where they practice high-speed chase.

We went across the boulevard to the county portion of the Plains, which is quite different: treed with red oak and pitch pine and hillier, its hollows filled with blueberries, huckleberries, and sumac. Large swaths had been burned; this was curious because scheduled burns are problematical in this location. The law forbids burning on weekends or at any time that the wind could carry smoke across Meadowbrook Parkway, just a block away, or toward a nearby old age home. And, when all conditions can be met, the fire must be doused every fifty minutes so students at the college may change classes smokelessly.

The fires had been started by homeless people camping on the Hempstead Plains.

I've become a meadow watcher. A field behaviorist. A grasser. There's no other way to learn their natural history and therefore how to treat them. The study sometimes has proved discouraging, as when I watched my neighbor's field go to vines and thorns and finally succumb to mile-a-minute during its years of neglect. But sometimes it has been a delight, as when this spring I witnessed Caliban's twin field on the other side of the old farm road arise like Ariel from three years beneath the mower.

Any such meadowed area on former agricultural land is called "old field," the general term used to describe grassy spaces that previously were farmed. The term doesn't imply any particular suite of vegetation, like terms describing native grassland ecosystems such as "shortgrass prairie" or "salt marsh meadow." An old field may be entirely alien, like ours in Maine that, when we mow it, passes for a lawn. Or it may be a mix, like a quackgrass field I've kept an eye on where equally aggressive native species—common milkweed, smooth sumac, rough-stemmed goldenrod—have held their own. Only rarely is there a preponderance of native species, such as the broomsedge or little bluestem grass that may occupy old fields on barren ground. The composition depends on the kind of soil, the amount of moisture, what seed was in the ground at the time of the field's abandonment, how it was used previously, and how it has been treated since.

My neighbor's twin fields, separated only by the wagonway that runs between them from what had been the farmyard to what is now our pond, were as alike as old fields can be when we first saw them eighteen years ago.

232   *Planting Noah's Garden*

They slope downhill from Long Ridge, the high road along which the farmhouse and barns originally stood, then level out to mucky bottomland drenched in the spring and moist all through the summer. The upper portions had been typical dry pasture—a rather fine grass, perhaps Kentucky blue, studded with similarly European clovers, buttercups, and daisies which, like the grass, bespeak their pastoral history by spreading along shallow runners through the sod.

The wet portions were more American. Flag iris bloomed in the spring; swamp milkweed flowered later in the summer. The north field, the one that is now overgrown, had a little pond with pussy willows around it.

I came to know the old farmer who was hired to mow these fields annually years ago. He was in his eighties and not on anybody's schedule. He mowed "whenever"—whenever the ground firmed up, whenever the days cooled down, whenever he felt like it. The owner at that time wanted only to keep her meadows free of brush.

Then she stopped mowing the north field. Finally, she sold the land.

The next owner also left the north field neglected—mile-a-minute arrived during his brief tenure—but took to mowing the south field as though it were a lawn. (*Clank-clank* went the Saturday ritual; "They're mowing the rocks again," Marty would note.) That regime lasted for three years, until last spring, when the soggy soil burst into such a spangle of blue-eyed grass that I felt I was looking back through time at this dainty iris relative, growing like stars in the meadow of my childhood frog pond. Flag iris had also survived, and two-flowered Cynthia, and a brilliant tapestry of sedges and rushes in the grass. The swamp milkweed was gone, though.

The upper portion of the field seemed not to have changed at all. Maybe it couldn't tell the difference between a sheep and a lawnmower. Ginny Weinland, the doyenne of ALFASAC and a professional wildflower photographer, showed me a slide of a meadow much like it, dressed in June pastels of daisy, buttercup, and clover blooming in unison with the grass. Such fields may have been in place for a century or longer and possibly could go on and on that way if treated in an Old Country fashion. I imagine, if I had a field like that, I wouldn't interfere with its natural tendencies except, with Caliban lurking so close across the farm road, maybe give it two more mowings past the haying season to check young bittersweet and roses.

Ginny didn't have any photos in her vast collection to match the sedge meadow that came up where swamp milkweed had dominated during the years the fields were mowed annually and whenever.

Since almost all the species in this wetland, both previous and present, are native, the question arose why an American type of grassland had survived a century of grazing or haying while the drier portion of the field was alienated. Yet why had the milkweed not survived a three-year stint of regular mowing? And what could explain not just the presence of blue-eyed grass—for surely some had been there all along—but its starry multitude, a galaxy in blue?

I don't think cattle graze much on sharp sedge and bitter milkweed; even muskrats, who try their very best to eat everything I offer, have left these two alone. The old farmer, however idiosyncratic his schedule, didn't risk his heavy tractor in the spongy soil until August anyhow, and often he didn't get around to mowing until fall. I wasn't watching closely enough in those days to notice whether swamp milkweed, a warm-season species, had released its seed by then, but it wouldn't have mattered much if it hadn't. Parent colonies of this species spread vegetatively by rhizomes; the tufted seeds are meant to start new colonies where the wind may take them. Treating them as lawn, though, deprived them of the foliage needed to stuff their roots with starch, so during that three-year period they died.

The remaining vegetation—sedges, rushes, and the several flowers—was in bloom or beyond that June when I first saw it. Checking in again during July, I found that it had finished setting seed and was beginning to ripen. I figured this must be a cool-season community, a native wetland group whose moist natural history never required the water conservation tactics that evolved on high ground or under less reliable conditions. Though some weeks behind the drier upper portion, the lowland could have coped with the old farmer's sooner or later ways. No sexual timing, however, could explain surviving three years beneath the mower, for, as my poacher's spade revealed, none of these species had the crabwise habit of vegetative evasion. Much less did there leap to mind any obvious reason why blue-eyed grass had arisen from the mower in such celestial abundance.

Searching for a clue, I looked up Sisyrinchium, the genus of blue-eyed grass, in Dr. Deno's germination guide. His generic advice was: "Light and outdoor conditions should be tried." I could see why. The results of his experiments with this species, S. angustifolium, had been no germination at all in the dark under any temperature regime and only desultory and sparse germination in light under the simple temperature regimes he tried. He must have guessed—and the shorn meadow seemed to verify—that blue-eyed grass seed is prepared to wait out however many seasons among taller wetland species for whatever natural or gas-driven disaster gives it at last its own place in the sun. That's all the sedges in the resurrected meadow in Maine had been waiting for in the shadow of the spruces that finally blew down. Most, and possibly all, of this lush growth could have come up from seed as opportunistically as opium in a backhoe's wake.

Or I may be spinning tales as fantastical as those the drug induces. I have at my disposal for such detective work no more than most people have: some books, two eyes, a spade. I can only imagine, watching others' meadows, what I would do or not do and guess what then might happen.

When we left for Maine last summer, the new owner of the twin fields, moved in just four weeks earlier, was working his way downhill with a weed-whacker through the dry hay toward his wetland Ariel. He reached it too soon; the

Ariel, the wet meadow that arose from the mowed side of my neighbor's twin fields. The starry flowers in the tapestry of sedges and rushes are blue-eyed grass, Sisyrinchium angustifolium, an iris relative. (Sara Stein)

seeds weren't ripe. If Ariel were mine, I would have watched and waited.

A few feet beyond our common boundary wall, in the same muck soil as his, our own less dainty wet meadow was in full bloom with ironweed, boneset, Joe-Pye weed, Turk's cap lily, Culver's root, and sweet black-eyed Susan. He could have them all for free; the breeze would blow their seed to him. All he'd have to do is keep the whacker in the shed until about November—much later than the old farmer used to mow and when even our New England asters have fluffed their windborne seed—and rake the litter off next March, just when lawns are raked clean of winter debris. That way, the ground would be open to the blue-eyed grass in the spring but available also for the taller, slower, summer sorts to repopulate.

I watched that happen in our swamp in a smallish clearing among red maples where the outlet stream from the pond divides into a maze of rivulets. The area had become overgrown with multiflora roses. I don't know when they started to take over; I wasn't watching in those days. By the time we noticed them, they were a head-high thicket that shaded the ground completely. We cleared them out in the fall. The following spring there appeared in their place

Caliban, the other of the twin fields, after a decade of neglect. Mile-a-minute grows in the foreground; its straw from the previous year still clings among the grapevines beyond. The multiflora rose that supports the grapevine, and the vine itself, would have been blanketed in mile-a-minute by summer's end if it had not been killed. (Sara Stein)

Planting Noah's Garden

cattails, tussock sedge, flag iris, tall meadowrue, swamp rose, marsh fern, and a gorgeous stand of milkweed.

But there also appeared purple loosestrife, Lythrum salicaria. If it's not one weed, it's another.

This one could eliminate by its aggressive growth all the other species, as rough-stemmed goldenrod (Solidago rugosa) attempted to do in our wet meadow, as mugwort (Artemesia vulgaris) is doing at the edges of the Hempstead Plains, as the Japanese knotweed (Polygonum cuspidatum) perched on my neighbor's hill may well do even to his well-established European hayfield if it aims its thirty-foot-a-season rhizomes in that direction. He ought to dig a bit to observe its root behavior. The art of meadow management requires a continuing curiosity about new plants that arrive.

But my neighbor must be peculiarly incurious. Can you imagine buying five acres of land, occupying it for a month, and not exploring it? He had not, until we showed it to him, ventured into his nightmare field.

I must say he was suitably appalled and perfectly cooperative with the government authorities when they came with sprayers to kill the mile-a-minute—but perfectly innocent, as well, of what he ought to do next. A cover crop, he thought aloud as a tentacle of bittersweet reached toward him eagerly. Maybe a wildflower meadow mix, he mused, standing inches from the clutches of a gigantic multiflora rose. He could sow this fall, he thought, kicking at the ground which, invisibly, was already percolating with mile-a-minute's ripe and purple fruit.

What should I have said? The truth? The truth is that there are many kinds of old field that can be improved by changes in management, the control of invasive species, or the introduction of additional ones by seed or transplant.

The truth is that Caliban should be put to death.

When I first saw the house in Maine, I thought the grass was a meadow, so I made a fool of myself like any summer jerk by having a tractor hay it. On a tiny lot, on a village street, where all the houses are white.

It turns out the meadow was a lawn, the same kind everyone else has, but let go. There's not a big market on the island for lawn seed; people just mow what grows, as people used to. Lawns when I was little had all sorts of things growing in them—plantains, hawkweeds, clovers. We sometimes stepped on thistles in the grass.

The grass on the island lot is mostly quackgrass, what my father used to call "witchgrass" because of the sharp, mean way it claws through gardens. There's some timothy, too, and ryegrass. The reason we had to use a backhoe to dig a curtain drain is that, the year before, a backhoe we'd had in to dig a hole for a septic tank broke the water line and the backhoe we had in to fix the water line broke the curtain drain that someone built a hundred years ago. That was the granite wreckage that surfaced in the latest digging, where the opium poppies grow.

The other two episodes in this digging history are visible, too. A line of Queen Anne's lace marks the route of the water line. A patch of sow thistle shows where the hole for the septic tank was dug. We put in a vegetable garden years and years ago. That's where the goutweed, another remnant of some former tenant's garden, grows in rectangular formation. Daylilies indicate where the edge of the driveway used to be before it unaccountably chose its own route from the street. A lack of any recent history other than neglect is marked by alder thickets.

Really, nothing in the yard appeals to my sensibilities except the pitch pines we planted and some wild roses that, now that I think about it, must have been responsible for nudging the driveway over. My dissatisfaction is shared. The only butterflies interested in the landscape are cabbage whites laying eggs on mustard weeds. In a day's drive, we trade a zillion singing birds for yammering gulls and shags. I like them fine, but I miss the wrens and robins. Why, under the porch roof and in the open barn, have no swallows built their nests? How come I can leave dog chow over the winter and the mice don't eat it? Every year, that first evening back home in September, I'm startled by the loudness of crickets and katydids after a month of silent nights.

It's not that the island lacks wildlife. Berry thickets burst with birds; monarchs emerge by the thousands in the fall. But they're out there somewhere in unkempt and unpeopled places, and I've gotten used to having lunch with animals in my own back yard. Only yellow jackets come to lunch with us in Maine.

My mistake in thinking the grass around the house was a meadow turned out to be more than just the social error it seemed at first. It was an ecological misunderstanding, the same one I discovered to be general during my year of traveling. By then, when I said "meadow," I was picturing our little bluestem meadow in New York. My audience was picturing a hayfield or an unmowed lawn and must have thought, as I once did, that all grasslands come with butterflies and birds.

They don't. The foreign portion of my neighbor's field comes only with the same cabbage whites that come with let-go lawns in Maine. I should have used the ecological term "eastern prairie." "Prairie" fits the grassland I had in mind when I was speaking, and prairies do come with all I spoke about.

"I look out my kitchen window over a dividing line of sorts," began a portion of my standard speech, "to one side, the lawn, just lying there looking green; to the other side, the little bluestem meadow, exuberant with life." I wasn't exaggerating. Even from a distance this native grassland is animated by butterflies and swallows. Hundreds of dragonflies and darning needles glint like jewels above it. The grass bows to the breeze; close up, it jerks to the kick of grasshoppers. A brush of the hand sends up a flurry of leafhoppers. Every flower is attended, some by aphids and their guardian ants, some by tiny gold and emerald flies and pollinating wasps, some by bumblebees, many by butterflies. Last summer one notably generous milkweed spent days doling meals to great spangled fritillaries, ten to a sitting.

Even at night one turns to hear the crickets and see the fireflies. Fall brings flocks of finches for the ripe grain and flower seeds and crops of mice and voles as well—or so I gather from the hawk parked on a hickory limb above the scattered sunflowers and from the fox that hunts the field in winter.

In the meantime and all the time, day and night in every season, the lawn just lies there, empty.

But the trouble with putting the contrast this way is that "dividing line" sounds like the mere physical difference between cutting grass and letting it grow. In fact, I had opened a marital wasps' nest. Half the women in America, it seems, want to let the grass grow, and half the men—their husbands—don't. I can resolve that argument forthwith. It doesn't matter. It will not in either case revive one's land.

The boundary of our neighbor's field and ours is the critical one. It looks like just a rubble wall, but climbing over it from his side to ours you pass abruptly into another time zone: American time.

Butterfly time, bird time, bee time, mouse time: native flora comes with native fauna because their seasons coincide.

The first monarchs appear in July, when the butterflyweed flashes into orange bloom. This is the earliest milkweed on our place. Swamp milkweed has just come into bloom when we leave for Maine, blunt-leaved follows shortly after. By then

A monarch in intimate contact with the milkweed Asclepias tuberosa, butterflyweed. (Virginia P. Weinland)

the monarchs have multiplied considerably. The milkweeds have finished blooming when the monarch population reaches its fall peak. That's the only generation that doesn't need to find its host plant, since it will not lay eggs until the following spring. What it needs is fuel for its migration. That's when goldenrods and asters bloom in such profusion.

Old fields look like fools to me in fall, decked in green to celebrate their obsolescent new year just as ours is bedding down for blizzards. Tallgrass prairie rises from June ripples, swells through summer into a great wave that, cresting in September, frothed with flowers, tipping under its weight of seed, slowly subsides to wash its countless offspring gently on their way, the mice to their grain-stocked burrows, the bees to their honeyed hollows, the fattened birds south to their winter homes with the north wind at their backs and the grass turned to copper in the lowering sun.

The wave deposits in its wake the riches nourished by its growth. I like to show visitors the misunderstood dividing line: to one side the lawn in hard dirt; to the other side the prairie in soft earth. Both were sowed at the same time in the same soil, a dense, inorganic clay dredged from the bottom of the pond. Now the difference is one the prairie has made for itself by rooting several feet deep instead of the few inches turfgrasses penetrate, by adding tonnage of organic matter to the soil instead of the light clippings lawns contribute, and by nourishing a rich zoology underground that can't thrive below the shallow roots of pasturage or lawn.

The little bluestem prairie is five years old now; it had all been lawn before. I knew vaguely when I sowed it that grassland would be better: less work at least, since no one has to water it or feed it, and nonpolluting, since it needs neither lawnmower nor pesticides. And certainly prettier to my eye and livelier. What I didn't know is that such a planting, designed to contain one's favorite forbs and grasses selected from a catalog, soon takes on a life of its own. I had chosen little bluestem grass: big bluestem, Indian grass, and purple top arrived by themselves. I had chosen milkweeds specifically to increase the monarch population, only to discover that the meadow was raising broods of skippers, too.

This sort of thing is happening everywhere we planted native grassland. We never planted monkey flower; it appeared on its own down toward the pond where dryland species give way to wetland ones. We had a single specimen of Culver's root up by the house; this year half a dozen plants joined the blue lobelia at the shore. I killed alien purple loosestrife last summer; this summer native yellow loosestrife filled the gaps.

You can't plan this sort of thing. I can't even find in my insect guide more than a few of the dozens of species of darning needle and dragonfly we see, much less guess why the one with amber wings flies upland and the one in velvet black flits low among the tussock sedges in the swamp, or which of the countless other insect species are their primary prey. I know their young must dine hugely on mosquito larvae: we haven't had to put up screens for years.

I asked a lepidopterist for a few words about the skippers and got a paragraph. Little bluestem, the grass we planted, is a larval food plant for swarthy, dusted, Indian, cobweb, and crossline skippers as well as common wood-nymph. Purple top, a grass that planted itself, feeds zabulon and crossline skippers and little glassywings. How could anyone plan for the exact species of ant that, in return for sweets the caterpillars provide, protect the larvae of gossamer-wings from predators?

Among the riches the prairie tide leaves in its wake each year are the surviving insects that will emerge the following spring to rebuild their populations in time to feed predatory dragonflies and their mosquito-greedy young, bass and bullfrogs, bats and swallows, the black and yellow argiope that spins her web on the terrace, and all those gaping mouths in the birdhouses Marty built. One can build a birdhouse and hang seed and suet to help designated species through the winter, but no one can plan for all the niches of a grassland habitat in which each insect species' eggs, larvae, or adults overwinter. The only practical way to proceed is to plant the habitat itself and let it sort out the details.

This, too, is a hard point to get across. The problem is the slides, the flowers, the gardening mind-set. Show gardeners shocking purple ironweed set off by ashy boneset, clumps of flaming butterflyweed or lacy meadowrue, and they will want to have them. And, halfway converted to the ecological view, they will want to have them growing in the grass, the grass they have already, the old field or the lawn let go.

I am so sorry. You cannot have your hayfield and your meadow lilies, too.

I'm sorry for myself. I can't plant New England aster in our island yard; the quackgrass will gobble up its space. I can't sow a prairie grass; the earlier grass will shade it out before it sees the sun. No mowing schedule will discourage the growth already there; it will be lawn, or it will be old field, or it will grow up in alders. I have no hope of resurrection. The digging we have done has shown what seeds lie hidden in the soil. Growing opium is against federal law.

So I will kill it off like Caliban and start again.

My heart beats with the thought. My mind is stuck on it. We're in Maine.

Marty is building a model of a tiny new barn to replace the decrepit one where swallows don't nest. The dining table here, as at home, is covered with his drawings. He's worried mostly that he might run out of rock works to keep him busy if, as the plan is now, we retire here someday. He's planned what seems to me a mile or so of granite retaining walls. On a drawing of the house (bigger bathroom for the old folks, better kitchen), he's added a sunroom where I can grow seeds.

I awoke with the cat at 4:00 A.M. That's William's time for hunting Friskies Fancy Feast Savory Salmon. I had coffee with Girl, the dog, and *Maine's Natural Heritage*, which was no help. Neither of them: Girl nagged me to go back to bed to keep her warm; the book told me all about rare flora.

I'm looking for the common community, the coastal grassland that probably no more exists here than does eastern prairie in New York. Driving up along the turnpike, the last wisp of little bluestem seems to give out in southern Maine, where white oak, white pine, and shagbark hickory give way to red spruce and balsam fir. I don't even know the basic *grass*, for heaven's sake.

Suddenly I feel lonely. I know my little bluestem so well; knew it from childhood. My father called Schizachyrium scoparius "poverty grass," a name traditionally given to several unrelated species that inhabit sterile ground. It's not that little bluestem "wants" poor soil—just that it can eke out a living where others can't. In my father's day, little bluestem indicated worn-out plowland no longer able to support a crop of corn. Those are the circumstances in which I see it on the way to Ellen's house along Route 1 in New Jersey. The same species waved to me from old apple orchards in the foothills of the Blue Ridge of Virginia, greeted me familiarly from Milwaukee yards, conversed with me about its ancient history on the Hempstead Plains, and kept in touch with me all through our mowing days at home from rocky outcrops too dry for other vegetation. Not about to go away. Just reminding me, in its congenial way, of its willingness.

Books say little bluestem is our commonest and most widespread prairie bunchgrass, occurring from the Atlantic coast to the Rocky Mountains, on both shortgrass and tallgrass prairie, and from Texas north into Canada. I looked again through Steve Rothe's snapshots of his urban Omaha yard, where mice harvest blazingstars and monarchs find New England asters. *He* has little bluestem. But I can't find it on this island, fifteen miles out to sea.

I took a three-day grass class one year at the New York Botanical Garden. The teacher, a grower from California, showed a grassy glade similar to midwestern oak savanna and planted, if I recall correctly, with California fescue. Judith Lowry lists in the Larner Seeds catalog twenty-six native western grasses, from a rare bottlebrush to a delicious vanilla grass. There is no such nursery in Maine.

The state doesn't have a native plant society. Or a newsletter like "Growing

Native" that my California pen pal, Louise Lacey, publishes on fortitude alone from a rented shack somewhere in the hills near Berkeley. I save every issue of that journal just in case my son in El Cerrito ever escapes his English ivy to plant a little grassland somewhere along the Pacific. Louise has devoted whole issues just to California grasses, dozens and dozens of species, page after page replete with photos and descriptions of their respective communities. Want to know how to restore a vernal pool? What fruiting shrubs to plant for birds in every one of California's many habitats? Read "Growing Native." Ask Louise. But don't ask her Atlantic questions.

And it's not as though I can call the Wild Ones in Wisconsin to my rescue. The tables have turned and it's my turn to complain. All you midwestern prairie folks are so parochial, never considering us outlanders here in Maine, writing as though we northeastern gardeners had your limestone rocks, your sandy loams, your broiling summers to bake our native grasses. And so smug in your historical correctness, your John Curtis and Aldo Leopold! What do you, luxuriating in your tallgrass prairie yards, know about this granite island where the winter sun sets halfway through the afternoon and tomatoes hang green past September?

The awful thought occurs to me that native grassland flora here might be cool-season species.

Now there would be a real predicament. Because of the weeds.

I remember Ruth in Arizona pointing out to me over the fence of her desert yard the one weed she contends with, an alien grass. She pulls it up when it appears. I asked her what grew in the yard before she scattered seed on it. Pretty much bare dirt, she said. The grass grower in whose class I saw the photo of restored West Coast grassland swore he had planted it just as one plants a lawn: till the ground, rake it smooth, sow it. We easterners, with our proud tradition of three centuries of farming, have three centuries' accumulation of weed seeds in our old fields. I note below the window, where the new septic tank is buried, a newcomer to the "garden": a Russian thistle, just waiting for me to open the ground to its multitudinous progeny. Or to cut it into pieces to spawn vegetatively. Tilling quackgrass is like chopping up Medusa.

So okay, midwesterners have old fields, too, and prairie recipes: you spend a season encouraging the weeds so you can kill them all and sow onto clean soil. Then—and here's the rub—you discourage any *cool-season* species that appear by burning or mowing early in the spring to give the *warm-season* species the advantage. I've seen this work. The little bluestem orchard in Virginia had once been mostly cool-season forage grasses; the owner switched the mowing schedule from July to March, and sure enough, the warm-season native bunchgrass was

able to take over. I've even done the trick myself, by burning Kentucky bluegrass in mid-April so that when the little bluestem surveyed the blackened field in May, it found itself the master.

There's no trick to encouraging good cool-seasoners at the expense of bad ones. It simply can't be done.

So I find myself in the extraordinary position of having to follow my own advice.

Beginning with page 268: "How to Kill a Lawn."

Shaping on the survey a plan for this new field.

Contemplating a pioneer community.

Researching the species.

Finding sources.

Collecting seed and growing it.

Developing, as I have advised you to do, a grassland restoration planting and management strategy that will bring back the butterflies.

*F*unny thing is, among the vegetation that came up where the spruces blew down at the north end of the island is my old nemesis, Eragrostis spectabilis, purple lovegrass. I went back to check it out. There, also, is the sedge whose seed I collected and that now is growing nicely in the vegetable garden back home. Also tufted hairgrass, Deschampsia flexuosa, whose seed is sold by several growers. I identified angelica, fireweed, three species of goldenrod, and two asters. Judging by their bloom time, these, like the sedge and grasses, are warm-season sorts.

Too bad about cool lupines, which turn the island blue in the spring.

But I can grow them in the stone terrace, the new one, here in Maine. Marty has been busy with his rocky plans.

Funny that for all those years of wanting a quarry garden on a backyard lawn, after all that lugging of Pennsylvania stone and moving of crowberry and cranberry and creeping potentilla from Maine to Westchester County, we didn't think much about the quarry in our own yard here.

It's not a big quarry. It's what islanders call a "motion," a granite face that was cut for cobbles in the nineteenth century. We park the car there now, over the excavated portion. We planted the pitch pines to one side—the pitch pines that didn't seem right for the terrace back home but that naturally grow here among bayberries and roses on this dry and gritty ground.

In considering future excavations, Marty recalled that there once had been a hollow at rock bottom below the motion, where rain and runoff water made a shallow pool. We had it filled so we could park the car. We'll scrape it out again and have a wetland: hear frogs again, plant chokeberry and blueberry and the hobblebush viburnum that grows here in roadside drainage ditches, and let the songbirds come. Bluebirds nested on the island when the land was farmed. We'll build some boxes.

Behind the barn along the shore of an inlet is a remnant of salt marsh. A great blue heron fishes there just as one does at home along the pond.

Above the quarry face is a small woods, not ours but not threatened by clearing, either. And on the quarry ledges, creeping from the cracks and spreading over granite, there is moss—Polytrichum, Leucobryum, and two others. I'll bring back samples for Chris to identify.

We will lack nothing here. We will have lunch with animals: in a village, one block from the library, at the dead end of a residential street, on a lot that measures a scant three-quarter acre.

Alas! The best time to burn a meadow is when the daffodils bloom. (Michael McKeag)

15 Ladies of the Club on Tour

*I*T'S ALMOST THANKSGIVING. Sondra Peterson reports that the turkeys are back, but it's a different crew this fall, more nervous and cautious, less domestic in their behavior than the previous flock of six. She reports, too, that foresters are becoming alarmed at their increasing population.

Wild turkeys are eating all the young sprouts in the woods.

Did you know, though, that they aren't really the wild ones, the ones that Audubon painted? They're a mixed breed, part farm turkey, released for the enjoyment of hunters.

This isn't a simple business, this living on the land. Or writing about it: things change too fast. One learns too much too quickly to keep up. One is always wrong.

Did I really say that I welcome the social butterfly bush into my garden? I take it back. Buddleia davidii turned up on a national list of invasive aliens—in ten eastern states and on the West Coast, too. Perhaps I gave the impression that I recommend Jerusalem artichoke as a perennial sunflower appropriate to a small garden, like the tight bed outside the kitchen door where I planted it to replace the previous year's annual sunflowers. The Jerusalem artichokes were brushing the first-floor windowsill when we left for Maine. Five weeks later, they were halfway up the second-story window, fourteen feet tall and branched like trees. Nancy the Master Gardener says I might as well get used to them. The tubers in her vegetable garden have proved ineradicable.

Pickerel frogs that I'd long searched for in vain around the pond turned out to be a summer inhabitant of meadows, which I discovered when they appeared in numbers on the terrace. The tiny annual rushes among which they live in that stone-dry environment turned out to be a sedge, Fimbristylis autumnalis, an inhabitant of moist soil, says the book. The "southern" ladybug that I had mistakenly claimed as my own home-grown meadow product is not, after all, a meadow but a woodland species and is not descended from USDA releases, but arrived independently by boat as a stowaway from Japan. The ladybug goes by the name Halloween beetle. I was tricked twice. Or thrice.

I can't keep count of the surprises that continually occur: the lupines that "turn the island blue in spring" were somehow transformed into the garden escape Lupinus polyphyllus, not our rightful native Lupinus perennis; some of the resprouting multiflora roses in the wetland clearing miraculously turned into swamp rose, Rosa palustris, when I wasn't looking.

It isn't fair.

It isn't fair, when escorting visitors through that swamp improved without a permit that one of them is a wetlands inspector for a neighboring town. Nor should it happen that, after amply explaining how the summer's drought had caused all the ferns to go into early dormancy, curled and crisp as though toasted in an oven, that the same botanist should point out the one exception: the most delicate, most rare, hardest to grow and treasured maidenhair.

Then again, isn't this the point of restoration? That we should be surprised, fooled, teased, tested in our limitations until the one blunt truth gets through to us: we really don't know very much.

Sondra's fall report continued. Because of her wildlife feeding habits and as a result of a telephone call to inquire if oral rabies vaccine for raccoons was yet available to homeowners (it wasn't), she had been chosen to participate in a study of bait preference. A camera will be mounted at the feeding ledge above the swimming pool. Various foods will be offered to see which the raccoons like. Some preferences are already known.

In rural countryside, raccoons prefer fish.

In cities, their favorite food is marshmallows.

And in the suburbs? Maybe a turkey club on toast, hold the mayo.

I picked up the August mail held for us at the post office during vacation. Among the letters was a time warp: an envelope postmarked June 9 with footprints on it. Lost in the shuffle, dead on the P.O. floor.

I looked up the date on my calendar. June 9, 1995, was when the Naturals came to help me weed the morning after my computer lost its mind. I retrieved the calendars for 1994 and 1993 and leafed back through the time that had passed since *Noah's Garden* was published and the curtain had been whisked away to reveal, I now realize, not only me to others but those others to myself. The same date the year before had been a garden club tour, and the year before that, an interview. The first talk I gave was in March of 1993 at the New York Flower Show to an empty hall, on the tail of a blizzard. The last was in March 1995 to a full auditorium in Madison, Wisconsin, the weekend I walked through the windy prairie with Lorrie Otto and Robert Ahrenhoerster. Two years altogether, from the first flutter to the last.

I'm in a time warp of my own or my sense of time is warped: scrunched, compressed like computer files obeying the program Stuff It. Time is filled with unrecorded holes that, because one can't remember them, collapse and are gone. What happened during the blank days? I read once that a decision one has made only comes into awareness after it has actually been formulated: the mental sequence is to make a choice and then to be informed of what it was. I won't find in the recorded events of those calendars the thought processes by which I came to appreciate what my role as reluctant wizard had actually revealed: not audiences who wished to be dazzled but people who wanted to learn; not a leader with booming drums and flashing lights but a rather plain woman who knew some things that they might like to know.

There is no record before '93; I'd never kept a calendar before. My correspondence file begins in February 1992, with Mike McKeag's first letter in response not to *Noah's Garden*, which was then in the writing, but to *My Weeds*, the previous book on gardeners' botany that had led in some circuitous way to all that followed. I never kept letters before that; it seemed to me self-conscious to preserve one's correspondence.

The month's mail included a letter from Lorrie Otto. A chipmunk's nest had clogged her downspout and the basement flooded. The Wildest One, Rochelle Whiteman, had the goofy thought that she ought to ask speakers staying at her home to sign the mattress: So-and-So slept here. Mike McKeag wrote about a workshop he'd been planning in which participants are to plant a children's garden at a Portland hospital. Jo Ann Teas found a huge beetle lumbering past her bedroom door; it was a female Ox beetle, two inches wide by two and a half long. There were several thank-you notes from people who had visited our garden in July. One mentioned the homemade cookies the Naturals had provided; another remarked on Chris's Leucobryum eyes, which matched her moss-green shirt.

Who can toss such letters? Are they even mine? Something must have flagged that first note from Mike nearly a year before the publication of *Noah's Garden*, and I'd like to claim that I realized right away how many other people were out there exploring similar terrain, but the fact is that I don't remember at all why I saved it.

The August letter that most moved me was from Steve Rothe in Omaha. I hadn't heard from him in nearly a year. He is a serious, indeed, a religious man; I once chided him for his gravity. (I don't know what he looks like; perhaps I'll make him laugh by confiding that I picture him as Walter Mondale.) His transformation, though, from gardener to restorer had been strikingly similar to mine, caught up at first in colors and cultivars, as real gardeners are, then summoned like sparrows to a field of grain by the flora of Nebraska. Now he too had stepped into the public light.

In June, Steve wrote, more than a thousand people had toured his city yard. He had labeled the hundred natives he grows, supplied his visitors with a printout of Nebraska species, given out seedlings from those he propagates. Steve's church had agreed to let him try small native plantings on its grounds, though it wasn't ready yet to replace lawn with the tallgrass prairie he envisions as a church's proper setting in the land of *My Ántonia* and *O Pioneers!* He was hoping to excise the last of his own lawn, helping neighbors join their garden beds to his. He was going to conferences. He was giving a talk.

I asked Steve to describe his feelings about this stewardship and leadership, this living in a private garden that so soon and so perversely exposes one to view.

"Scary," was the first adjective in his reply—scary, that is, to be mentioned in a book. Then, "To add to the story of the asters, this week we have witnessed a gathering of butterflies, this time sulphurs, crowding the few New England asters and azure asters every sunny day, twinkling about in a loosely scattered cloud. They each or severally flutter up briefly, long enough to light upon the next open flower, spend a minute or less at that flower, then flutter up again so there is a steady show of yellow flutters with brief rests."

He had given extras of his asters to several of his coworkers; they, too, reported their delight in the clouds of sulphur butterflies come to nectar in their yards. He's trashing what exotics remain from former days; he won't give them away. But, he added, "the Painted Ladies do seem to prefer the non-native sedums (I may keep these)."

(I was sure I knew which sedum: 'Autumn Joy'; I've kept mine, too. I could see them out the window as I read the letter, the only attractive plants among dead peony stalks and seedy asters.)

The letter continued. It's been hard to accept sprawling flower stalks, Steve admitted—although he realizes that their sprawl is a "logical dispersal mechanism" where light is limited. It has taken an effort to become accustomed to brown seed heads waiting for winter finches or dead stems that, sticking through the snow, serve as their perches. He is frustrated, too, that a restored lot in Omaha can never be a real prairie: it "lacks that sweep, that blended beauty, seems amateurish, isolated." And he is embarrassed that he displays himself in front of rush-hour traffic, pulling dandelions from the lawn, because he can't bear others to think he has abandoned it to weeds.

The letter spoke of the "sacredness of place," of responsibility for "creatures vulnerable to our will," of pride in "having the grace to provide room for other lives." This man who had prepared a hundred labels and several times that many potted plants for the education of the garden touring crowd concluded that "it is what we do as an individual that matters, not what we can get others to do."

I smiled, of course. Ours is a comic nature. We are uplifted by butterflies and hunkering to dandelions all in the same summer afternoon.

The Garden Conservancy is a national group that encourages public interest in the preservation of fine and historic gardens. In 1995 the Conservancy began an Open Days Directory, similar to the British program that opens noted gardens to the public on scheduled dates. To qualify, a garden must be interesting for its plant selection, design, or philosophy, and it must be well groomed. A hundred gardens were chosen in this trial effort, ours among them. The date we were inspected for our grooming must lie in one of those blank areas in my calendar: presumably the garden was buried in fall leaves at the time.

One can name one's Open Day—or two or three days if the garden commands such attention—on Saturdays or Sundays from May until October. I happen to think, and I'm sure Steve Rothe would agree, that every season is of interest in a natural garden—if one is, at heart, a naturalist. What gardeners might think of burnt-black meadow in May, though, excluded that month, especially because nothing is drearier than fried daffodils.

I guess planting daffodils was one of the silliest things we ever did, but it can't be undone. We planted fifteen hundred bulbs in the little bluestem meadow in its first year, thinking in English still, not well translated into American. I can't tell you how arduous it was, five hundred bulbs a day over a long fall weekend, planted by mattock in that hard, pond-bottom clay. Now they're burned annually just as the flowers open: they sizzle.

But they don't die. Lorrie Otto doesn't want you to know about her crocuses, either, but there they are (I saw them): once the bulbs are in, you can't ever get them out.

And so to June: the glory month for English borders, rockeries, and roses.

Not to mention dandelions in the lawn.

August certainly was out, since we wouldn't be here to escort guests through our native northeastern landscape at its summer height.

So was September impossible because of the requisite grooming. On the day we ultimately chose, a Sunday in late July, one of the other open gardens was a fifty-one-acre estate attended by a staff of thirty gardeners, each responsible by category for rose or perennial—or, arithmetically, for about 1.6 acres each. Our property is around five acres, roughly 2.5 acres per gardener (Marty and me), both of whom have other jobs and garden only on weekends. Labor Day weekend finds the place at its most disreputable.

As it was, we needed help, and if Steve is embarrassed about being seen beheading blowballs, so I am embarrassed to admit that we hired Chilo Duarte—and sometimes his brother Dimas or their brother-in-law Rolando—to do just such work. My ethics allow the hiring of labor for great and noble works: felling trees, setting boulders. One ought to edge one's own beds.

The whole business of edges is problematical in this sort of landscape. They keep getting longer. Figure it: connect islands, extend peninsulas, build isthmuses, and before you know it you've created the shoreline of Greece. And what is the sea around it?

It is lawn.

Usually I edge only the gardens close to the house—Peony, for instance, to keep her corners in kilter—but most areas I leave blurry, just let the lawn peter out among fallen leaves and prairie grass.

We edged everywhere on the landscaped grounds that July.

I am against mulching. Plants are supposed to mulch themselves. It's not for me to feed their nematodes and mycorrhizae, their annelids, bacteria, arthropods, and protozoans. Wouldn't it be rash, in fact, to dose the living earth with shredded bark when its accustomed diet is grass blades and goldenrod? And why waste the trees? I practiced such lines for visitors-to-be often that month as I neatly mulched the edges.

The effect was wonderful, though! It made the lawn look so much bigger.

I was too busy with esthetic propriety to bother reading the Garden Conservancy's instructions for Open Days. You get a whole kit: road signs to direct people to your property, name badges for the guides, a cash box for the ticket taker. I figured you got the guides, too, and the ticket taker, and the sign erector, all dressed in swishy skirts with pretty hats, as is customary when garden clubs come touring. I planned for the ladies to set up their folding table with their flower arrangement, plates of cookies, and pitcher of iced tea in the shady White Garden.

The Naturals pricked that fantasy—one week before the great event.

Anyway, there wasn't any shade in the White Garden. The crabapples were infected with the most disgusting case of cedar-apple rust I've ever seen. The twigs were oozing orange fungus. All the leaves had dropped.

I don't believe in prophylactic spraying.

*T*wo hundred eighty-eight people visited that Sunday. The first couple arrived by mistake a day early, all the way from Philadelphia. Another couple called to ask for driving instructions from Detroit; sure enough, they got here. A woman who had hoped to visit from Ohio deputized her sister to videotape the garden. A woman who came alone around midday left and returned late in the afternoon with her husband and their children.

From the first, it was unlike any previous garden tour recorded on my calendars. Visitors before had clearly been ladies of the club and addressed me as Mrs. Stein. "You must be Sara" was the greeting I most often got that day, as though we were old friends come together for reunion. "There wasn't a single error," a woman declared to me as she approached my station on the terrace. She introduced herself as the head of the Biology Department at a state college not far from here. She meant there were no errors in the science of *My Weeds*. So she'd known me even then, before I'd ever met a real gardener and when Rose was still alive.

The sense of reunion was fortified by an uncanny incident. "You're Alice Covell," said a woman to Alice Ballin, née Covell, one of the Naturals, who was taking tickets at a card table in the shade of the lonesome oak along the driveway. The two had gone to school together: grade school. They hadn't set eyes on each other in fifty years.

Others, too, met again here: local naturalists, fellow birders, friends of ALFASAC. The three years since the curtain had dropped from my attic hideaway looped back on me as though I were treading a Möbius strip. There appeared the president of a New Jersey garden club whose name is on the calendar from 1993; Polly Townsend, whose hole-in-the-hill frog pond had belied my pessimism; a psychiatrist who had asked for help in planning a meadow and in whose yard I had first seen pawpaws and persimmons.

The demographics of this group also were different. Usually one is startled if there is a man among the women, but nearly half the visitors that day were men. Most guests before had been of an age that any children they might have brought (but didn't) would have been their grandchildren. Many who came to the Garden Conservancy Open Day were in their thirties and came with sons and daughters. They wore plain clothes and carried field lenses, binoculars, butterfly guides.

A red-spotted purple emerged from its chrysalis to pump its wings on the driveway for a circle of admirers. Girl tried to eat it; Saint Sondra stepped through the crowd and saved it. Monarchs, of which we'd seen only a few so far, chose that day to bat one after the other across the terrace as though we'd trained them for a parade. A butterflier identified tiger swallowtails, red admirals, painted ladies, and mourning cloaks. Someone took a picture of a monarch and a sphinx moth nectaring at the same flower on the terrace.

Chris was stationed at the moss garden. We had put up a sign asking guests to follow the stepping-stones because the moss wasn't well enough established to be walked on yet. The exercise was instructive. A meander of "one foot" stones is too subtle a path to follow. The moss didn't really suffer much (Chris may have), but there was a crisis with the wrens living in the church birdhouse at the center of the clearing. Their babies had hatched only the day before; the parents were feeding them at two-minute intervals—as fast as they could fill those gaping maws. We knew the routine because we'd been plugging in moss until the last minute, and the wrens had been popping in and out like clockwork as we worked. The birdhouse entrance, though, faced the flow of visitors, and the looming quality of oncoming bipeds made it impossible for the parents to reenter the hole once they began arriving. One or the other would zoom in with a fat moth, hover nervously, and retreat. The babies' hungry cheeps took on a frantic note; we felt as helpless as when infants screech with colic, and presumably the wrens were just as disturbed. Finally they solved the problem by stuffing moths through a rear ventilation hole, to the applause of the assembled crowd.

I had thought no freshwater snails lived in the pond; a five-year-old named Tess found two species, one conical, one flat. Bullfrogs garumphed through the day, interrupted occasionally by another croaker whose identity is still unknown to me. Nothing, though, beats the showoff blacksnake who chose that Sunday to swallow a frog in front of three eyewitnesses.

On the stone terrace.

Of course the terrace was popular that day, if for no other reason than the cookies the Naturals had made: vanilla chocolate chip, chocolate chocolate chip, peanut butter, mandarin orange, lemon with poppy seeds, and squares of Alma's squash bread and heaps of bite-size pecan pies baked by Chris's mother. There was icewater flavored with mint sprigs and lemon slices and a rosy herbal tea brewed in batches through the day. I was into beer, myself, by midafternoon, dazed ultimately not by alcohol so much as by the sheer eventfulness of the day.

We had put up signs. One said to compare the lawn with the meadow next to it. I saw a man read the sign, lift his eyes to the meadow, lower them to the lawn, and repeat the gesture several times in rapt obedience. Another sign invited

William courting admiration on Open Day in the meadow, where daffodils sizzled in the spring. (C. Filipacchi/ EarthBase)

guests to search for cranberries on the terrace. I wanted them to notice the insignificant plants that grow there, to look down to the level where the action is. And they did, and noticed—every one of them, it seemed to me—the little sedge that grows between the paving stones. Naturally people wanted to know its name, for their own garden; naturally it was the only plant I couldn't identify. No one found the cranberries, but many asked me to point them out. I began to feel like Mother Wren, with so many mouths to feed, but just as proud.

People had begun arriving a half hour before opening and lingered for an hour and a half after closing. Twenty, thirty cars were parked along the road all day. A neighbor dropped by, thinking we were having a garage sale. We ran out of registry sheets. William the cat, long-haired and weighing more than twenty pounds, lay spreadeagled on the grass, accepting tribute to his size and majesty almost until the very end. Girl, at first official greeter and escort of each new arrival, soon retired to the less demanding job of cookie guardian. The last guest to leave was the young woman who had gone home and returned with her family. The wrens came to bathe in the basin. Marty took down the signs and closed the gate. It was dusk when the trespassers arrived.

I heard them in the woods behind the pond: two young women, weekend guests of my weed-whacking neighbor. They had walked down the hill and through the Ariel meadow, climbed over the rubble wall, and squeezed through the wires of the deer fence. They had thought, from the day's activity, that this was a public nature preserve.

*W*riters choose words, painters create images, gardeners plant scenes. All are sincere in their intent to present the truth as they believe it to be, but to express anything at all is to plead for one's point of view, to slant and shape and shade in order to convince. We worked very hard, and frankly in the mode of any gardener, to convince visitors on Open Day of the ease and naturalness of this landscape. An hour earlier, they would have found Marty in a cock-eyed straw hat tied under his chin with butcher's string, baggy muddy pants, cracked boots, frayed shirt. They would have found me sweeping up the rusted apple leaves and disposing of the evidence.

The virtue that Steve Rothe upholds—that we are to measure our lives by what we do, not by what we get others to do—is an ideal that can't be attained by any human being. From the moment of birth, from the infant's first cry, we press others to do what we want, and even if, as adults, we assiduously avoid influencing opinion, by so doing we press others to take note of our example.

We had a local hermit once, the Leather Man, who wore skins and lived in caves in the woods. He subsisted on food left for him by farmers, cadged cigarettes, and died eventually of lung cancer. This least of men—whom no one knew, who never spoke a word—could not help but leave a story. Uncounted people year after year trek to see the Leather Man's caves, and surely they don't leave without a thought, a doubt, a wondering, they did not have before.

I have gathered here my and other people's stories. None is complete, and all of them together amount to polka dots. I'd like to wrap the volume up in panorama paper, combine the little stories into a glorious impression of the larger future, but that isn't possible.

Niece Ellen ordered plum trees but didn't plant the meadow. The cedar waxwings that have returned every fall to our crabapples flew on without stopping this year at the fruitless, rusted trees. Jo Ann in Arkansas is reconsidering the wisdom of letting her wintercreeper run free. Ruth in Arizona writes of seedling oaks that tempt her to collection. Mike in Oregon is surfing the Internet with dangerous abandon (my fault: I asked him to explore for me). Polly Law installed her pond. Rochelle Whiteman is sending me a snapshot of a KEEP OFF THE POI-

SONED GRASS sign put up by the Barefoot Grass Company on the grounds of her synagogue two days before Yom Kippur, the Day of Atonement. The women of ALFASAC just keep on walking.

In other words, not much is happening, not at the myopic scale I can address.

Marty comes home each evening and genially asks how the manuscript is coming. I said the other night that I thought it was fairly rounded, fairly honest, fairly finished, but lacking some fillip at the end, like a pig without a tail.

I love this man. He consented to replace fragrant lilacs with the nominally "aromatic" sumac and has stood by me through even frozen pizza. This fall Marty stripped and killed another loop of lawn and opened for me slots to receive nerve-racking numbers of plants that, contrary to both our expectations, did indeed grow from seedling to transplant size in the former vegetable garden. He doesn't know their names; he misses the tomatoes. His labor is an act of faith.

So I will finish the story with his rock.

This is the rock that Marty saw years ago at the stone yard when we went to buy some bricks. It's the one that was "thigh-high and long enough to lie on, as rectilinear as rocks come, and still wearing the lichens and mosses of its origin somewhere in the Pennsylvania woods." It happens that the years of constructing the stone terrace coincide with the first two of my calendars, and in all that time, as he paved and I planted and the intended and unintended gardens became superimposed on one another, as grasshoppers grew to flying size and bluebirds multiplied, the rock stood in the masonry yard. The great stele had been ordered by a landscaper for clients who changed their minds, and there had been no other takers. Its lichens spread; its moss greened and browned with the seasons.

We went to the yard a dozen times during that period. Shipments of Pennsylvania stone came in once a week. Each pallet differed. Those with the best stones usually were sold within a day. Sometimes we chose smaller stepping stones for narrow paths; sometimes we needed large ones for open spaces. One winter was so icy that we couldn't work on the terrace from November until March. Christmas and birthday pallets lay stacked and heaped with snow; flocks of juncoes sheltering in them from the wind swirled up like a blizzard from their hideaway each time we passed.

Still the rock stood in the stone yard. And still Marty gazed at it and stroked it on each visit.

The last trip, for the last pallets we needed, was in anticipation of our thirty-sixth wedding anniversary. By then we were well known to the owners, as you can imagine, and Marty's lingering at the big rock had not gone unnoticed. In the

Marty, at work.
(Sara Stein)

office, writing out the check whose sum Marty didn't want to know, I was offered a bargain price for the rock. I took it. The stone was ours.

Or mine—my secret. For where it would go, how it would get there, and when I should spring this great surprise on Marty was a matter to be considered carefully lest, after all, we end up with a gigantic garden bench in the driveway.

In the end the solution was quite simple because, as the John Wayne double who had delivered stone and sand to us so many times pointed out to me, his truck can back off the driveway when the ground is frozen solid, and the truck's hydraulic crane, which swings heavy loads into place, has a certain reach as well. I had only to time the delivery to Marty's birthday on January 1 and choose a spot within the truck's technical capability: the juncture of three paths that meet at the edge of the birch and bracken grove, thirty feet to the right of the driveway as you enter.

And there the stone now stands: out-of-state and out of place, odder than erratics left by glaciers, too high to sit on unless your legs are very long, more awkward than ornamental, rather large to excuse ecologically—were it not for the small hole beneath the far left corner.

I guess the chipmunk doesn't care what fools we mortals be.

PART TWO

*How to Plant
Noah's Garden*

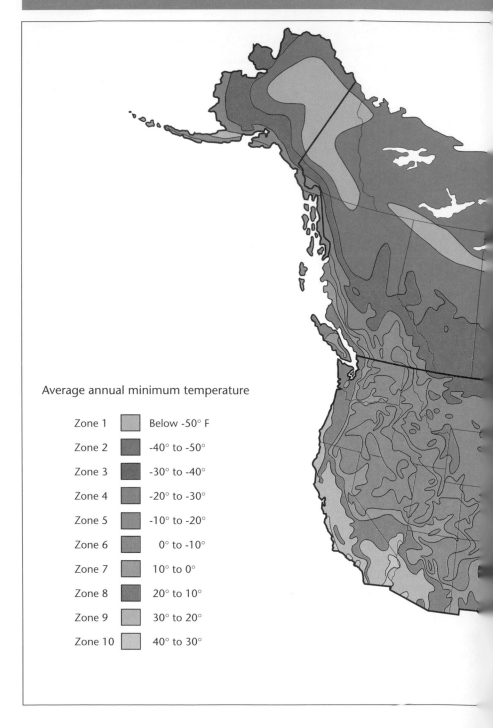

Average annual minimum temperature

Zone 1	Below -50° F
Zone 2	-40° to -50°
Zone 3	-30° to -40°
Zone 4	-20° to -30°
Zone 5	-10° to -20°
Zone 6	0° to -10°
Zone 7	10° to 0°
Zone 8	20° to 10°
Zone 9	30° to 20°
Zone 10	40° to 30°

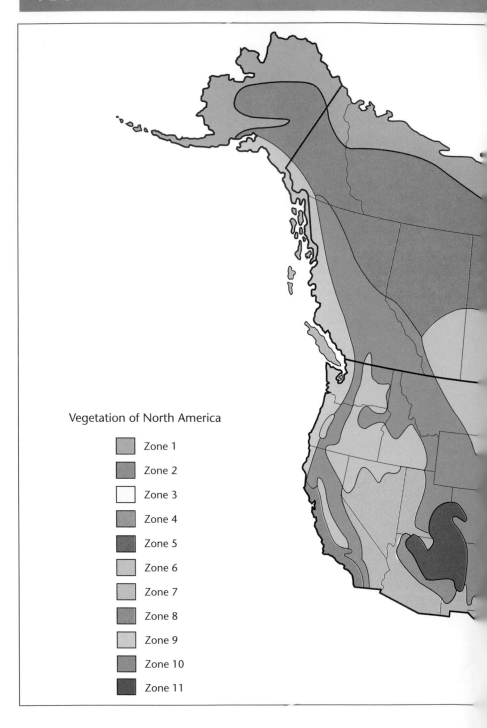

Vegetation of North America

■	Zone 1
■	Zone 2
□	Zone 3
■	Zone 4
■	Zone 5
■	Zone 6
■	Zone 7
■	Zone 8
■	Zone 9
■	Zone 10
■	Zone 11

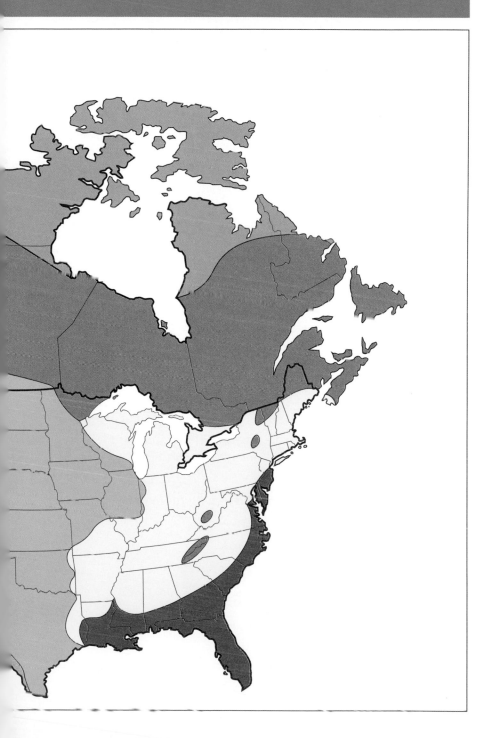

How to use the plant charts

The plant charts in this book are not exhaustive; they are just sufficient —enough species to get you started, not so many as to overwhelm you. Vegetation region and USDA Hardiness Zone maps are on pages 264–65 and 262–63. Vegetation regions refer to broad types of ecosystem— desert scrub, deciduous forest, tallgrass prairie, and so on. Hardiness zones are based on average minimum annual temperature. If just one zone is given, it means that's as cold as the plant can stand; sometimes a range is given instead. Locate yourself on the map and memorize the numerals for your zone and your region. For example, my town is in Zone 6, Region 2. That doesn't mean every plant that's assigned both those numerals on a chart occurs in the wild in southern New York. If you want to be a stickler for accuracy, you'll have to do further research (see page 304).

Other necessary information is either spelled out or depicted by a symbol.

Height is in feet (') or inches (").

Season is early, mid, or late. Seasons vary by altitude and latitude. "Early" roughly means spring, "mid" means summer, and "late" means fall.

Soil texture and moisture are represented by patterns that suggest density:

    = sandy or light soil that drains easily

    = loam or ordinary garden soil

    = clay or heavy soil that drains poorly

    = a dry, often upland or rocky site

    = a medium moist site

    = a wet, usually lowland site

Light requirement is represented by shaded circles:

◯ = *full sun*

◔ = *light shade, dappled shade, or afternoon shade*

● = *full shade*

Habitat is designated by glyphs that can't possibly do justice to any actual ecosystems, but roughly correspond to:

🌾 = *grassland* (field, roadside, woodland edge or clearing)

🌲 = *woodland* (any gathering of large trees)

🌿 = *wetland* (swamp, marsh, shore, saturated or soggy ground)

These are independent variables. A plant may be able to cope with dense clay soil, but needs a high, dry site. Many native species can tolerate a broad range of conditions:

≡ to ▰ , and ≋ to ≋ , and ◯ to ● .

The same plant may occupy more than one habitat—even, as with certain ferns, all three habitats.

The best way to proceed with deciding which species to use for a new planting is to draw on the top of your planning sheet the abbreviation and symbols that apply to your region and circumstances, then list the plants that fit those criteria. See the index for names of charts.

16 *Starting the Garden*

🍂 A NOTE ON LAWN NEGLECT

In the days before herbicides, sprinklers, commercial fertilizers, and self-conscious suburbs, the common lawn was what we would now consider neglected. That is, it was left to grow as a composite of different sorts of plants, both broad-leaved ones and grasses, and mowed only a few times a season. You might want to let an experimental patch of lawn go about its business for a while just to see what happens. In shade you might get drifts of bluets or violets or an interesting texture of moss with grass; in sun, some of the more attractive creeping weeds such as ground ivy (Glechoma hederacea, also called gill-over-the-ground) might come up. The only turf weed you can buy as seed is white clover. White clover, although an alien like most other weeds, is a source of nectar and also feeds the grass nitrogen. Sometimes bluets can be bought as sods; a friend might let you dig plugs of bluets or violets to transplant into your turf, where they will spread by themselves.

🍂 HOW TO KILL A LAWN

Start with a small project, such as expanding an existing bed or creating a new one that incorporates an existing feature. Some ideas: a new planting in front of foundation shrubbery; a new bed along a path; an island bed around an ornamental tree. You won't need to dig the bed or amend the soil; just kill the grass. The less you disturb the area, the fewer weeds you'll have to contend with. Don't "improve" the soil. Enriched soil encourages weeds; native species don't need feeding.

Lay out the shape of the new area

Use stakes and string to lay out a rectilinear bed. Measure the long edge from a parallel reference point, such as the house wall, a boundary fence, sidewalk, path, or patio. For a small bed, you can check that the corners are right angles with a carpenter's square, but for large beds a more accurate method is the 3-4-5 rule, illustrated here. Lay out curves with a hose. Tug the hose gently to take up slack. Fine-tune the curve by shuffling along it, letting the hose slide over one foot while the other stabilizes it. Hold the finished portion of a long curve in place with rocks or bricks while you perfect the rest of it.

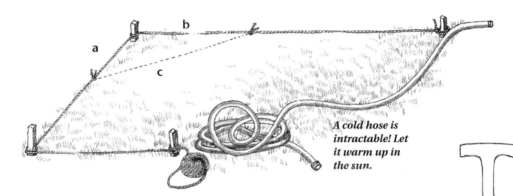

A cold hose is intractable! Let it warm up in the sun.

Use mason's line, a firm, nonstretchy string. Pull it taut and wrap it around each stake several times to keep it from slipping or getting loose. The string should hug the ground.

Square corners using the 3-4-5 rule. Tie a bit of string to each of two adjoining sides to serve as a measure. Slide the ties into place so that a=3 feet and b=4 feet. If the sides form a right angle, the diagonal between them will measure 5 feet (remember the Pythagorean theorem?). Adjust the angle (by moving a stake) until the measurement comes out right.

Trench the edge

Use an edger or a small spade to trench the perimeter of the bed. First, cut a vertical incision around the perimeter. Then, working from inside the bed, remove wedges of turf to form a deep, narrow trench. If the string or hose impedes your progress, spray-paint along the edge and use that line for guidance.

Kill the turf

The traditional—but least effective—method of preparing a bed is to till the ground. Repeated tillings are necessary; each new disturbance brings more weed seeds to the surface. Choose one of the following methods instead.

An edger. A short-handled type is easier to use than a long-handled one.

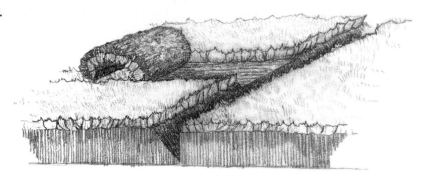

The edger's first cut is vertical. A second, angled cut from inside the bed removes a wedge of turf.

Strips of turf are incised with an edger and peeled back using a mattock or grub hoe.

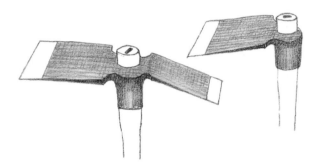

A mattock has two blades and a short handle; it's used for chopping out roots as well as for stripping turf. A grub hoe is a lighter tool with one blade and a long handle; it's used mostly for working hard soil. The blades of both tools come in various shapes and widths and may be set straight or at an angle. Test the heft and action of these tools before choosing one.

Strip the turf by hand for a small bed or with a rented stripper for a large one. The soil should be moist but not sodden. To strip by hand, incise the turf into narrow strips with an ax or edger. Use a mattock or grub hoe to detach the strips by cutting through their roots. Start at the far end of a strip; the chopping motion of the blade will roll the sod toward you. Gas strippers work on the same principle. Although stripping turf is the fastest method to get rid of lawn and may leave a surface quite free of weed seeds, topsoil is lost, and the sod you remove takes a long time to rot. Cover the pile with leaves or other compost to speed decay.

Smother the turf by covering it. You can smother grass with an organic mulch, such as thick layers of newspaper either weighted with stones or held in place by additional layers of grass clippings, raked leaves, or commercial mulch. Or you can spread plastic over the turf. Organic covers speed decay and improve soil texture, but they don't kill weed seeds. Black plastic, by absorbing heat, may kill weed seeds at the surface. Clear plastic kills by heat alone; it may kill weed seeds to a depth of several inches, but it is effective only during hot weather. Allow six months for smothering.

Planting Noah's Garden

Poison the turf with herbicide. Roundup and other brands whose active ingredient is glyphosate are effective and environmentally benign. The ready-mixed product can be used straight from the bottle; the concentrate must first be mixed with water to the recommended dilution. A hand-held sprayer is adequate for a small bed. Choose a still, clear day. Spray from the trenched edge toward the interior of the bed (spray that drifts onto the edge of the surrounding lawn may kill whole patches of grass). Weed seeds newly exposed to light will sprout in the dead turf. Repeat the spraying as necessary. (See page 370 for a detailed discussion of glyphosate herbicides.)

An excellent 2½-pint hand sprayer is made by Olympic Company, P.O. Box K, Mainland, Pennsylvania 19451. Set the adjustable nozzle to a large drop pattern; fine mist sprays are impossible to confine to the target area.

What next?

No method assures that the area will be free of weed seeds. This is okay if you're using plants and mulching around them. If you're going to seed the area, rake the surface lightly, let weeds sprout, and kill them. Repeat this several times before sowing. Other than weed control, do nothing to prepare the bed for planting. Don't turn the soil. Don't break up the surface with a hoe. Don't spread fertilizer. But do "hold" the bed with grasses or ferns even if you're not ready for (or don't want) a fancier planting.

For more information:
How to Know Your Dirt, page 286

How to Sow Wild Seeds, page 312

How to Handle Bareroot Stock, page 325

A FEW GOOD GRASSES
(AND SOME FERNS)

A new bed can be planted just with native grasses—for instance, in an area that incorporates existing shrubs—or it can be "held" by grass until you decide what you want to add to the planting. In shady areas, ferns can be used instead. Measure the area to get the approximate square footage. Catalogs usually give the area covered per ounce or packet of seed. To cover an area with grass or fern plants, space them a foot apart. Plant just before the fall rainy season in arid areas, in spring or fall elsewhere.

See pages 266–67 for instructions on how to read the symbols on the chart on the next two pages.

A FEW GOOD GRASSES (AND SOME FERNS)

Use ferns or grasses to fill in a new bed temporarily while you work out the design of a meadow or woodland garden, or consider them an alternative groundcover to replace a section of lawn. These are chosen for their good looks, modest height, adaptability, and availability as either seed or transplants.

GRASSES Lawn grasses spread sideways to form a dense turf. Most of these native perennial bunch grasses instead grow in clumps with space between for flowers. A few do spread, but not so vigorously as to exclude other plants. Some are cool-season species: they bloom early in the season; others are warm-season species that bloom midsummer into fall. Two useful sedges are also included. A visual reference for foliage color and bloom is the *Encyclopedia of Ornamental Grasses* by John Greenlee (Rodale).

name	habit, texture, color	height	soil density	moisture	light	season	zone	region
Andropogon virginicus (broomsedge)	clumps, medium, light green turning copper	12 - 24"				late	4 - 9	2, 3, 4
Bouteloua curtipendula (sideoats grama)	clumps, medium, blue green turning gold	12 - 24"				mid	4 - 9	2, 4, 5, 8
B. gracilis (blue grama)	clumps, fine, gray green turning purple to tan	8 - 14"				early	3 - 10	5, 7, 8
Buchloe dactyloides (buffalograss)	spreads, fine, blue green turning purple to tan	4 - 6"				early	3 - 9	4, 5, 7, 8
Carex pensylvanica (Pennsylvania sedge)	spreads, fine, light green turning tan	4 - 6"				early	4 - 8	2, 3, 4, 5, 6, 10
C. muskigumensis (palm sedge)	spreads, fine, light green turning tan	24 - 36"				early	4 - 9	2, 4
Deschampsia flexuosa (wavy hairgrass)	clumps, fine, medium green turning orange to tan	12 - 24"				mid	4 - 8	2, 4
D. caespitosa (tufted hairgrass)	clumps, fine, medium green turning tan	12 - 24"				early	4 - 9	throughout
Eragrostis trichoides (sand lovegrass)	clumps, fine, dark green turning rusty tan	12 - 24"				mid	5 - 9	2, 3, 4, 5, 7
E. spectabilis (purple lovegrass)	clumps, coarse, light green turning purple to tan	12 - 18"				mid	5 - 9	2, 3, 4, 5, 6, 7, 8
Festuca californica (California fescue)	clumps, fine, blue gray turning tan	12 - 24"				early	8 - 10	6, 9, 10
Hystrix patula (bottlebrush grass)	clumps, coarse, light green turning tan	8 - 12"				mid	5 - 9	2, 3
Koeleria cristata (June grass)	clumps, medium, medium green turning tan	12 - 24"				early	4 - 9	2, 3, 4, 5, 6, 7, 8, 10
Muhlenbergia filipes (purple muhly)	clumps, coarse, medium green turning tan	12 - 18"				late	7 - 9	3, 4

name	habit, texture, color	height	soil density	moisture	light	habitat	zone	region
Oryzopsis hymenoides (Indian rice grass)	clumps, fine, bright green turning gold to tan	6 - 8"				early	8 - 10	5, 7, 8, 10
Schizachyrium scoparium (little bluestem)	clumps, medium, blue green turning copper	18 - 24"				late	3 - 8	2, 3, 4, 5, 7, 8
Sporobolus airoides (alkali dropseed)	clumps, fine, gray green turning gold to tan	24 - 36"				mid	7 - 9	5, 6, 7, 8, 10
S. heterolepsis (prairie or northern dropseed)	clumps, fine, bright green turning orange to tan	12 - 24"				late	3 - 9	2, 3, 4, 5

FERNS For all their delicate looks, ferns are hardy, practical plants for difficult sites. Although many form clumps, most also spread by sprouting new clumps along creeping rhizomes. A few nonclumping aggressive spreaders are included here for their usefulness as groundcover. Heights are for optimal habitat; most ferns will be shorter under back-yard conditions. Predominantly eastern species usually have western counterparts of the same genus.

name	habit, texture, color	height	soil density	moisture	light	habitat	zone	region
Athyrium filix-femina (lady fern)	clumps, fine, medium green	30"					3 - 8	1, 2, 3, 4, 5, 6, 9, 10
Dennstaedtia punctiloba (hay-scented fern)	spreads aggressively, fine, yellow green	16"					3 - 7	1, 2, 3, 4
Dryopteris marginalis (marginal woodfern)	clumps, medium, dark green (evergreen)	18"					3 - 8	1, 2, 3, 4, 5, 6, 9, 10
Matteuccia struthiopteris (ostrich fern)	clumps, fine, medium green	60"					3 - 6	1, 2, 3, 4, 6
Onoclea sensibilis (sensitive fern)	spreads aggressively, coarse, light green	12"					3 - 8	1, 2, 3, 4
Osmunda cinnamomea (cinnamon fern)	clumps, coarse, medium green	30"					3 - 8	1, 2, 3, 4, 5, 6
O. claytoniana (interrupted fern)	clumps, coarse, medium green	30"					3 - 7	1, 2, 3, 4
Polystichum acrostichoides (Christmas fern)	clumps, coarse, dark green (evergreen)	24"					3 - 8	1, 2, 3, 4
Pteridium aquilinum (bracken)	spreads aggressively, coarse, medium green	30'					3 - 8	throughout
Thelypteris noveboracensis (New York fern)	spreads, fine, yellow green	18"					3 - 7	1, 2, 3, 4
Woodsia ilvensis (rusty woodsia)	clumps, coarse, light green	10"					1 - 7	1, 2, 3, 4

17 Assessing the Yard

HOW TO IDENTIFY PLANT SPECIES AND INVENTORY YOUR LAND

You ought to know what's growing on your land. There may be, either growing wild or as cultivated specimens, invasive weed species that will sabotage any attempts at restoration. Or there may be species valuable to wildlife that could be encouraged or incorporated into improved habitat. Naturally occurring native species will give you an indication of what sorts of companions could be added to enhance a plant community.

Purchase field guides

The best series for identifying plants is the Peterson Field Guides (Houghton Mifflin). The basic wildflower guides come in Eastern and Western editions; there are also more specific titles such as *Rocky Mountain Wildflowers, Pacific States Wildflowers,* and *Southwestern and Texas Wildflowers.* You'll need a tree guide, too; Peterson's Eastern and Western tree guides include shrubs. Houghton Mifflin also offers the *Peterson Field Guide to Ferns.*

For those who live east of the Mississippi and north of North Carolina, *Newcomb's Wildflower Guide* (Little, Brown) is an excellent addition. It has a unique identification system and very clear botanical illustrations and includes some shrubs and vines.

One other guide that may be of interest is *Grasses: An Identification Guide,* by Lauren Brown (Houghton Mifflin). Although it covers only a selection of grasses, most of them common to the Northeast and North Central states, it is a good primer for learning what details to look for when identifying these more difficult plants.

Study the guides! Each relies on a vocabulary that, though not especially technical, is nevertheless indispensable to understanding the text. Each also uses a key, a systematic procedure for identifying species. Vocabulary and procedure are clearly explained, illustrated, and demonstrated by examples.

Take samples

Trees can usually be identified by their leaves, twigs, and bark; most plants, though, are most easily identified by their flower, fruit, or seed. Grassy plants—rushes and sedges as well as grasses—are notoriously difficult to identify. Ferns aren't easy, either. Start with the largest, most obvious plants. Snip a good-size sample. You may need to note whether the leaves are opposite one another or occur at alternate intervals along the stem, or whether the leaves at the base of a plant are different from those farther up the stalk.

To keep samples fresh, put each in a plastic food storage bag. Use a marking pen to label the bag with the location of the plant from which you took the sample, and store it in the refrigerator until you have time to identify it.

Samples are easiest to identify when they are in flower, fruit, or seed. These samples are, from left to right, swamp goldenrod, Solidago uliginosa; highbush blueberry, Vaccinium corymbosum; and sea oats, Chasmanthium latifolium. Use botanical names to identify species. Common names, such as sea oats, may be used for several species, or the same plant may have another common name, such as wild oats. The botanical name is unique to the species.

A sample in a labeled plastic bag ready to be sent to the Agricultural Extension Service for identification. Keep a second sample, also in a plastic bag with the same label, in the refrigerator.

The grass specimen placed in waxed paper before pressing. Note that the label identifies it as Uniola latifolia, whereas the illustration on page 275 calls it Chasmanthium latifolium. Taxonomists change botanical names as new research more clearly reveals a plant's kinship with other plants. To avoid mistakes, check the copyright date of the guide you use for identification. Old guides may use outdated names.

If you can't identify the plant, contact your county's Agricultural Extension Service, found under the name of your county in the government section of the telephone book. (If you can't find such a listing, call your state university's agricultural college to locate the Extension Service in your area.) The Agricultural Extension offers a species identification service for a small fee per sample. Take in or mail the sample, preferably in fruit, flower, or seed, enclosed in a plastic bag to keep it fresh. Label the bag with a code of some sort: Sample A or Front Yard Tree #1. Keep a second sample, labeled with the same code, in a bag in the refrigerator. That way, when you receive the identification, you'll know which plant it is. Noting a location that describes habitat, such as "swamp edge," is more helpful to those determining the species than one that has meaning only to you, such as "bottom of back yard." Dating the samples is a good practice, too.

Ornamentals can be hard to identify because there are so many of them and, unless they have become naturalized in the wild, they aren't included in field guides. A local garden club or botanical garden may help you with these.

Keep a record of plants you have identified

The most dramatic and satisfying way to record the plants on your property is to press a sample of each one, mount it on a sheet of paper, and have a color photocopy made. The resulting image is startlingly three-dimensional, and your record will not be fragile or subject to deterioration like the actual specimen.

Press the sample. Tear off a piece of waxed paper about twice the width of a standard letter sheet. Fold it in half, crease it, and position the sample in the fold. The waxed paper will make delicate samples easier to handle. Sandwich the folded sheet between layers of newspaper to cushion it. Place the sandwich on a flat surface and weight it with heavy books. The drying time depends on the temperature and humidity as well as the thickness of the sample. Two or three weeks is usually long enough. (It's also long enough to forget the specimen's identity; slip a label into the sandwich before you press it.)

Remove the pressed specimen from the waxed paper and mount it on a sheet of standard, letter-size paper. You can use transparent tape to hold it in place, but the tape will show on the color copy. A better method is to position the sample with spray-mount adhesive (available at art stores). Place the pressed specimen upside down on a sheet of newspaper. Spray it lightly according to the directions on the label. The spray will leave the bottom surface of the specimen

A photocopy of the pressed specimen. Yours, of course, will be in color.

tacky. Pick it up, turn it over, and position it on the mounting sheet in such a way that you have room for notes. Write at least the name of the plant on the sheet before making a color duplicate.

Duplicate the sheet. Color xerography is now widely available, and the quality is very good to excellent. (The color faithfulness depends to some extent on the operator's willingness to make fine adjustments.)

Create a notebook. There are all sorts of binders available. For a large record, an old-fashioned three-ring binder is best, but you'll have to hole-punch the sheets.

Add to the record any helpful information—especially the location of that species on your property, but also whether it is native or alien, aggressively spreading, or important to wildlife. You may also want to note the bloom or fruiting time, habitat, and names of plants with which this one is normally associated in the wild. The value of these sheets is that you can add more data over the years without harming the sample, and on the back as well as the front of the sheet. As you add more information and new species, the notebook will become a valuable botanical inventory of your property.

HOW TO ASSESS BACKYARD HABITATS

One way to rate the existing landscape is to note its value to birds in terms of food (fruit, insects, edible seed) and shelter (evergreens, thickets, brambles). A yard that isn't inhabited or frequented by birds is probably not suitable to other wildlife (except pest species!). A second way to assess your yard is in terms of its cost in labor and materials. A poor habitat—a lawn or a bed of tulips—requires materials such as water, fertilizer, and mulch as well as considerable work. A good habitat—woods, thickets, or meadow—requires no material, very little labor, and improves its own conditions over time. Later instructions describe the preparation and planting of basic ecosystems. Before considering the details, try to see in existing growth such as shade trees or foundation planting an opportunity to convert an area to a natural habitat, or at least to improve its quality.

Quiet observation and casual research

As the weather grows warm, remove any birdfeeders you may have and spend some time just watching and listening for bird and insect activity in your yard. For comparison, you might also join birders or butterfliers on a few walks to get a sense of the habitats they know to be productive. Casual reading can also help you develop a clearer idea of what sorts of habitat to aim for.

Read about plant communities. Field guides give at least a general idea, such as that a species you may find in your yard inhabits "dry, rocky woods" or "roadsides." You may learn indirectly in this way that a species is apt to do better as part of a hedgerow than as an understory species, or vice versa. More helpful in imagining where your plants "belong" in their natural habitats are nature guides and books devoted to regional ecology. Information on how to go about this research begins on page 304.

Read about the food preferences of birds and mammals in *American Wildlife & Plants, A Guide to Wildlife Food Habits* (U.S. Department of the Interior; now a Dover reprint). You'll come away with the distinct impression that a weedy vacant lot is of far greater value to wildlife than the typical yard. Not that you should let your land go to weeds, but do notice that the most productive species in terms of food value tend to grow on open, sunny ground that is mostly wasted on lawn in the suburbs.

Tree and shrub habitats

Large trees are generally forest species. Exposure on a lawn is stressful to them and precludes their natural role in environmental conservation: maintaining soil, conserving water, moderating temperature, and protecting the smaller species that ordinarily grow with them in the woods. These other species typically form layers: understory trees that mature at 20 feet or so, shrubs that are shorter still, and a ground cover of ferns and wildflowers. Once properly assembled, even a small woodland habitat can take care of itself with little or no intervention. The soil, webbed with roots to a depth of several feet, holds moisture even during a drought. Nourished on naturally shed debris, it becomes a rich organic humus. In summer, evaporation from woodland foliage cools the air by as much as 20°F. In winter, the undergrowth cuts the wind. Many of the birds that visit winter feeders are woodland species that nest in tree cavities and eat tree-dwelling insects and their eggs and larvae.

Consider whether large trees can be joined by planting additional species among them. Even a single specimen tree can be incorporated into a more valuable shady habitat by underplanting it with smaller trees and shrubs. These can be planted directly below the crown of taprooted canopy trees, such as oaks, or at the perimeter of the crown of heavy surface feeders, such as beech and maples. Conifers create heavy shade and acid soil that discourage most deciduous understory species. They are better thought of as background for other plantings or as a canopy for a woodland flower garden. However, needled evergreens make better windbreaks than deciduous trees and provide the best wind shelter for overwintering birds.

Consider whether small trees and shrubs can be grouped to form a woodland edge or a freestanding thicket. Some ornamentals commonly planted as specimens on the lawn are actually woodland understory species that would eventually benefit were saplings of canopy species planted among them. Others that require more light are typical of woodland edges. These species grow also in freestanding thickets between fields or along roadsides. Isolated specimens may be joined by the addition of other species to form such a hedgerow. Among both groups of ornamental trees and shrubs are found the fruiting species most valuable to birds. Woodland edges and hedgerows also provide nesting sites and winter shelter.

Grass, wildflowers, and other ground-cover habitats

Turfgrass is, of course, the major vegetation in American yards. Second in popularity are aggressively spreading and usually exotic ground covers, such as English ivy and pachysandra. Neither has wildlife value as food or shelter, and both preclude diversity by excluding native species. Flower gardens are notably rare in the suburban landscape, perhaps for the good reason that they require a gardener's care. Regardless, in the course of their breeding most cultivated flowers have lost the enticements, especially copious amounts of nectar and pollen, that in the wild courted insect pollinators.

Any remaining open ground in most yards is mulched. Organic mulches, while they do more for soil than paving or gravel, are not as effective in conditioning and enriching soil as the natural plant debris that accumulates in a meadow or on the woodland floor. Natural debris also houses myriad insects and other arthropods that are staple items in the diet of many birds.

Measure the area of your yard that is taken up by nonproductive ground covers, including lawn and mulch. Roughly measure as well the area that you actually use—for seating, as a play area, or as a route from one place to another. Any portion of the remainder that is sunny all or most of the day could be meadow. Any portion that is in shade all or most of the day could be woodland ferns and wild-flowers—or at least be left unraked to accumulate a natural mulch of leaf litter.

Calculate, if you have the data available, the amount you spend on lawn care and other routine yard maintenance, such as watering, fertilizing, and replenishing mulch. A portion of that budget could be spent instead on habitat improvements that ultimately would reduce your annual expenditure.

Amenities

A good habitat may also require specific amenities, such as drinking and bathing water and natural or manmade housing. These, like butterfly host plants and hummingbird nectar flowers, need not be in your own back yard. They should, though, be part of a general assessment of your neighborhood. If you find that amenities are lacking in your immediate area, consider providing them. The construction of birdhouses is explained beginning on page 361. A simple way to make a birdbath is described on page 369.

For more information:

Fruit Trees and Shrubs for Bird Hedgerows, pages 282–83

How to Start a Tree Island, page 405

How to Prepare a Grassland Site, page 426

🍂 A NOTE ON DOCTORING PHOTOGRAPHS

Color duplication offers a new opportunity to play around with different ways to change the landscape. Take color photographs of the areas where you're considering improvements. (Prints come out better on a color copier than transparencies do.) Try to keep the views simple: straight-on shots of the front or rear of the house or straight-on shots of the perimeter as seen from a living room window or a patio. The best time to do this is in the winter, when there is the least foliage and colors are pale and dull. An overcast day is preferable, to reduce harsh shadows.

Have each print duplicated and enlarged on a color copier to fill a sheet of paper, which can be up to 11 x 17 inches. You may want several copies of each. Purchase at an art store Prismacolor pencils in an array of colors—greens for foliage, brown for tree trunks, straw for grasses (as they would look in the fall), and colors that match the house. You can use the pencils both to cover up features on the paper duplicate and to add new ones. For example, "erase" existing shrubs against the house by penciling the house color over them, or modify their appearance by sketching other vegetation in front of them. Or change lawn to meadow, trees to woods, fence to hedgerow. You needn't delineate these changes carefully; just suggest bulk and texture by crude strokes and scribbles.

For more information:

How to Make a Scale Drawing of Your Lot, page 294

A typical suburban home with an equally typical front yard and foundation planting

A duplicate of the photo (yours would be in color) doctored to give an idea of how the landscape could be redesigned as quality habitat. A portion of the lawn has been replaced by meadow. The young conifers at the foundation have been moved out to form a hedgerow along the driveway. A small grove of trees—a pocket woodland—has been added, along with an edging of fruiting shrubs.

FRUIT TREES AND SHRUBS FOR BIRD HEDGEROWS

Birds use hedgerows in three ways: for food (insects as well as fruit), safe nesting sites, and shelter in the winter. The most useful hedgerows include a variety of species laced together with suckering or thicketing shrubs such as roses or red osier dogwood. Aim for a long fruiting period. Punctuate the hedgerow with small trees, not only the crabapples suggested here, but any of the pioneer species listed in Pioneer Trees and Shrubs (page 302) or the smaller nuts and acorns (page 420). Hedgerow species may also be planted along a sunny woodland edge. On small properties, contain the hedgerow's spread between mowed paths. A plus sign (+) added to the season indicates that the fruit persists on the plant, and therefore is available to wildlife over a long period.

name	fruit color	season	height	soil texture	moisture	light	habitat	zone	region

ARCTOSTAPHYLOS (manzanitas) Most Arctostaphylos species are low, trailing plants, but these Pacific Coast species grow to hedgerow size. Fruits are consumed especially by grouse and quail.

name	fruit color	season	height	soil texture	moisture	light	habitat	zone	region
Arctostaphylos glauca (bigberry manzanita)	brown	early	6 - 12'			○		10	9, 10
A. manzanita (common manzanita)	red	early	10 - 12'			○○		7	6

CORNUS (dogwoods) Dogwood species include both trees and shrubs. The small, abundant fruits are rich in starch and oils, and ripen all at once in late summer or fall when birds flock and begin their fall migration. Shrub species form thickets; control their spread with mowed paths.

name	fruit color	season	height	soil texture	moisture	light	habitat	zone	region
Cornus florida (flowering dogwood)	red	late	10 - 40'			○○●		4	2, 3, 4
C. stolonifera (red osier dogwood)	white	late	6 - 12'			○		2	1, 2, 4, 5, 6, 9
C. racemosa (gray dogwood)	white	late	10 - 15'			○		4	1, 2, 3, 4

ILEX (hollies) The best-known hollies are evergreen, like inkberry, but the others here are deciduous species whose fruit, persisting into spring, are of great value to overwintering birds.

name	fruit color	season	height	soil texture	moisture	light	habitat	zone	region
Ilex decidua (possumhaw)	orange/red	late +	12 - 20'			○○		5	2, 3, 4
I. glabra (inkberry)	black	late +	6 - 9'			○○●		3	3
I. verticillata (winterberry)	red	late +	6 - 12'			○○		3	2, 3, 4

MAHONIA (mahonias) There are other Mahonias whose berries are relished by birds and other wildlife, but most are low groundcovers of limited use in a hedgerow.

name	fruit color	season	height	soil texture	moisture	light	habitat	zone	region
Mahonia aquifolium (Oregon-grape)	blue	mid +	3 - 6'			○○		5	6, 9

name	fruit color	season	height	soil texture	moisture	light	habitat	zone	region
MALUS (crabapples) All the crabapples have high wildlife value, but the one-inch fruits of native species are not as valuable to birds as the quarter-inch fruits of ornamental crabs, many of which are of Japanese descent. Fruits may be red, yellow, or orange; all ripen in fall and some are most palatable and nutritious after they have been softened by frost. Height ranges from a shrubby 6 feet to trees of over 20 feet. Requirements are typified by the two examples here.									
Malus floribunda	yellow/red	late	15 - 25'			◯		4	(NA)
M. sargentii (Sargent's crabapple)	red	late +	6 - 8'			◯		4	(NA)
PRUNUS (plums and cherries) These selections from a very large group are thicketing shrubs that spread by root suckers. A few Prunus species that grow to be single-stemmed trees are listed as Pioneers on page 303, but the shrub forms, too, thrive on neglect.									
Prunus americana (American plum)	yellow/red	early	15 - 25'			◯		3	2, 3, 4, 5
P. angustifolia (chickasaw plum)	yellow/red	mid	4 - 10'			◯		6	3
P. besseyi (sand cherry)	black	mid	4 - 6'			◯		3	4, 5, 8
P. caroliniana (Carolina cherry-laurel)	black	late +	20 - 30'			⬤		7	2, 3
P. ilicifolia (holly-leaved cherry)	red	late	10 - 25'			◯		9	10
RIBES (currants and gooseberries) Currants and gooseberries are among the few summer fruits that remain on the bush for weeks after ripening. They are particularly valuable to ground-nesting birds such as quail and pheasant.									
Ribes odoratum (clove currant)	red	mid	6 - 9'			◯		4	5, 6, 7, 8
R. sanguineum (red-flowering currant)	blue/black	mid	10 - 12'			◯◐⬤		5	6, 9

ROSA (roses) The small hips of wild roses remain on the branches for several months, providing food for overwintering birds. Flowers are single, pink or white, and bloom in late spring. Expect all these species to sucker somewhat through the hedgerow, and welcome the habit: birds prefer to nest in well-knit thickets.

name	fruit color	season	height	soil texture	moisture	light	habitat	zone	region
Rosa blanda (northern prairie rose)	red	late +	3'					2	2, 4
R. californica (California rose)	orange	late +	3 - 9'					5	9
R. carolina (Carolina rose)	red	late +	3'					4	1, 2, 3, 4
R. gymnocarpa (little woods rose)	red	late +	1 - 3'					3	6, 9
R. nitida (shining rose)	red	late +	2'					3	1, 2
R. nutkana (nutka rose)	red	late +	3 - 6'					3	6, 9
R. setigera (prairie rose)	red	late +	6 - 12'					4	2, 3, 4
R. virginiana (Virginia rose)	red	late +	6'					3	1, 2, 3, 4

RUBUS (blackberries, raspberries, etc.) The sweet summer fruits of the Rubus genus are among the most popular with birds. They are generally brambles-prickly shrubs that spread by suckering-but except for blackcap raspberry, the species here are less aggressive than the common wild blackberry. Keep their spread in check by a mowed path to both sides of the hedgerow. American red raspberry is available only as named varieties.

name	fruit color	season	height	soil texture	moisture	light	habitat	zone	region
Rubus deliciosus (boulder raspberry)	purple	mid	2 - 5'					5	6
R. odoratus (pink-flowered thimbleberry)	red	mid	6 - 9'					3	1, 2,
R. parviflorus (western thimbleberry)	red	mid	3 - 6'					3	2, 4, 6, 7, 9
R. occidentalis (blackcap raspberry)	black	mid	3 - 6'					3	2, 4
R. strigosus (American red raspberry)	red	mid	3 - 6'					3	1, 2, 4, 6

SYMPHORICARPUS (snowberries, coralberries) Symphoricarpus species are fine-branched, mounding shrubs found mostly in north central and northwestern regions. Branches may become weighted to the ground with ripened fruit.

name	fruit color	season	height	soil texture	moisture	light	habitat	zone	region
Symphoricarpus albus (common snowberry)	pink	early +	3 - 4'						1, 2, 6, 10
S. occidentalis (western snowberry)	white	late	3 - 4'						4, 5, 6
S. orbiculatus (coralberry, Indian currant)	magenta	late +	3 - 4'						2, 4

VACCINEUM (blueberries)

There are many Vaccineum species in northern regions of the country, somewhat fewer to the south. All require acid soil, but their tolerance of a wide range of conditions is otherwise remarkable. Crops of the wild but not the commercial species ripen over weeks during the summer, and are much sought out by birds.

name	fruit color	season	height	soil texture	moisture	light	habitat	zone	region
Vaccineum angustifolium (lowbush blueberry)	blue	mid	1 - 2'					2	1, 2, 4
V. corymbosum (highbush blueberry)	blue	mid	6 - 12'					3	2, 3
V. stamineum (deerberry)	blue	late	6 - 12'					5	2, 3

VIBURNUM (viburnums, haws)

Most native viburnums are southeastern shrubs, but a few range north into New England and the Great Lakes or west onto the central plains. There are no truly western species. Ripening is quite variable among the species, ranging from summer fruits to ones timed for fall migration, a few clinging into winter.

name	fruit color	season	height	soil texture	moisture	light	habitat	zone	region
Viburnum acerifolium (mapleleaf viburnum)	blue/black	mid +	3 - 6'					3	2
V. dentatum (arrowwood viburnum)	blue	late	6 - 12'					2	2, 3
V. nudum (possumhaw)	pink/blue	late	12 - 20'					6	2, 3
V. prunifolium (blackhaw)	black	late	12 - 15'					3	2, 4
V. rufidulum (rusty blackhaw)	black	late	10 - 20'					5	2, 3, 4
V. trilobum (cranberrybush viburnum)	red	late +	6 - 12'					2	1, 2, 4

18 Planning the Landscape

🍃 HOW TO KNOW YOUR DIRT

The existing vegetation on your land may already have assessed the soil for you. Plants that are growing well indicate at least an average garden soil, adequate in moisture, texture, and fertility for the majority of native species. Consistent plant failure may indicate that the soil isn't average, but it doesn't necessarily mean that anything is "wrong"—except the choice of plants. To choose the right plants, get to know your dirt. The simple investigations here address soil texture, moisture, and fertility. They will help you use the corresponding symbols on the species charts. Catalogs and research materials use much the same vocabulary.

Dig a big hole

Do this when the soil is moist. To learn in general about your soil, choose a spot away from the house where possibly the ground hasn't been disturbed by regrading or backfilling during construction. To learn about a "trouble spot," dig there. If the area is lawn, first cut out a generous circle of turf and put it aside to replace later. You'll be digging the hole about a foot and a half deep, in stages.

Test the texture of the top layer. Rub a little soil between your thumb and fingers to feel its texture. Sand feels gritty, and you can see the particles. Silt feels silky or floury, but not sticky, and you can see the particles with a magnifying glass. Clay particles are too fine to see even with a magnifying glass, and though clay feels smooth, it is also sticky and plastic. Most soils contain combinations of these particle sizes. Medium-texture soil, called loam, is made up of equal portions of sand, silt, and clay. Soils are further categorized as clay loam, silt loam, or sandy loam, depending on the predominant particle size. Pick up a handful of moist soil and squeeze it into a ball. Clay loam is a dense "heavy" soil that holds its molded shape and dries hard. Silt loam is lighter; it holds its shape somewhat but crumbles at the edges. Sandy loam is a "light" soil; it holds its molded shape only momentarily and falls apart if jiggled. Terms like "good garden soil" or "rich woodland humus" imply the medium crumbly texture of loam, whose proportions of sand, silt, and clay are more or less equal and which also contains plenty of organic matter.

Sniff the soil. A rich, earthy fragrance indicates that the soil is high in organic matter—decaying animal and vegetable debris. A merely mineral scent indicates that it's low in organic matter. Minerals—phosphate, potassium, and nitrogen, plus smaller amounts of such items as iron, calcium, and magnesium—are the only nutrients that plants need. They become available for roots to absorb in two ways: sparely and slowly, as water dissolves the minerals from particles of dirt, or abundantly and rapidly, as soil microbes decay debris. Nitrogen, the major ingredient of fertilizers, can be delivered to plants in usable form only by soil organisms. A rich scent suggests a large reservoir of "fertilizer." A lack of much odor suggests sterile soil.

Dig out the top layer and put it to one side. You'll know you've removed the "topsoil" when the color or texture of the dirt changes. Regardless of whether the topsoil is light or heavy, it is usually darker than the underlying soil because it contains brown or black organic matter. Any dirt below this layer is subsoil—inorganic clay, silt, sand, or loam. The change from topsoil to subsoil could be just inches below the surface or down a foot or more. On new lots, there may be no topsoil at all. Although plants may anchor deep in subsoil, most of their feeder roots obtain nourishment from the top layer.

Continue digging, but keep the different kinds of dirt in separate piles. You may come on another layer, again of a different color or texture, or even a lens of sand or a streak of solid clay. You may find that what you're digging out is mostly stones: your ground is "rocky." You may hit bedrock at less than 20 inches: your soil is "thin." Water may seep into the hole: the soil is "wet" or "saturated." If the soil is so hard that you'll need a pickax to loosen it before you can dig it out, the ground may be "compacted" by construction equipment or foot traffic, or you may have hit a cement-like layer of hardpan (don't try to dig any farther in this case). When you're finished digging, scrape one side of the hole clean so that you can clearly see the "profile" of the layers you've removed.* The underground condi-

---

* In undisturbed ground, the various colors and textures in this depth of soil will match those described in a soil profile for your area. If you're interested in pursuing the subject (it's fun but not really necessary), ask your Agricultural Extension Service where to obtain a profile—most likely from a county department called Soil and Water Conservation or a similar name.

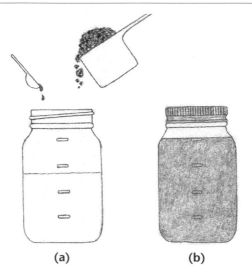

(a)   (b)

To determine soil texture by a method more accurate than a mere squeeze, measure its sedimentation rate. You'll need a ruler and a clock or watch with a sweep second hand.

(a) Fill a 1-quart canning jar two-thirds full with water. Add a tablespoon of a nonsudsing liquid dishwasher detergent, then add enough soil to bring the level to the 1-quart mark. The soil should be free of debris, such as sticks, stones, and fragments of dried leaves.

(b) Screw on the lid and shake the jar vigorously for however long it takes to mix the soil and water thoroughly. There shouldn't be any lumps or soil stuck to the sides.

(c) Put the jar on a flat surface and time 1 minute. Measure the sediment that settles to the bottom of the jar: that's the amount of sand in your soil sample. Jot down the measurement (1 inch in this example).

(d) In 1 hour, measure the sediment again. This time, the additional amount will be silt. Measure the total (1.5 inches here) and subtract from the

tions you've uncovered are the conditions that roots, too, will have to cope with.

Fill the hole with water. Watch the water level over the next few hours. If the water subsides at the rate of about an inch an hour, the soil is "well drained." Faster subsidence means the soil is "excessively drained"; slower subsidence means it's "poorly drained." Drainage is affected by soil texture: sand drains fastest, clay slowest. It's also affected by the lay of the land—you may have dug your hole up on a hilltop or down in a sump—and by what lies underneath, like a bowl of bedrock. Although "well drained" describes the middling ground idealized by gardeners, many plants do best under more extreme conditions. Species adapted to excessively drained sites have evolved water conservation technologies that allow them to live through

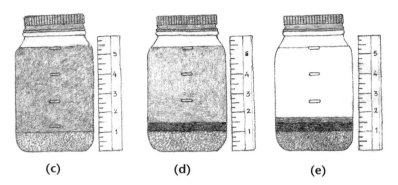

(c)	(d)	(e)

total the amount of sand (1.5 minus 1 inch of sand equals 0.5 inch silt).
(e) Leave the jar undisturbed for a day or longer. Clay particles are so small that they can take as long as a week to settle. When the water in the jar clears, measure a third time. Subtract the previous two layers from the total. Here, the figure for the clay layer is 0.25 inch.

To convert these measurements to percentages, first divide 100 by the total sediment height (1.75 inches). That figure comes out to 57.1, which represents the whole sample, 100%. Multiply this result by the amount of each component to find the percentages of sand, silt, and clay:

> *57.1 x 1.0 (sand) = 57.1% sand*
> *57.1 x 0.5 (silt) = 28.6% silt*
> *57.1 x 0.25 (clay) = 14.3% clay*

This soil sample would be classified as sandy loam.

drought. The same species would die in waterlogged, poorly drained sites for lack of oxygen to their roots or by decay. Species adapted to flooded soil take in the necessary oxygen through pores in their aboveground stem or air pockets in their underground parts; they have evolved chemical defenses against decay organisms.

Before you fill the hole, you may want to take soil samples for analysis of fertility and acidity. Soil analysis is offered for a modest fee by your Agricultural Extension Service. It may also provide a form to fill out and instructions on how to submit samples. If not, just set aside a small amount of topsoil, mix it well, and submit the sample in a plastic bag. This is not an important exercise, but soil testing is so emphasized in horticultural literature that you may feel less than thorough if you don't give it a try.

The dirt on the left is sand and clay subsoil that may have a vaguely mineral smell. The soil on the right, rich with organic debris as evidenced by its deeper color (and the earthworm!), should have a rich, woodsy smell.

Open test slots through the season

There's no guarantee that the soil in your yard is uniform from site to site. Regrading may have changed the surface considerably; erosion may have thinned the soil over rocks and silted lower areas. Soil will be drier uphill, moister downhill. Windy areas dry out faster than sheltered ones. South or west exposures are drier than east or north ones. Existing vegetation also affects moisture. Surface-rooted trees, such as maple or elm, dry the soil around them; plants that shade and mulch the ground, such as ferns or bunchgrasses, conserve moisture. To choose suitable species, you'll need to know which areas are dry (or "xeric"), which are medium (or "mesic"), and which are wet.

This is a matter of observation over the full growing season. From time to time, open a slot in the soil with a spade at various sites in the yard. The deeper you have to penetrate to reach soil that feels moist to the touch, the drier the site. There may be dramatic differences over the course of the seasons. Poorly drained areas that are inundated in the spring may bake dry later in the summer. Even this condition can be accommodated, for quite a few "wetland" species are actually "bipolar." They manage in both flood and drought.

WHAT NOT TO DO WHEN THE SOIL TEST ARRIVES

Soil analysis reports are usually returned to you within a month. The results can be alarming. The analysis may indicate that your soil has too little organic matter to provide sufficient nitrogen, that the sam-

Planting Noah's Garden

ple is low in one or more other minerals, or that its pH—a measure of soil acidity or alkalinity—is too high or too low. The assumption is that your purpose in obtaining the analysis is to "correct" these "deficiencies" by soil amendment, such as fertilizer to provide minerals, sulfur to increase acidity, or lime to decrease acidity. The analysis will include these recommendations. Don't follow them. There is no soil to which some form of vegetation is not adapted. The right choice of vegetation will do well under existing conditions and in time improve them. Use the soil analysis merely to get some notion of the existing conditions.

The pH factor. The pH of soil, measured on a scale from 1.0 (most acidic) to 14.0 (most alkaline), affects the solubility of minerals. Each mineral dissolves optimally at a different pH. Nitrogen is most soluble in the middle range, between 6.0 and 8.0 (a pH of 7.0 indicates a "neutral" soil, neither acid nor alkaline). Phosphorus and potassium dissolve better in more alkaline (or limey, "sweet," calcareous) soil; iron dissolves better in more acid ("sour") soil. The pH of soil over large areas is determined by the nature of the bedrock from which the soil particles are derived. Much of the central portion of the country lies over limestone and so tends toward alkaline soil; naturally, it's not rich in iron. Elsewhere, the bedrock may be granite, and the acidic soil derived from it tends to be richer in iron, poorer in phosphorus and potassium. Soil pH also varies locally. There may be pockets of limestone in otherwise granite areas. Lime leaching from a concrete foundation may lower the acidity in only one bed. Oak leaves or conifer needles raise soil acidity in the area of their leaf fall.

Plants don't need acid, nor do they need antacid (calcium carbonate, or lime). They do need dissolved minerals. Plant species that have evolved in alkaline soil adapted their mineral requirements to what was available, and the same is true of those that evolved in acid soil. Blueberries (Vaccinium species) fail to thrive in central portions of the country because they're accustomed to more iron than lime soils provide, but the buffaloberries (Shepherdia species) that do well there would be a poor choice for more eastern areas, where very acid soil can't provide them with enough calcium. There's no reason to correct the pH as long as you respect its limitation on plant choice.

Soil low in organic content can't support a large population of microorganisms that subsist on debris, and therefore it is also low in nitrogen, which ordinarily is made available by certain soil bacteria. Depending on the chemical composition of the underlying rock,

For more information:

How to Prepare
a Grassland Site,
page 426

soil lacking an organic reservoir may be impoverished in other minerals, too. Pioneer species are unusually efficient at obtaining what
minerals are available in even sterile soils; some have their own bacteria for supplying nitrogen. The minerals accumulate in their
leaves. The shed leaves create the organic reservoir that will nourish
more demanding plants in the future. In extreme cases, pioneer
species can be used as temporary cover, to be tilled into the soil to
improve texture and fertility.

HOW TO ROUGHLY PLAN YOUR LOT

The survey that accompanied the deed to your lot can be used as the
basis for planning the landscape. If you can't find the survey, get a
duplicate from your building department or from the county court-
house where the deed is filed. The instructions that follow are based on
a small lot. The same principles apply if you have acreage, but in that
case you may want to plan the landscape on only a portion of the
property.

This rough plan is a small sketch called a thumbnail: it's bigger than
a thumb, but small enough that you can grasp it at a glance.
Thumbnail sketches are just for playing with general ideas—what
might be open space, tall growth, or shorter shrubbery, where paths
lead, and what sorts of places they lead to. The survey size is usually
about right for this doodling.

You probably have a ruler, an eraser, and pencils. You'll also need a
pad of inexpensive tracing paper large enough to trace the lot boundary from the survey. You'll be layering these sheets on top of one another, so the more transparent they are, the better.

Trace the survey

Trace the survey or the portion of it under consideration. You don't
need detailed information—just the boundary and immovable objects
like the house and driveway. Guess the location and size of important
trees, and add them to the tracing along with any other landscape features that you consider permanent, such as a hedge or walk. When
you're satisfied with this basic sketch, darken the lines so they'll be easily visible through other layers of tracing paper.

Sketch your ideas on tracing paper overlays

You can use sheet after sheet—or smaller pieces taped in place—each
overlay changing, correcting, or refining the previous layout. Tape the
layout you like best into position over the original tracing, which
shows permanent features. This sketch is all you need to guide the general shape of your future planting.

(a)

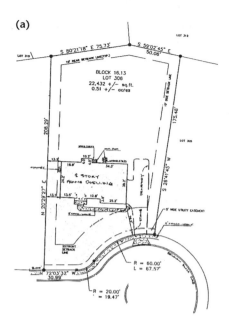

(b)

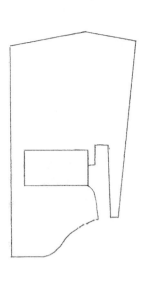

(a) The survey of a typical lot

(b) A simplified tracing of the lot

(c)

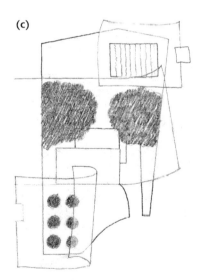

(d)

(c) Scraps of tracing paper show several ideas: a vegetable garden, rows of fruit trees, a patio, and a belt of woodland.

(d) The final thumbnail pulls the ideas together. The fruit trees are staggered to follow the curve at the front of the lot. The woods have moved to a rear corner. The perimeter of the lot is enclosed by shrubs.

To create a landscape plan in any greater detail than a thumbnail sketch, you'll have to work at a larger scale. If you have available a copying machine that can enlarge a drawing, simply have the original survey or your thumbnail doubled in size and work from that. But it takes only a few minutes to double the survey size on a tracing.

Eventually you'll also need to figure accurate dimensions on your landscape plan: the width of a path, the size of a play area. The survey indicates the distance in feet from angle to angle along the boundary lines. There's also a notation such as Scale: 1"=30'. It ought to mean that if you measured, say, the length of the driveway on the drawing and it was 1.75 inches, the actual driveway is 52.5 feet long. Often, though, the original survey has been reduced to a convenient size on a copying machine, so the scale is no longer accurate. This doesn't affect the proportions, however. If the driveway was twice as long as the front walk on the original survey, it's still twice as long on the copy. But if you wanted the vegetable garden to be 15 x 20 feet, how would you draw it correctly? The procedure described here shows not only how to enlarge a survey, but also how to create a scale that you can use as a ruler.

You need:

Graphed tracing paper, either several single sheets or a pad (available at art stores). An 11 x 17-inch sheet will let you double the size of a typical lot survey. Check that the paper is thin enough to trace through.

An inexpensive compass, the kind children use at school, and a 12-inch ruler.

A steel tape for measuring the actual dimensions of your yard. Hardware stores sell steel tapes in various lengths; a 100-foot one is advisable.

Double the survey size

The principle here is simple. Trace onto the graph paper each segment of the boundary line twice, end to end, to double it. At the end of each segment, trace the corner angle and double the next segment. The illustrations on the next two pages show you how. Use the ruler to draw the lines straight.

Construct a scale

The enlarged drawing doesn't indicate how the graph paper grid relates to the actual measurements of your house and lot, nor would the ruler help you represent accurately the placement of major features whose location you merely guessed in your thumbnail sketches. You

A 100-foot steel tape

need to construct a scale. Since the scale will be drawn on the same sort of graph paper as the enlarged survey, it will also give you a sense of how the grid relates to actual dimension in feet.

Choose on your enlarged survey any long boundary line whose dimension is more or less divisible by 5 or 10. This is usually a side lot line: for instance, a lot line of 110 or 86 feet. It doesn't matter if there's a small remainder; the scale will be accurate enough. In the example here, the chosen boundary line measures 90 feet.

(a)

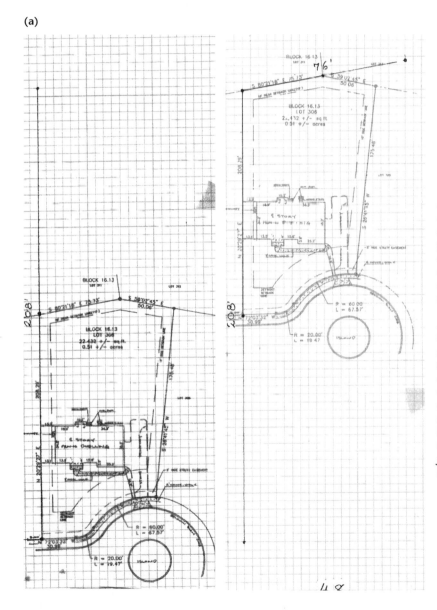

(a) *Left: Trace the far left boundary line from the survey onto the graph paper. Make a dot at both ends of the line for emphasis. Lengthen the line somewhat using the ruler.*

Right: Reposition the tracing over the survey and use the same boundary segment as a measure to double the length of the line on the tracing. Make another dot to mark where the next segment begins. Copy from the survey the actual number of feet this first boundary line represents.

(b) Reposition the survey under the tracing, trace the next boundary segment, and double it in the same way as you did before. You have now reproduced the boundary angle exactly but "blown it up" to twice its original size. Again, copy from the survey the actual measurement in feet.

(c) Repeat the tracing of angle and doubling of line until the boundary is complete. (If there's a curved boundary line, as there is here, draw it by eye on the tracing after all the straight segments are done.)

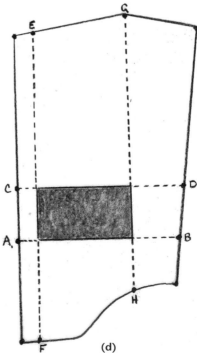

(b)

(c)

(d) To position the house correctly (and at twice the size) on your tracing, first extend the house walls on the survey so they cross the boundaries. These guidelines give you a new set of measures a-b, b-c, c-d, and so on. To locate the intersecting points on your tracing, use the same technique you used to double the boundary segments. Connect the points with a ruler to define the perimeter of the house, then erase the extra portions of the guidelines.

(d)

Planting Noah's Garden

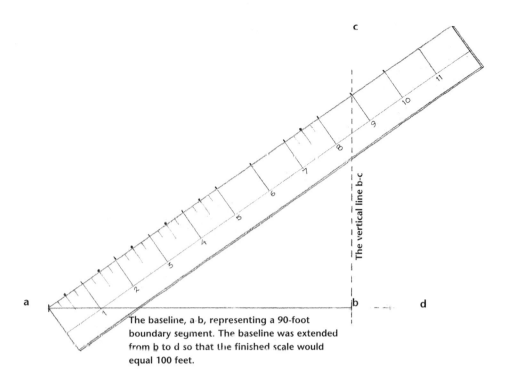

The baseline, a-b, representing a 90-foot boundary segment. The baseline was extended from b to d so that the finished scale would equal 100 feet.

The vertical line b-c

Draw the line you've chosen horizontally on a fresh piece of tracing paper toward the bottom left of the sheet; use the grid to keep the line straight. This is your baseline, a-b. Hatch a short vertical mark, as on a ruler, at each end of the line for emphasis.

Figure the number of 10-foot (or 5-foot) segments into which the baseline could be divided. This one can be divided into nine equal 10-foot segments.

Draw a long vertical line, b-c, up the page as shown.

Now draw a diagonal to form a triangle. The diagonal will measure, in inches, whatever number of segments you figured—in this case, nine. Another way of putting it is that the scale of the diagonal line will be 1 inch = 10 feet (½ inch = 5 feet). Hold the ruler so that its first hatch is on the baseline's left end marker, a, and its 9-inch hatch crosses the vertical line, b-c. Draw the diagonal and, with the ruler still in place, make hatch marks along it at ½-inch (5-foot) and 1-inch (10-foot) intervals, as shown. Make the last hatch at the 10-inch mark so the finished scale will represent 100 feet rather than just 90. Jot numerals along the diagonal to indicate the lengths represented by the hatches.

Using the grid for guidance, draw verticals between the baseline and each of the hatch marks on the diagonal. The baseline is now a scale marked off into segments representing the same lengths as those

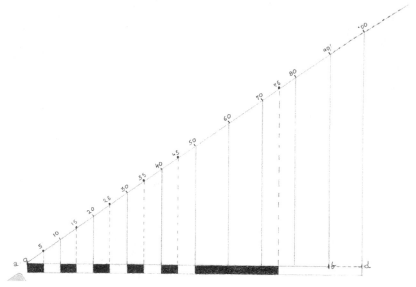

To make the scale easier to read, add a bar along the bottom of the baseline and shade the segments.

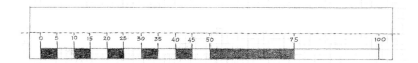

Fold the scale on the dotted line.

on the diagonal. Each short segment equals 5 feet; each longer segment equals 10 feet; the longest segments equal 25 feet.

So that you can use the scale as a ruler, add a numeral at each mark to indicate the number of feet; for convenience, this scale was numbered at 5-foot intervals up to 50 feet, with a mark added at 75 feet. Cut the scale out, fold it in half lengthwise to strengthen it, and use it to measure any new dimension you wish to add on your drawing. You may also want to trace the scale onto the drawing, as is done on maps.

Note also that the marks on your scale probably coincide well enough with the graph paper grid that you can roughly figure a dimension by counting squares. On this scale, three squares equal a little less than 5 feet.

Add detail to your drawing
Now that you have a scale, you can accurately position permanent features. Make a list. You need to know the locations of the front and back

doors and such items as the meter box, condenser, swing set, garbage pails, mailbox, and so on, as well as the features whose locations you merely guessed on the thumbnail. You'll need a pad of paper for taking notes and someone to help you measure with the steel tape.

Measure locations by referring to one or two points already represented on your drawing. To place the mailbox, for instance, measure its distance from the driveway. Locating a tree in the yard requires two measurements: for example, its distance from the right rear corner of the house and its distance from the left rear corner. Jot down the dimensions. Locate only a few items at first. When added to the drawing, they will give you more fixed reference points from which to measure others.

Transfer the locations to the drawing. For the mailbox, just use your scale to mark its distance from the driveway. You'll need the compass to locate the tree. Using the scale, set the compass to the first of the two dimensions. Place the point at the house corner from which you took the measurement and draw an arc. Reset the compass to the second dimension, taken at the other corner of the house, and again describe an arc. Where the arcs intersect is the location of the tree.

Measure areas, too, such as the patio or vegetable garden, and add them to the drawing. If such areas don't yet exist but you hope to include them in your future landscape, figure the approximate size you'd like them to be, use the scale to draw them separately on another sheet of graph paper, and cut them out. That way, you can move the shapes around on your drawing until you're satisfied with their location.

Sketch in the vegetation

Refer back to your thumbnail now to copy your rough design. Using tracing paper overlays on the drawing, sketch in the contours of paths, clearings, and vegetation. They'll change, of course, now that you know where things really are. Also, you now can measure with your scale to adjust the width of a path or the depth of a planting area. Play with the design on overlay after overlay, just as you did with the thumbnail. When you're pleased, darken the lines on the final version. Put the sketch under the drawing, and trace it. The new drawing is now an accurately scaled landscape plan.

🍂 A SHORT LESSON IN VEGETABLE TEXTURE

A landscape plan is easier to visualize if the vegetation is filled in with texture rather than just a tone or outline. The textures can be rubbings, like those done by children to make the image of a penny. Use Prismacolor pencils. They are richly pigmented, come in black and a huge range of colors, and don't smear like ordinary pencils.

You may want to work on a fresh tracing for this finished drawing; the first one may have become smeared, or it isn't lettered as nicely as you'd like, or you can see that you'd rather position it better on the sheet of paper. Lightly trace all the outlines onto a fresh sheet with a Prismacolor pencil. (You don't have to copy the numerals that give dimension since you now have a permanent scale.) Darken the lines only when you're sure you like them—these pencils are difficult to erase.

Most of the textures here are rubbings of book covers. Use a piece of scrap paper to experiment. Lay the paper on the textured object and pencil over the surface lightly, using either the blunted point or the side of the lead. Darken the texture gradually until you achieve an effect you like. When you rub texture onto your drawing, tape the sheet of paper down so it doesn't move while you work.

These rubbings (from left to right and top to bottom) are taken from a catalog cover, a piece of watercolor paper, a book bound in fake leather, a checkbook, a book bound in buckram, another clothbound book, a Valentine's Day card, and an encyclopedia.

Planting Noah's Garden

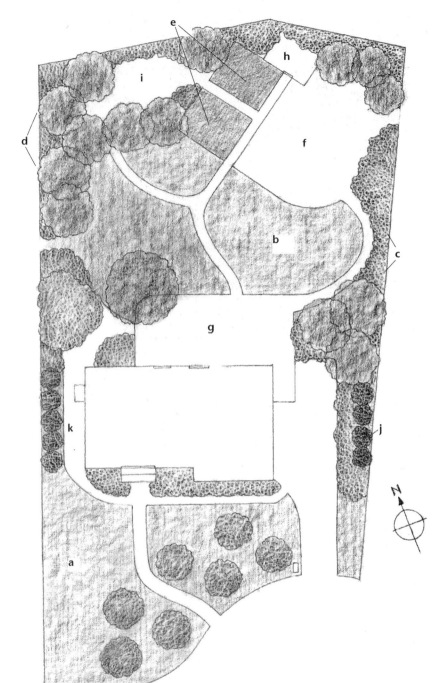

The finished landscape plan:

a. Shortgrass meadow
b. Tallgrass meadow
c. Fruiting thickets,
   brambles, hedgerows
d. Pioneer trees, wood-
   land trees
e. Vegetable garden
f. Children's play area
g. Future patio
h. Future tool shed
i. Fern glade
j. Conifer screen
k. Service path

PIONEER TREES AND SHRUBS

Pioneer species are by definition ones that populate open, sunny ground. Most grow quickly, fruit vigorously, cope with poor soil, flood, or drought, but are considered "short-lived" plants: that is, they live less than a hundred years. Those listed here were chosen partly for their modest size: pines and spruces, for instance, aren't included, and oaks and other pioneering nut trees are listed separately on page 420.

name	height	soil texture	moisture	light	habitat	zone	region

ALNUS (alders) Alders are of ecological importance not only for repopulating stream banks after floods or blowdowns, but for their ability to add nitrogen to infertile soils. Eastern alders are coarse, thicketing shrubs that few are fond of. These western species are attractive trees.

name	height	soil texture	moisture	light	habitat	zone	region
Alnus rubra (red alder)	40 - 60'					4	9, 10
A. rhombifolia (white alder)	60 - 80'					5	6, 9, 10
A. tenuifolia (mountain alder)	20 - 30'					3	6

BETULA (birches) Birches naturally sprout in groves on disturbed land and abandoned fields. Foliage is airy; bark ornamental, and the buds are an important food for wildlife.

name	height	soil texture	moisture	light	habitat	zone	region
Betula lenta (sweet or black birch)	50 - 70'					3	1, 2
B. nigra (river birch)	60 - 80'					4	2, 3, 4
B. occidentalis (western red or water birch)	15 - 25'					3	6, 7
B. papyrifera (paper or canoe birch)	70 - 80'					2	1, 2, 4, 6
B. populifolia (gray birch)	20 - 30'					4	1, 2

JUNIPERUS (junipers, red cedar) Unlike most pioneers, junipers grow slowly but may live for centuries. The resinous gray to blue fruits persist over several seasons, providing a ready food source for many animals, and the dense foliage serves as windbreak and winter shelter.

name	height	soil texture	moisture	light	habitat	zone	region
Juniperus communis (dwarf juniper)	1 - 4'					2	1, 2, 3, 4
J. occidentalis (western or Sierra juniper)	10 - 25'					4	7, 10
J. virginiana (eastern red cedar)	40 - 50'					2	2, 3, 4, 5
J. scopulorum (Rocky Mountain juniper)	15 - 30'					3	6, 7, 8, 9

POPULUS (poplars, aspens, cottonwoods) Poplars grow at an astounding rate—as much as 4 feet a year for quaking aspen. Leaf buds and catkins are eaten by birds and mammals in the spring.

name	height	soil texture	moisture	light	habitat	zone	region
Populus angustifolia (narrow-leaved poplar)	40 - 60'					3	5, 6, 8
P. balsamifera (balsam poplar)	30 - 80'					2	1, 2, 6
P. deltoides (eastern cottonwood)	40 - 80'					2	1, 2, 3, 4, 5, 6
P. fremontii (Fremont's cottonwood)	80 - 100'					3	6, 8
P. tremuloides (quaking aspen)	20 - 50'					1	1, 2, 4, 5, 6, 8
P. trichocarpa (black cottonwood)	40 - 80'					3	6, 7, 9, 10

PRUNUS (plums and cherries) Although most native Prunus species are thicketing shrubs, these grow to be small trees. The fruit ranks very high among wildlife.

name	height	soil texture	moisture	light	habitat	zone	region
Prunus pensylvanica (bird or pin cherry)	25 - 40'					2	1, 2, 3, 4, 6
P. serotina (wild black cherry)	50 - 60'					3	1, 2, 3, 4
P. virginiana (common chokecherry)	20 - 30'					2	1, 2, 3, 4, 5, 6

RHUS (sumacs) Sumacs are much looked down on in this country as weeds, but elsewhere they are valued as ornamentals for their "tropical" compound leaves, brilliant orange to scarlet fall color, and mounding, thicketing habit.

name	height	soil texture	moisture	light	habitat	zone	region
Rhus aromatica (fragrant sumac)	6 - 12'					3	2, 3, 4, 5
R. copallina (shining sumac)	10 - 20'					4	2, 3, 4
R. trilobata (skunkbush)	2 - 6'					4	4, 5, 6

SAMBUCUS (elderberries) Elderberries are among the most common and least fussy roadside pioneers. Their lacy bloom is followed by abundant juicy summer fruit.

name	height	soil texture	moisture	light	habitat	zone	region
Sambucus canadensis (common elderberry)	6 - 12'					3	1, 2, 3, 4
S. cerulea (blue elderberry)	15 - 25'					5	

19 *Choosing the Species*

🍂 HOW TO LEARN THE COMMON FLORA OF YOUR REGION

Only the rare expert can be said to know the flora of his or her own county, much less state or region. As a practical matter, such huge familiarity isn't that helpful anyway, since only a small percentage of native species are commercially available. Still, you have to know some common ones at least in order to revise existing plantings intelligently or carry forth a landscape plan. There is no step-by-step way to do it. The following means of gaining knowledge are interdependent; try them all at once.

Buy a few basic reference books

The most helpful home reference library focuses on field guides, to identify species you find, and natural history texts, to help you place species in context according to their habitats. Horticultural reference books are less helpful because so much of the information involves exotic species and irrelevant cultural instruction, but you may want to consult them for photographs and descriptions.

General identification guides. In addition to the Peterson Field Guide series suggested earlier (page 274) for identifying trees, shrubs, and wildflowers, consider the Audubon Field Guides. These are not as efficient for identification, and the series lacks the regional guides included in the Peterson series, but the descriptions of the natural distribution of each species are more exact, and plants are illustrated with color photographs, which may help you to picture them better in a garden. For those who live in the eastern half of the country, *The Tree Identification Book* and *The Shrub Identification*

Book, companion volumes by George W. D. Symonds (William Morrow), feature a photographic key that many consider the easiest to use. Lauren Brown's *Grasses: An Identification Guide* (Houghton Mifflin) is useful over most of the country. Look for more narrowly focused field guides to plants of unique or geographically limited ecosystems in conservation-minded bookstores—for example, at bird sanctuaries, nature centers, natural history museums, botanical gardens, arboretums, parks, preserves, and college or university bookstores.

Natural history texts. The Sierra Club Naturalist's Guide series, with nine titles so far, provides regional explorations of, for example, the Piedmont, Southwest Deserts, and North Woods. Another source is Patricia Ledlie Bookseller, a mail-order company that issues five catalogs a year listing current titles in natural science and conservation biology. Among its offerings are specialized books on regional flora unlikely to be covered in more general volumes; for example: *Native Plants of Southeast Alaska, Common Wetland Plants of Coastal California, The Vegetation of the New Jersey Pine Barrens, Intermountain Flora,* and *Trees, Shrubs, and Woody Vines of Northern Florida and Adjacent Southern Georgia and Alabama.* Write to Patricia Ledlie Bookseller, One Bean Road, P.O. Box 90, Buckfield, Maine 04220, or call 207-336-2778.

General cultural information. Horticultural encyclopedias, including *Wyman's Gardening Encyclopedia,* by Donald Wyman (Macmillan), and the Taylor Guide series (Houghton Mifflin) offer good descriptions and some practical gardening advice. Species covered in the Taylor Guides (to shrubs, trees, and so on) are illustrated by color photographs. Woody species are more extensively treated in *Manual of Woody Landscape Plants,* by Michael Dirr (Stipes). None of these texts emphasizes native plants. The one indispensable guide to American woody plants is *Native Trees, Shrubs, and Vines for Urban and Rural North America,* by Gary Hightshoe (Van Nostrand Reinhold). This splendid volume includes an excellent selection of species (though not as many western plants as one could wish for), and offers more—and more valuable—information than any other native plant reference. Black-and-white photographs and illustrations are exceptionally clear. Each species description covers not only the usual data, such as height, spread, habit, foliage, bloom time, and so on, but also habitat, wildlife value, pH range, drought and flood tolerance, and shrub and tree associates within the species' natural community. In addition, the plant's distribution in the wild is indicated on a map scaled to show county boundaries.

Contact government agencies and nonprofit conservation groups

Often, the most practical regional information is offered by state conservation departments (such as Fish and Wildlife), forestry or agricultural colleges at state universities, and private conservation organizations. Call around (one call will lead to another, but a good starting point would be a botanist or ecologist at your state university). Explain that you wish to learn more about native plants and natural habitats in your area and ask what materials the person would suggest. Here's a sample of some of the items turned up by such a search in the Northeast:

Plant Communities of New Jersey: A Study in Landscape Diversity, by Beryl Collins and Karl Anderson (Rutgers University Press), describes and lists the flora of every sort of habitat in that state from ridge top to sand dune, including not only trees and shrubs but their commonly associated ferns, forbs, and grasses (native and alien). Pioneer communities are also covered.

Native Species Planting Guide for New York City and Vicinity (City of New York Parks and Recreation) is a planting guide for habitat restoration. Species are grouped by community. Grasses are included; aliens are not. Commercial sources (some mail order) and planting instructions are given for each species.

Wetlands of Connecticut, by Ken Metzler and Ralph Tiner (State Geological and Natural History Survey of Connecticut in cooperation with the U.S. Fish and Wildlife Service National Wetlands Inventory), is an example of a thorough treatment of more specific habitats. Or one might choose instead *Wetland Planting Guide for the Northeastern United States,* by Gwendolyn Thunhorst (Environmental Concern), for its more instructional how-to-plant and where-to-get approach.

Use the library

Any library can track subjects by computer and obtain books from other collections through interlibrary loan. Ask the research librarian to help you do a search, which is based on key words such as "ecology, desert" or "plants, native, southwest." A book labeled "reference" can't be loaned; you would have to go to that library to consult it. Books not cataloged by any library (because none has bought them) won't turn up in the search. It's unlikely, for example, that *Native Species Planting Guide for New York City and Vicinity* would come to the attention of librarians. Sometimes, though, larger libraries keep files of ephemera—uncataloged pamphlets or booklets arranged by subject, such as trees or conservation.

Join conservation groups and native plant societies

You may, of course, join national groups as a charitable venture and out of general environmental concern, but to learn about your own region's plant communities, local groups or chapters are more helpful.

The Nature Conservancy is a group that buys and manages critical habitats threatened by development. Regional chapters publish newsletters about local conservation issues and offer guided nature walks and other educational opportunities. Staff naturalists are available to answer specific questions. Find your regional chapter in the telephone book or call the Nature Conservancy's main office in Arlington, Virginia: 703-841-5300.

The National Wildflower Research Center is worth joining for its clearinghouse service. Through the clearinghouse you can get regional bibliographies of native plant publications, state lists of species and sources, and addresses of native plant societies. The emphasis is on wildflowers, not plant communities, so you may find the bibliographies and species lists thin. Do send for the list of the native plant societies in your region; write to the National Wildflower Research Center, 4001 La Crosse Avenue, Austin, Texas 78739.

Native plant societies are advocacy, public service, and educational groups—some well established and well funded, others young and struggling. The least you'll get through membership is support from others who share your interest; you may also get a newsletter (the quality varies), discounts on publications, guided field trips, and a program of speakers. The most valuable learning experience may be public service work to preserve natural habitats. Locate native plant societies through the National Wildflower Research Center (see above) or *Gardening by Mail* (see below), in the Society Index under "Native Plants & Wildflowers."

Collect catalogs

Collecting catalogs will introduce you to the still rather small and manageable world of commercially available native species. Two source books will help you find growers who ship by mail order. Both of these oversize paperbacks are regularly updated, so consult the latest edition.

Gardening by Mail: A Source Book, by Barbara Barton (Houghton Mifflin). Growers are listed alphabetically by the name of the nursery and cross-referenced with an extensive plant source index. Using the index, you can find growers by type of plant ("Trees, flowering" or "Trees, seedling"), by type of plant within a region ("Grasses, prairie" or "Wildflowers, Rocky Mountain"), by region alone ("Native plants, southeastern U.S."), by habitat ("Desert plants" or "Wetland plants"), or by the common or botanic name of the genus ("Oak" or "Penstemon"). Turning from the index to the nurseries listed in that category, you will find a brief description of each catalog. The description will help you decide whether to send for the catalog. You may be referred by "Desert plants" to several growers, one of whom specializes in Arizona species, but another of whom just happens to carry some American cacti in a catalog otherwise devoted to exotic succulents. The description also gives you the price of the catalog; some are free or the cost is refundable with your first order.

Source List of Plants and Seeds (Andersen Horticultural Library). Some 47,000 plants are listed by botanical name and variety, each followed by a set of numbers designating the mail-order growers who carry them. There is a cross-reference of common names. Catalogs aren't described, so you have no way of knowing whether the grower emphasizes native species. Nevertheless, this book is invaluable if you know the species you want and can't find it in the catalogs you've already collected using Barton's book. The book is available only from the publisher: Andersen Horticultural Library, Minnesota Landscape Arboretum, 3675 Arboretum Boulevard, P.O. Box 39, Chanhassen, Minnesota 55317; or call 612-443-2440.

Evaluate the catalogs first by reading them. Responsible growers list species by botanical name; common names can apply to any number of species. Look for complete information, especially habitat requirements. Value especially growers with an obvious interest in—even a dedication to—native plants and plant communities. Try not to judge by marketing ploys such as color photography or a sophisticated layout. Compare prices, of course—but be aware that prices aren't necessarily based on the quality of the plant. When you've pared the stack down to a chosen few, place a sample order to compare the quality of the stock. An order also entitles you to a free "subscription" to the catalog, which will extend at least through the following year. A nicely honed collection of half a dozen catalogs is plenty to begin with.

Talk to growers; visit the nurseries. Once you've identified by catalog the growers whose interests seem best to coincide with yours, don't be shy. Call with any questions you may have or arrange to visit a nursery that's not too far away. *Gardening by Mail* and *Source List of*

Plants and Seeds both give the nurseries' telephone numbers and group them by state. *Gardening by Mail* also gives the grower's name. The catalog will tell you whether you need an appointment to visit the nursery.

Subscribe to publications

Gardening by Mail includes a Magazine Index, which lists hundreds of specialized journals, quarterlies, bulletins, and newsletters. Every sort of horticultural interest is represented, but a portion relates to native plants on a regional basis—and some of them are treasures (for example, the bimonthly newsletter *Growing Native*, P.O. Box 489, Berkeley, California 94701). Ask for a sample issue before committing to a subscription.

Obtain species lists through your state's Natural Heritage or Natural Areas Program

This isn't easy! The Natural Heritage Program, also known in some states as the Natural Areas Program, is an offshoot of the Nature Conservancy, whose mission is to identify and map the location of species needing protection in each state, each province of Canada, and several other countries. In the United States, its botanists and naturalists sometimes are paid by the Nature Conservancy but may instead be on the state government payroll and therefore based at one or another bureaucracy in the capital or hidden somewhere at the state agricultural college. Write to the Nature Conservancy, Conservation Science Division, 1815 North Lynn Street, Arlington, Virginia 22209, for a complete list of all the Natural Heritage Programs. Or call 703-841-5300 to find the program in your state. All Natural Heritage or Natural Area programs will send you without charge a list of the species protected in your state. More valuable, but not always available, is a "Check List of Vascular Plants" for your state. It differentiates aliens from natives and is sometimes broken down by county. County lists, of course, are the most valuable. Some offices will compile a list of plants in your county for a fee.

Take a walk!

Book learning quickly blurs unless you support it with actual experience. Guided nature walks are offered by the Audubon Society, Nature Conservancy, nature centers, native plant societies, all sorts of other conservation groups, specialist groups such as mushroomers, as well as public parks and preserves of every description. Look for offerings in your newspaper and try a few. You may well find compatible people with whom to start a walking group of your own.

The old way to accumulate written knowledge is to keep a notebook. The new way is to maintain a computer database. The old way takes a lot of work and entries are difficult to find (where is that note on wild petunias?). The new way is just as tedious to assemble, but the information is instantly accessible. Using the database software FileMaker Pro (Claris Corporation), for example, you can enter a species under its botanical and common names and create fields for any other attributes you wish: height, color, period of bloom, habitat, community, culture, importance to wildlife, or where you saw it growing, where you planted it, or from which growers it is available—or even a scanned image, such as a botanical drawing or your own pressed specimen. You can then perform a search using any of these attributes or any combination of them. A search for "Ruellia humilis" would find the wild petunia. A search for "lavender," "0.5 to 1.5 feet," and "sandy soil" would find the petunia as well as any other species you entered with the same characteristics, such as purple lovegrass.

It is no exaggeration to say that the Internet is revolutionizing the way we gain information, how fast we can do so, and the scope of information available to untrained researchers. The Internet connects by telephone thousands of computers, worldwide, that are able to communicate with one another through a common system of formatting. You, in turn, can read this immense store of information over your telephone through your computer and a modem. A rapidly increasing portion of the Net, called the World Wide Web, features graphics, sound, and video as well as the text that was once the only resource. Internet service providers, including AT&T, offer ways to navigate the Web through easy "gateways," such as NetScape. You don't have to know the route to the information you're seeking or even where it resides (or even necessarily what you're looking for!): the navigator lets you explore freely.

Here is an example that, in four clicks of the mouse (and without any typing), will take you from a general directory covering broad topics, such as art, education, religion, and science, to a list of the vascular plants of the Baker Wetlands in Kansas. The first click, on the topic "science" in a general directory, takes you to a choice of science disciplines. There, a click on "ecology" takes you to an index of subtopics, such as "Illinois Natural History" or "Great Smoky Mountains Bibliography." Choosing the less specific "General Biodiversity Related Resources" takes you to a long list of possible "home pages" (title pages that introduce more extensive material), one of which is "Biotic list for the Baker Wetlands in Kansas." One more click and you're there.

Already, knowledgeable native plant gardeners are creating their own home pages that link with their or others' databases, articles, online newsletters, and groups of like-minded people who exchange information and opinion by e-mail (electronic mail). An example is Pacific Northwest Native Wildlife Gardening, a Web site maintained by a gardener in her spare time. The site provides plant and wildlife data, an extensive bibliography, sources for Pacific Northwest native species, a plant and seed exchange, a subscription to an e-mail discussion group, and links to related organizations. (The Net address is http://chemwww.chem.washington.edu/natives/.) The number of such sites will grow in days to come, as will the number of links among them and the depth of information they provide. In preparation even now are online field guides to native species, with graphics and keys to all plant parts and links to associated plants and wildlife. Don't toss your reference books yet, but do consider exploring this new research landscape.

20 *Growing the Seeds*

🍂 HOW TO SOW WILD SEEDS

Cultivated plants that have traditionally been raised from seed germinate promptly and in unison. This is because gardeners understandably became impatient with seeds that were slow to sprout and tossed the flat or turned the bed that held them. Seeds that did sprout soon and more or less together therefore became the parent plants from which seeds thenceforth were harvested. In this way, through a perfectly natural form of Darwinian selection, the germination of cultivated annuals and vegetables has become predictable: at a given soil temperature, all the seeds of a given species will sprout in a certain number of days.

Natural selection has had the opposite effect on wild species. In the history of their evolution, those whose seeds germinated all at once risked dying of drought, flood, or frost in unison, while those whose seeds germinated over a period of time—some now, some later, some even after years—might produce at least a few offspring to grow to maturity. This ploy is called staggered germination, and it frustrates would-be wild gardeners to whom time and bedding space are precious. If you have the space and patience, though, sowing seed outdoors directly into nursery beds is less fussy than starting them indoors.

What wild seeds are like

The seeds of some wild species are so tiny that they appear to be dust. Others are firmly attached to fluffs or barbs of appendage that, in nature, are meant for their dispersal. Such "encasements" may not have been removed by the grower or collector. Seeds like whiskered little bluestem and cotton-wrapped thimbleweed are particularly hard to

312

clean. The seeds of berries, such as strawberries, may come in their own dried flesh. Only a few, like the large seeds of lupines, are as easy to handle as peas.

Seeds can be bought wild-collected or harvested from crops planted by the grower. Since the seeds harvested as field crops have undergone some selection—parent seed that failed to germinate in time never made it to the field—their rate or speed of germination may be more reliable than that of seed collected in the wild.

When to order and sow

Before ordering seeds, read the catalog copy to see if there are specific seasons or special instructions for the species you're interested in. If not, these rules generally apply.

Spring-blooming wildflowers may germinate only when fresh. Order them in the spring for moist shipment at the grower's discretion, usually in early fall. Sow them as soon as they arrive. Woodland species may need a partially shaded bed. Order winter- or spring-blooming desert species before the rainy season for planting just as the rains begin.

Summer-blooming wildflowers often germinate best if planted in the fall and left to overwinter under natural conditions. The difference isn't so great, though, that you can't order for planting in either season. If the order arrives before planting time, store the seeds in their original packets at room temperature or in the refrigerator unless the grower gives other instructions. In the spring, sow the seeds outdoors when late crops like corn or squash are ordinarily planted in your region. In the fall, sow them outdoors after the weather is reliably cold (you don't want them to germinate until the following spring). Grassland species do best in full sun.

Grasses that bloom early are often planted in the fall; those that bloom late are best planted in the spring. Again, though, the difference isn't great. In either case, plant in full sun.

Prepare the beds and seeds for sowing

The catalog or seed packet should indicate how large an area to prepare per weight or packet of seeds. Loosen the soil to the depth of a garden fork as you would for vegetables, but don't add fertilizer or compost. Rake the surface very smooth for the smallest seeds. Lay straw or salt hay mulch between the beds (not the ordinary hay used for livestock, which has grass and weed seeds in it). Prepare wood, plastic, or metal labels, using a soft pencil or a nonfading, waterproof marking pen. The labels have to last at least a season.

Legume seeds—lupines or baptisias, for example—require their own kind of nitrogen-fixing bacteria for their growth. A packet of this "inoculum" should come with your order. Mix the seeds with the powder in a little warm water just before sowing. Once moist, the inoculum dies if exposed to sun or drying. Sow these large seeds in furrows, like peas or beans, and cover them right away with a half inch of soil.

Minute seeds or those with dispersal devices still attached can't be handled individually. You'll need a sowing medium in which the seeds can be separated from one another and evenly distributed. The easiest medium is builder's sand, sold by the bag at lumber-yards and nurseries. The sand should be just damp, not wet. Figure a quarter of a mop pail per packet and mix by hand. Sprinkle the seed-sand mixture evenly over the bed by the handful through slightly opened fingers. The seeds must be in contact with the soil for successful germination. For tiny seeds, pat the surface of the sanded bed with your hands to assure contact. For medium-size seeds, rake the bed lightly. For large seeds, sprinkle soil over the bed.

Keep the beds evenly moist. Planted seeds immediately begin to absorb water. From this point on, and even though signs of germination may not be visible for weeks or months, the seeds will die if they dry out. Use the color of the sand as a moisture indicator. It will begin to pale as it dries, so beds should be watered. You may have to water the beds daily during hot, dry weather (early morning is the best time). Some germination may be visible as early as two weeks after sowing and continue sporadically through the season. Just as likely, you may see nothing for six weeks or longer (or, with fall planting, until the next spring).

Weed the beds by hand. If you're not sure whether what's come up is weeds or the seeds you planted, look elsewhere in the garden. Weeds coming up in one place are bound to come up in others.

What about thinning? Should you be so lucky that the bed is crowded with seedlings, you could pull some up (groan!) or move them to larger quarters (see How to Transplant Tiny Seedlings, page 320).

When seedlings can be transplanted to permanent locations
One-year plants—that is, those entering their second season of growth—are usually ready to be moved to permanent locations. Move them just as they are beginning to resprout from dormancy, before the leaves are fully open. The season would be fall in arid locations, spring in moister areas. Some species are still so small at one year that they can be left in the nursery bed for another season. But

taprooted species, even if the tops are quite small, may have too deep a root to excavate by the time they're two years old. If in doubt, dig one out.

🍃 HOW TO START WILD SEEDS INDOORS

For more information:

How to Handle Bareroot Stock, page 325

The instructions here assume that you have a copy of Norman Deno's *Seed Germination Theory and Practice* to refer to. The technique aims to mimic in an abbreviated time frame and in the small space of a moist paper towel pad the natural conditioning seeds receive when they are dispersed over the ground in the wild. Seeds that, when ripe, would have remained on the parent plant for a while, waiting to be dispersed, expect a period of drying before being moistened. Those that would have been buried in the soil immediately upon ripening die if they dry out. The "ground" from which seeds obtain moisture in this method is the damp pad. "Winter" is a three-month period in the refrigerator (40°); "summer" is a three-month period at room temperature (70°). Some species need to experience the oscillating temperatures of spring and fall: they need to be moved repeatedly between cool and warm or stored in an unheated garage.

If you don't have Dr. Deno's book, feel free to experiment. You might have to anyway. The book covers quite a few native plants, but it is not devoted exclusively to them, and some that you wish to try may not be included. A reasonable approach is to proceed by analogy. Although a genus of plants may include species that require quite different conditioning regimes to germinate, totally unrelated plants that share similar habitats tend to have similar requirements. So if you wish to start a prairie species, look up other species that grow with it and follow that regime; or, if a species grows in a wetland habitat, look up one of its marsh companions. Remember that the regimes are not artificial constructs that some mad chemist has thought up but survival strategies that the plants themselves have worked out in the course of their evolution.

To order *Seed Germination Theory and Practice,* write to Dr. Norman C. Deno, 139 Lenor Drive, State College, Pennsylvania 16801. The price of his privately published book at this writing is $20.

The most practical plants to germinate by the moist pad method

A 3.5-inch-square plastic pot holds nine seedlings. (Don't forget to order labels, too.)

are wildflowers native to grassland habitats. The seeds must be large enough to be manipulated with forceps after sprouting. Dr. Deno describes special methods for germinating tiny seeds and other difficult types not covered here. Grasses are needed in such quantity that they are better sowed outdoors in nursery beds or permanent locations. Use purchased seed, or see How to Collect Wild Seeds (page 346).

Equipment for raising plants indoors

Some of the items used to start vegetables indoors aren't good for wild seeds. Flats are too shallow for the deep-rooted species. Peat pots don't last long enough for the slow-growing ones. Forget egg and milk cartons, too. The "sunny window" where you might grow young tomatoes will cook these seedlings to death because they are raised in plastic-covered pots that act as greenhouses.

All the equipment suggested here is available from Grower's Supply Company, P.O. Box 1123, Ann Arbor, Michigan 48106; call 313-426-5852 for a catalog.

Pots and plant trays. Choose square plastic pots, 3.5 inches to a side and 3.5 inches deep. These will hold nine seedlings in three rows of three plants each. A standard plant tray, 11 x 22 inches, holds fifteen of these pots. The trays should be thick, sturdy plastic, not flexible or floppy.

Artificial lights. Only fluorescent lighting is cool enough. Gro-Lite or other brands sold especially for raising plants indoors are expensive and not necessary. Use ordinary 40-watt daylight fluorescent tubes. A 48-inch-long fixture that holds two tubes gives even light over two standard plant trays placed end to end.

Timer. A timer attached to the fluorescent fixture turns the lights on in the morning and off again at night. Choose an inexpensive one; it doesn't need to be fancy.

Plant stand. Although a plant stand isn't necessary, it is convenient. If you don't have one, maybe wait to purchase it until you see how your first germination experiment goes. The sturdiest stands are made from 1-inch-square aluminum tubing.

Plan the germination regimes

Seeds ordered in January or February from the latest catalog usually arrive by March. They have already undergone dry storage in the interval since they were harvested and can be started in moist paper towel pads when they arrive. Check for any special instructions from the grower before planning your own regimes.

Arrange the packets in alphabetical order by botanical name. Look up each in Deno (or look up another species from the same habitat to use as an analogy) and jot down on the packet the regime you intend to use. Some may need light (L) for germination. (The need for gibberellin, GA-3, is infrequent, and there is apparently no commercial source for it in practical quantities for home use.) Early spring bloomers may do better if started at 40° even if they share a habitat with summer-blooming species that are started at 70°. You may also want to split a packet and try two different regimes for the same species.

Divide the packets into batches according to regime—for example, one batch that will be germinated at 70°, another that will be germinated at 40°, and other batches that need multiple three-month cycles alternating between the two temperatures.

Prepare the pads

You'll need paper towels for the pads and sandwich bags for storage. Choose bags made of thin polyethylene film, such as Baggies. This material keeps moisture in while allowing oxygen to permeate. Thick storage bags such as Ziploc or similar brands prevent oxygen from reaching the seeds. The paper towels should be plain white ones with good wet strength (or they will turn to mush); try Scots or Bounty.

Fold single sheets of paper towel first in half, then in quarters. Fold one more time to form the rectangular pad.

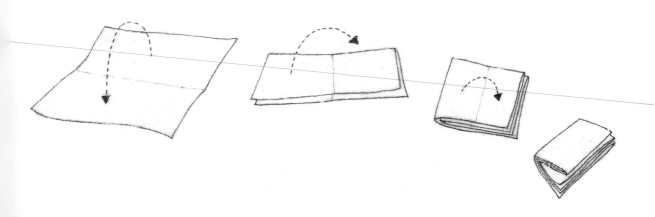

Moisten the pad before spreading seeds on it. Add water by the teaspoon; the pad should be moist, not wet. Open the pad to spread the seeds on half of it.

Tap the seeds out evenly through a cut corner of the packet. Bunched-up seeds can be spread with the edge of a table knife. Use a second pad if there are too many seeds for a single layer.

Write the necessary data for each species on a Post-it so you can stick it to the outside of the storage bag. Minimal data are the name of the species, the germination regime, and the date you started the regime: Liatris spicata (dense blazing-star), 70°, 2/10/97. For seeds you've collected yourself, add the collection date and location (so you can get more next season if these work out). For seeds that require more than one three-month cycle, note the date(s) the pad should be moved from refrigerator to room temperature or vice versa: Started 40° March 3, move to 70° June 3, back to 40° Sept 3.

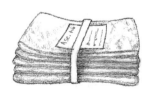

Fold the pad shut (unless the regime calls for light, in which case fold it the other way so the seeds remain on the surface). Lay it in its storage bag, fold the top of the bag under, and stick its Post-it label on the outside. Continue until you've completed that batch so all the species in it can be checked or moved together.

If the regime calls for oscillating temperatures, store the pads in their bags in an unheated shed or garage where the temperature will vary naturally. Keep them in a metal cracker or cookie box, or the mice will eat them!

Check the seeds

Check the batches occasionally for moisture, mold, and germination. Those at 40° need checking only once a month. Check those at 70° more frequently; some species may germinate in as little as a week. When germination begins, check the pads daily so you can move the sprouts to pots before they root into the towel.

Planting Noah's Garden

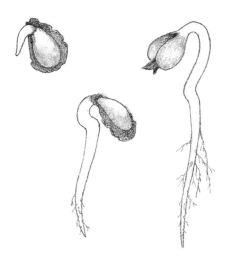

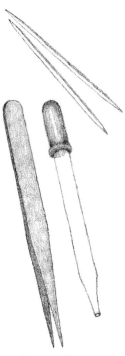

Germination has started when you can see a rootlike projection, called a radical, emerging from the seed. The milkweed seed to the left is ready to plant. The longer radical on the middle seed may have grown into the paper towel; you'll have a hard time teasing it out without breaking it. The last one, with its cotyledons (seed leaves) already opening, has definitely been in the pad too long; possibly you can rescue it by removing it along with the shred of towel it's grown into.

Moisture slowly decreases over time from evaporation, more so at room temperature than in the refrigerator. Add a few drops of water to the pad with an eyedropper if it's becoming dry.

Mold may form on the pads. Look for fuzz or stains. Live seeds rarely grow mold. Usually the growth is around dead seeds or debris from incompletely cleaned ones. Prepare a fresh pad. Move the unaffected seeds to it with forceps or by scraping them up with the edge of a table knife.

Plant the sprouts

The germinated seed can be planted as soon as the radical—the embryonic root—has emerged or a day or so later, when you can also see the leaflike cotyledons emerging from the seed. A few species germinate in two steps. Many lilies, for example, produce a root and bulb at 70°, then must be returned to 40° for an additional cycle before, at 70° again, they also form a leaf.

Fill the pots with a mixture of sand and soil—half and half potting soil and builder's sand, or an even higher proportion of sand for dryland species. Moisten the soil carefully; it should be damp, not wet. The mixing and moistening can be done in a bucket or, to prepare a lot of soil mix, outdoors in a wheelbarrow.

A good pair of forceps, available from medical pharmacies, is the best tool for moving sprouted seeds from pad to pot. An eyedropper is a help in adding small amounts of water as a pad dries. Round toothpicks are for digging tiny holes.

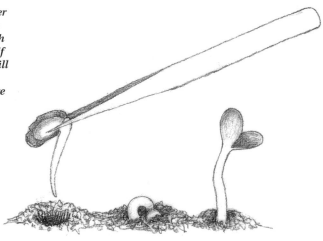

Pick the sprout up by its neck and stick it all the way into the soil. Cover it with soil, using a toothpick or fingertip. The elongating stem will push the seed leaves up through the soil. If not enough seeds have sprouted to fill the pot, mark the empty locations with toothpicks so you'll know where to plant the others when they're ready.

An almost full pot ready to go under lights; the toothpicks mark spots where two more sprouts can go when more seeds germinate.

Transfer the seedlings to the pot with forceps. Gently poke the sprouts into the soil surface or, if the radicals are quite long, use a toothpick to form small holes in which to plant them. As many as nine seedlings can share a pot. Don't forget to label the pots!

Place each pot in a medium-size food storage bag. Draw the top together and close it with a twist-tie. (Keep unplanted pots and extra soil in plastic, too, so you don't have to moisten every time you have more seedlings to plant.)

Keep the planted pots under artificial light. Hang the fluorescent fixture 4 inches above the pots; raise the height as necessary. Set the timer for 12 hours on, 12 hours off. Temperature is probably not critical, but growth will be slow below 60°, faster at 70° or higher.

Check the pots every two months. They will stay moist for up to a year as long as the bag remains intact, but most grassland species will be ready to go into a nursery or garden bed long before that.

HOW TO TRANSPLANT TINY SEEDLINGS

Seedlings are ready to go into prepared beds when their roots are well developed and the season is suitable. You can't, of course, move seedlings outdoors in the middle of the winter or during a desert drought. Any time during the growing season is probably okay as long as you can keep an eye on them for a while, as you would for baby tomato plants. Unlike tomatoes, though, the seedlings' "readiness" can't be judged by top growth. Some species with a few puny leaves may already have grown roots twice or more the depth of the pot and need to get outside before they strangle.

Planting Noah's Garden

Check for root development

Take off the plastic bag. Tip the seedlings into the palm of your hand by turning the pot upside down, tapping its edge on the side of a table, and catching the plants with their soil. If the roots are well developed, you'll see them along the sides and at the bottom of the soil mass. Seedlings of the same species and age will be at the same stage of development, so you need check only one pot of that group. Put the seedlings in their soil back into the pot either to grow some more or, if there's plenty of root, to "harden off" before transplanting. In either case, recover the pot with its plastic bag.

Harden off the seedlings

Hardening off is a physiological process comparable to what you would go through to acclimatize to rarefied mountain air or tropical temperatures. For plants, the process involves adjustments to drier air, more intense light, and possibly changes in temperature as well. The seedlings have been growing at 100% humidity in their plastic bags, in light much less intense than full sun, and at a steady indoor temperature. Allow ten days for hardening off. The pots are easier to handle if you keep them in plant trays.

These seedlings have been in their pot too long. Even though they have just one pair of leaves, their roots are getting tangled, and the seedlings will be hard to shake loose from one another at planting time.

Days 1–3: Accustom seedlings to the ambient humidity. Slash each bag a few times with a paring knife, but keep the top closed with the twist-tie. The next day, slash the bags a little more. On the third day, open the tops of the bags (don't remove them yet).

Days 4–6: Move the tray of plants outdoors—but into the shade—to get used to the changing temperature. The open plastic bags still offer some protection. Check for moisture, and water the pots if the soil is dry.

Days 7–10: Move the plants gradually from partial to full sun. Species with thin or juicy leaves may take longer to adjust to heat and light than those with thick, leathery, or hairy foliage. Sunburned foliage means you're going too fast, and the seedlings need to recover for a while in partial shade. Start with dappled shade or morning sun. The next day, remove the plastic bags, water the pots if necessary, and try full afternoon sun for an hour or two. If the foliage still looks fine, try three or four hours in the sun the next day. Seedlings that still look brisk are now ready to be transplanted into nursery beds.

Use this style of trowel, sometimes called a transplanter, for prying slots. It has a narrow, slightly curved blade about 2 inches wide by 6 inches long, sometimes incised with inch marks to gauge depth.

Loosen the soil in the bed to the depth of a garden fork, but don't "improve" the soil in any other way. If the ground is dry, water it well the day before you plant. Assuming you're going to move these plants to permanent locations when they're a year old, you can plant them as close as 8 inches apart. Use a narrow trowel; you'll be plunging it in deep to pry a slot, not dig a hole.

Work early in the morning before the sun is high or on a cloudy or misty day. The only hazard in transplanting seedlings is that the roots can dry out before you get them in the ground.

Dump the pot of seedlings into your hand. The roots are likely tangled with one another and have grown longer than the pot. Grasp the mass of plants near the top and shake or bang out the sandy soil until the roots hang loose and free. Grasp a seedling by its crown (where the roots join the stem) and gently pull it away from the others. Separate all nine seedlings in this way, but keep them piled together so they don't dry out as you plant them.

A potful of seedlings after the soil has been shaken from their roots

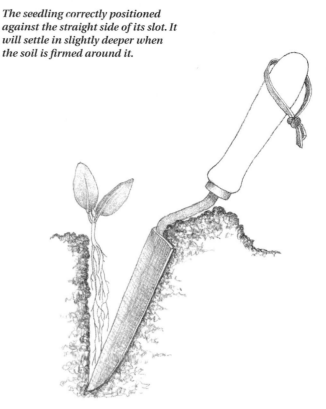

The seedling correctly positioned against the straight side of its slot. It will settle in slightly deeper when the soil is firmed around it.

A single seedling separated from the others, ready to transplant

Plunge the trowel into the soil to its hilt, and push it to one side to create a slot. With the other hand, lower a seedling into the slot, and hold its crown at ground level with a thumb. Pull out the trowel, push the soil back around the seedling, and go on to the next one. Figure about five minutes per pot of nine seedlings to get the lot into the ground.

Watering isn't necessary at transplanting if the soil is moist. The seedlings may have to be watered every week thereafter in their first season if there is no rain. Don't overdo it. Wilting isn't a sign that a seedling is about to kick the bucket. Plants wilt in hot weather to prevent excessive evaporation, just as people sweat to prevent over-heating. A plant is "thirsty" when, after the relief of a cool night, its leaves still haven't recovered their normal crispness.

21 Planting the Plants

🍃 DIGGING TOOLS

Most people's first serious digging tool is a full-size common shovel, the kind used to excavate big holes or toss dirt around. A first trowel is usually an average sort with a slightly concave, medium-width, medium-length blade. These standard tools are not the right shape for the more precise digging that is most efficient for planting large numbers of plants, for planting small woodland sorts, or for planting the easy way, in slots rather than holes. The more specialized digging tools described here will save you a lot of time and effort, but hardware stores may not carry them. A mail-order source for these and other professional tools is A. M. Leonard, 241 Fox Drive, P.O. Box 816, Piqua, Ohio 45356; call 800-543-8955 for a catalog.

The difference between spades and shovels is in the handle—a spade has a short handle with a hand grip. Transplanting spades, also called drain spades, have a long, narrow blade useful for slot-planting. An example is Ames transplanting/drain spade, with a round, turned-step blade 5¼ inches wide by 16 inches long on a 27-inch D-grip ash handle. The True Temper model L III is an example of a scaled-down version of an ordinary shovel. The ash handle measures 42 inches from tip to blade. The blade is 6 inches wide by 8 inches long and has a turned step.

The slightly curved blade of the transplanting trowel on page 322 is fine for most jobs, but one with a deeply curved blade works better when jabbing holes in woodland soil for bulbs and rhizomes. I prefer a wood handle (plastic and metal slip in sweaty hands).

Small shovel

Transplanting or drain spade

A transplanting trowel

Planting Noah's Garden

Traditional transplanting methods described by gardeners seldom apply to habitat restoration. Your plants are to be members of communities, not specimens. They are usually bareroot and must be put promptly into the ground. You may be faced with several hundred to install on a weekend. The methods here are practical, fast, and easy. Some, though, require two people, one digging and the other planting.

Planting seasons

Dormant plants are shipped in spring or fall; the catalog will give the range of dates based on the climate in that region. Note that this isn't necessarily *your* region's climate. The shipping seasons of northern and southern nurseries, for example, may differ by a month or more. If you can't plant immediately, store the shipment in its original packaging in a cool, dark place (preferably the refrigerator). How long the plants will last depends on how well they were packed. The dense roots of forbs and grasses store better than the scantier roots of trees and shrubs. Check the packing material. It should be evenly damp (not wet) throughout. If portions of it begin to dry out, plant immediately! Remoistening may cause mold to grow.

Southwestern and other arid-region species are usually planted in the fall, as the rainy season begins. If planted in the spring, they may not survive the ensuing drought.

Spring-blooming wildflowers may also be shipped only in the fall; they tend to come out of dormancy too early in the season to risk spring shipment. Check the catalog.

Ferns hold their dormancy longer and do better if planted in the spring, when there is less danger of their shallow rhizomes drying out.

Summer-blooming flowers and grasses are better planted during the spring in northern climates to avoid frost heave; either season is okay where winters are mild.

Trees and shrubs generally transplant as easily in fall as in spring, but there are exceptions. Check with the grower to be sure.

Preparing the soil

Only very compacted soil, such as on construction sites or severely trampled areas, may need a period of conditioning before it can be planted (see How to Start a Tree Island, page 405). Otherwise, if you have chosen plants that suit your soil, there is no reason to dig the bed or amend it with extra ingredients. Turning soil disturbs its structure,

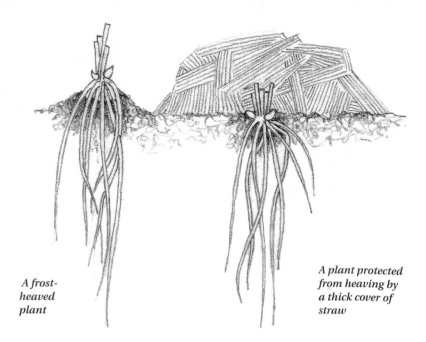

Successive frosts and thaws can push a new plant right out of the ground. The crown then dries out, and the plant dies. If you must plant forbs and grasses in the fall, mulch the planted area after the ground is deeply frozen; the idea is to keep it frozen until spring! Use 6 inches of salt hay or straw—not hay with seeds in it, as the seeds will germinate. Don't use chips; raking them off the following spring could injure the resprouting crowns. Salt hay or straw can be lifted off with a pitchfork after the soil is thoroughly thawed.

A frost-heaved plant

A plant protected from heaving by a thick cover of straw

upsets the microbial population, and invites a crop of weeds. Feeding native species causes lank stems that can't stand up and tender growth that is vulnerable to insects. Even organic fertilizers injure valuable soil microorganisms. Forbs and grasses should be planted in open soil or through dead turf (see How to Kill a Lawn, page 268, and How to Prepare a Grassland Site, page 426). Trees and shrubs can be planted through living turf.

Choose the day

Most losses of bareroot plants are due to their roots' drying before they are safely in the ground. This can happen in minutes on a hot, dry, sunny, windy day. Choose a day when the weather is cool, cloudy, and still, or humid, foggy, or drizzling.

Prepare the plants

Plants may come wrapped in foil, plastic wrap, or heavy paper, held with rubber bands or string. These wraps are irritating when you're on your hands and knees with muddy fingers and will only slow your work. Unwrap the plants one package or layer at a time. Rewrap multiples of five or ten according to one of the following methods. Prepare only as many plants as you can get into the ground in the next hour. For instance, prepare a box of fifty grasses, plant them, then prepare another batch.

Planting Noah's Garden

A basketful of bareroot grass plants bundled in cornucopias. To make a cornucopia, place the plants diagonally across a double thickness of wet newspaper. Roll the sheets around the plants from the near corner, then fold up the bottom to enclose the roots.

Forbs, grasses, and small bareroot shrubs can be rewrapped in a double thickness of wet newspaper rolled around them like a cornucopia and folded up at the bottom. Stack the cornucopias upright in a carton or basket that you can easily move along with you as you work. The wet newspaper will keep the roots safely moist while you plant from one cornucopia at a time. Keep even the package you're planting from loosely rolled to protect the roots from drying.

Fern rhizomes are usually too bulky for cornucopias. If they are well layered in moist material, plant them from the shipping carton. If not, divide them among large food storage bags.

Woodland wildflower rhizomes, bulbs, corms, tubers, and even whole plants are so small that twenty-five or more may fit easily into a sandwich bag.

What about the labels? Usually plants come with at least one label per species. Drop a label into one of the cornucopias holding that species so you'll know what you're planting. If you plant in single-species groups, stick the label in the ground where that group is planted. For the most natural look in a meadow garden, you may want to plant the flower species at random, choosing a variety to make up the five or ten plants per cornucopia. In that case, the labels aren't much use; you can always identify the species with a field guide as they mature.

Planting ferns and woodland wildflowers

The difficulty here is not in the planting—the hole is so little and so shallow that planting is a snap—but in seeing where to plant, for each individual immediately becomes invisible—the tuber buried, the rhizome disappeared. Plant in patches—five clumping ferns, ten slender Solomon's seal, twenty little bloodroots—each patch separated from the next

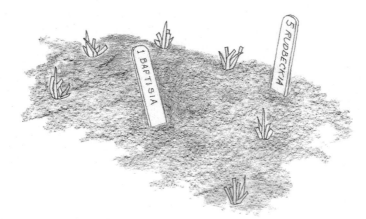

You can't see most dormant plants once they're in the ground. To avoid utter confusion, lay out and label planting areas with the name and number of plants before you begin. In woodland, rake the areas to be planted so you can see the whole scheme at once.

Elsewhere, outline your plan on the soil surface with crushed limestone. Or use grass plants, whose dried tufts remain visible above the ground, to define the areas that will be filled with forbs.

by an area of unplanted woodland floor. Give ferns a square foot or more; only inches for small woodland flowers. Scrape each patch clean of debris with a rake or shovel. Stick a label in the ground with the name of the species and the number to be planted. Continue to clear patches until all the plants you ordered have an assigned place. In this way the entire arrangement will be clear before you start to plant.

Plant ferns according to the physical form of their rhizomes: knobs in holes, sticks in grooves, mats in shallow depressions. A narrow trowel can excavate all three. Make the number of excavations the label calls for. Place the rhizomes in each one, top side up. Cover each plant with a thin layer of soil; the buds should be almost even with the surface. Then rake the original debris back over the area. The buds will easily unfurl through this loose mulch. (If there was no natural mulch in the area, scatter dried leaves gathered elsewhere or a light commercial preparation of shredded bark.)

Plant woodland wildflowers according to their physical form, too: whole plants in root-deep holes; rhizomes sideways, just below the surface; bulbs, corms, and tubers at a depth about twice their height. For these last nugget types, a deeply curved, narrow trowel works best. Jab it in and twist it to ream out a plug of soil. Drop the nugget in and bury it with the plug. Cover the other types lightly with soil. Rake the original debris back over each planted area as you complete it. Wildflowers may not be able to push through either as much or as heavy a mulch as ferns. If you must supplement their cover, use pine needles or oak leaves (not maple leaves, which mat like felt). Shredded bark may be too heavy.

Planting bareroot grasses and meadow flowers

The difficulty with bareroot meadow flowers is the same as that with woodland ones: once they're in the ground, you can't see them. At least

Planting Noah's Garden

woodland species can be planted in separate patches, but a meadow garden looks most natural when flowers of several kinds drift more or less continuously through a matrix of grass. The lime-and-grass technique for dividing the planting area, explained below, should minimize confusion. And, even though the roots of prairie species are very deep, two people can install from fifty to a hundred plants an hour by prying slots instead of digging holes.

You need a bag of crushed limestone, the kitchen scissors, a carton or basket of the wrapped plants (grasses first), a narrow spade, and a helper. A plan is optional; you can simply fill space as you go.

Delineate the areas where grasses will mark the general design. The easiest way is to trail crushed limestone along the curves or at the spots where grass is to be planted.

Plant the grasses. Most prairie grasses eventually grow to clumps about 2 feet across, so they're usually planted 2 feet apart. For smaller grasses or a planting that will fill in more quickly, plant them 1 to $1^1/_2$ feet apart. Work with one cornucopia at a time. One person steps on the spade to push it deep into the soil and pries open a slot without removing the blade. The other person places a grass plant against the flat side of the slot and holds the crown against the rim of the slot with the thumb of one hand; with the other hand, the planter fans the roots out flat against the side. The digger then withdraws the spade and stamps the slot closed. In heavy clay, it may be necessary to break the soil up to close the slot. Roots not in contact with the soil will dry and die. Keep unplanted grasses loosely wrapped in wet newspaper as you work. If you can't dig slots deep

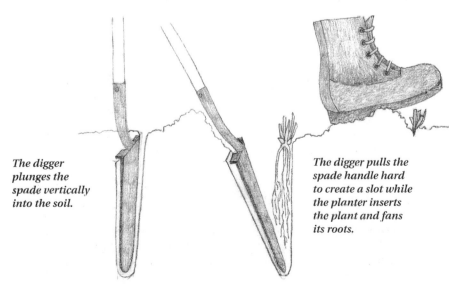

The digger stamps the slot shut.

The digger plunges the spade vertically into the soil.

The digger pulls the spade handle hard to create a slot while the planter inserts the plant and fans its roots.

enough to accommodate the grass roots, cut them to fit with the scissors. Plant all the grasses before starting the flowers.

Plant the flowers. The technique is the same as with grasses except, of course, that taproots don't fan out. Again, allow 1 to 2 square feet per plant, depending on how broad the crown will grow; a few species need more like a yard of space (see the catalog description). Finish planting one area before going on to the next. When deciding at what level to place the crown, err on the deeper side. Crowns that stick up from the soil will dry out and die.

Water the plants? Mulch them? Soil is ordinarily moist at bareroot planting time. The plants have no leaves from which to lose moisture; the roots need only be damp. There is no particular reason to water them after transplanting. Mulching isn't possible because you can't see the flower crowns to avoid smothering or crushing them. Small gardens can be mulched with a light material such as shredded bark or leaves later in the season, when the plants have grown some. Mulch will help keep weeds down. (For large plantings, see Some Grassland Management Regimes, page 432.)

Planting bareroot shrubs and trees

Whips—unbranched stems with slender roots—can be planted by the slot method described for meadow flowers and grasses. Branched trees or shrubs with more elaborate roots must be planted in holes. They can be planted directly in turf. Deturf just the spot where the hole is to go. If you're working alone, you may want to dig all the holes first, then put in the plants. If you have a helper, one can dig while the other plants.

Dig the hole somewhat deeper and wider than the roots. It isn't necessary to dig the enormous holes often advised. You need only to be able to lower the plant into place without cramming it. The hole should be rounded, with rough sides. Chop at the sides with the shovel to roughen the surface; this will leave some loose dirt in the bottom, too. If you hit roots, cut them off with loppers or a hatchet. Don't worry about stones; roots will grow around them. If you hit a boulder, choose another spot. Break up any clods you've dug out so the soil can more easily be pulled back in.

If the digging is very hard, cut the roots of the plant to fit the hole. Usually the problem is just one or two especially long roots that the plant can manage without. (If you are really worried about this, prune away some top growth, too.)

Stick in the plant. Hold the stem above the hole with the crown about level with the soil surface. Pull dirt around it until the plant stands up by itself. The former depth of planting may be revealed by

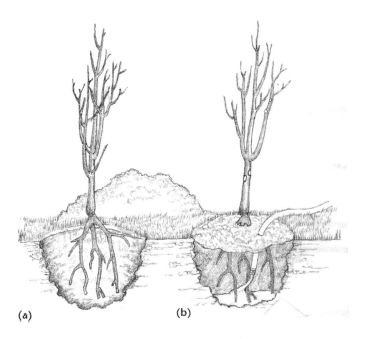

(a) (b)

(a) The rough, bowl-shaped hole is big enough to accommodate roots with just enough extra room at the sides for refilling with soil. A few extra-long roots have been trimmed off.

(b) In the next step, some branches are pruned to compensate. After back-filling, a hose is jammed deep among the roots and allowed to trickle until the soil is soupy. The tree has been placed too high. It can be pushed deeper now, or more soil can be piled up to meet the crown, where the trunk joins the roots. Also, the tree was set crooked into the hole; it can easily be jiggled straight at this point.

a line of soil still clinging near the crown. This "proper depth" is less critical than it is made out to be. You can always dig away soil that is too high or mound up soil that is too low. Or, after soaking, you can jiggle the plant up or down.

Soak it. The purpose of this maneuver is not to water the plant but to get rid of air pockets in which roots could dry out. Turn the hose to a trickle and jam the nozzle deep into the hole. If you can't get it through the soil at first, you'll be able to as it softens. Leave the hose trickling until the soil is mushy—a good ten minutes or more. Jiggle the tree or shrub to settle it in (and, if necessary, adjust its height and tilt). Don't stamp or tamp the soil. Time-honored as that practice is, compressed soil suffocates roots.

Mulch the plant? Build a moat around it? Stake it? No niceties are necessary in woodland. Just kick some dead leaves around the plant. A 3-inch mulch of wood chips or shredded bark is helpful elsewhere to keep moisture in and weeds out. If planting in a lawn, mulch just the hole. If planting in an open bed, mulch the whole area. Moats are necessary only if you will be watering each plant individually by hose and only if, as you do so, the water runs right off (moats aren't necessary if you use a soaking hose or sprinkler). If you do create a moat, rake it off after two months. By that time the roots will have grown beyond the original hole, and the moat will prevent water from reaching them. Staking is a waste of time with

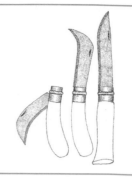

These pocket knives don't have the spring mechanism that makes the blades of other folding knives hard to manipulate with muddy fingers. Instead, they feature a simple twist band that locks the blade in the open position. The lightweight wood handle is a generous size and shaped to fit the hand without slipping. The one with the hooked blade is especially useful for slashing through potbound roots. Both are available from Smith & Hawken and other garden catalogs.

bareroot stock; the plants aren't bushy enough to be toppled by the wind. More important in some areas is to protect the plant from browsers; see A Note on Rabbits, Rodents, and Deer, page 407.

A NOTE ON POTTED STOCK

You won't always be able to get bareroot stock. Trees may come bareroot only in quantities too large for you to use, or a particular species may be carried only by nurseries that grow their stock in containers. The roots almost always will be potbound to some degree—massed against the sides, coiled at the bottom, or crowded throughout the soil. In this case, a hole based on the size of the container will be too small to accommodate the actual extent of the roots. Start the hole; finish it after you see how extensive the root system really is.

Examine the roots

Bang the rim of the container smartly against a rock or the edge of a wheelbarrow and tip the rootball out into your hand. If it is a solid mass that doesn't fall apart, the plant is potbound. The roots will have to be loosened, untangled, uncoiled, or slashed to free them.

Free the roots and spread them out

With any sort of root system, start by banging the whole mass hard against the ground or the sloped front of the wheelbarrow to loosen the soil. As it falls away, unwind any roots that have coiled in the pot. They will be both around the sides and at the bottom. Some will break as you try to free them. Don't worry about it. The more fibrous-rooted species may have grown into a solid mesh at the sides or even tighter at the bottom. Pull the mesh apart with your fingers until the roots hang loose. There will be some breakage with this maneuver, too. If the roots are webbed so tightly that you can't free them with your fingers, use a knife with a hooked blade to slash them vertically down the sides; hook out or slash the bottom, too. Hose the roots if necessary to keep them moist while you finish digging the hole. Proceed as with a bareroot plant—which, now, the potted one should resemble.

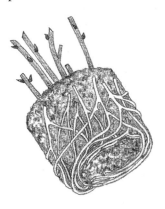

Potbound plants. The thick roots of the first plant coiled against the pot; the fibrous roots of the second plant webbed the entire rootball into a solid, feltlike mass.

Banging the first plant hard against the ground loosened its thick roots considerably, and some of the soil fell away. Banging had no effect on the potbound fibrous root mass. To begin to loosen it, the matted surface had to be slashed vertically all around, using a knife with a hooked blade. Now the bottom surface also will have to be hooked out to free the roots.

With a little more hanging, teasing, untangling, and—in the case of the fibrous-rooted species—scrabbling with fingernails, the roots of both plants now hang free. Notice that their root systems are bigger than their pots.

22 *Buying on a Budget*

HOW TO HANDLE GROUP WHOLESALE ORDERS

Group ordering can be accomplished smoothly, though not without effort. It requires considerable preparation followed by large doses of paperwork, calculation, and telephoning. Labor is involved, too, to move and unpack cartons and to rewrap and distribute orders.

A critical ingredient is having at least one person who feels comfortable talking to and placing orders with wholesale growers. A computer with spreadsheet software is invaluable.* Costs such as the telephone, copying, and rewrapping materials can be volunteered, or factored in as a percentage of each member's total order.

You'll need several months to do the research, make basic decisions, and give members time to prepare their individual orders.

Create the group

It's important that the group be made up of people whom you know to be reliable, compatible, and with a common interest in native plants and habitat restoration. Fewer than six people won't be able to generate large enough quantities. More than twelve people generate chaos.

The suggestions that follow are directed at the few people who will actually handle the ordering. The process involves communicating with growers, selecting appropriate plants, creating computer forms and spreadsheets, and coordinating the effort. The Naturals appoint teams of two to handle the group order with each selected grower. One (the

---

* The Naturals got along without computers for its first group order. It was, however, a bruising experience. Our next order—with the help of a computer—went smoothly and with a fraction of the time and effort. If you have to do the paperwork by hand, the forms illustrated in this chapter will help you keep your order information organized and accessible.

Selector) chooses which plants to buy; the other (the Orderer) attends to the business of ordering. For consistency, it's advisable that someone be chosen especially to create the computer forms and spreadsheets. Once they're on disk, anyone else with a compatible computer and software can enter the data, and the same forms can be used year after year.

Choose the growers

Use Barbara Barton's *Gardening by Mail* (see page 307) to send for catalogs that deal in plants for habitats such as woodland, prairie, or wetland. Prefer growers in your region and plants shipped bareroot. Group ordering of seed isn't feasible because the bulk seed would have to be weighed and redistributed by the ounce. Choose growers listed as either R&W (retail and wholesale) or W (wholesale only). Call them to discuss your plans. Some wholesalers simply will not sell to nonprofit, amateur groups or will not give them wholesale prices. Others require a minimum quantity or dollar value that a small group can't meet. Select from the remaining possibilities the fewest possible growers from whom you can order the species your members are most interested in and at the best price breaks for large quantities. Explain what you wish to do and that you will abide by the following ground rules:

You will pay in advance if necessary and pay tax where appropriate.

The entire order will be shipped to one address.

You will be responsible for the distribution of bulk shipments.

Strike from the list of candidates those who are grumpy about your plan. The growers you want to work with will want to work with you.

Set up a timetable

Ask each grower by what date you should send in your order for the best availability of plants, and work back from there. Members need a good chunk of time to figure their budget and plan their landscape. A sample timetable formated as a flow chart, using the spreadsheet program Excel (it could also be done by hand on graph paper), appears on page 336. Each step is described below.

1. Appoint an ordering group

The process starts with naming the members of the group who will be responsible for selecting plants and placing the orders.

2. Request and receive catalogs

Each member of the full group needs a copy of each of the catalogs from which you'll be ordering. It's wise to order them early in case the grower runs out, and have them sent to one address for later distribution. Note that the catalogs may be out of date by ordering time, but you have no

GROUP ORDER - SAMPLE TIMETABLE

Task	September	October	November	December	January	February
Compose ordering group	▌Sept 1					
Request & recieve catalogs	███					
Select species & create order forms	███					
Set up group order spreadsheets	███					
Distribute catalogs & order forms		▌Oct. 1				
Member's plan & complete forms		████████████				
Receive completed order forms				▌Dec 15		
Compile order quantity worksheets				████		
Hold order meeting					▌Jan 5	
Confirm orders with growers					████	
Bill members					Jan 21 ▌	
Receive payment						███
Place final orders						▌Feb 7

A sample timetable based on the grower's advice to order by the first week in February.

choice. By the time new catalogs are sent out at the beginning of the new year, there won't be enough time to coordinate a group order.

3. Select species and create order forms

Each grower may list scores of species. If you allow members to order from the full list, you're unlikely to reach wholesale quantities of any one species. Twenty species per catalog is a reasonable limit for a group of twelve; the selection might be limited to ten species for a group of six. Limit the choice to species native in your own region. If plants come in several sizes, list one size only. Select the most basic species: pioneer plants and those of easy cultivation.

The Selectors can work on their own or in committee, but either way it's important that they know what kinds of plantings the members have in mind so they don't, for example, choose half a dozen grasses when no one is doing a prairie restoration. Probably the best approach is for the Selectors to coordinate their choices on the basis of habitat. If many members are working on woodland, one Selector can choose woodland ferns and wildflowers from one catalog while another chooses understory shrubs from a different catalog.

Although you can use the catalog form for actually placing the final group order—and the grower may prefer that you do—having your own forms for members to fill out saves time and spares confusion. The formating of a form is a one-time thing: once you're pleased with the layout, save it to use over and over again. The blank should have only two columns: plant species and quantity. Leave enough space in the quantity column so members can jot down the price for their own information, but don't make a formal price column. You won't know the quantity breaks until all the members' orders are compiled, and prices are likely to change by ordering time. Enter on the standard layout the name of the nursery and those species that members may order through the group. List the plants alphabetically by botanical name. If you like, include on the order blank a one-line description of each species:

> Rudbeckia hirta (black-eyed Susan); orange-yellow, early summer; self-sowing biennial; 2 to 3 feet; full sun; dry to mesic; sand, loam, clay

EASTERN PRAIRIES, INC. ORDER FOR: _____   ____

PRAIRIE GRASSES & FORBS	QUANTITY
Asclepias incarnata (swamp milkweed)	
Asclepias tuberosa (butterflyweed)	
Aster laevis (smooth aster)	
Aster novae-angliae (New England aster)	
Echinacea pallida (pale coneflower)	
Eupatorium maculatum (Joe-Pye weed)	
Eupatorium perfoliatum (boneset)	
Helianthus mollis (downy sunflower)	
Liatris spicata (dense blazingstar)	
Lobelia siphilitica (great blue lobelia)	
Penstemon digitalis (foxglove penstemon)	
Ratibida pinnata (gray-headed coneflower)	
Solidago rigida (stiff goldenrod)	

A sample group order form listing species from the Eastern Prairies catalog. You'll need a separate order form for each grower and a copy for each member in the group.

Make a copy of your order for own records
Return the completed form by December 15 to:

> Pam Wye
> 15 Oak Street
> Stone Ridge, NY 12345

Include the name of the nursery and a line for the member's name. State the date by which the order is to be completed and returned. Remind members to make a copy of their order for their own records before returning it to the Orderer.

4. Set up group order spreadsheets

Setting up the basic spreadsheet is also a one-time effort. From then on, it's only a matter of filling in member names, plant species, and numbers (quantities, prices, and percentages, such as tax and shipping charges). Spreadsheet programs allow you to manipulate the data and to print it out in various ways, so you can use the same basic setup to compile quantities, to calculate price, to track changes in quantities and prices, to bill individual members, and to confirm the final order.

EASTERN PRAIRIES, INC.
GROUP ORDER - QUANTITY WORKSHEET

A sample worksheet for tracking quantities.

PRAIRIE GRASSES & FORBS	ALMA	CARM	DIANE	ELLIOT	SONDRA	GROUP TOTAL
Asclepias incarnata						
Asclepias tuberosa						
Aster laevis						
Aster novae-angliae						
Echinacea pallida						
Eupatorium maculatum						
Eupatorium perfoliatum						
Helianthus mollis						
Liatris spicata						
Lobelia siphilitica						
Penstemon digitalis						
Ratibida pinnata						
Solidago rigida						
INDIVIDUAL TOTALS						

The first format you'll need is a quantity worksheet, to keep track of the number of plants per species and per person as members return their order forms. Once the quantities are compiled, you'll need to calculate prices on a cost worksheet.

All these figurings can be done by hand, but not easily. Prices may change; members may change quantities at the order meeting; some items may prove to be out of stock or available only in a smaller or larger size. With a spreadsheet you can enter these changes as they occur. The program will automatically revise the figures.

5. Distribute catalogs and order forms

It's best to do this at a meeting so you can both save on postage and make clear that any orders not returned on time won't be included in the group order. If members want a species not on the list, they can buy as individuals provided they can meet the grower's minimum for quantity and dollar value. The best bargains will be those species ordered in large quantities by the group.

6. Plan and complete forms

Quite a bit of time is set aside for planning, partly because the holidays intervene and partly because members need leisure to consider buying in larger quantities than they're used to. Ideally, members will do their own research, using catalogs, field guides, and other resources (see research resources, beginning on page 304), but it's helpful if one or a few of the more experienced people in the group are available for informal advice.

7. Receive completed forms

You may have to nag. One person who's late can mess up the whole schedule.

8. Compile order quantity worksheets

Enter each individual's order on the quantity worksheet for that nursery. Once these preliminary figures are compiled, you'll be able to see at a glance those species for which the group could reduce the price per plant by a modest increase in quantity. For example, the price break for New England aster might be 51 plants, but the group total is 48 plants. If one member increases his order by 3 plants, everyone will benefit from a lower price for that species.

These calculations and possible order revisions are the subject of the order meeting, which comes next in the timetable. Prepare for the meeting by completing a cost worksheet of dollar amounts for the order as it stands. Note any opportunities for further savings.

9. Hold the order meeting

If you've compiled the orders on a spreadsheet, hold the order meeting where the computer resides or bring a laptop with the spreadsheet on

The quantity worksheet filled in with the number of plants each member wishes to order from Eastern Prairies. This simplified example illustrates why the membership should number at least six people: only a few of the group totals per species approach the quantities needed to get a good price. Price breaks commonly occur at more than 10, 25, 50, and 100 plants per species.

EASTERN PRAIRIES, INC.
GROUP ORDER - QUANTITY WORKSHEET

PRAIRIE GRASSES & FORBS	ALMA	CARM	DIANE	ELLIOT	SONDRA	GROUP TOTAL
Asclepias incarnata						
Asclepias tuberosa	20			10	10	40
Aster laevis						
Aster novae-angliae		5	25	3	15	48
Echinacea pallida			5			5
Eupatorium maculatum				5		5
Eupatorium perfoliatum	10					10
Helianthus mollis				3		3
Liatris spicata		3	3			6
Lobelia siphilitica						
Penstemon digitalis			3	3		6
Ratibida pinnata	10					10
Solidago rigida			3		20	23
INDIVIDUAL TOTALS	40	8	39	24	45	156

disk. A pocket calculator will be helpful if you've compiled the worksheets by hand.

Make a copy of the quantity worksheet for each member. Highlight those species for which the quantity is just short of a price break.

Go down the order form for each grower alphabetically by botanical name. You may find that a minimum order for a species hasn't been met. Also, members may have doubts or questions regarding their choices. They can make changes based on discussions during the meeting.

Enter changes on the quantity worksheet (members can make notes on their own copies of their orders) and see how they are reflected on the cost spreadsheet.

Planting Noah's Garden

Remind people that even with these adjustments, you can't guarantee either prices or availability until the orders are confirmed by the growers. Don't allow any more changes once final quantities are entered and the meeting ends. Be sure everyone understands when invoices will be sent out and by what date they must be paid.

Before closing the meeting, decide where the plants will be delivered. Until now, the grower has been dealing with the Orderer, but that person may not be conveniently located for distributing the plants to the other members, or the work should be spread out more equably within the group. Read ahead to see what's involved when plants arrive. Choose who will receive the shipment.

EASTERN PRAIRIES, INC.
GROUP ORDER - COST WORKSHEET

PRAIRIE GRASSES & FORBS	ALMA	CARM	DIANE	ELLIOT	SONDRA	GROUP TOTAL
Asclepias incarnata						
Asclepias tuberosa	20.00			10.00	10.00	40.00
Aster laevis						
Aster novae-angliae		5.00	25.00	3.00	15.00	48.00
Echinacea pallida			5.00			5.00
Eupatorium maculatum				5.00		5.00
Eupatorium perfoliatum	10.00					10.00
Helianthus mollis				3.00		3.00
Liatris spicata		3.00	3.00			6.00
Lobelia siphilitica						
Penstemon digitalis			3.00	3.00		6.00
Ratibida pinnata	10.00					10.00
Solidago rigida			3.00		20.00	23.00
SUBTOTAL	40.00	8.00	39.00	24.00	45.00	156.00
SHIPPING @10%	4.00	0.80	3.90	2.40	4.50	15.60
TAX @ 6.75%	2.97	0.59	2.90	1.78	3.34	11.58
TOTAL	46.97	9.39	45.80	28.18	52.84	183.18

The Eastern Prairie cost worksheet, including tax and shipping. Again for simplicity, the quantities weren't changed and all the plants are a dollar each. The actual picture would be more complicated, but the setup is the same. This spreadsheet can be used both to confirm the order and, when any necessary adjustments are made, to create individual invoices for members.

10. Confirm orders with growers

You still may not have received the current catalog, and prices may have changed. Even if you have the latest one, some species may be out of stock or not available in the desired quantity or size. You'll save time and grief by calling the grower and discussing the order or by faxing the cost spreadsheet with a note asking for confirmation of price and availability before preparing the final order. You may be given a choice, such as substituting a similar species for one that's out of stock, back-ordering it to the next planting season, or accepting it in a different size. Any adjustments are up to the Orderer. Usually they're minor.

An individual invoice derived from the spreadsheet.

EASTERN PRAIRIES, INC.
GROUP ORDER - INVOICE

PRAIRIE GRASSES & FORBS	ALMA
Asclepias incarnata	
Asclepias tuberosa	20.00
Aster laevis	
Aster novae-angliae	
Echinacea pallida	
Eupatorium maculatum	
Eupatorium perfoliatum	10.00
Helianthus mollis	
Liatris spicata	
Lobelia siphilitica	
Penstemon digitalis	
Ratibida pinnata	10.00
Solidago rigida	
SUBTOTAL	40.00
SHIPPING @10%	4.00
TAX @ 6.75%	2.97
TOTAL	46.97

11. Bill members

By printing only the species column and the column for that recipient, you can easily create individual invoices using the spreadsheet pro-gram. If the calculations have been done by hand, duplicate the final worksheet and give a copy of it to each member with his or her own total circled. Checks should be made payable to the Orderer unless your group has its own bank account.

12. Receive payment

Although growers with whom you have dealt before may not require payment in advance and others may ask that only a percentage of the total be paid when the order is placed, members should pay in full up front. Otherwise, the accounting is too difficult, and the Orderer may have to risk his or her own funds. A bank account that would cover such a risk is a possibility, but banks that accept small balances and whose service charges are reasonable for a small nonprofit group are becoming rare.

13. Place final orders

Use the catalog order blank. Your group order blank isn't as detailed and lacks information the nursery needs for its own records. Indicate on the final, confirmed order the payment method (credit card or check) and delivery method (usually UPS ground service, but there are other options). Fill in the preferred shipping date, or ask the nursery to tell you when the order will be shipped. Most growers ship early in the week, for delivery on Thursday or Friday. Orders may arrive in several batches rather than all at once.

If the order is to be received by someone other than

the Orderer, indicate that person's name and address in the SHIP TO space on the order blank, as though the order were a gift. Enter the Orderer's name and address in the SOLD TO space. That will keep straight in the nursery's computer the record of who actually placed the order. Even clearer, of course, is to have a group name such as the Naturals. The address might change as the job of Orderer rotates, but the group name stays the same. Some catalogs don't have order blanks. In that case, the spreadsheet can be made to serve the purpose, or just write a letter with the necessary information.

WHAT TO DO WHEN ORDERS ARRIVE

The person who receives the plants should be responsible for them for three days, no longer. Put the carton(s) temporarily in a cool, shady place. Choose the day of distribution, and arrange for members to pick up their plants that day. Repackage the plants for distribution first thing in the morning; a typical shipment takes three people about one hour. The procedure is to rewrap plants, one species at a time, in damp newspaper and plastic bags, label each package with the recipient's name and the number and identity of the plants, and group the packages for pickup. Have on hand the following materials for rewrapping, labeling, and keeping track of distribution.

The quantity worksheet for the order, so you know who gets how many of each species and you can tick off each individual's order for a species as it is repackaged, labeled, and set aside for pickup. Cartons may contain several species stacked in layers between damp sphagnum moss or newspapers, bundled in separate parcels, or simply piled in however best they fit. Orders also may arrive incomplete, with other species to come later.

Packaging materials, including plastic bags in various sizes, from sandwich to garbage, depending on the numbers and sizes of plants to be repackaged, and newspapers. You'll also need a source of water to moisten the newspapers: they may be dipped in a tub or sink or sprayed lightly with a hose.

Wood or plastic plant labels for identifying repackaged plants and a waterproof marking pen.

Signs designating where each order is to be picked up. Outdoors, these can be stakes labeled with the person's name and stuck into the ground (in the shade!). Indoors, they can be sheets of paper or shirt cardboards placed on the floor. Packages can just be stacked at each sign or accumulated in a labeled carton or large plastic bag.

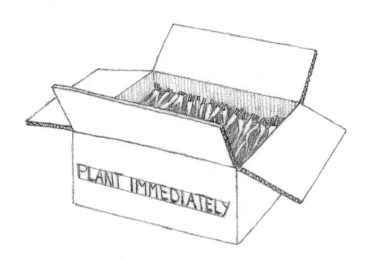

An efficient repackaging procedure

This takes three people—a Checker, a Counter, and a Wrapper. Before you begin, lay out the name signs where each order will be organized. Unwrap the first species to be rewrapped.

This may sound ridiculously detailed, but when a dozen people have each ordered varying numbers of plants out of a total of sixty possible species from three different nurseries, strict procedure is all that stands between you and insanity.

(a)

(a) The Checker consults the shipping bill and worksheet and prepares a label for each member who ordered the species in that shipment. The total of the numbers on the individual labels should equal the total number of plants in the order.

Use abbreviations: "Alma - 5 Asc tub" means Alma is to get five Asclepias tuberosa, or butterflyweed. "Pen dig" would be Penstemon digitalis (foxglove penstemon); "Rat pin" would be Ratibida pinnata (gray-headed coneflower). Not only do abbreviations take much less space (and so save time) but they often help rather than hinder learning botanical names.

Planting Noah's Garden

(b)

(b) The Counter consults each label in turn to determine the right number of plants for that person and places them on a double sheet of damp newspaper along with the label.

(c) The Wrapper folds the newspaper around the order and places it in a plastic bag—still with its label.

(c)

(d)

(d) The Checker then deposits the package at the right sign and ticks the species off that member's order. Repeat the procedure for each species until all the plants are repackaged.

23 Collecting Wild Seeds

🌿 HOW TO COLLECT WILD SEEDS

The novice may easily become greedy, taking more seeds than can possibly be grown and without discrimination among species. A disciplined approach is to work from a list of species you'd like to add to a particular habitat, just as you would if you were preparing to order seeds from a nursery, and to collect in similar quantity—a single packet of seed per species. The goal should be to increase the diversity of a chosen habitat with plants that, based on research and observation, "ought" to be there but aren't. The hunt for plants on your list will lead you to others still unknown to you that grow in the same community. These will provide still more opportunities to identify plants, and later collect seeds, to add new species to your increasingly complex habitat.

Some basic rules of collection

Collect seeds only from plant communities similar to your own. These are likely to be disturbed areas, not pristine ones where rare plants survive in conditions you can't replicate. Any community that looks unusual compared to communities that are common in surrounding areas should be left undisturbed. Even in a community that appears to be common, any species represented by only a few individuals, or that grows in a patch not repeated elsewhere in the community, should also be left undisturbed. Don't take seeds from plants you haven't identified.

Collect from different plants, just a few seeds from each. This preserves any unique characteristics that an individual parent may pass on to succeeding generations.

Choose species most likely to be successful. In general, prairie and meadow forbs and grasses are the easiest to germinate. Consider, when making your list, whether you really are up to the technical demands of germinating woodland wildflowers (see page 315) or have the patience to care for trees or shrubs while they grow to transplant size. Buying the more difficult species as bareroot plants may be a better option.

A folding pocket hand lens. "10x" means it magnifies the object to ten times actual size.

Don't collect seeds from alien species. Most flourish at the expense of natives and are doing fine without your encouragement. Save your energy for native species that will benefit from your effort.

Assemble the equipment
The equipment you need takes very little space; the difficulty is having the items on hand when you want them unexpectedly. Keep what you need in a backpack (or whatever carryall you use out walking) and stow it in the car, not the closet. You'll want the equipment for scouting likely sites as well as for collecting.

A field guide and hand lens to identify a species when the plant is in flower.

Plastic sandwich bags to collect seeds that have to stay fresh and moist and as sample bags for species you can't identify on the spot (see page 275).

Small envelopes for collecting seeds that can easily be stripped from the plant. Seeds spill out the corners of ordinary envelopes. Look in stationery stores for manila envelopes about the size of a seed packet, with the flap at the narrow end.

Small paper bags for collecting bulky material from which you can't remove the seeds in the field.

A pruner or pocket knife for snipping off flower heads when the seeds don't strip off easily.

A pencil and notepad to keep a record of your venture. Although the date, location, and species should be recorded on the paper bag or envelope in which you collect the seeds, you always need to jot down other species that grow at a certain spot or ones whose seeds you were too late or too early to harvest this time around.

Don't collect seeds of protected species

A list of protected plants is available from your state's Natural Heritage or Natural Areas Program (see page 309). Strike any protected species from your list. Check also whether your state has "beauty" laws, which forbid picking flowers along public roads. Although such laws don't usually apply to collecting seeds, a state trooper may misunderstand your intentions. Public lands specifically set aside as nature preserves may require a permit for seed collection. Again, these requirements are intended to protect rare, endangered, or overcollected plants, but it's wise to be sure you have permission to collect the seeds on your list. Collecting from private land without permission is trespassing, which is against the law in every state.

Scout for likely sites

Likely sites are often common roadside ones: ditches, old fields, hedgerows, or woodland edges. You may be able to spot a promising area from the car by its general look—rocky and dry or wet enough that skunk cabbage grows there—or because you recognize a showy flower on your list. Disused areas in cemeteries, under power lines, and along railroad tracks are worth investigating, too.

Explore promising areas with your field guide to identify species that are in bloom at that visit.

Take a sample in a plastic bag of each species you identify and wish to collect from; later, press it so that you'll be able to recognize it by its leaf or other characteristics after it's in seed. If you can't identify a species, take a sample to send to your Agricultural Extension Service (see page 275).

Note on a slip of paper the plant's name (or description) and where you found it—for example, "Solidago speciosa, Rte. 172 at north entrance to Thruway, in front of the sumacs." Or "Short, fine-textured bunchgrass on rock outcropping beyond apple tree, Carver's Cemetery." Note the date, too, and keep the note with the sample.

Visit the site at intervals during the growing season to see if other plants of interest also grow there; note these as well. At each visit, check on the plants you already know to see how its seeds are progressing. Bloom time doesn't necessarily indicate when seeds will ripen, since flowering may be timed for pollinators and ripening for dispersers.

An excellent book for identifying wildflowers past their blooming season is *Guide to Wildflowers in Winter,* by Carol Levine (Yale University Press). Unlike other flower guides, it has keys that direct you to stems, leaves, and—most important for the seed collector—the plant's dried fruits.

Harvest the seeds

There may be only a small window of time between when seed becomes ripe and when it disperses from the parent plant (or is eaten by birds!). Luckily, neither individual plants nor colonies of a species ripen all their seeds simultaneously, so if you arrive earlier or later than peak ripening time, you may still find enough seed. Collect seeds in capsules or pods when the container is dry or beginning to split open; seeds of grasses when they are hard and brown; seeds with chaffy attachments when the chaff is dry and fluffy; seeds in fleshy fruits when the fruit is ripe. In many cases, seeds will continue to ripen on the cut stalk during the drying period. Below and on page 350 are some examples of seeds and how to harvest them.

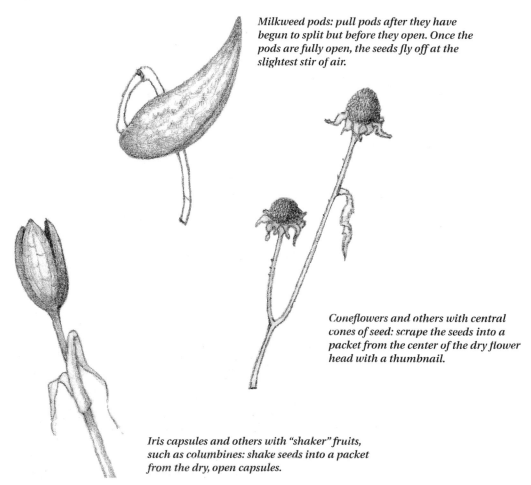

Milkweed pods: pull pods after they have begun to split but before they open. Once the pods are fully open, the seeds fly off at the slightest stir of air.

Coneflowers and others with central cones of seed: scrape the seeds into a packet from the center of the dry flower head with a thumbnail.

Iris capsules and others with "shaker" fruits, such as columbines: shake seeds into a packet from the dry, open capsules.

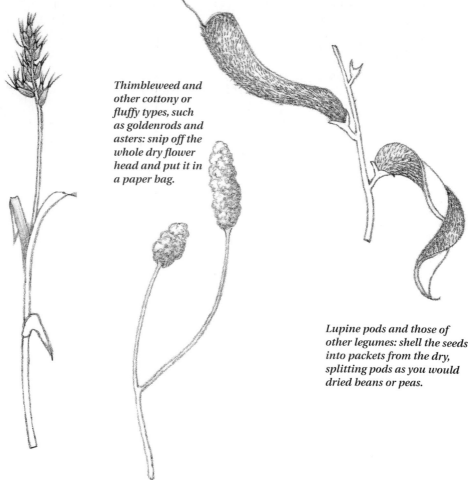

Grasses, sedges, and rushes: strip seeds from the stalk between thumb and finger in a "milking" motion into your palm and thence into a paper bag or packet.

Thimbleweed and other cottony or fluffy types, such as goldenrods and asters: snip off the whole dry flower head and put it in a paper bag.

Lupine pods and those of other legumes: shell the seeds into packets from the dry, splitting pods as you would dried beans or peas.

Process the seeds

Seeds that will be planted outdoors when fresh don't need further treatment. Seeds that you were able to shake, shell, or strip easily need only a period of drying. Seeds harvested slightly prematurely need to continue ripening on the stalk or in the capsule until they detach easily. Probably successful germination doesn't demand that seeds also be cleaned of encasements and debris—and some can't be without special equipment—but clean seed is easier to handle. Seeds embedded in fleshy fruits won't sprout unless cleaned because the flesh contains germination inhibitors (fruit seeds normally would be cleaned as they pass through the gut of the animal that disperses them).

Ripen immature seed stalks in open paper bags where the air circulates freely. There is often enough moisture and nutrition to complete seed maturation, but lack of air circulation could cause the whole lot to grow mold and die. Seeds as they ripen become darker and harder and finally come free from the stalk, pod, or capsule just as they would had they been collected when fully mature.

Free ripe, dry seeds from stalks and encasements by hand threshing or extraction. Rub the flower stalks between your palms to free the seeds, or scratch the seeds from flower heads with your fingers. To separate milkweed seeds from their fluff, strip them while the silk lies flat. Grasp the silk firmly with the fingers of one hand, and scrape off the seeds with the other. Other pods and capsules can often just be spilled out. Hard, closed capsules can be cracked individually with pliers or lightly tapped between two bricks to break them open.

Separate the seeds from the chaff. Professionals sieve seeds through several grades of mesh to clean them. The idea is to choose a mesh that traps debris but lets the seeds drop through. You can approximate this procedure using fine to coarse kitchen strainers. Rub the material lightly against the mesh, then shake the strainer to let the seeds fall onto a piece of paper. Fine-clean the seeds by shaking the paper to pool them, then brush the debris aside with a soft artist's brush. Or pick the seeds out individually with forceps. Sometimes vigorous shaking in a paper bag will pool the seeds at the bottom, leaving the chaff on top to be disposed of. Don't worry about seeds that can't be nicely cleaned; they'll germinate regardless.

Soak fleshy fruits in water for at least a week. Soft fruits can be mashed first; cut hard fruits open to reveal the flesh. Germination inhibitors in oily seeds may not be water soluble; add detergent to their soaking liquid. Rinse the soaking fruit daily in a strainer under running water, and change the water in the soaking dish. As the flesh softens, free the seeds by rubbing the mush against a strainer set into a bowl of water. Much of the pulp will float and can be skimmed off the surface. What's left can usually be cleaned by rolling the seeds on a paper towel with your fingers, then picking out the wiped seeds with forceps. Wash the seeds well again and let them dry thoroughly before storing.

Store clean, hard, ripe seeds in paper packets at room temperature. This assures that they'll get whatever additional drying they may need. Three months in dry storage is probably enough. If you don't intend to start germination at that point, store them in the refrigerator.

For more information:

How to Start Wild Seeds Indoors, page 315

24 Constructing Habitats

 THOUGHTS ON CONSTRUCTED ENVIRONMENTS

Patio is not an ecological term; neither is a stone wall a recognized habitat, a basin a wetland, or a birdbox a natural cavity. Yet these man-made structures offer improved living standards for many small animals: the patio by its unique microclimate favorable to a rich diversity of food plants, the stone wall by its extended shelter, the basin for its convenience, the box for its cleanliness. Some thought is required to combine these elements into a living space that is also comfortable for humans.

If you already have a patio, consider upgrading it by replacing some paving with planting beds and adding wildlife amenities.

The site

Warm, sunny sites support more vegetation attractive to wildlife than do woodsy ones, but for more variety of habitat and some welcome shade, the paving can turn a corner of the house or incorporate an existing tree. Except in the seating area, the site needn't be level. Paving can follow gentle contours; steeper changes in grade can be terraced. The patio surface should drain away from the house, toward the perimeter.

The surface

Masonry absorbs and retains heat; the soil below stays warmer overnight and in the winter. Heat radiating from the stone or brick heats the air as well; the "climate" is hotter than on a lawn, and evaporation at the surface is more rapid. Yet beneath the paving, the soil is

Although this patio is a generous size—the main portion is 22 x 40 feet—only about half of it is paved. The smaller portion, facing west and convenient to the back door, is an herb garden.

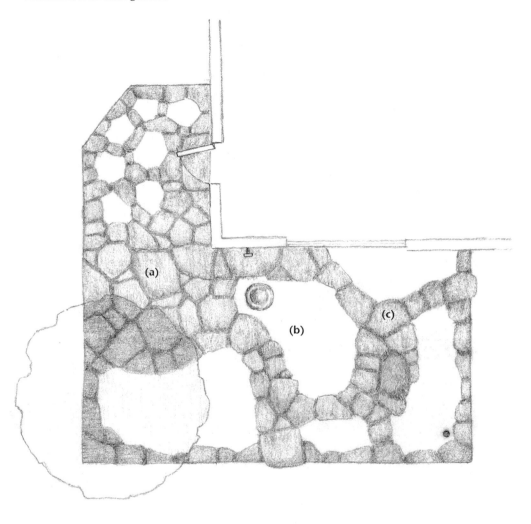

(a) Paved areas should include one generous level surface for seating and perhaps for outdoor cooking. Smaller open areas are needed, too—for putting down a tool basket, piling weeds, or setting out plants to be installed. An open area to the right includes a seating rock.

(b) Beds can be as small as the space left between stones that don't meet at their corners or large enough to hold a small tree or incorporate existing shrubbery. This one includes a birdbath next to the hose outlet. The corner bed to the right includes a post for a birdhouse.

(c) Paths can range in width from one that accommodates a wheelbarrow or garden cart to very narrow footpaths among the beds.

protected from evaporation, and moisture is surprisingly constant even though the sand in which the masonry is set offers excellent aeration and an easy run for roots.

Patio construction is described step-by-step in books on the subject published by Ortho or Sunset, available at bookstores and garden centers. Choose a technique that uses sand or gravel, not concrete, as the base and filler. To make planting and weeding easier, leave wider spaces between large pavers than the book advises. Where the surrounding area is lawn, install a cemented masonry edge or a concrete footing to keep turf from intruding.

Masonry paving. Natural fieldstone—lime, shale, sandstone, granite—is nice if you can get it, but bricks, tiles, flags, slate, cut stone, or recycled concrete pavement can all be used. The larger the individual pavers, the fewer cracks there will be between them to plant and maintain and the more easily they can be laid over a contoured surface.

Steps and walls

Enclosing walls, retaining walls, and steps are good habitats for small creatures only if they are constructed without concrete. A good reference book on how to acquire and handle rock, lay slabs, and construct steps and walls is *Building with Stone,* by Charles McRaven (Garden Way). Orders can be placed by calling the publisher at 800-827-8673.

Vegetation

Choice of species, of course, depends on where you live and will vary also according to the degree of light in different portions of the patio.

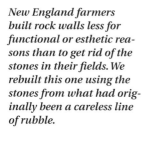

New England farmers built rock walls less for functional or esthetic reasons than to get rid of the stones in their fields. We rebuilt this one using the stones from what had originally been a careless line of rubble.

In general, plant communities suitable to this created microclimate are made up of drought-tolerant species with leathery, waxy, or succulent foliage that resists desiccation, often of low or creeping habit, and perhaps more typical of warmer areas to your south.

Choose wildlife food species. A "balanced diet" will include bunchgrasses for grain, fruiting shrubs and ground covers, and flowers popular for their nectar and their seeds. Catalogs often give such information. The Dover reprint *American Wildlife & Plants: A Guide to Wildlife Food Habits* includes cross-referenced indexes that allow you to look up either the name of the plant, to learn which birds or mammals it supports, or the name of the animal, to learn its food preferences. Peterson's Field Guides *Eastern Butterflies* and *Western Butterflies* include an index to butterfly host and nectar plants. *The Audubon Society Guide to Attracting Birds,* by Stephen Kress (Scribner's) and Kress's more recent *Bird Gardens* (Dorling Kindersley) list favorite bird fruits for all regions of the country and suggest popular hummingbird flowers, too.

Layer plantings for wildlife shelter. Use bunchgrasses, sedges, rushes, and low wildflowers instead of mulch as the filler in beds and in the spaces between pavers to provide shelter at ground level. The next level should include dense shrubbery; evergreen shrubs provide winter protection for birds. Incorporate a few small fruit trees into the beds for perches where birds can retreat between forays.

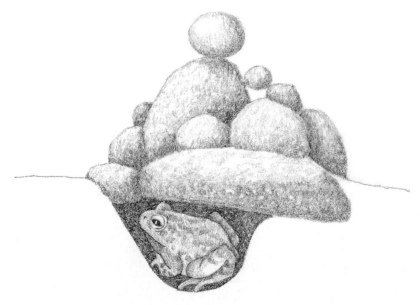

A toad in its burrow beneath a stone cairn. By moderating the temperature and conserving moisture in the soil below, stone constructions of even the most casual sort create a specialized niche for many animals. Place the large roof stone first. Dig out a small cavity below it, and line it with sand or dried leaves. If you have children, they'd probably love to build the rest of the cairn.

Amenities

Informally heaped rock shelters or arrangements of boulders will harbor small animals if walls aren't part of your plan. A water basin, filled by hose or equipped with a dripper, will prove to be a great attractor. You might consider also a little bog or pond (see How to Build Small Bogs and Ponds, page 393). One or more birdboxes will be appreciated. Bird feeders may not be advisable. Sunflower seed hulls contain a toxin that inhibits the germination and growth of other plants; thistle is usually irradiated to make it sterile, but if it hasn't been, the seeds sprout into troublesome weeds. The plantings themselves will produce quite a bit of seed, and plant debris left in the beds over the winter will harbor insect food as well.

🍃 HOW TO MOVE A HEAVY STONE

Moving big stones is heavy work—too heavy for brute strength alone. It always requires two people, the right tools, and a degree of cleverness. That said—and with a warning that this is not work for anyone

Rock varies in density, but this common sort of fieldstone weighs about 100 pounds per cubic foot, or nearly 300 pounds for a slab this size.

with back problems—stones weighing up to several hundred pounds can be moved into place with precision, and with less effort than you might imagine. These instructions will let you move large slabs and unearth boulders.

What you need

A tractor with a cart is a great help; so is a friend with a front-end loader. If you have neither, though, most stones can be moved by two workers using primitive equipment.

Prybars (also called crowbars, or just bars). The terminology is fuzzy here, as short wrecking bars go by the same names. You want long, straight steel bars with one end shaped like a chisel. Prybars are used in two ways: to lift the edge of a stone (so it can be manipulated) and to nudge a stone forward. The longer the bar, the greater the leverage—but the heavier it is and the harder to wield. Choose one large and one medium bar (small ones aren't very useful).

A wheelbarrow. Any stone that can more or less fit into the bed of a barrow, and that can be rolled or tipped into it using sheer muscle or the prybars, can be wheeled into place. Garden carts and plastic wheelbarrows aren't strong enough. Choose a steel barrow with a medium (not deep or steep) bed and hardwood handles.

A plank, 2 inches thick by 8 inches wide by 6 feet long, and sizable plywood scraps whose exact thickness and dimension don't matter much. The plank and plywood are used with log rollers to move stones along the ground and into place.

Log rollers. Nothing fancy here: just unsplit fireplace wood 3 or 4 inches in diameter, 2 feet long or so, smooth and straight. You'll need about six logs.

A prybar

The rest of the technical equipment: a plank, scrapwood, logs, stones

Small to medium stones (softball to football size) to use as fulcrums for the prybars and as wedges for lifting rocks. You can substitute bricks or broken concrete blocks if necessary.

The workers need not be twin strong men! One can be the muscle person who lifts and holds a stone in place while the other, nimbler sort uses the smaller bar to stabilize the rock and insert wedges, planks, or rollers.

The techniques

Start with something the size of a rural tombstone to get the knack of things before you try to move a huge slab or boulder.

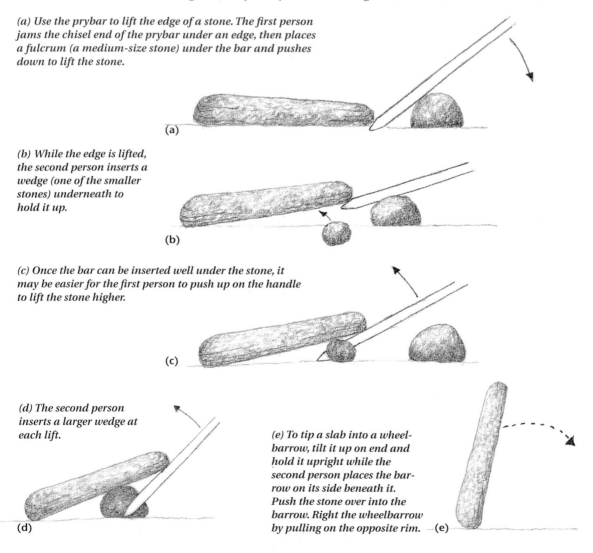

(a) Use the prybar to lift the edge of a stone. The first person jams the chisel end of the prybar under an edge, then places a fulcrum (a medium-size stone) under the bar and pushes down to lift the stone.

(a)

(b) While the edge is lifted, the second person inserts a wedge (one of the smaller stones) underneath to hold it up.

(b)

(c) Once the bar can be inserted well under the stone, it may be easier for the first person to push up on the handle to lift the stone higher.

(c)

(d) The second person inserts a larger wedge at each lift.

(d)

(e) To tip a slab into a wheelbarrow, tilt it up on end and hold it upright while the second person places the barrow on its side beneath it. Push the stone over into the barrow. Right the wheelbarrow by pulling on the opposite rim. **(e)**

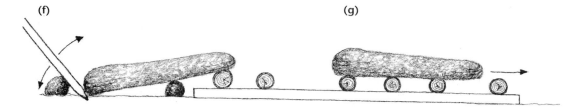

(f)   (g)

If a stone is too large to move by wheelbarrow, use a plank, plywood, and rollers to push it forward. While one person lifts the forward edge of the stone with the bar, the other person shoves the plank under the edge. At the next lift, a log roller is placed between the plank and the belly of the stone.

(f) The stone is urged onto the roller by prying it forward with the bar from the rear, with or without a fulcrum. As it rolls onto the first log, another is placed in its path along the plank.

(g) When lifted entirely onto rollers, even a very heavy slab becomes easy to handle. Add rollers at the front as the stone slides off those to the rear. Use plywood scraps when you get to the end of the plank; the sturdy plank is a good starter, but the broader, more supple plywood scraps are easier to manipulate.

(h) Bellied slabs or round boulders can be moved by a variation of the log roller method. Pry or tumble the stone onto a plywood scrap. Proceed as before, but place rollers under the plywood instead of under the stone, and move the stone with its wooden base as a unit.

(h)

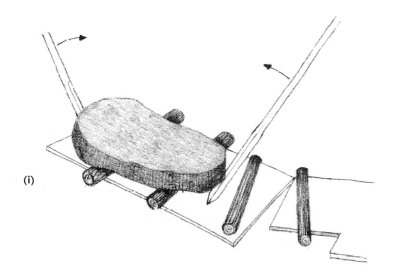

(i) When moving a stone uphill or downhill, use a second bar to brake it so that it doesn't slide too fast or in the wrong direction on its rollers. By placing log rollers at an angle and prying from one or the other rear corner with the bar, you'll be able to direct the stone accurately toward its goal.

(i)

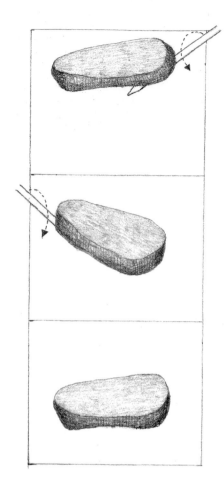

Left: Use the prybar to move a stone off the plank into place or to position it accurately on the ground. While a stone is on logs, it can be nudged along by placing the bar under the rear edge and pushing forward on the handle. Once off the logs, though, that action tilts the forward edge of the stone into the ground, with the frequent result that it won't budge unless it happens to be round and headed downhill. Instead, sidle the stone forward, first from one side, then the other, each time lifting an edge and moving the bar in an arc. Use this method to position a large stone precisely once it's roughly in place. It's too painstaking for moving stones any distance.

Below: To lift a boulder out of the ground, first dig out the surrounding soil.

(a)

(a) Use the bar with a fulcrum stone to tip the boulder to one side; slip a wedging rock under the boulder to hold it in the tilted position.

(b)   (c)

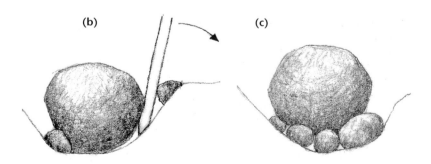

(b) Move to the opposite side and repeat the maneuver. Each wedge will hold the boulder higher.

(c) As the boulder approaches the surface, you'll be able to slip a plank and rollers beneath it to move it out of the hole.

All these birdhouses, none of them standard, were immediately occupied by a variety of cavity nesters. Birds also use them for shelter in the winter.

🍂 HOW TO BUILD A BIRDHOUSE

The Audubon Society Guide to Attracting Birds (see page 304) includes detailed instructions for building nesting shelves and boxes for any number of species. Home carpenters may enjoy the challenge, especially if they wish to house demanding tenants such as wood ducks, owls, or purple martins. Anyone, though, can nail together boxes for bluebirds, tree swallows, chickadees, wrens, and other easily pleased backyard birds. For creative freedom, the instructions here are for building a box by eye, without a dimensioned drawing (though you may want to sketch your idea) and without using a ruler. The entry hole must be accurate. Holes larger than 1½ inches will let starlings take over your housing; fledglings may have difficulty climbing out of a hole placed higher than 6 inches from the floor.

Tools

You need a hammer, a saw, a drill with a 1½-inch circle bit, and a 90°-45°-45° triangle. Improvise a work surface, such as an old wooden chair and some C-clamps to hold the wood.

Materials

Scrap wood will do. For basic construction, use lengths of 1 x 6 or 1 x 8 boards, leftover pieces of exterior-grade plywood, old siding from demolished buildings, and discarded wood shingles for roofing.

Construction sites are a good source; some lumberyards keep bins of free or cheap scraps. Wood putty comes in handy for filling inadvertent gaps, and carpenter's glue is helpful, too. Decorative materials include strips of bark, grapevines, pinecones, or anything that you can nail down. (Nail length will depend on lumber thickness.) Sandpaper, varnish, or paint is optional.

Basic design

The basic designs are a peaked-roof house and a shed-roof box. Both begin with cutting the floor, but the sequence of constructing the walls differs. Instructions for a shed-roof box begin below. Instructions for a peaked-roof house begin on page 365.

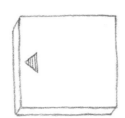

For both designs, cut the floor first. So you can nail the walls into the floor edge, cut it from a 1-inch board or 3/4-inch plywood. The length and width aren't critical. A square measuring 4 by 4 inches accommodates a small nest, like that of a chickadee; 6 by 6 is more than enough for any backyard species. Larger floor areas are okay, too, and birds aren't prejudiced against rectangles. Approximate the size: there's no need to use a ruler. Use the triangle to mark straight lines and right angles.

Cutting and assembling a shed-roof box

(a)

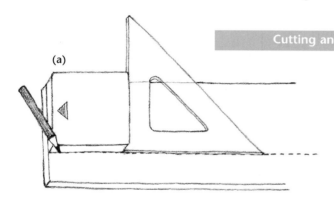

(a) You'll be cutting the front and rear walls before the side walls. Mark on the floor piece which edge is the front. Lay the floor piece flush with one corner of a board, and use it to mark the width of the front and rear walls. Extend that mark vertically along the board with the triangle. The line should be quite long, because both front and back walls will be cut to that width.

(b) Decide the height of the front wall. It's the low end, where the slanted roof hangs over the entrance hole. With the triangle, mark the height at right angles to the first line and cut out that piece.

(b)

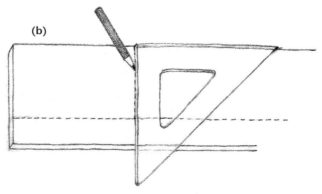

(c)

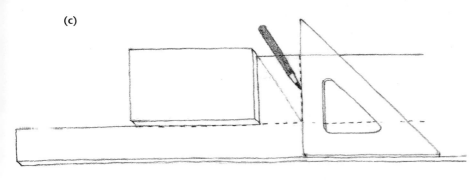

(c) To figure the height of the rear wall, lay the front wall on the board and sketch a slanted line as though you were drawing the slope of the roof. The top of the slanted line is the height of the rear wall. Mark that height with the triangle and cut the rear wall.

(d)

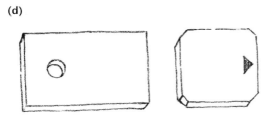

(d) Before you assemble the pieces you've cut so far, finish the floor and front wall. Nick off the corners of the floor piece to allow drainage. Cut the entrance hole in the front wall.

(e)

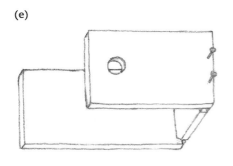

(e) Nail the rear wall to the rear edge of the floor. Tack the front wall to the front edge of the floor, but don't hammer the nails all the way in; you take them out after you assemble the side walls.

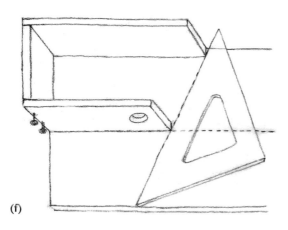

(f) Lay the assembly on its side flush with the corner of a board to mark the width of the first side wall; extend the width line using the triangle. Lay the triangle against the top edges, as shown, to mark the height and slant of the first side wall.

(f)

(g)

(g) Cut out the first side wall and lay it back on the board flipped over so the slants are flush. Mark the height of the second side. The two should match exactly. Cut out the second side wall.

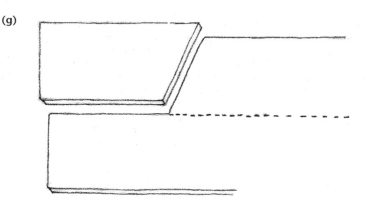

(h)

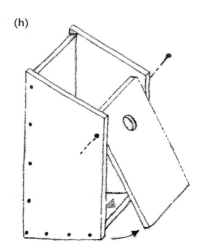

(h) Nail the side walls to the edges of the floor and rear wall, but not to the front wall. The front wall is going to swing up between the side walls on pivots so the box can be opened for cleaning. The pivots are just long nails. Place them exactly opposite each other, as shown, and hammer them in straight. Now pull out the tacks holding the bottom of the front wall and check that the "door" pivots smoothly.

(i)

(i) Use the slanted top of the assembled box to mark the size of the roof. Make the roof big enough to project a little all around. Cut the roof and nail it into place along the top edges of the side pieces. The top edges at the front and rear walls aren't at the right angle to butt against the roof. That's okay; the poor fit provides ventilation. The box is now finished. Page 367 shows how to mount it on a post.

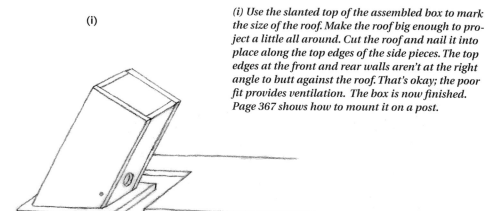

Planting Noah's Garden

The methods of measuring and marking the pieces are the same as for a shed roof house, but the sequence is different. The two side walls are attached to the floor first, and that assembly is used to figure the angled front and rear walls. Also, the pivoting "door" is in this case one of the side walls, not the front wall.

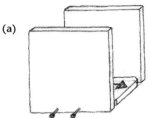

(a)

(a) Cut the side walls first; they will match in width and height. Mark the width using one side of the floor piece and extend the line with the triangle. The height is up to you; it will be the eave line of the roof. Cut the first side wall and use it to mark the height of the second one. Nick the corners off the floor piece for drainage. Nail one side into the edge of the floor, but just tack the other one into place so you can remove those nails later.

(b)

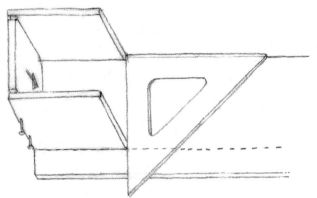

(b) Lay the assembly down flush with one corner of the board. Mark the width of the end walls and the height of the eave line. Draw a horizontal line between the eave line marks. Put the assembly aside while you draw the roof angle on the board.

(c) To draw the roof angle accurately, place the triangle at the eave line, as shown, to make first one diagonal line and then another diagonal intersecting the first. The diagonals mark the pitched roof line; their intersection is the peak. Extend the pitch lines the full width of the wall so they form an X; this will assure that the two walls match exactly.

(c)

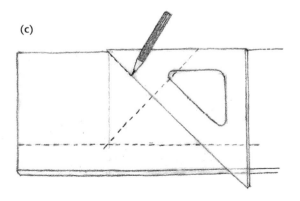

(d) Cut the first end wall.

(d)

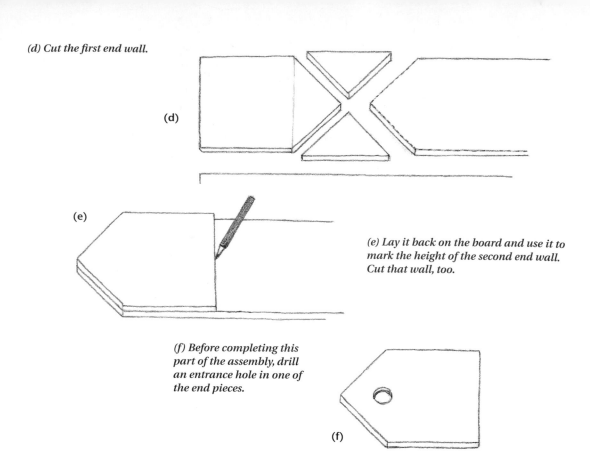

(e)

(e) Lay it back on the board and use it to mark the height of the second end wall. Cut that wall, too.

(f) Before completing this part of the assembly, drill an entrance hole in one of the end pieces.

(f)

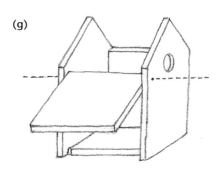

(g)

(g) Nail the end wall into the edge of the floor and into the side wall that was previously nailed in place, but don't nail into the other side wall that you merely tacked in place. This is the side that's going to pivot up for cleaning. Place the two pivot nails exactly opposite each other, as shown, and hammer them in straight. Now you can pull out the temporary tacks.

(h)

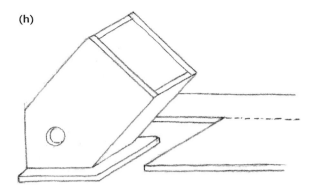

(h) Use the nearly completed box to mark the first roof piece. Lay it on the board so the peak is flush with the edge, but allow a little extra board on the other three sides of the roof piece, to project as eaves. Just do it by eye, then use the triangle to draw the edges straight and at right angles. Cut out the first roof piece. Position it on the house so that the eaves project equally front and rear and the top edge is flush with the peak. Nail it into the top edges of both end walls.

(i) The second roof piece is the same width as the first one, but because it overlaps the edge of the first piece, it's longer by the thickness of the board. Lay the assembly on the board as before, then butt a scrap of the same board against the roof peak to mark the total length. Cut this last piece and nail it into the end walls. (As with the shed roof box, there will be cracks where the pitched roof doesn't properly meet the flat tops of the side walls. The cracks are for ventilation.)

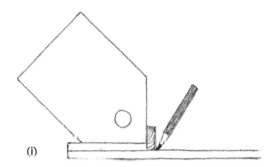

(i)

Before mounting the house, you may want to paint or decorate it. Do whatever you want to the outside of the box, but leave the inside raw wood. Some cavity nesting birds don't actually build nests. They just nestle down in the soft decaying wood that accumulates in natural cavities. Give them a generous cushion of wood shavings or coarse sawdust instead.

The mounting post can be a 2 x 2 or a 4 x 4. Ask for treated lumber or paint the bottom few feet with a wood preservative to keep it from rotting. Red cedar posts—the trunk with just the branches removed—naturally resist decay. Allow an extra 20 inches at least for burying the post securely in the ground.

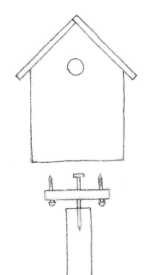

To mount a house on top of a post, cut a base plate slightly smaller than the floor. Drill a screw hole in each corner of the plate and nail it firmly to the post. Hold the box in position against the plate, stick an awl through each screw hole in turn to make matching holes in the box, and screw the box to the plate using brass screws (they don't rust).

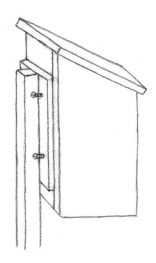

Mounting a box to the side of a post is similar. Cut the plate somewhat smaller than the back.

A dead tree trunk makes a handy post; you don't have to dig it in! The top has to be cut straight, though, or the box will lean.

Dig a hole 20 to 24 inches deep, stand the post in it, and have someone hold it while you fill the hole. Wedge the post with a few rocks if they're handy. Stamp the dirt in hard.

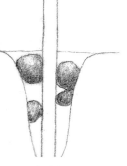

 ### A NOTE ON BIRD BASINS

Many commercial bird basins are available; most come with stands to keep the birds safe from marauding cats. However, placing the basin on a stand also places it beyond the reach of small animals like ground squirrels that would otherwise come to drink, and birds prefer to bathe the old-fashioned way, at ground level. Shy species, both birds and mammals, will be more apt to use the basin if they can pop in and out safely from adjacent shrubbery.

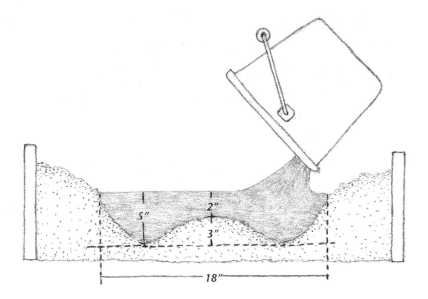

Sand casting is an easy way to make a natural-looking basin. Heap a pile of damp mason's sand in a child's sandbox, or slap together a temporary frame from scrap lumber. Scoop and mold the sand into a shallow mound surrounded by a moat. The mound will be the inside of the basin; the moat will be the rim. The dimensions here are approximate. If you like, the surface can be decorated with gravel or pebbles for an interesting texture.

Prepare a batch of ready-mix concrete in a wheelbarrow or a tub (the instructions are on the bag). You'll need about two bucketsful for an 18-inch basin. Add enough water to make a thick but pourable mix. Spoon the concrete over the mold to cover the surface, then pour the rest of it in to the height of the rim. Level the bottom with a scrap of board.

Let the concrete cure for at least a week before lifting the basin from the mold.

25 Controlling Weeds

NOTES ON HERBICIDE: GLYPHOSATE

Glyphosate, a clear, odorless, amber liquid, is commonly used in ecological restoration to kill invasive weeds. Other herbicides that work as well (or better for some species and in some circumstances) are used too, but this one has found the widest acceptance among conservationists. Weed species can also be controlled by uprooting or repeated cutting, but the judicious use of glyphosate is wise not only for your own convenience but for the environment. Please read the following information before deciding whether to use this herbicide.

Problems of cutting and uprooting

Cutting down a tree, shrub, or vine isn't guaranteed to kill it. The occasional plant may die; most species will resprout from dormant buds in the stub. Cutting down a plant is the physiological equivalent of pruning it to encourage new growth. A hormone called auxin, produced in the growing tips of plants, inhibits the sprouting of dormant buds farther down the stem. You can't see these microscopic buds, for they're beneath the bark. When you cut off the tips of a plant (or the whole stem or trunk), you remove the source of auxin and thus its inhibition. As a result, buds awaken and grow in the remaining stub. These new sprouts, nourished by the plant's full root system, are likely to be more numerous than the original stems. To finally kill the plant, the sprouts have to be cut repeatedly until the roots are depleted of stored nourishment and the plant starves.

Uprooting by plow or backhoe is the brute-force method most often used for clearing vegetation on a large scale, but the obvious problems created—drying, erosion, and the reinvasion of the disturbed soil by the same or other aggressive species—occur also at the smallest scale of pulling out a vine or grubbing out a shrub. Uprooting may not be an option for other reasons. Taprooted plants are hard to pull out even as seedlings; the roots of thicketing shrubs and vines are often too tangled with those of other, valued species to wrench them out; the work to grub out even an isolated, moderate-size shrub is exhausting; the plant may resprout anyhow from root fragments left in the ground.

That said, perhaps the worst result of both repeated cutting and uprooting is that this arduous and discouraging work may lead you to abandon the project altogether.

A cut stub resprouts vigorously from dormant buds. In some species, cutting encourages the buds' spread along the roots as well as at the stub, so the area of infestation increases.

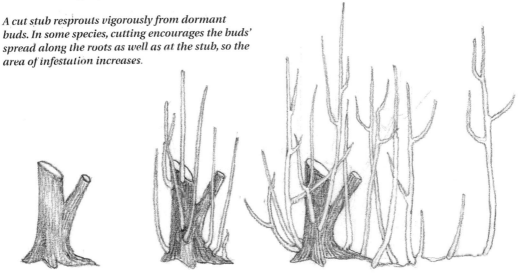

Facts about glyphosate

Although herbicides may be sold under seemingly generic labels such as "Lawn Weed Killer," "Brush Killer," "Poison Ivy Killer," and so on, they may all contain the same active ingredient or different ones of differing toxicity, leaving you confused about both efficacy and hazard. You can get along with just one herbicide, glyphosate, and it is the safest one to use. "Safe" means that the product does not leave a residue that is harmful to life in soil or groundwater, and that the chemical itself would be toxic to animals only in quantities unlikely or impossible to ingest.

Glyphosate adheres to soil particles, so it does not enter groundwater. Soil microorganisms rapidly break it down to phosphate, a plant nutrient that occurs naturally in soil and is a component of most fertilizers, and glycine, an amino acid that exists in all body proteins and is further broken down into nitrogen, carbon dioxide, and water.

Toxicity to animals is expressed as an LD_{50} (Lethal Dose, 50) value. This is the oral dose, in milligrams of the substance per kilogram of body weight, that kills 50 percent of the animals tested. Susceptibility varies with the kind of animal; birds in general are more easily poisoned than

Newer measuring cups are marked in milliliters on one side. These decimal units make it easy to measure small quantities of strong solutions. Here, a 20% solution is made from 50 ml of concentrated herbicide and 200 ml of water. The suds on top, caused by a surfactant, are a nuisance. Avoid sudsing by measuring the water first, then adding the herbicide. The total amount, somewhat more than a pint, is enough for cut-stem application over several days of clearing.

Screw-top rubber cement jars are sold empty; the glass is impervious to the chemicals used in a herbicide. To avoid dripping, adjust the brush height so the tip just touches the liquid.

mammals. Pesticides with an LD_{50} value of 5,000 or higher are generally considered nontoxic. The LD_{50} value for glyphosate when tested on birds is over 2,000, which makes it "slightly toxic." * For example, it could kill a song sparrow only in the unlikely event that the ⅔-ounce (19-gram) bird could ingest 38 milligrams of the chemical. No animal kills have ever been reported from its use.

Glyphosate is a nonspecific herbicide: it kills every kind of vegetation. For this reason, and despite its low toxicity to animals, it should be used only in the most precise manner to avoid injuring any but the target species.

Choosing the most useful glyphosate product

Glyphosate is manufactured by Monsanto and sold under the brand names Roundup and Rodeo. Monsanto also has licensed its use in products made by other companies under various brand names. These diluted formulations ("premixed" or "ready to use") may contain either a greater percentage of glyphosate than is necessary for weed control or too low a proportion to be effective. Roundup and Rodeo are sold in both diluted and concentrated form. Choose the concentrate; it can be diluted in water to the percentage most effective for the control method you're using.

Roundup contains a surfactant (a detergent that spreads the chemical over leaf surfaces), which can be harmful to fish and so is not approved for use in or near wetlands. Rodeo is approved for wetland use.

Using glyphosate for cut-surface application

In most cases, invasive trees and shrubs can be killed by brushing a small amount of herbicide onto the freshly cut surface of the stem or trunk. This method, called cut-surface application, uses the least possible chemical and delivers it precisely to the target plant.

The chemical must be applied to a fresh wound. Within an hour or less, the stem or trunk begins to form callus tissue that bars the entry of the herbicide.

Treatment is most effective toward the end of summer, when plants are storing nutrients in preparation for dormancy and sap is descending to their roots. Rising sap early in the growing season may exclude the herbicide.

Use a concentrated solution. The manufacturer suggests anywhere from a 50% solution (half concentrate, half water) to the undiluted

* According to *Pesticides and Wildlife: A Guide to Reducing Impacts on Animals and Their Habitat,* jointly prepared by the Virginia Department of Game and Inland Fisheries and the Virginia Cooperative Extension.

Planting Noah's Garden

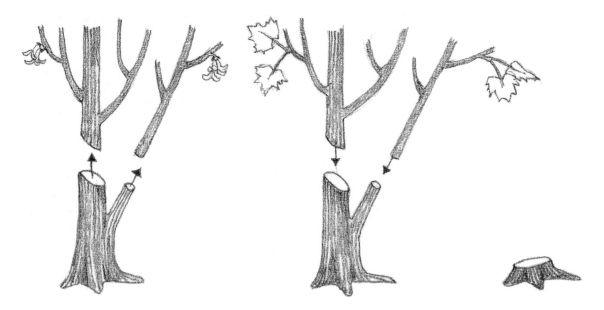

concentrate (100% solution), depending on the species. Those experienced in cut-surface application have found a 20% solution (1 part concentrate to 4 parts water) sufficient for most species. You need only a very small amount: 1 cup (8 ounces) is enough for a weekend's work.

Prevent spills by keeping the mixture in a jar with a screw top that you can close when you're not using it. A rubber cement jar, sold in art stores, makes an excellent container. The screw top has a brush that's adjustable in height so the bristles are moistened but not dripping.

In spring, rising sap pushes out herbicide applied to the cut surface. Cut the stem and apply herbicide later in the summer, when roots are taking nutrients from the leaves. The stem was cut high just for convenience in applying herbicide. Eventually, you can cut the dead stub down to the ground.

Using glyphosate for foliar spraying

Foliar spraying is the most widely practiced, wasteful, and potentially destructive use of herbicide. A spray solution of glyphosate kills any plant that's in leaf and photosynthesizing. To be effective, the spray must wet the entire leaf surface of the target plant; to be safe, it must not wet the leaves of other plants around or drip onto other plants below. To achieve this degree of control, you must be able to aim the spray down over the target plant. Therefore spraying is best reserved for low, thicketing shrubs, whose many stems would be tedious to treat individually with herbicide, and to vines and ground covers.

Cut the vegetation back early in the season to shorten stems; sever ascending vine stems from their supports. Any regrowth from this "pruning" will concentrate the foliar surface, giving you a clearer target for the spray.

Plants are most susceptible to glyphosate when they reach peak growth, when the mature foliage is most actively photosynthesizing.

Glyphosate is not absorbed by tree trunks or woody stems in the concentration used for spraying. By aiming the sprayer low over an invasive ground cover, the target species can be killed without harming any trees and shrubs that grow through it.

Choose a clear, still day for spraying. Wind carries the spray through the air; rain washes it off the leaves (and onto other plants). If rain is forecast within six hours of spraying, put the job off to another day.

Use a sprayer with a flat, fan-type nozzle. Chapin manufactures both shoulder-strap and backpack sprayers with interchangeable, high-quality brass nozzles. The fan type produces a larger droplet than round, adjustable nozzles, and the flat spray pattern gives more efficient coverage. Use a hand-held sprayer for small jobs and for spot-spraying the occasional invader.

A fan-type spray nozzle

Read the label information that comes with the product; mix glyphosate with water according to the manufacturer's instructions. If proportions aren't given for the species you're killing, choose the most dilute solution, not the most concentrated. A 3% solution—2 ounces (¼ cup) of the concentrate to 1 gallon of water—may well be strong enough. To avoid having to get rid of leftover chemical, mix only a half gallon at first. Get a feel for how far this quantity goes before mixing a larger amount.

Glyphosate doesn't harm plants that are fully dormant. Since quite a few invasive aliens are still in full leaf when native species have dropped their leaves, there may be a window of time late in the season when the target species can be safely killed without harming adjacent plants. Here, alien garlic mustard, Alliaria officinalis—a weed that is rapidly invading woodland in nearly a third of the country—is still green, but the leaves of native Virginia creeper, Parthenocissus quinquefolia, growing with it are paling and dropping from the vine. Spraying at this stage will kill the garlic mustard without hurting the dormant creeper.

There may seem to be an equivalent window early in the season when aliens have leafed out but natives haven't. Spraying at this time, though, risks killing germinating and resprouting plants whose foliage is not yet obvious. Evergreen species are vulnerable to glyphosate all through the year.

Sweep each plant once; spray it again from another angle only if some foliage escaped the first sweep. The foliage doesn't have to be sopping and shouldn't drip; it need only be moist. For very large areas, see How to Prepare a Grassland Site, page 426.

For more information:

Notes on Herbicide: Triclopyr and Fluazifop, page 437

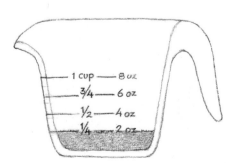

Add 2 ounces ($1/_4$ cup, or $1/_8$ pint) of concentrated Roundup to 1 gallon of water in the spray tank to make a 1.5% solution. A more usual strength recommended by the manufacturer is twice as strong—4 ounces ($1/_2$ cup, or $1/_4$ pint) herbicide to 1 gallon of water, or a 3% solution.

Whether or not you use herbicides to kill invasives, the first step is to cut them down or back. A good number of these species are tangled, thorny, crowded, or otherwise unpleasant to deal with. To spare yourself additional aggravation, use top-quality cutting tools, and have them sharpened professionally once a year. Carry a pocket hone to touch up blades as you work. Usually you'll need several kinds of tools for the same job. Get belt sheaths to hold the smaller ones, such as a pruner and hand saw. When you're finished for the day, spray the blades and working parts of the tools with silicone (available at hardware stores in aerosol cans) to lubricate the joints and prevent rust.

Most of the tools described here are available by mail order from A. M. Leonard (see page 324). The blades of Japanese tools are made of superior steel, which takes a sharper edge and holds it longer than American blades. The tools also tend to be lighter and better balanced. A limited selection of Japanese cutting tools is offered by Smith & Hawken, Two Arbor Lane, P.O. Box 6900, Florence, Kentucky 41002; or call 800-776-3336.

Loppers are the most useful cutting tool for clearing the stems of brush or vines up to an inch in diameter. Look for lightweight loppers with long handles, such as those made by Corona Clipper; their length lets you cut the base of a stem without painful stooping. Less weight is less wearying to your arms, especially when reaching. In addition, this brand features a shock-absorbing joint that cushions the palms; the model shown has wood handles that don't slip in sweaty hands.

A hatchet is used to kill trees by girdling. Choose the kind with a curved handle that looks like a small ax. Carpenters' shingle hatchets, which have a hammer opposite the blade, are not as effective. Choose the more expensive hatchet; its blade is likely to be a better-quality steel.

Planting Noah's Garden

Other tools you may need depend on the type of plant you're clearing. A strong steel rake is useful for "combing" thin-stemmed vines before cutting them back or uprooting them by hand. A mattock (see page 270) is good for exposing and cutting through shrub roots.

A Weed Wrench is a unique tool that uproots shrubs and trees by a lever action. The jaws, supported by a steel plate that acts as the fulcrum, clamp to the base of the stem; you pull the handle toward you to uproot the plant. Weed Wrench comes in three sizes. The lightest one uproots shrubs and saplings up to 1 inch in diameter, the medium weight handles those up to 2 inches; the heavy model uproots trees up to 2½ inches or shallower-rooted shrubs as thick as 6 inches. All work best on single-stemmed species; they are less effective on multistemmed ones. Consider this expensive, heavy tool only if you have a large property to manage and don't intend to use herbicide or if you are purchasing it for a community project. It's available only from New Tribe, 5517 Riverbanks Road, Grants Pass, Oregon 97527; or call 503-476-9492.

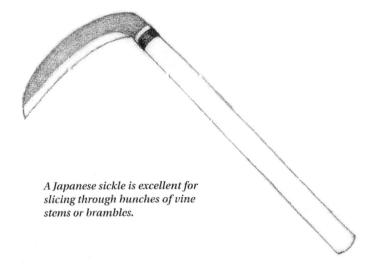

A Japanese sickle is excellent for slicing through bunches of vine stems or brambles.

A hand saw will cut through larger stems, from 1 to 4 inches. Bow saws, often recommended for light clearing, are too large for working in thicketed or overgrown areas. Choose a pruning saw instead. Look for one with a wood pistol grip and a gently curved blade that cuts on the pull, not on the push. (Pushing uses the triceps muscle, which is much weaker and tires more easily than the biceps muscle, with which you pull.)

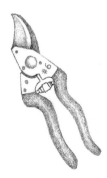

Hand pruning shears are needed to remove twigs that get in the way and to cut vines from trees. Felco makes high-quality pruners in many styles and sizes. Choose the one that fits your hand the best. Practice a cutting motion over and over again with the pruner before you buy it.

Gardeners in general are familiar with the weeds that beset their gardens, but the weeds that beset natural habitats are themselves garden plants, and for that reason they go unnoticed or are even applauded for their looks, vigor, or value to wildlife. Their control ultimately will depend on a change of attitude—and this is not easy when, as is the case in portions of ten states so far, a seemingly innocent species like common lilac is among the enemy. A special responsibility therefore devolves on those who become aware of the threat. As you learn which species damage habitat in your area, tell your friends, your garden club, and, most of all, the nurseries that sell the plants.

Recognize the enemy

Field guides don't distinguish between species that are merely "wild" and those that are barbaric. Agricultural Extension Services, though they may offer lists of field weeds and advice on their control, may not list those that infest natural areas (and may even recommend their use). State conservation agencies are better sources: inquire at Conservation, Forestry, or Fish & Wildlife whether a list of invasive aliens is available for your area. Native plant societies and other conservation groups are also likely to have information. Most helpful are illustrated sheets describing each plant and suggesting ways to control it.

Suspect woody species or ground covers that grow rampantly, spread to the exclusion of other vegetation, or show out-of-season behavior. Identify the species using a field guide, or send a sample to your Agricultural Extension Service for a positive ID. It is not sufficient to know just the genus of the plant, such as honeysuckle (Lonicera

To the unpracticed eye, these two honeysuckles are similar, but the one on the left is our reasonably civil native, Lonicera sempervirens (flame honeysuckle), while the other is the extremely invasive L. japonica (Japanese honeysuckle). Even when they're not in bloom, you can distinguish them by the leaf pairs at the ends of their stems. On the native honeysuckle, the upper leaves are connate, joined like Siamese twins. Those on Japanese species are separate.

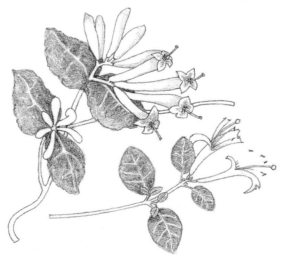

This white pine snag belongs to Stephen Kress, author of The Bird Garden *and* The Audubon Society Guide to Attracting Birds. *The tree is in his front yard. Rather than having the tree felled when it died a natural death, Steve had the top and branches lopped for safety and added several large birdboxes. The snag has provided homes for wood ducks, hooded mergansers, screech owls, gray squirrels, and honeybees. Sharp-shinned hawks perch on it to scan for prey.*

spp.). Be sure you can distinguish the suspect species from other similar, noninvasive or native ones of the same genus.

Check the suspect against a list of invasive aliens for your area. An example of illustrated sheets are those published by the Virginia Native Plant Society. They apply over large portions of the Northeast and Mid-Atlantic states and, for some species, the Southeast and Midwest as well. Instructions for control are suggested for each species. The fact sheets are sold individually by the Virginia Native Plant Society, P.O. Box 844, Annandale, Virginia 22003.

A complete list of invasive woody vines, shrubs, and trees (as well as herbaceous species) for every state and region is available from the Exotic Pest Plant Council. Write to the EPPC Governmental Liaison, 8208 Dabney Avenue, Springfield, Virginia 22153. While this list is not illustrated and has no instructions, it names all the states in which each species has been reported to be invasive.

Killing trees

Unless you're a professional, don't attempt to cut down large trees. The job is too dangerous; so are chain saws. Hire a licensed arborist to fell trees in the winter, when prices are lowest. An alternative to felling the entire tree is to have the arborist remove only the upper trunk and branches, leaving the bottom 20 to 30 feet as a snag. You can kill large trees yourself by girdling them; cut down small ones with a hand saw.

Cut small trees by first sawing a notch on the side where the tree is most likely to fall. Then saw through to the notch from the other side. Saplings can be sawed straight through without notching. Sever the trunk at any convenient height, but cut any remaining stub to ground level so people don't trip over it.

Girdling large trees is an option in woods where dead trees are a natural part of the landscape. The living tissue in a tree is a thin layer just beneath the bark. When the bark is cut through to the wood below, the tree above the cut dies. Girdle the tree at about the height of your thigh, using an ax or hatchet. The rougher the cut, the less likely the tree is to resprout from the base.

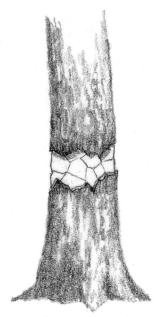

The cut-surface application of herbicide will prevent the resprouting of girdled or felled trees. This method works only if the cut is fresh, and it works best late in the growing season, just before dormancy, when the sap is descending toward the roots (see page 373). Paint the solution over the freshly cut surface with a brush according to the directions on page 372.

Uprooting small trees is feasible only with the Weed Wrench, described above, but it is the surest way to prevent resprouting short of using herbicide.

Killing shrubs

Killing an isolated shrub is no different from killing a tree, but when invasive shrubs grow in thickets or are crowded among other species that you wish to save, your options are more limited and the working conditions are trying. These suggestions may be helpful.

Be sure you can recognize the target species by its stem. Otherwise you may lop off the wrong plant by mistake. Or tag the species you want to save by tying a bit of plastic ribbon to it low on a stem where you'll see it while cutting.

Multiple stems of a single plant may range from slender twigs to thick trunks. Keep with you all three cutting tools: hand pruners, hand saw, and loppers.

Planting Noah's Garden

Typically for this annoying species, a buckthorn, Rhamnus frangula, has come up smack in the middle of a blueberry bush. The best way to handle these sneak attacks is to flag the invader with a Day-Glo pink plastic ribbon tie as soon as you notice it. That way, when you're on weed patrol, you can easily find it to kill it. Keep the roll of ribbon in your back pocket with the free end dangling; pull the end and tear off a piece as needed. Another hint: as you learn of each invasive woody species, cut a length of stem to use as a field reference.

Make your first cuts high; pile the brush out of the way so you can see what you're doing. If you're not using herbicide, make a second cut at ground level so people don't trip over the stubs. If you are using herbicide, leave the stubs high, where you can see the tips to paint them. The dead stems can eventually be recut level with the ground. Don't leave sharply angled cuts at any height. Always trim them flat so that they won't impale anyone who steps or falls on them.

Take down arching, thorny canes stepwise. Wear leather gloves! Start by lopping off whatever portions of the canes you can reach from the perimeter of the stand. Cut the canes into short lengths and stack them out of the way. Make a second series of cuts, and repeat until the stems are reduced to a tractable length. Species like multiflora rose, which grows from a central crown, can then be handled like any other shrub. Species like Himalayan blackberry, which spreads underground by rhizomes, are better controlled as though they were vines.

The cut-surface application of herbicide prevents otherwise inevitable resprouting, but one person can't simultaneously cut the stems and paint the stubs. Get a second person to paint the tips as they're cut. Follow the label instructions for mixing the herbicide. Dab the solution on the freshly cut surface with a brush.

The distinctive warty bark of this buckthorn provides a handy check against lopping the wrong stem by mistake.

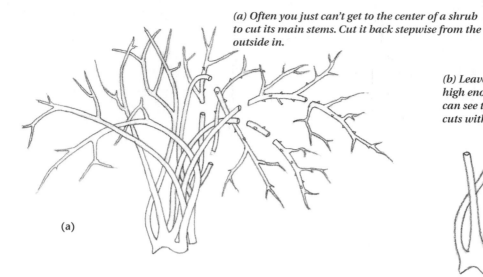

(a) Often you just can't get to the center of a shrub to cut its main stems. Cut it back stepwise from the outside in.

(a)

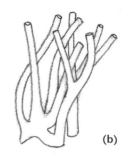

(b) Leave the middle stubs high enough so that you can see them to paint the cuts with herbicide.

(b)

(c)

(d)

(c) Later, when the plant is dead, you can cut it lower to the ground.

(d) Old stubs get easier to uproot as they dry and rot.

To grub out a shrub, first lop the stems to about 6 inches. Then use a mattock to hack around the base of the plant to loosen and cut through the roots until the central portion comes free of the soil. Grubbing is difficult if not impossible in rocky soil, with thicket-forming species, and where the roots of desirable plants would be injured in the process.

Killing vines

Getting rid of vines requires a combination of techniques that depend on the species and the form of infestation. An old vine that has sparse but thick stems can be handled like a shrub. Eradicating younger infestations or controlling species with numerous small or matting stems is more like killing lawn. Vines are exceptionally irksome; don't expect to work more than two hours at a time without relief.

Clear from the least to the most infested area. This may be from the perimeter where plants are youngest to the center where they originally took root, or from the dark interior where they grow sparsely to the bright edge where they grow thickest.

This is a simplification of actual conditions in a vine-infested area. Cut high, cut low, stack neatly, and take lots of breaks. It's okay if you can't handle lopping and herbiciding at the same time. Let foliage regrow from the stubs, and zap them another time.

Sever ascending stems first. Cut them low to the ground where they climb a tree or other support, then again as high as you can reach. Pull away these short pieces and stack them out of the way. The idea is to see where you're going and give yourself maximum free space in which to maneuver.

Clear the intervening ground before attacking the next group of ascending stems. Where vines mat along the ground like ivy, use a steel rake to lift or comb them to reveal their stems. Pull what stems you can by hand, or gather them into bunches and sever them with a Japanese sickle. If you run into a major root mass, you may be able to grub it out with a mattock (see page 270). Thicker-stemmed and deeper-rooted species can't be raised by rake or pulled by hand unless they're very young. For these, shuffle your feet along the ground to locate recumbent stems. Lop them off as best you can and pile them out of your way. You should now have a visually clear space that you can also walk through, but the vines have not been killed and will resprout. As with shrubs, you can uproot, recut repeatedly (with a weed eater, perhaps), or use herbicide.

Herbicidal options depend on the number of stems. If the growth is made up of a small number of thick stems, the vines can be killed by cut-surface application. This method, however, is impractical for vines made up of many slender stems; the better way is to spray the foliage when it resprouts. This new foliage will be dense, making it an

Light gloves suitable for most gardening aren't up to thorns and brambles. Work gloves in men's sizes are easy to find. Thick, well-made leather work gloves proportioned to fit women's hands are available from Womanswork, P.O. Box 543, York, Maine 03909.

easier target for the sprayer, and because you have cut off all the ascending stems, you can aim the sprayer low to avoid harming other plants. There may also be a window of time late in the season when only the target species is still in leaf; surrounding species won't be injured by glyphosate if they are leafless and fully dormant. The root systems of vining species may be so extensive, with such reserves of energy, that resprouting may occur and spraying has to be repeated.

Don't pull off the dead vines that remain in shrubbery or trees after you've severed them below; you'll just break branches if you try. Even massive quantities of dead vine that still drape shrubs or cover the woodland canopy will rather quickly dry, break, and drop away.

Managing reinfestation

Clearing disturbs the soil and opens it to light, thereby encouraging the germination of whatever seeds lie in the ground. In areas infested with invasive aliens, those seeds are likely to be of the very species that were removed. Until and unless invasive aliens are eradicated from the surrounding areas, their seeds will continually reinvade.

Practice an annual weed patrol late in the season. At that time most invasive aliens, even that year's seedlings, reveal their locations in full color. Choose a day after there's been rain, when the soil is moist and roots come easily, and simply pull the plants up by hand. You may be able to get away with patrolling only every other year. (Two-year plants are still fairly easy to pull by hand.)

What to do with the debris

A dense area strewn with cut brush quickly becomes impossible to navigate. Take the time to stack debris neatly out of your way as you work. Stack brush in separate piles according to length. Cut ungainly stems into more manageable pieces. Lay the brush with stems facing in the same direction and lined up so that later you can drag the stacks to other locations if necessary.

Large brush piles provide valuable wind shelter for overwintering birds. Small piles are not unsightly in the woods, and their gradual decay enriches the soil.

Brush and smaller tree branches can be chipped to use as mulch. Chips from toxic trees remain toxic for some time; use them to mulch paths, not plantings. Some towns maintain a center where debris can be brought for composting or chipping; the compost and mulch are then made available free to residents. If your town doesn't have this

A one-year woody vine, still easy to pull by hand

Planting Noah's Garden

Small mammals, such as weasels and ground squirrels, seek temporary shelter in wood piles and use them as secret highways, hidden escape routes, and roofs over the burrows in which they raise their young. The much longer list of occupants includes frogs, toads, salamanders, lizards, snakes, snails, spiders, and insects. The total number of creatures sheltered by a wood pile is much greater than that of creatures in a living tree.

service or if there is too much brush for you to transport, pay to have the job done professionally. Although chippers can be rented and small ones are sold for home use, they are dangerous machines.

Vines and brambles pose the most difficult problem of disposal because they're hard to handle and don't stack compactly. The extra labor involved in feeding them into a chipper raises the cost of that option considerably. Try to find an unobtrusive area where the pile can dry for a year or so. You may then be able to flail or trample the brittle stems flat to the ground.

Tree trunks can be cut into logs for firewood. If you don't need firewood, trunks are better left in large sections to decay on the ground, where they'll support a great deal more life than do living trees. Or trunks can be cut into shorter lengths, stacked, and left in place as wildlife shelter.

26 Creating Wetlands

The "hard" approach to controlling erosion along shores, banks, and streambeds is to line the area with reinforced concrete or to cover the soil surface with rip-rap—broken rock, sometimes held in place with wire mesh. These engineering methods are ugly and ungenerous. The "soft" approach to wetland restoration is to replant the surface with the help of various fiber products that stabilize the soil while the plants become established. Replanting creates wildlife habitat, and the vegetation evolves over time from the original pioneer community to one of more complexity and diversity.

Growers and suppliers

The greatest obstacle to home wetland restoration is the difficulty in finding sources. Only a few mail-order growers offer wetland and aquatic species as plugs that can be purchased inexpensively in quantity; more offer these species as seed or sometimes as tubers, bulbs, and rhizomes. Most commonly, though, you'll have to search the Yellow Pages for wetland mitigation companies and pick up the order yourself. Erosion control products aren't available directly from the manufacturer but are distributed by mitigation and restoration contractors. You may have to call the manufacturer for the names of distributors in your area. The specific products described here are made by BonTerra, P.O. Box 9485, Moscow, Idaho 83843; 800-882-9489.

Erosion control products

Fiber products serve several functions while new plantings get established. They stabilize the soil by cushioning the blow of raindrops and by slowing the flow of water over the surface; they hold moisture and buffer the soil temperature so the seedbed is warmer in spring and cooler in summer; and they provide a fibrous material in which seedlings quickly take root. Various natural fibers are used. Straw is the cheapest but decays fastest. Coconut fiber, called coir, is more expensive but lasts longer.

Erosion control blankets are a layer of fibrous material about ⅓ inch thick, sandwiched in plastic mesh (a stronger type for very steep slopes is made of coir bonded with latex to resist tearing). The plastic mesh eventually disintegrates, along with the fiber. The blanket sizes vary: 7½ feet wide by 90 feet long is typical. They come rolled like carpeting, and the material can be cut with scissors into smaller pieces of any shape—for instance, to fit a curved bed along a bank. They are intended for slopes, swales, or other situations where seasonal flooding or heavy rainfall causes erosion. The blankets are laid lengthwise in the direction of the water flow, with the top end tucked into a narrow trench and the sides of the strips overlapped like clapboards. The strips are anchored in the ground by large staples hammered through the blanket into the soil. They can be used in areas that are to be either seeded or planted with plugs, but because the material must be laid smoothly against the soil, they can't be used on rocky surfaces.

Erosion shows clearly at the top of this bed, where we ran out of erosion control blanket to cover the soil. Seeds of the sedge meadow mix we sowed washed off this portion in the first hard rain.

Where the surface was protected, growth was fast and lush. This picture was taken toward the end of the sedge meadow's first summer.

Left: A piece of bog mat planted with plugs of pickerel weed, Pontederia cordata, in shallow water at the pond edge. The picture was taken a few days after planting.

Right: A piece of bog mat, this one planted with plugs of arrowhead, Sagittaria latifolia, was completely hidden in foliage by late the same summer.

Bog mats are similar to erosion control blankets but thicker—up to 2 inches—and are intended for underwater use in eroding streambeds or along crumbling banks. These smaller mats—usually about 3 feet wide—also come in rolls, can be cut with scissors, are laid in the direction of the water flow, and are anchored by staples. They are planted with plugs, not seeds; roots grow into and through the material. Cut into smaller pieces, bog mats are useful for establishing underwater beds of aquatic plants, which, when planted in muck without this anchor, tend to loosen and float away. The bed in which bog mats are laid must be smooth so the mats touch the bottom.

Coir logs (BonTerra's brand name is BioLog) look like long loofah sponges. The standard length is about 20 feet, but the logs, made of the same coconut fiber as bog mats, can be cut shorter. Coir logs are used to hold the base of a steep grade along a watercourse where the current undercuts the bank. They're placed in a shallow channel right along the stream edge with the bottom of the logs below water, held in place with wood stakes. Planting is the same as for bog mats:

plugs are inserted in torn or slashed holes along the top of the log. Lengths of coir logs can be fitted between rocks if necessary, and any eroded bank behind them can be backfilled, covered with erosion control blankets, and reseeded to stabilize the entire bank.

Fascines are living material, bundled wands of thicketing wetland shrubs, ready to sprout both roots and shoots like pussy willows put into a vase of water in the spring. Like fiber logs, they're used to control erosion on steep banks, but whereas the logs are partially submerged at the bottom of the slope where the bank meets the water, fascines can be trenched into place stepwise higher up along the slope. Fascines can be ordered in specific lengths from wetlands mitigation nurseries, or you can make them yourself from budded branches of suitable wetland species such as shrub willows, osier dogwoods, and alders.

Wetland seeds

Mail-order growers specializing in prairie restoration offer wetland mixes of grass, sedge, rush, and forb seeds suitable for wet meadow plantings or shore revegetation. Species also can be ordered individu-

Erosion control products can be used in combination to stabilize and restore even steep banks. The coir log, staked in at the water's edge, prevents the undercutting of the bank. Behind it, where a previously eroded section was filled with soil, living fascines are beginning to sprout. The rest of the bank is covered with erosion control blanket seeded with a mix of wetland species.

ally. Quantities are based on area—500 or 1,000 square feet, for example. Regrade eroded sites first and remove the stones. Prepare the surface as for any grassland sowing (see How to Prepare a Grassland Site, page 426). If you're using erosion control blankets, the manufacturer may recommend sowing the seed on the soil before the material is laid; seedlings easily grow through the fiber. However, the tiny seeds of sedges and some other aquatic species need light to germinate. Consult the grower about what strategy to use or, for species that are hard to germinate, use plugs instead of seed. You can combine seeds and plugs in the same planting.

Wetland plugs

Young transplants, called plugs, establish faster than seed and may be necessary to hold steep grades quickly. The plugs come in trays like egg cartons that hold 50 or 100 plants grown from seed, bulb, tuber, or rhizome. You can order large quantities by contract; that is, you can place an order a season in advance, and it will be specially grown for you. Any number of herbaceous species are available, either from stock or by contract as well as both those in the catalog and others the grower may obtain for you.

A plug of blue flag, Iris versicolor. It won't bloom in its first year, but at this size, ten plants cost about the same as one mature plant at retail, and they'll bloom the second year.

Decide how many plugs you'll need. One plant per square foot will give you good cover, but you can figure up to 2 square feet per plant for species that spread rapidly or form large clumps. Plugs of smaller aquatic plants can be spaced as close as 6 inches.

Choose only a few species. Plugs for wetland restoration aren't sold in three-of-this, five-of-that quantities. For eroded surfaces, where the soil is generally sterile, choose tough, pioneer species such as common rushes, sedges, and wetland grasses. Forbs can be added later as the soil improves. You have more options if the area to be planted is in—not along—a pond or stream, or if the site is the wet, fertile soil of a marsh or swamp.

Order well ahead of time. Nurseries that supply plants in plug form often handle such a high volume that they may not be able to guarantee the availability of stock once the season is under way.

To plant plugs through erosion control blankets, use a dibble to open holes in the fiber into the soil below. If the soil is too hard for the dibble to penetrate or the roots of the plugs too long, slash holes in the fiber with a knife or make crosscuts with scissors. Then use a narrow trowel to open the soil. Space the holes a foot or so apart. Release each plug from its tray by pushing up against its bottom with your thumb.

A dibble. This tool, intended for planting small bulbs, works fine for plugging plants through fiber blankets if the soil below is soft.

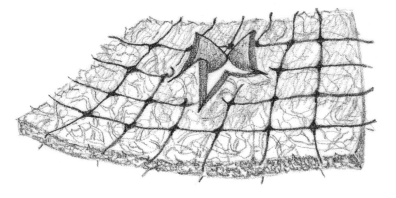

If the soil is too hard to penetrate with a dibble, either rip openings in the fiber blanket or make crosscuts big enough so you can jab a trowel through to plant the plugs.

To plant plugs into bog mat, soak it down well to soften the fiber. Slash the matting at intervals with a knife, then use both thumbs to tear openings in the fiber. Push the plugs into the holes; the thick fiber will hold them snugly. Contractors can handle whole rolls of planted bog mat and may line an entire streambed with them, or they may divert the water to regrade the bed and plant the mats in situ. This work is too taxing for amateurs. Use the material to establish patches of aquatics in shallow water in marshy areas or at the edge of a pond or stream. Cut the roll into manageable pieces, insert the plugs, then lower the planted pieces into the water. Staple them into the mud. If the staples don't seem to hold, weight the mats with rocks or bricks.

To plant plugs in fiber logs, stake them into position along the shore first according to the manufacturer's instructions and let them get saturated with water to soften the fiber. Then slit and rip the top surface at intervals, just as for bog mats. You can plant fiber logs with plugs of wetland herbaceous species or with rooted cuttings of woody wetland shrubs.

Fascines

Fascines are freshly cut wands of willow, osier dogwood, alder, or other thicketing wetland shrubs bundled and wrapped with twine or wire. The bundles are usually about 6 inches thick and can be ordered from

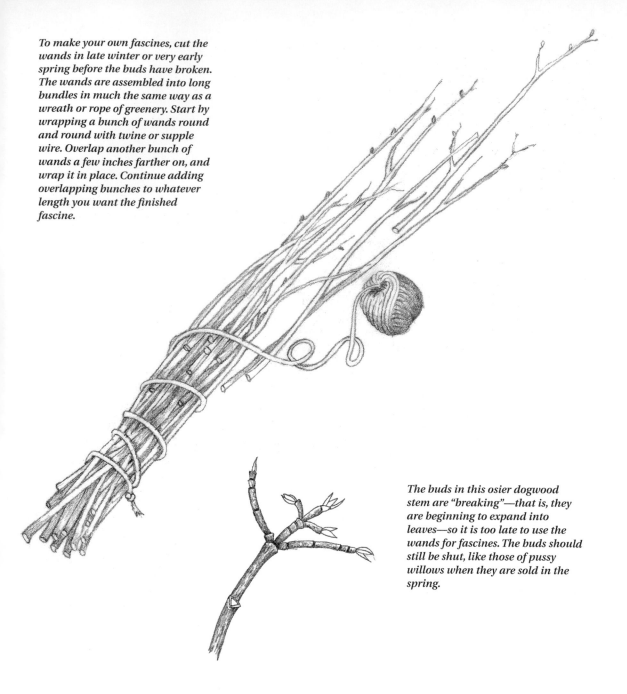

To make your own fascines, cut the wands in late winter or very early spring before the buds have broken. The wands are assembled into long bundles in much the same way as a wreath or rope of greenery. Start by wrapping a bunch of wands round and round with twine or supple wire. Overlap another bunch of wands a few inches farther on, and wrap it in place. Continue adding overlapping bunches to whatever length you want the finished fascine.

The buds in this osier dogwood stem are "breaking"—that is, they are beginning to expand into leaves—so it is too late to use the wands for fascines. The buds should still be shut, like those of pussy willows when they are sold in the spring.

a few feet to 20 feet or more in length. They are buried in trenches along disintegrating stream banks, where they quickly root and hold the slipping soil. Order fascines in the winter; they can be made up only during a short period in the spring. Prepare the bank ahead of time, as fascines have to be planted promptly.

The basic form of small backyard bogs and ponds is just a hole in the ground lined to prevent water from escaping. The suggestions here are for the simplest backyard wetlands to serve as summer habitat for insects, amphibians, and other visitors. They don't need pumps, filters, or wiring; they are merely basins of stagnant water that is renewed by hose or irrigation line as it evaporates. More extensive wetlands, including sizable clay-lined ponds where fish can live year-round or waterworks featuring streams and falls, require substantial excavation and mechanical and electrical installations that are better done by professional contractors.

The shape and size of the hole

Natural bogs and ponds are bowl-shaped, and there's no reason to deviate from this pattern for an artificial bog. Artificial ponds, though, don't have earth bottoms. Some portion of the perimeter is usually terraced to accommodate potted plants. The bog or pond can be round, oval, or irregularly curved; sharp corners are both unnatural and hard to line smoothly.

The area is a practical matter. You're not limited by the liner, which comes in even huge sizes, but by the amount of digging you can realistically manage and by the volume of dirt you'll have to dispose of. To do it yourself, figure a minimum of 25 square feet (5 x 5 or 4 x 6 feet) and a maximum of 50 (5 x 10 or 6 x 8). The depth should be at least 18 inches at the center. A bog can be shallower: 10 inches will do, though 12 is better. If you want some portion of a pond to serve as a birdbath, it should be no more than a few inches deep.

Don't buy the liner until you've dug the hole—it may not turn out quite the way you planned it.

Choose the site. Bog plants are available for both sunny and shady sites. Pond plants do best in full sun—but so do algae. A good compromise is a spot that gets several hours of afternoon shade. You don't have to decide between bog and pond. The two kinds of wetland can adjoin each other or part of a pond can have a boggy edge. The water supply is the nearest hose spigot; don't go too far afield. The site has to be pretty level, too. A spot that already tends to collect water is a good candidate; putting a wetland there will turn a problem into an asset. If, within these limits, you still have a choice, choose the spot that's easiest to dig!

Lay out the contour with a garden hose. The procedure is the same as for laying out a garden bed (see How to Kill a Lawn, page 268).

Dig the hole. Figure out first where you're going to put the soil; there's going to be a pretty big pile. (A good way to use it is to build

Layers and levels of a pond. The hole is basically a bowl with a flat shelf 9 to 12 inches below the water level to hold submerged pots of plants. An upper rim, shallow but slightly sloped, will hold a fieldstone coping to edge the pond and anchor the liner. A layer of sand can be smoothed over rough spots in the excavation to cushion the liner, but it isn't necessary if your soil is smooth. As the pond is filled and the liner pleats into place, the excess is trimmed with scissors about level with the surrounding sod. When the water reaches to just above the base of the coping, the liner won't be visible and frogs will be able to climb ashore.

a berm or mound elsewhere in your yard. A raised area can give you more privacy along the street or lot line or, gently contoured, add a little movement to a flat back yard.) Start by trenching the edge so you can get the hose out of the way. Then move to the middle and dig out the deepest portion. That way, as you continue to dig, you'll be able to grade the hole smoothly from the center depth up the gradually sloping sides. For a pond, terrace the contour to form a shelf that will hold potted plants. Rocks and roots can puncture the liner: pry or grub them out.

Finishing the surface and installing the liner

Buy the liner. Measure the excavation: depth, width, and length. The supplier—a mail-order water garden source or a pool company—should be able to figure from these dimensions the size of liner you need. There are many kinds, of various materials and thicknesses.

Planting Noah's Garden

The best are textile bonded to rubber for elasticity. Thickness is measured in mils (thousandths of an inch). The thickest and costliest liners—but also the most durable and least likely to get punctured—are 60 mils. Cheaper products are 32 or 45 mils thick. Wait until you have the liner in hand before you put finishing touches on the excavation.

Grade and level the edge. In a bog, the liner can just peter out at the edge under a few inches of dirt or sod to hold it in place. A portion of a pond may be similarly graded along part of the edge for a boggy extension: slope the bog bottom slightly toward the pond. Elsewhere you may want a sharp shoreline: shape a cut and ramped margin along which you can lay flat stones to define the edge and weight the liner. The top of a pond rim has to be level in all directions or the liner will show at the high spots: use a straight board and a carpenter's level to check the rim. Remove the soil in the high spots until the rim is level all around. A bog doesn't have to be so perfect because it will be filled with soil.

Spread a layer of sand over the excavation. Use mason's sand (available by the bag at lumberyards). Spread an inch of dampened sand over the interior of the hole to smooth the surface and cushion the liner. (If your soil is very smooth and your liner very thick, you probably can safely skip this step.)

Lay the liner. At least two people are needed to handle the large, cumbersome, and heavy liner; four may be better. Try to lower the liner gently into place so you don't disturb the grading or sand cushion. When the sheet lies smoothly over the center and you're

Laying the liner for a backyard pond

sure there's enough margin all around, start to weight it down by running water from a hose into the bottom of the excavation. As the water rises, tug at the edges of the liner to encourage it to pleat neatly against the curved or terraced sides. For a pond, fill the bowl almost to the top. Fill just the bottom of a bog, then install the irrigation line if you plan to use one. Shovel soil up to the rim before trimming the liner edge.

Trim and secure the liner edge. Use scissors to cut off any excess liner around the perimeter. Weight a bog edge with soil. Weight a pond edge with stones. Some of the stones should be flat and dip to the water's edge so they can be negotiated by small animals, but the shore will look more natural if some of the stones are large (and mossy!). Smooth pebbles can pave a shallow area for birds to bathe.

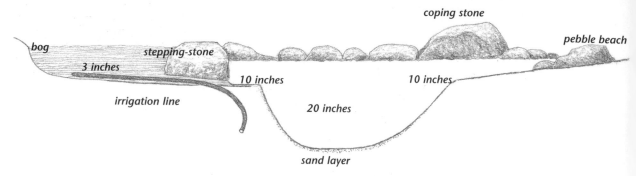

A combined pond and bog in cross section. The bog has an extra piece of liner, weighted with a large stepping-stone where the pond's liner overlaps it. An irrigation line is snaked between the two liners, beneath the stone. At the other end is a pebble beach and bathing area for birds. Notice that the water level of the pond is below the bog's surface and that the bog drains slightly toward the pond.

Pond and bog, seen from above. A little extra excavation is needed at the edges to accommodate various sizes of stones. The perforated irrigation line lies in a loop at the bottom of the bog (the far end of the line is plugged).

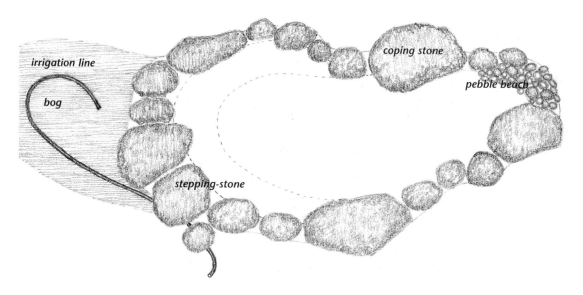

The pond and bog in perspective. The large stones between the two are stepping-stones. They could be part of a path. A few extra rocks make the bog look more natural. The pebble beach continues into the water to give birds a secure footing when they bathe.

Installing the irrigation line

A buried irrigation line spares your having to drag the hose around, but you can, if you like, just skip the whole business and water by hand. Or, now or at any time in the future, you can have the work done by an irrigation contractor (listed in the Yellow Pages under "Sprinklers—Garden and Lawn"). You might also then connect a line from the hose spigot to the pond for easy filling.

To do it yourself, look for a supplier under "Irrigation Systems and Equipment." Prepare a simple dimensioned sketch so the supplier can advise on installation and help you choose the right pipe materials, lengths, and connectors. Piping comes in two kinds: PVC (semirigid) plastic and poly (flexible) plastic. Netafin is a high tech brand of sub-surface irrigation line developed by farmers in Israel, but simpler types are more widely available.

Filling and planting a bog

Bog soils aren't commercially available, nor can you replicate any of the various kinds of soil that occur naturally in bogs. Some are sticky, but others are sandy. Some are extremely acidic, but others are limy. The soil you excavated, mixed equally with one part peat and one part commercial compost, should support species common in saturated soil. (The mix will not support insectivorous or other rare bog species

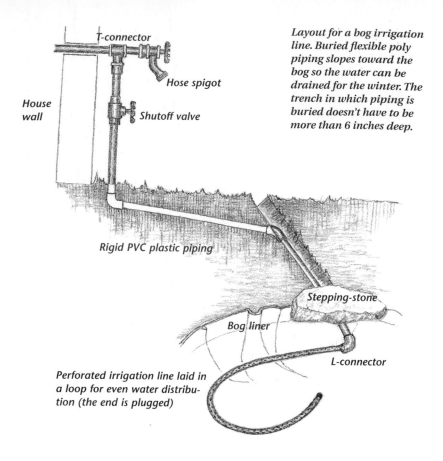

T-connector

Hose spigot

House wall

Shutoff valve

Layout for a bog irrigation line. Buried flexible poly piping slopes toward the bog so the water can be drained for the winter. The trench in which piping is buried doesn't have to be more than 6 inches deep.

Rigid PVC plastic piping

Stepping-stone

Bog liner

L-connector

Perforated irrigation line laid in a loop for even water distribution (the end is plugged)

adapted to anaerobic and nitrogen-poor sphagnum soils.) Fill the bog to the top. Walk over the soil to settle it in, then overfill the hole somewhat with more soil. When wet, the fill will settle even more, but if you irrigate it to a muck at this point, you'll sink into the bog when you try to plant it. Do the planting first, then saturate the soil.

Planting a pond

The edges of small ponds can be planted like any other wetland shore, with species common to pond and streamside—and, if you've designed an adjoining area of saturated soil, with bog plants, too. Aquatic species that root below the water line but extend their foliage above it have to be potted. Use clay pots filled with regular garden soil, not potting mixes (they're so light they float away); after planting, the surface can be covered with small cobbles to hold the soil. Choose at least one species whose floating leaves will shade the water. The plants you order will usually come with instructions on how deep each species can be sunk below the surface.

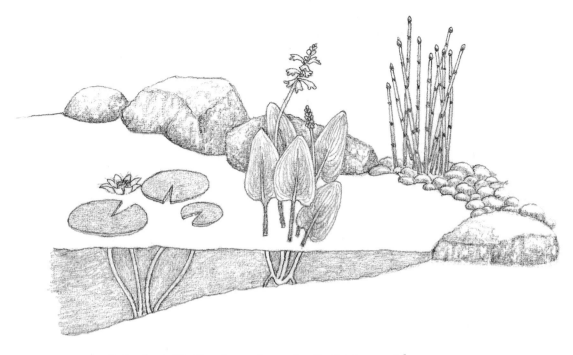

From left to right: Native water lily, Nymphaea odorata, has floating leaves; pickerelweed, Pontederia cordata, is an example of an emergent aquatic—one whose roots are in the water but whose leaves rise above it; scouring rushes, Equisetum species, really are terrestrial plants that can tolerate standing water but aren't obligated to grow in it.

Maintaining the water level

Check the pond water level or bog moisture every few days in hot, dry weather, or take a few minutes to irrigate daily. You probably won't have to water or fill at all during cool or rainy weather.

The last-resort yuck method for controlling algae

Controlling pond scum

Green pond scum is algae. Bright light, warmth, and excess nutrients cause an algal "bloom." This always happens in a new pond. The water usually clears in a few weeks as the other aquatic plants compete for nutrients and shade the surface. If the scum persists, it may be because there is fertilizer runoff from the lawn or garden or not enough floating plants to provide shade. Stop fertilizing! Add more floating species. You can also try adding algae-eating water snails.

🍃 SOPHISTICATED WATERWORKS

Many books explain how to construct complicated water gardens with circulating water and fountains, falls, and streams. Mail-order sources for liners, tubing, pumps, filters, and so on are listed in Barbara Barton's *Gardening by Mail* in the Product Sources Index under "Ponds and Pools" or "Water Garden Supplies" (see page 307). However, most of the waterworks so temptingly photographed for books and catalogs are professional installations, not do-it-yourself projects. You might want at least to speak to an expert to appreciate what's involved. Look in the Yellow Pages under categories such as "Landscape Contractors" and "Swimming Pool Contractors, Dealers, and Designers" for people who specialize in this kind of work. Some professionals offer workshops for homeowners who want to do their own installation, or they offer partial installations that you can finish yourself.

🍃 SOME COMMON WATER PLANTS

Wetland vegetation is more similar across the country than that of other ecosystems. Bodies of water maintain a more constant temperature than the surrounding land, and waterways provide easy transit. The floating seeds of some wetland plants are carried by the current; others have burrlike or sticky seeds that are dispersed by waterfowl. All the species here are broadly distributed, and some range nationwide, as much at home in the Southwest as in the Northeast. They are available from mail-order growers who specialize in water gardens and artificial ponds. For wetland ferns, see the chart on page 273; some wetland shrubs are listed in the chart on pages 282–84.

Submerged species
These grow in the water, never breaking through the surface. They hold the soil in earth-bottomed ponds and help to keep water oxygenated. Both are sold at pet stores for fish tanks.

Elodea canadensis (anacharis)
Vallisneria americana (vallisneria)

Floating species
True floaters such as water lettuce, Pistia stratiotes, drift on the surface with their roots dangling, and multiply so quickly that it is all right to scoop up a few if you find them growing in the wild. The leaves of water lily and water pennywort float, but the plant is rooted in the soil. Floating plants help to keep down the growth of algae by shading the water.

Hydrocotyle verticillata (water pennywort)
Nymphaea odorata (common water lily)

Emergent species

Emergent plants are those that root under water but raise their stems above the surface. The sedge and the cattail are grassy plants; wildflower guides will have pictures of the others.

Carex stricta (tussock sedge)
Orontium aquaticum (golden club)
Nuphar luteum (spatterdock, cow lily)
Poltandra virginica (water arum)
Pontederia cordata (pickerelweed)
Sagittaria latifolia (arrowhead, duck potato)
Saururus cernus (lizard's tail)
Typha latifolia (cattail)

Margin species

In natural wetlands, these plants grow in the water when it's high, but they can tolerate being stranded on the shore during drought. Look for the iris and sweetflag in a wildflower guide; the grassy plants in the list are depicted in *Grasses: An Identification Guide*, by Lauren Brown.

Acorus calamus (sweetflag)
Iris versicolor (blue flag iris)
Eleocharis montevidensis (spike rush)
Equisetum hyemale (scouring rush)
Juncus effusus (soft rush)
Scirpus cyperinus (woolgrass)
Sparganium americanum (lesser bur reed)

27 *Improving Woodlands*

 THE LINGO OF SIZE

Whether you buy woody stock in small sizes from a wholesale grower or in large sizes, as landscapers do, from a rewholesale yard, you have to know enough to ask for what you want, not only by species, but by size. These places deal with professionals in the shared terminology of the trade, yet size designations may baffle initiates, and their abbreviations in catalogs are more cryptic still. Here are the commonly used terms, their meanings, and their abbreviations.

Developmental stage

In their early life, trees and shrubs may be described by their stage of development. A liner (L) is a seedling or a rooted cutting, probably in its first season. The following year, if it is still unbranched, it is a whip (W). When branches develop, it is a transplant (T). Such young plants are used in large woodland restorations, but their mortality rate is high unless they are watered and protected from browsing during their first year or so.

Age

Age is more often used to describe the maturity of herbaceous species than to indicate the size of woody stock. Nevertheless, a catalog may describe a shrub as 2-year or 3-year. Figure that the plant is pretty skimpy, probably the equivalent of minimal transplant size. If the shrub or tree were larger, the grower would more likely offer a dimension.

Container size

Potted plants are moved into a larger container each year. If it is measured in inches of diameter, as in 3-inch pot (3"), the shrub or tree is

A seedling tree, or liner

likely a mere liner. Larger pot sizes are measured by volume, beginning with 1 quart. A quart pot suggests that a shrub has reached transplant size, but a tree in so small a pot is probably still a whip (fruit trees are sometimes sold this young). The next step up is usually to a 1-gallon pot (1 gal) or—another way of expressing the same volume—a number one can (#1 can). The following season, the plant might go into a 2-gallon container (#2 can) or, more usually, jump to a 3-gal (#3) can. All you really know from these designations is the approximate age of the plant—perhaps 4 years for a plant in a 3-gallon container—and the volume of its root system. You're safe, though, in picturing the top growth of a shrub as at least equivalent in volume to the container and probably broader. Where height is of greater interest, as it is with trees, that figure is usually given along with the container size (3–4' #3 can).

Height

Height measurements are typically given as ranges for two reasons. Plants of the same age, whether field-grown or raised in containers, may vary in height, and the height of an individual plant will increase in the course of the selling season. The height of plants is given in inches in the case of slow-growing species, such as dwarf conifers—for example, 6 to 8 inches (6–8", or 18–24"). More commonly, the height is expressed in feet, at first in 1-foot increments (1 to 2 feet, or 3–4'). Beyond 6 feet, the interval increases to 2 feet (6 to 8', or 8–10') and may again increase at heights over 12 feet (12 to 15', 15–18').

Width and foliage density

Occasionally a grower gives width dimensions for species where spread is an important consideration, such as for a plant like prostrate juniper, which is used for ground cover. Less often, a grower may want to convey how bushy the plants are by giving both height and width (2–3' h x 3' w). "Landscape size" may also be used to suggest bulk, regardless of height. Density of foliage and compactness of shape are often achieved by pruning. Growers may offer the same species at the same height in two versions—plain and heavy (6–8' hvy). Heavy means the plant has been pruned to make it bushier. For woodland restoration, width, bulk, and foliage density are not worth paying a premium for.

Caliper

At some point in a tree's growth, the diameter of its trunk becomes as important as its height in judging its landscape value. Trees that have been grown closely spaced may be tall but spindly. Trees of the same age grown widely spaced may be shorter but stouter of trunk. However,

An unbranched tree, or whip

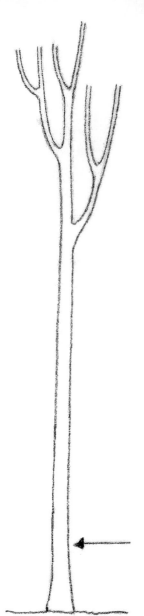

as a tree approaches maturity, trunk diameter is the better indicator of age. It is measured with an instrument called a caliper at the point where the trunk narrows from its base, a foot or so from the ground. Caliper is expressed in inches, in either ½- or 1-inch increments, sometimes as the only measurement and sometimes in conjunction with the tree's height (8–10', 2–2½" cal, or just 3–4" cal). For woodland restoration, youth and height give a tree a better competitive advantage than age or thickness does.

Cultivation history

The same nursery may offer plants—even plants of the same species and in the same sizes—in containers, bareroot, or balled-and-burlapped (the excavated rootball wrapped in fabric). Potted plants may

A field-grown balled-and-burlapped tree. This style of wrapping is called drum lacing.

Caliper is measured at the point where a trunk narrows from its base.

have been field-grown at some period in their lives (they may have been dug from the field and potted up for sale), but you can be pretty sure that bareroot shrubs and trees and balled-and-burlapped stock have been grown in the field. These plants are preferable for the rugged conditions of woodland restoration, but do be sure when you order to differentiate between a bareroot (BR) plant and a balled-and-burlapped (BB or B&B) one.

Yardmen may assume, when you designate B&B, that you merely mean big. Recently, nurseries have begun to offer trees in 30-gallon tubs that they claim to be equivalent to B&B plants and that may be substituted in an order that the buyer assumed would be dug from the field.

🍃 HOW TO START A TREE ISLAND

You can start a tree island by judiciously neglecting an area where trees are already established, encourage such an area by conditioning the soil and adding young plants, or develop an island from scratch using pioneer species. In all cases, identify seedlings that appear and weed out aggressive volunteers.

Neglect

Neglect is an appropriate way to start a wooded island where turf grass has failed. Mark off the perimeter of the island—an area roughly corresponding to the spread of foliage above—and stop mowing. Allow fallen leaves to accumulate. If native woodland species appear, the island

This typical suburban stand of trees is a good candidate for restoration. With encouragement, such as loosening the compacted soil and mulching it with leaves, and with the addition of young understory trees, shrubs, and ferns, it could become a cool and leafy wooded island in five years.

may be left to develop without further interference (except for weeding out unwanted species).

Encouragement

Possible problems that can't be overcome by sheer neglect include an existing ground cover that precludes the germination of other species, compacted soil, a windblown surface that doesn't retain fallen leaves, and no nearby source of woodland seeds. Here are some suggestions for encouraging a tree island.

Kill ground covers such as English ivy (Hedera helix), myrtle (Vinca minor, also known as periwinkle), wintercreeper (Euonymous fortunei), and pachysandra (Pachysandra terminales). See How to Kill Invasive Trees, Shrubs, and Vines (page 378).

Loosen compacted soil. A hard surface may not be able to support seedlings or incorporate decaying leaves. Break the surface into rough clods with a mattock or fork hoe before letting leaves accumulate.

Plant evergreen ferns such as Christmas fern (Polystichum acrostichoides) in the East or sword fern (Polystichum munitum) in the West to anchor fallen leaves against the wind. This is particularly helpful on high ground or steep slopes.

Enclose the island with a low fence of 12-inch poultry or plastic-coated wire mesh staked at 2-foot intervals. Add more leaves to compost in the enclosure. If you use leaves that neighbors are discarding, check the species first. You don't want to import the seeds of weed trees such as Norway maple and ailanthus by mistake. Oaks make the best mulch.

Plant seedling trees and shrubs. If you don't have nearby woodland to provide seeds, contact your state forestry department or Agricul-

A fork hoe. This heavy-duty tool loosens compacted soil with less injury to roots than a mattock. Lighter, four-pronged versions suitable for vegetable gardens aren't up to the job.

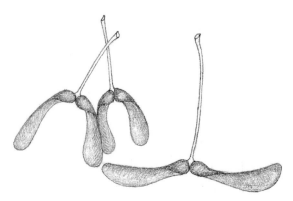

To avoid planting Norway maples by mistake, check the wings, or samaras, among discarded maple leaves before using them for mulch. The wings of native species droop, like those of sugar maple (left) and red maple (center). The wings of Norway maple (right) are wide open, almost horizontal.

tural Extension. One of them may offer seedling canopy and understory species. They'll need watering the first year.

Start an island from scratch

Choose from the chart Pioneer Trees and Shrubs (page 302) a fast-growing tree species native to your area or several associated trees and shrubs. Buy them as whips or in larger sizes and plant them directly in the lawn. Water the stock the first season, and mulch the island area until its own leaves keep the ground covered.

🍃 A NOTE ON RABBITS, RODENTS, AND DEER

Rabbits chew the tops of young woody plants; rodents girdle the stems. Where deer are overpopulated, their browsing is so heavy that few or no young shrubs or trees survive. As predators have become scarce and hunting illegal in developed areas, it has become nearly impossible to restore woodland and woodland edge without protecting the young plants at least until they grow beyond browsing height and develop thick, unappetizing bark.

Deterrent sprays

Sprays are mostly sulfur-based—they smell like rotten eggs. They do work, and they are practical for nearby plantings. But because they have to be renewed often and after every rain, they are not feasible for plantings at any distance from the house.

Plastic netting

Enclosures of black plastic netting staked into the ground work well for groups of shrubs or young trees where deer are the major problem, for the netting is nearly invisible from even a few feet away. It comes in rolls and is easily erected. Four-foot netting is sufficient against deer if it closely surrounds the plantings. Heavy net fencing for large areas that deer can jump into has to be at least twice as high. Although deer are good jumpers, however, their poor distance perception makes them reluctant to attempt broad jumps. Therefore an alternative to a single high fence to enclose a sizable planting is two parallel fences 4 feet apart and 4 feet high. The entire area, including the strip between the two fences, will be safe from deer.

Tree shelters

Netting doesn't bar mice and voles, and it's too much work to erect separate enclosures around dozens of individual plants. The better solution for isolated, individual woody plants is tree shelters, translucent

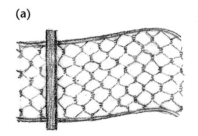

(a) One-foot poultry wire secured by wood stakes keeps leaf mulch from blowing off a tree island during its early years, but it doesn't bar browsing animals.

(a)

(b)

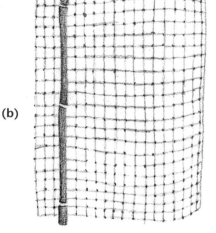

(c)

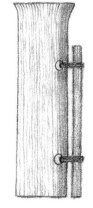

(b) Four-foot plastic netting tied to bamboo or other wood or plastic poles keeps rabbits and deer from browsing on young stock. Use this defense where shrubs and trees are planted in groups that can be protected as a unit. Two parallel fences 4 feet apart are effective in barring deer from larger plantings or whole properties.

(c) Translucent plastic tree shelters protect isolated trees from browsers and shield bark from gnawing rodents. By raising the temperature and humidity in the enclosure, they also dramatically increase growth. Tree shelters come with a stake and bands to secure them.

corrugated tubes that enclose young shrubs and trees. They were developed for growers and foresters, partly to protect young stock from browsers and partly to increase the growth rate, to minimize the amount of time a plant needs protection. The growth rate is accelerated because tree shelters, like greenhouses, increase the warmth and humidity around the plant. An oak seedling surrounded by a tree shelter typically grows in its first season to 4 feet—nearly the maximum browse height of deer. Rodents and rabbits are also excluded. The tubes, while perhaps the best temporary protection for young stock, are not attractive. Those made of polyethylene can be used for five years; those made of polycarbon break down after two years. Some tree growers offer shelters in their catalogs. Tree Pro is one mail-order source for flexible tree shelter systems for any width or height of stock. Call 800-875-8071 for a brochure.

HOW TO HANDLE B&B STOCK

Balled-and-burlapped stock may well represent the largest single investment you'll make in the course of restoration. Whether you're choosing and installing the plants yourself or hiring a landscaper, you'll need to judge the quality of the stock and see that it's correctly planted.

When to buy

Woody stock is available most of the year, leading one to assume that it also can be transplanted at any season. However, plants available in fall may have been dug the spring before and have sat around at the yard ever since. Planting during a dry season is not a good idea: irrigation can't make up for lack of rain. Some species, such as oaks, must be planted before they come out of dormancy in spring. For any species, planting timed to coincide with budbreak (the unfolding of the new leaves) is probably wisest.

Judging the stock

Select the plants yourself if you can, but don't limit yourself to esthetic judgments such as pleasing shape or heavy branching. The health of the tree or shrub is more important. Don't hesitate to ask the yardman to pull plants out of the block (the area where that species is stockpiled) so you can look them over carefully.

Signs of injury include split branches, scraped bark, or old wounds that show signs of decay. Don't worry about wounds healing with fresh callus tissue over sound, hard wood.

Compare the leaf size and bud density among trees of that species in the block. Opened leaves that are abnormally small for the species are a sign that the plant is in "shock" because root mass was lost in the digging. A sparse number of leaves or opening buds, or buds that are failing to open on time compared to those of others, also indicate shock.

Compare rootballs. You needn't choose the largest, but don't accept the skimpiest, either.

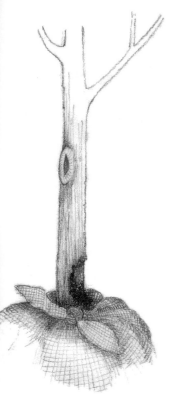

The old wound partway up the trunk is healing well; the callus tissue is fresh, the bare wood in the center is dry and firm. The wound at the base of the tree isn't healing; there's no callus around the edges, and the bare wood is soft with decay. Poor healing is most likely where water collects, such as in a ragged wound or at the base of a tree under the damp burlap.

Check the wrapping for type and condition. Any of three materials may be used: woven plastic fabric (usually green), synthetic burlap, and the real thing—burlap made of jute or hemp. Roots don't grow through plastic or synthetic burlap, nor do these materials rot. They have to be completely removed at planting. Genuine burlap allows roots to grow naturally and rots away in a year or less. Soft spots, a collapsed bottom, leaking dirt, or loose wrapping may indicate that the plant has been dropped and its rootball broken. (An exception is a shallow-rooted plant such as blueberry or rhododendron. They often can't be wrapped firmly in the first place.)

Don't choose trees too heavy for you to handle! Just to give you an idea of possible loads, the rootball of a deciduous tree 2- to 2½-inch caliper or of an evergreen 5 to 6 feet high measures 24 inches across by 16 inches deep and weighs 300 pounds. The next size up weighs twice as much—600 pounds.

Managing the unloading

The rootball of field-grown stock is very heavy and, unlike the pot-bound rootball of a container shrub or tree, it may be quite fragile. If the mass of soil breaks, roots may be badly torn and the plant's life jeopardized. This most often happens because the plant has been dropped off the bucket of a backhoe or the tailgate of a truck. Dragging the plant or lifting it by the lacing that holds the wrapping is less likely to injure it. Mishandling when the stock is unloaded at your home is more common than mishandling at the yard, and unloading may be your responsibility.

Decide where the stock will be kept before it's planted. The plants will have to be watered until they're in the ground. Choose a place that a truck can back up to, near a hose spigot, and preferably in the shade.

If you're using a landscaper, he or she will most likely deliver the order by truck. Be there to supervise: the stock should be lifted—not dropped—from the tailgate.

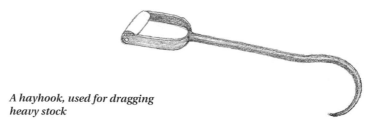

A hayhook, used for dragging heavy stock

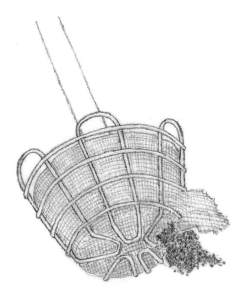

Burlap that has decayed beneath the rootball suggests that the plant has been sitting around for some months since it was dug. A second layer of wrapping signals the same thing: the first layer rotted through, and the plant has been rewrapped. A freshly dug specimen is always preferable.

If you pick up stock yourself, the yard will load it into your car or van. Don't leave stock in a closed vehicle: it can roast to death.

If the yard will deliver your order, ask whether the driver is responsible for unloading. Often drivers are not. Yards are accustomed to delivering to landscapers, who have the labor and equipment to unload stock. If unloading will be up to you, you'll have to know when the delivery will arrive and in what kind of truck. Good news is a truck with a hydraulic tailgate for lowering the stock to the ground. Bad news is a flatbed trailer 5 feet off the ground.

Aids to unloading include a plank ramp, wheelbarrow, hayhook, ballcart, two strong people, and possibly tip money. The plank should be a 10-foot 2 x 8 if the truckbed is high off the ground (you'll need it anyway for moving heavy stock to the planting site). The wheelbarrow is something you ought to have for moving anything heavy. Ask the yard to load a hayhook and a ballcart with the delivery: the hayhook is for dragging rootballs by their twine lacing; the ballcart, for wheeling stock into place. Two strong people needs no explanation, but if the trucker is willing to help with the unloading—as is often the case even when it's not part of the job description—a tip is in order.

Check the plants for new injuries before accepting them. Trees and shrubs are wound with cord to draw in their branches and hold them tight during shipment and transplanting. If a major branch splits or breaks under the pressure, you can request an exchange.

The lowest branch of this tree was broken in the course of tightening the binding cord.

Caring for stock before it's planted

All you have to do is keep the rootballs moist with a hose or sprinkler. If there's going to be a substantial delay before planting, heap mulch around the rootballs to cut down on evaporation.

Don't remove the cord that holds the foliage yet. Although it's tempting to free the branches to admire the stock, moving and transplanting are much easier with the branches bound.

Moving stock to the planting site

The no-sweat way to move weighty B&B stock is with a ballcart designed for the purpose. The plant is tipped on its side while the ballcart is wheeled beneath the rootball, then the two together are tipped back so that the plant rests in the cart's curved bed. Large, professional ballcarts have generous pneumatic tires that make rolling heavy stock around surprisingly easy. For some reason, though, companies that rent every imaginable electric or gas-driven tool don't carry this simple mechanical one. Before resorting to more arduous methods, see if you can borrow a ballcart from a landscaper or nursery. If you intend to plant promptly, the yard where you bought the plants may lend you a ballcart for a weekend. Otherwise, use one or more of the methods here. Most require two people.

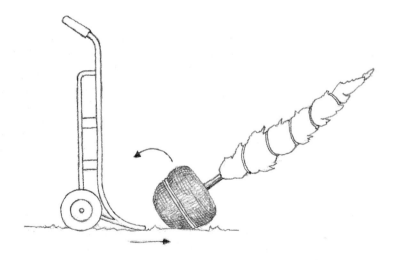

To get a plant into a ballcart, tip it over and maneuver the cart under it in an upright position until the bed of the cart is under the rootball. Push the plant up so it stands vertically in the cart. Then tip the cart and plant back toward you to wheel the stock into place.

Planting Noah's Garden

Short moves. Small plants with firm, light rootballs can be lifted by their stem or trunk to carry into place. Lift heavier plants by the lacings; otherwise the roots might tear from the soil. The rootball can also be dragged by its lacings over smooth ground or along a plank. Often even very heavy stock can be tipped over on its side and the rootball rolled into place along the ground.

A tree is tipped on its side, ready to be rolled onto a plank. Once on the smooth plank, it can be dragged by its lacing with hands or a hayhook.

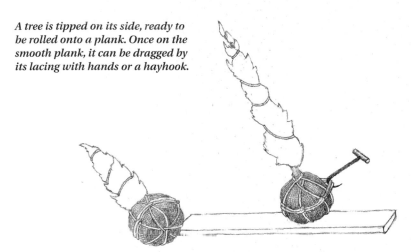

Hauling by wheelbarrow. Lift lighter stock into the bed by its lacing. For bigger rootballs, tip the plant over and lay the barrow down on its side so that the rim is under the ball. Drag the plant into the bed of the wheelbarrow by its lacing or roll it in. Rotate the rootball so that the trunk and branches are aimed forward. To right the wheel-

Weighting the load toward the front of the barrow makes it easier to push. There's a chance that when you right the barrow or lift the handles to push it, the trunk of the plant will hit the rim; cushion the rim with an old blanket or other padding.

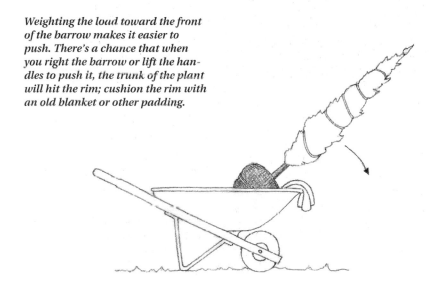

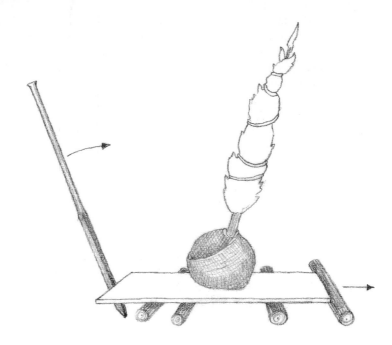

barrow, one person pulls the up side of the rim while the other pushes from the down side against the rootball. You may also have to steady the plant as it's wheeled into place and brake its movement as the wheelbarrow is tipped to spill it out.

Rolling by plank and logs. This is similar to moving stones on log rollers (see How to Move a Heavy Stone, page 356), except that here the logs are placed between the plank and the ground instead of between the plank and the object to be moved. Whereas a stone is rolled from board to board like a train on a railroad track, a plant stays on the same piece of wood throughout its trip. Tip the plant over and shove the board beneath the rootball (for very large rootballs, a wider piece of ¾-inch plywood makes a steadier base). Before righting the plant, ramp the board onto a log roller. Push the plant upright onto the board and drag it forward until the rootball is well supported. Lay a few other logs below the board and pry it (not the plant!) forward with a bar until it's up on the rollers. From then on you have only to nudge the board forward with the bar, replacing logs at the front as they fall away to the rear. Control direction both with the bar and by angling the rollers; use a second bar to act as a brake when moving up or down a grade. Leave the plant on the board when you get to your destination; you may need it as a ramp when you roll or slide the plant into its hole.

Digging the hole

Small shovels used for planting bareroot or potted stock aren't up to digging big holes. Use a full-size shovel. Except for the difference in scale, digging holes for B&B stock is the same as for potted plants (see A Note on Potted Stock, page 331).

Gauge the size of the hole with the shovel handle by holding it upright against the rootball to get a rough measurement of depth. Keep your hand at that level on the handle, and move the shovel into the hole to check if it's deep enough. To check the width, lay the handle across the top of the rootball and compare that measurement with the diameter of the hole. You'll need extra maneuvering space around the rootball for removing wrappings and for replacing soil. You don't have to dig the hole any deeper than the rootball, but you do have to loosen several inches of soil at the bottom and grade it flat so the plant will sit nicely. Roughen the entire bowl by jabbing with the spade before lowering the plant into place.

If you run into digging trouble, get help. You may hit hardpan that can be broken up only by a pickax. You may hit a boulder. The most difficult circumstance of all is thoroughly rooted woodland floor. Plants may be able to withstand these conditions, but you may not. If you haven't already hired a landscaper, consider getting trained laborers or a person with a Bobcat to dig the holes for you. Holes can be drilled in thickly rooted soil with a gas-driven augur operated by two people. This is definitely not a machine to be tried by amateurs!

To check whether a hole is large enough, use the shovel handle to gauge the depth (left) and width (right) of the rootball.

Planting the stock

Getting a really heavy rootball into its hole and maneuvering it into position at the bottom is hard work, and clumsy handling at this point can damage the roots. Plan your moves; take your time!

Lower the plant into the hole simply by lifting it if it's light enough; if it's too heavy to lift, drag it along a ramp. If the plant was moved by wheelbarrow, lean a plywood scrap against the side of the hole and tip the plant onto it. Drag or roll the plant to the bottom of the ramp; tip the rootball over to pull the plywood out. If the plant was moved on plank and rollers, maneuver the forward edge of the plank to a position over the hole, use a prybar to lift the rear edge, and drag the plant down the incline. The weight of the plant will tip the plank into the hole like a seesaw, and you can then extricate the board.

Position the plant in the hole. The trunk should be vertical and the surface of the rootball approximately level with the surrounding grade. To make adjustments, one person tilts the plant while the other digs out or adds soil beneath the rootball to lower it, heighten it, or straighten it. Maneuvering the rootball with a prybar is apt to damage it. If proper depth can be achieved by leaving a depression around the plant or banking soil higher around it, that is preferable.

Cut the cords that bind the branches. When the branches are free, you may see that the plant would look better turned a bit this way or that. Make any final adjustments now, while the rootball is still wrapped.

Remove the wrappings. Sever the twine around the trunk or stems. Cut away all the other cords you can reach. Take out the nails that also hold the fabric and pull it away from the rootball. If the fabric is jute or hemp burlap, you can just tuck it down firmly around the base of the rootball, where it will soon rot. Plastic or synthetic fabric must be removed completely. Cut it away from the sides with scissors or a sharp knife; tilt the rootball to cut or pull the remnant from underneath the bottom. (If the wraps aren't removed, the growing stem becomes strangled by the cords around it, and roots may never grow through the fabric. Landscapers, sad to say, often just shovel dirt over the intact wrapping; they are long gone by the time the plant dies.)

There may be a wire cage around the rootball. It won't interfere with root growth, but it is a nuisance. Cut it apart with wire snips, or step hard on the loops to bend them back from the rootball and out of your way.

Removing the cords and wrapping is a tedious but critical operation. The number of cords can be astounding! Both ties and burlap were cut away to below the soil line before this tree was backfilled.

Backfill the hole. Break up clods and remove turf or other debris from the soil you dug out. Shovel the loosened soil around the rootball or pull it into the hole with rake or hoe.

Soak the plant. Turn the hose to a trickle, and shove the nozzle as deep into the backfill as you can get it (see page 331). In a few minutes, as the dirt softens, you'll be able to push it farther. Let the water run until the soil is a soupy mush (move the nozzle a few times if necessary). The idea is to make the soil runny enough to fill any air pockets left around the rootball.

Staking may be necessary. Until their roots grow firmly into the surrounding soil, trees with small rootballs and heavy foliage—conifers in particular—may be tipped over by wind during rainstorms. Staking kits are sold at hardware stores and garden centers. Shrubs don't need staking, nor do trees with sparse branching and light foliage.

Finish the grading. Rake over the surface around the plant to smooth it. You may want to form a temporary moat around larger plants to hold water for irrigation. A 3-inch layer of mulch cuts down on evaporation.

You often see street trees supported between two tall, stout poles, but an easier way is with three short stakes. Kits come with the stakes, sections of tubing or straps to protect the tree's bark, and a roll of wire.

A moat is an aid to watering transplanted stock, but within two months, as new roots grow beyond its circumference, the moat prevents water from reaching them and should be raked away.

Planting Noah's Garden

Prune the plant. Thin the plant somewhat to decrease the amount of foliage the roots have to support. Clean out twiggy growth in the center; remove crowding branches; shorten the other branches. Growers suggest reducing the total top growth by about a third. You don't have to prune conifers.

For more information:

How to Move a Heavy Stone, page 356

OAKS AND OTHER NUT TREES

Taprooted oaks and hickories are best moved in early spring as young trees grown in tall containers. A few lowland oaks with more fibrous roots transplant successfully in larger sizes as balled and burlapped stock. Hazelnuts can be transplanted bareroot. Although the habitat of mature trees may be woodland, most need sun during their early years. With a few exceptions, fall foliage is yellow-brown. All these species ripen their nuts in fall, and range from intermediate to very high wildlife value. Walnuts (Juglans spp.) aren't included because although humans love to eat them, few other animals do.

name	remarks	height	soil	moisture	light	habitat	zone	region

CARYA (hickories) Although the three species here are avidly eaten by small mammals, only the pecan is palatable to humans. The wild pecan has a thicker shell than commercial varieties, and a smaller nut. All eventually grow very large, but smaller understory trees thrive in their open shade.

name	remarks	height	soil	moisture	light	habitat	zone	region
Carya cordiformis (bitternut hickory)	broad graceful crown	75 - 100'					4	2, 4
C. illinoensis (pecan)	massive structure	75 - 100'					5	2, 4, 5
C. ovata (shagbark hickory)	thick plates of flaking bark	75 - 100'					4	2, 4

CORYLUS (hazelnuts, filberts) Hazelnuts are woodland understory shrubs that tolerate shade even as saplings. Wild filberts are smaller than commercial varieties, which are partially descended from European hazelnuts. Don't expect to harvest the nuts: birds and mammals will get to them first.

name	remarks	height	soil	moisture	light	habitat	zone	region
Corylus americana (American hazelnut)	somewhat coarse thicketing shrub	6 - 12'					4	2, 4, 5
C. cornuta (beaked hazelnut)	slender, graceful, thicketing shrub	6 - 12'					4	1, 2, 4, 9

QUERCUS (oaks) Oaks are the most numerous species of nut trees, and certainly the most ornamental. Those here include shrubby forms that can be incorporated into hedgerows, medium-size trees useful for shading the small yard, and ones that eventually grow to be very large. Oaks provide a basic fall and winter crop for numerous animals.

name	remarks	height	soil	moisture	light	habitat	zone	region
Quercus agrifolia (coast live oak)	evergreen, holly-like foliage	30 - 50'					9	10
Q. alba (white oak)	very broad, rugged branching	75 - 100'					4	2, 3, 4
Q. rubra (northern red oak)	transplants well, shade-tolerant, very hardy	75 - 100'					3	1, 2, 4
Q. coccinea (scarlet oak)	shiny foliage, scarlet fall color	50 - 75'					4	2
Q. douglasii (blue oak)	blue-green foliage, medium height	40 - 60'					9	10
Q. gambelii (gambel oak)	glossy foliage, shrubby habit	10 - 15'					3	6

CUERCUS (oaks) *(continued)*

name	remarks	height	soil	moisture	light	habitat	zone	region
Q. garryana (Oregon white or garry oak)	shiny, leathery foliage; medium height	40 - 65'			◯		6	9
Q. macrocarpa (bur oak)	very broad, open branching	75 - 100'			◯		2	1, 2, 4, 5
Q. palustris (pin oak)	transplants well	50 - 75'			◯		4	2, 4
Q. prinoides (dwarf chinkapin oak)	shrubby habit, may be used in hedgerow	12 - 20'			◯	fields	6	2, 3, 4, 5
Q. lobata (valley oak)	small-leaved largest of western oaks	40 - 100'			◯	woods, fields	9	10
Q. shumardii (shumard oak)	large, shiny foliage, scarlet fall color	70 - 100'			◯	woods, fields	5	2, 3, 4, 5
C. stellata (post oak)	broad, chunky habit, cross-shape leaves	35 - 50'			◯	woods, fields	5	2, 3, 4, 5
Q. virginiana (Virginia live oak)	evergreen, shiny foliage, to 150' wide	60 - 75'			◯	woods, fields	8	3, 4, 5

421

28 Managing Grasslands

🍂 GARDEN VS. GRASSLAND

Restoring large areas of lawn or field to native grassland is a major undertaking. If your property is small, you're better off starting with a modest meadow or prairie garden that you can expand a little at a time. Keep weeding to a minimum by using just transplants and mulching between them until they fill in. Or, if you first "hold" a new bed by sowing it in native bunchgrasses, you can later dig out or herbicide clumps of grass where you wish to replace them with prairie forbs. A third option is to sow a permanent garden bed as you would a nursery bed, but using a mix of forb and grass seed. Previous sections describe the various techniques.

🍂 HOW TO PLAN A PRAIRIE

Although woods can be converted to grassland by clearing, the most obvious places to consider are lawn, old field, or clearings invaded by brush. Explore the area to see whether it's uniform in soil, moisture, and light or, instead, represents different conditions and therefore would support differing communities of plants. Consider also whether some features or some portions of the area could be improved without destroying the existing vegetation. Existing conditions will affect the design of your grassland ecosystem, including what suites of species are suitable and how the area might be divided for efficient management.

Identify any "good" portions that should be saved
The entire area, even if it's made up of alien species, may be attractive enough to you that it isn't worth the effort to destroy and replace it. Or, as you take an inventory of the area, you may find portions of it that

For more information:
How to Kill a Lawn, page 268
How to Sow Wild Seeds, page 312
How to Handle Bareroot Stock, page 325

show promise, perhaps a site where the plant community is mostly native or there is a nice stand of shrubs, a patch of wildflowers, or individual trees you wish to save. Segregate these portions so that they can be managed separately. Design mowed paths around them or, in the case of small patches of shrubs or wildflowers, plan to protect and encourage them with netting or shelters (see page 407) while you develop the surrounding area.

Investigate how conditions vary within the area

Soil, light, and moisture will affect which standard seed mixes will work best or give you and the grower you consult a basis on which to design the planting. The existing species in a meadow may give you clues about its nature. Even in an apparently uniform lawn, investigate whether there are drier and wetter portions, changes in soil texture, or differences in hours of sunlight.

Consider how the grassland could be divided for easier management

A small meadow can be managed as a unit, but a large grassland area is better divided by paths into smaller segments that can be managed separately in case you want to vary the regime for a particular portion or develop it specifically as a bird refuge or butterfly feeding station. Paths might lead to a special feature, such as a stand of trees, or divide moist from dry areas. If you intend to burn, incorporate broad mowed paths into the design to act as firebreaks, especially where the grassland abuts woodland or approaches buildings. Dividing a large area will also let you carry out the plan one segment at a time over a period of years.

On the next two pages is a strategic plan for restoring a large field to a variety of habitats using several different methods. The view is from a terrace overlooking the field. Several snapshots were overlapped to make a panorama (or you can use a panorama camera), then duplicated and enlarged on a color copier. The plan was first sketched on the copy with a pencil so it could be erased; final designations were made with a marking pen. Then the photocopy was traced, and vegetation was filled in using Prismacolor pencils (see page 302) to give an impression of what the restoration might look like some years in the future.

Learn what you can from prairie catalogs

You probably won't be able to draw up a detailed list of species at this strategic stage of planning, but catalogs will give you some broad categories to consider, such as "clay busters" for hard soil or "wet meadow mix" for soggy areas. At the very least, you'll learn what information growers will need in order to advise you on which standard seed mixes to choose or to design mixes best suited to your site. Note also any special criteria that interest you, such as species that attract butterflies, provide seed for birds, or add nitrogen to the soil.

For more information:

How to Make a Scale Drawing of Your Lot, page 294

How to Learn the Common Flora of Your Region, page 304

1. *A broad firebreak mowed against the woodland edge; other paths are planned for strolling through the meadow and for segregating portions according to their differing regimes. Mowed paths add flexibility to the plan because they can function as firebreaks if necessary.*

2. *A large red cedar, Juniperus virginiana, is to be the focus of a pioneer tree island that extends across a path to include several other trees. More red cedars will be added, along with birches and thicketing shrubs. Two invasive alien shrubs are marked for removal; the weeping willow, Salix babylonica, will be replaced with more productive native willows, such as pussy willow, Salix discolor.*

3. *A patch of shining rose, Rosa nitida, will be fenced off and encouraged to develop as a bramble. Raspberries may be added.*

4. *An area with a good deal of native little bluestem, Schizachyrium scoparius, will be restored by annual burning until the grass is reestablished as the dominant species.*

5. *The portion closest to the house, overgrown with multiflora rose and aggressive vines, will be cleared entirely, herbicided, and replanted with a preponderance of butterfly species.*

6. *For now, the largest segment will be mowed, raked, and lightly overseeded with a mix of native grasses and forbs. The hope is simply to improve it, not reclaim it. Other regimes, including burning, may be tried later.*

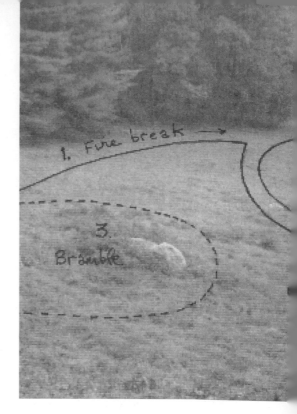

e island

(more trees)

← paths →

4 Burn this area

u & rake

rseed)

Replant w/ flowers →

5. Kill! →

Warning: Mugwort, Ar-
temesia vulgaris, is an
example of a perennial and
aggressively spreading
weed that may require two
full seasons to eradicate.
The root systems of such
species can completely mat
the soil, and even small
pieces broken off by culti-
vation resprout into new
plants. Any remnants can
rapidly and completely
overwhelm a new planting.

The failure of new grassland plantings sown from seed is usually due to overwhelming competition from weeds. In old fields, each cubic foot of soil may contain hundreds of thousands of weed seeds that remain viable for as long as fifty years and germinate as they are exposed at the surface. The existing vegetation may also include species that spread aggressively by rhizome and that resprout from rhizome fragments in the soil. Usually it takes a full growing season, from early spring to late fall, to prepare a site for reseeding with native grassland species. Exceptions may be lawn previously treated with herbicide to control broad-leaf weeds, recently abandoned fields of corn, soybeans, or wheat that also were treated with herbicide to keep down weeds, and new lots where the ground has been prepared for lawn but not yet seeded. You can cut short any of these preparation regimes if it's clear after a month or so that few or no new weeds are sprouting.

Clear, mow, and rake off existing vegetation

Cordon off any vegetation you wish to spare with stakes and plastic ribbon or protect it with tree shelters (page 407). Clear unwanted woody species using the methods described in How to Kill Invasive Trees, Shrubs, and Vines (page 378). If the area is large and badly over-grown, hire a professional to clear it for you with a bush hog. Mow the area very short, and rake it clean of debris and thatch.

Small areas (less than 1,000 square feet)

Use any of the three methods—smothering, stripping, or poisoning—described in How to Kill a Lawn (page 268). Or experiment with one of the cultivation methods described below on a small test plot (or one segment in the plan) before committing to preparing a large site for grassland restoration. This will take an extra year, but if you succeed your prairie is begun, and if you fail the loss won't be colossal.

Large areas (more than 1,000 square feet)

There are three options: spraying without cultivating, cultivating without spraying, and a combination of the two.

Spraying alone is the least work, gives maximum protection against soil erosion, is most effective with rhizomatous perennials, but cleanses the soil of weed seeds only at the surface and does not loosen the soil for resowing. Choose this method for slopes and places where the soil has a crumbly texture.

Cultivation alone is the most work, opens the soil to maximum ero-sion, is least effective for rhizomatous perennials, but cleanses weed seeds to a depth of several inches, prepares a loose seed bed, and doesn't use chemicals. Use this method only if you wish to avoid using chemicals.

Cultivation in combination with spraying has all the advantages of both methods but causes less erosion than cultivation alone and is more work than spraying alone. Use this method for heavy clay or compacted soils.

Cultivation without spraying

Machine cultivation is feasible for large areas in farm country where someone is available to do the tilling by disk harrow. You can use a rototiller on smaller areas, but the work is heavy, and the depth of the tines is hard to control. Heavily rooted soil, especially where brush has been removed, may have to be plowed before it can be tilled.

Cultivate to a depth of 4 to 5 inches, beginning in the spring to avoid erosion over the winter.

Repeat the cultivation at two-week intervals during the growing season straight through into the fall. This prolonged schedule assures that all weed species are eliminated, regardless of their germination time. Intervals any longer than two weeks will encourage rhizomatous weeds like mugwort and Johnsongrass.

Spraying without cultivation

Spray the area with a glyphosate herbicide when new growth is vigorous, in mid to late spring. Spray a second time when weeds green the area again in summer and a third time in fall to kill late-germinating weeds and any remnants of rhizomatous species that haven't succumbed to the previous two sprayings.

For even coverage, lay a string between two stakes for guidance, and use a fan spray nozzle (see page 374). About the right amount of wetness is achieved by walking briskly along the string lane with the fan spray held at knee height. At the end of the line, move the string over one spray width and repeat until the whole area has been treated.

A reel-type line is easier to handle than string wrapped around stakes. This one, made by Gardena, is widely available.

Cultivation in combination with spraying

Spray the area with herbicide when new growth is vigorous, in mid to late spring. Wait a few weeks until the vegetation dies, then cultivate shallowly—no deeper than 3 inches—to bring up more seeds. Spray again when a new crop of weeds appears, wait for that crop to die, then repeat the cultivation. You may have to repeat this sequence only three times: spring, summer, and fall.

Cover crops for erosion control

Where erosion is a problem, sow a temporary cover crop to hold the soil over the winter. Ask your Agricultural Extension Service which cover crops are used in your region and at what seeding rate. The ideal cover crop is a species that will germinate in early fall, root into the soil, but die before spring planting. A common choice is annual ryegrass, Lolium multiflorum.* Winter wheat holds the soil better but has to be killed in spring.

Conditioning crops for clay or compacted soil

If your soil is so hard that not even weeds thrive in it, it can be improved before planting with one or more conditioning crops (sometimes called green manure). Buckwheat, a summer crop, deeply penetrates even the hardest ground. Be sure to cut it down before it goes to seed, though, or you'll never see the end of it. Till the buckwheat thatch into the soil, and follow it with a cool-season species, such as winter wheat. Till the second crop into the soil in the spring. Your Agricultural Extension Service can suggest other soil-conditioning sequences for your region.

🍃 WHEN, WHAT, AND HOW TO SOW

Native grassland seeds can be sowed in fall or spring, but when is fall and when is spring in your region? In southern, arid areas, spring may begin in February and fall not start until late October, whereas in moister, more northern areas, spring may extend almost to July and fall begin in mid-September. Catalogs may also advise that grasses are best sowed at their natural germination time, whereas forbs germinate better if sowed in fall and left to the vicissitudes of weather during their dormancy. On problem soils with a high proportion of fast-drying sand or slow-draining clay, fall seeding also gives forbs a longer time to choose the best moisture conditions for sprouting. Rather than struggling to develop some optimal strategy for your circumstances, rely on the advice of the grower whose seed you order.

* There is a potentially hazardous confusion of common names here. Lolium multiflorum, sold in garden centers for seeding temporary lawns, is usually called annual rye, not ryegrass. But if you were to ask for annual rye at a grain supplier, you would get Secale cereale, the cereal rye that bread is made from. This species is allelopathic—toxic to other plants—and would seriously hinder the growth of your prairie. Also be sure that the ryegrass seed you purchase isn't the perennial species Lolium perenne, which is used for permanent lawns and will not die over the winter.

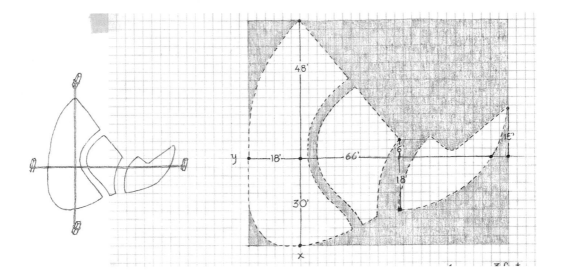

The grower from whom you order seed will need to know the area of your grassland planting in square feet. Sometimes this is easy to approximate: the area is
the whole (or a third or a half) of the front or back yard, and you can figure the
square footage well enough by sketching the planting area on your survey. But
grasslands on small properties may also assume strange shapes; the apparently
irrational irregularity of this one is explained by the plan on page 434. To figure
out the area of an irregular shape, plot it on graph paper as you were taught to do
in geometry, using x and y axes.

Out in the yard, use stakes, string, and a steel tape to measure two lines at right
angles to each other: the y axis is the maximum length of the area to be planted;
the x axis is the maximum width. The angles needn't be perfectly square; just do it
by eye. Make a rough sketch of the shape to record your measurements: you'll need
to measure the total lengths of the axes and the distance from the perimeter to the
center point where the axes intersect.

Draw the x and y axes to scale on graph paper. Choose any convenient scale;
here, each square equals 3 feet. Using the axes as a guide, sketch in any portions of
the area you can. The curve at the left here wasn't hard, but the rest of the pattern
didn't jell, based on such sparse information, so more points were measured in
the field and plotted on the graph. You can, of course, plot dozens of points measured from the x and y axes to achieve a really accurate curve on the drawing, but
you're aiming for only an approximation. A few additional points on the plan
were plotted here, and that was good enough to fill in the general shape.

There are a few ways to figure the area. For a simple shape, count the squares
in the shape. If each square measures 3 feet on a side, the area of each is 9 square
feet. The small portion on the right that looks like a rhinoceros horn contains
about 60 squares, or 540 square feet. For this complicated plan, it seemed easier to
enclose the shape in a rectangle and figure about what fraction of the rectangle
the area to be planted fills. The rectangle measures 26 x 30: 780 squares, or 7,020
square feet. The area to be planted appears to be about half of that, or 3,510
square feet. To be more exact, you could subtract from the rectangle the shaded
portion that lies outside the area to be planted. My result by that method was
3,447 square feet, not enough of a difference to be worth the extra arithmetic.

Contact one or two growers as you begin site preparation

This will give you plenty of time to order seed for either fall or spring. To help you choose species, a grower will need to know the site conditions for each portion of the planting. Jot down on your prairie plan what your investigations have revealed regarding light, moisture, and—very important!—soil texture (see page 286). Seed quantities are figured by area to be sown, in square feet, so roughly figure out the area of each portion before you call.

Standard and custom seed mixes

Pound for pound, standard mixes appear to be the best buy, but there's a catch. The grower, not knowing exactly what conditions to satisfy, may include a very broad range of species so that some portion is bound to be successful. You may therefore be paying for some species that aren't suitable for your site. Steer clear of vague descriptions, such as Northeastern Meadow Mix. Look instead for specifics, such as Short Sedge Meadow for Wet Mesic Soils. There are also mixes for particularly difficult conditions, such as dry sand soil or exposed clay subsoil. Custom mixes cost somewhat more than standard ones, but an optimal match of seed to site may be worth the extra expense.

The proportion of grass to forb seed will vary with the mix, but usually about half the seed—by number, not weight—should be grasses, the other half forbs. Of the forbs, approximately half should be pioneer species, such as aster, goldenrod, coneflower, and black-eyed Susan. These proportions will change as the prairie matures. Usually, the planting will settle down at about 80% grasses, 20% forbs, and short-lived species such as evening primrose and black-eyed Susan will give way to long-lived, deep-rooted perennials such as baptisia and butterflyweed.

Seeds in a standard mix will come in separate packages according to the way they're planted. Tiny seeds, like those of sedge and lobelia, may be combined for planting on the surface after other species are raked in, or a legume may be separately packed along with the inoculum (dried soil bacteria from which the plant obtains nitrogen) to mix with it at planting time.

Seeds in a custom order are all packed separately by species. This allows you to sow them at separate locations or to mix at sowing time groups of species that have similar needs.

The seeds of an annual grass or flax may be included in your order as a "nurse," to keep down weeds and shade the seedlings lightly in their first season. The nurse crop will die out in the winter. On erosional surfaces, you may want to add annual ryegrass to the mix whether it's supplied by the grower or not. You'll need 7 to 10 pounds per acre, sowed thinly.

A stratification medium, such as vermiculite, may also come with your order if the grower expects you to give the seeds some period of conditioning (see page 314) before planting. If so, the grower will include instructions.

Sowing the seed

Sort the packages according to where the various seeds or seed mixes will be sown. You can plant each species separately or combine those that go in the same area and have the same planting requirements. The bulk of the seed will be grasses, which you may want to sow separately from the forbs.

If necessary, give the area one last treatment to kill remaining weeds. You can sow right through vegetation that's been sprayed with a glyphosate herbicide without harming the seeds.

Rake the soil surface to roughen and soften it a bit. Use a steel rake on bare soil. A bamboo leaf rake will help to remove excess thatch from areas where you'll be planting through dead vegetation.

For a complicated plan—these five species in one segment, those two in another—prepare labels reflecting the groupings. Outline the segments on the ground with crushed limestone, and stick in the label to remind you what to sow there.

Mix one batch of seed at a time in a bucket with damp builder's sand or moistened vermiculite to whatever volume you think you need to sow evenly over the planned area. The proportion doesn't matter; it's perfectly all right to mix a mere teaspoon of seed with a half bucket of filler. Sand is easier to sow with but heavy to carry. Vermiculite weighs next to nothing but is harder to handle. In logging areas, you may be able to get rough sawdust, which is just about perfect.

So that you don't run out of seed before the area is covered, divide the batch of mixed seed and filler in half, and sow each separately. Sow one half while walking the area lengthwise, the other half while walking the area crosswise.

To distribute the seed evenly, walk at a leisurely pace while flinging handfuls of the seed-filler mix in broad, sweeping arcs as you would to sow a lawn. Don't sow the smallest seed until you've finished raking in the large and medium-size ones.

Rake in the large and medium-size seeds when all have been sowed. Just rake lightly to get the seeds in contact with the soil. Deep raking will bring up more weed seeds.

Sow tiny or dustlike seeds over the surface after the others are raked in. Most of them need light to germinate.

Compact the surface to settle the seeds in. Walk over the soil repeatedly, drive over it, or use a lawn roller.

How to tell weed seedlings from prairie seedlings

Compared to weeds, prairie species have a look of quality and substance even as tiny seedlings, but there are also two ways you can identify them. One is to cover a small patch of soil with a piece of cloth or sheet of plastic while you sow so that no prairie seeds fall on that spot. Anything that later sprouts there is bound to be a weed. The other way is to prepare a small garden bed in which to sow and label a sample of each species so that you can identify the seedlings as they germinate.

SOME GRASSLAND MANAGEMENT REGIMES

There is no one correct way to manage grassland, nor does a prairie or meadow planting ever stay the same from year to year. These are dynamic ecosystems that respond not only to your treatments but to whatever treats nature may have in store. Think of management as an ongoing experiment, and feel free to play around with the following suggestions.

The first two years

No matter how thoroughly you prepared the ground, there will be weeds. Prairie forbs and grasses may be so small their first year that they're not noticeable at all; even in the second year, weeds will be much more apparent than the species you planted, and the grassland will be disappointingly ugly. Management at this stage consists of keeping weeds from shading out the prairie and preventing weeds from going to seed.

Mow the grassland in the first year to 4 to 5 inches whenever the weeds exceed about 8 inches or before the weeds set seed. Rotary mowers and sickle bars leave heavy cuttings that cast too much shade. Use a reel-type hand mower set at the highest position, a weed whacker, or a flail-type mower that chops up the cuttings. You won't hurt the prairie plants by cutting off an occasional top or running over seedlings.

Continue mowing in the second year, but raise the height to 6 inches, then 12 inches over the course of the season.

The next three to five years

The fastest way to establish a young prairie is to burn it annually—at least for three years running, sometimes for as long as five years. Mid to late spring burning has several important effects. It shrivels cool-season weeds, which by their early growth otherwise have a competitive advantage over late-sprouting and slow-growing warm-season prairie species. Fire clears away the previous year's thatch, allowing maximum light to reach germinating seeds and resprouting plants. The blackened ash surface absorbs heat, warming the soil and jump-starting warm-season natives. The ash also fertilizes the soil.

Timing is important. If you burn too early in the spring, the weeds may not have grown high enough to be damaged by the fire. As a prairie becomes established, there may be reason to burn in the fall instead of spring, as explained later. Special schedules are also being developed to combat specific weeds, such as yellow star thistle, Centauria solstitialis, on Pacific coast grassland. The Exotic Pest Plant Council (see page 378) may be able to direct you to more information on fire management for stubborn infestations.

A permit to burn is necessary almost everywhere in the country. In some areas, it may be as simple as calling the fire department on the morning of the burn. Elsewhere, permits may be granted reluctantly and only under prescribed circumstances. Urban areas and places where air pollution is a chronic problem may not allow burning under any circumstances at all.

Research the burn regulations in your area. There is a hierarchy of authority. Your state may designate areas where burning is never allowed due to population density or other factors. Your county may

Don't play with fire! Before you consider burning, read How to Manage Small Prairie Fires, *by Wayne S. Pauly. This booklet, published in Madison, Wisconsin, by the Dane County Park Commission, is an invaluable guide to the safe and efficient burning of small meadows and prairies. It covers equipment, timing, wind and weather, firebreaks, and— most important— the hazards of burning. Most prairie nurseries offer it in their catalog, or write to Dane County Park Commission, 4318 Robertson Road, Madison, Wisconsin 53711*

restrict burning even where the state allows it. Your town, or even the subdivision where you live, may also regulate or forbid outdoor fires. You may have to contact each level to find out whether or how to proceed, but try county government first; county attorneys are likely to be familiar with the applicable statutes.

Burning for ecological reasons is more likely to be allowed than burning to get rid of brush, leaves, or construction debris. Certain words are handy: you are *restoring*—or preserving, or managing—a *native prairie ecosystem*. It is a *fire-adapted* or *fire-dependent* ecosystem. The rationale for burning is more powerful if your prairie ecosystem contains species that are protected in your state. Be sure to include a few in your planting plan!

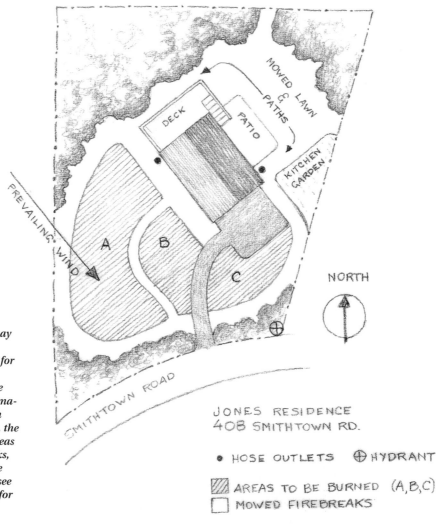

The sort of map you may be expected to submit with your application for a burn permit. Never mind the quality of the drawing; it's the information that counts: north arrow, wind direction, the location and size of areas to be burned, firebreaks, and water sources. Use your property survey (see page 293) as the basis for the map.

Planting Noah's Garden

The application form for a burn permit may be quite detailed. You may have to provide not only a map of the planting itself, with hose spigots and firebreaks clearly indicated, but also a map (available from your town office) showing the surrounding lots and access roads with the location of ponds or hydrants. Take your time; turn in an A+ piece of work. Be scrupulous, too, about complying with restrictions if and when the permit is granted. They may include weather conditions on the day of burning, prior notification of neighbors, site inspection by a government official, and supervision by your fire department. Realize that burning for environmental reasons is a controversial, even volatile issue, and mistakes on your part could result in others being denied permission to burn. Once you are granted a permit and have complied responsibly with any restrictions, annual renewal is nearly automatic.

If burning is not an option, mow instead. Schedule mowing in these years of establishment just as you would burning, in midspring when cool-season weeds are green and growing but warm-season natives are still dormant. Mow very close to the ground. Rake off clippings and thatch to expose the soil surface to sunlight.

Thereafter

As prairie species cover the ground and their roots form a thick sod, grassland becomes more difficult for weeds to invade. It never becomes immune to weeds, though, especially woody species. Continue to mow or burn annually for as long as five years where the growth is thin or weeds are thick. Gradually reduce the schedule in established areas—first to alternate years, then to every third or fourth year. Burn or mow only a half or a third of the total area in any given year. This will leave the untreated portion as a refuge for overwintering insects and nesting ground birds.

A bobwhite on her nest. Grassland habitat burned in the spring offers no cover in the nesting season. Overwintering insects may be killed by burning in the spring before eggs have hatched, larvae matured, or adults become active. Wildlife is best protected by a syncopated regime in which the total grassland area is divided into segments, each of which is managed differently (or not at all) in any given year.

Ordinary hedge shears are heavy and tiring to use. These light, well-balanced, and exceptionally sharp hedge shears sever even large bunches of stems at a single snip. The steel is Japanese; the shears are available by mail from A. M. Leonard (see page 324).

But stay flexible. No two grassland ecosystems are the same, and no one person's experience applies to them all. The "rules" below really amount to adages based on common observation and empirical research. For the most part, the reasons that grassland ecosystems respond differently to different regimes aren't yet understood.

Burning favors grasses; mowing favors forbs.

Spring burning or mowing favors grasses over forbs.

Fall burning or mowing favors forbs over grasses.

Use these adages as if you were a juggler. If your grasses seem to be thriving at the expense of wildflowers, mow and rake that section instead of burning it, or burn or mow in the fall instead of spring so the ground will be open early to germinating forbs. Shift the balance also in the more extreme habitats. Wet and arid grasslands are often composed of a mix of cool- and warm-season species—iris and dropseed grass in a marsh, anemone and bluestem grass on a sand moraine. The spring-blooming species are helped by a late fall regime of mowing or burning; the summer-blooming species by a midspring regime. Try shifting seasons occasionally or alternating them to keep the whole community in balance.

Special techniques for stubborn invaders

Most weeds that come up in new plantings are annuals. They're not usually a threat as long as you keep them short and don't let them go to seed; they won't be able to compete once the perennial prairie species fill out. Perennial weeds, especially those that spread aggressively by rhizomes, may take over as time goes on regardless of which regime you use. This is especially true of warm-season weeds, which include some native species such as rough-stemmed and Canada goldenrod as well as aliens like purple loosestrife and black swallow-wort. Woody shrubs and vines will inevitably colonize grassland, too, and these again may be aliens, such as Asian bittersweet, multiflora rose, Russian olive, and tree-of-heaven, or natives, such as grape, blackberry, birch, and cherry. Control them promptly before they get completely out of hand.

Hand pulling works well with woody species in their first year, when their roots are meager. It is less effective with spreading weeds. Rhizome fragments that break off in the soil grow into new plants. There is always a risk that hand pulling will uproot nearby seedlings and that the patch of disturbed soil will invite another weed.

A cut-stem application of glyphosate herbicide (see page 370) in late summer will kill older woody plants that resprout after fire or mowing. Use a special variation of this technique for rhizomatous herba-

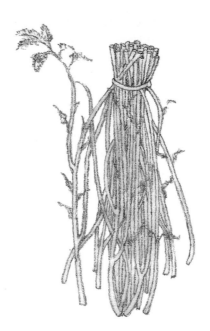

When herbiciding invasive species, avoid harming the surrounding plants by bundling the target plants into sheaves and applying herbicide just to the surface of the freshly cut stems.

ceous species. Wait until the plants are in bloom so you can identify them easily by their flowers. Bundle their stems into groups with string like sheaves of corn or wheat. Tie the string high on the stems but below the flowers. Use hedge shears to cut through the bundled stems above the tie, and immediately paint the cuts with herbicide.

🍃 NOTES ON HERBICIDE: TRICLOPYR AND FLUAZIFOP

Monocot- and dicot-specific herbicides may be helpful in grassland management if used carefully. Monocots are plants that, at germination, sprout a single cotyledon (seed leaf or storage leaf). All grasses are monocots, but so are lily, blazingstar, iris, and onion. Dicots sprout a pair of cotyledons. Most prairie wildflowers are dicots. Sometimes you may get a patch of native grass in which the only dicot is an invasive weed—for instance, bindweed in an otherwise pure stand of switchgrass. Or you may have a patch of prairie forbs in which the only grass is an invasive weed—for instance, quack grass in a patch of asters. Both these examples are of common weeds that aren't controlled by burning or mowing and that don't lend themselves to cut stem application with glyphosate. More specific herbicides are a possible answer.

Triclopyr is the active ingredient in herbicides such as Garlon, Crossbow, Turflon-D, and Confront, products used to control broad-leaved weeds and brush in situations where grass is to be

The single seed leaf of a monocot, a lily, and the paired seed leaves of a dicot, a milkweed. There are other differences: monocots usually have parallel leaf veins, and their flowers have three petals or multiples of three. Dicots usually have netted leaf veins and four or five petals, or multiples of four or five.

spared. The chemical is classed "slightly toxic" (the same as glyphosate) by the Virginia Department of Game and Inland Fisheries and is the preferred dicot-specific herbicide in restoration work. Unfortunately, few of the brands are labeled for homeowners,* and those that are (such as Confront) are available only through distributors, not retail stores. An exception is the Ortho product Brush-B-Gon, but the label restricts its use to woody species. Ironically, your best recourse may be to call in a lawn care or landscape maintenance company to spot spray for you! The job should be done early in summer when the grass is short and you can clearly see both the target weed and any valued forbs that would also be killed by triclopyr. One other possibility is Dow Elanco's product Turflon D, but it contains the more toxic 2,4-D as well as triclopyr.

Fluazifop has the opposite effect of triclopyr: it kills monocots, not dicots. It is the active ingredient in herbicides labeled "grass killer," including Fusilade. Fluazifop is classed as the least toxic of all herbicides. Remember, though, when spraying with this chemical, that sedge, rush, lily, blazingstar, and all members of the iris and onion families are also monocots and could be killed along with the grass if you're not careful.

* This is not because of toxicity or difficulty of application but a corporate decision based on profitability and other marketing considerations.

Planting Noah's Garden

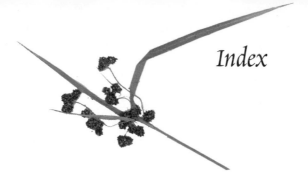

Index

Harebell (*Campanula rotundifolia*), 87, 100
Hedgerows, 41, 43, 278
  to attract birds (chart), 282–85
  dispersed by birds, 53
  workshop on, 38
Heirloom vegetables, 90
Hempstead Plains (Long Island), 134, 227, 228, 230–32, 242
Herbicides, 15, 21, 63, 180
  glyphosate, 271, 370–75, 383, 427, 431, 437, 438
  to kill invasives, 181, 370–75, 424, 436–38
  to kill lawn, 271
  to kill trees, shrubs, vines, 379, 381, 383
  toxicity of, 371–72, 438
  triclopyr and fluazifop, 437–38
  See also Chemicals, use of; Spraying
Hightshoe, Gary, 217
Honeysuckle (*Lonicera*), 174, 195, 212
  native and invasive, *379*
Honeysuckle Sipping (Chesanow), 69
Horticulture magazine, 52, 174
Horticulture vs. ecology. *See* Ecology
Hose, garden, *269*, 393
Housing developments, *48*, 49–51, 52, 147–48
  and children, 64, 65
  and natural habitats, 53–54, 203
  and obliteration of ecosystem, 12
  soil in, 26–27, 49, 50, 55–56, 58
  See also Suburbia
How to Manage Small Prairie Fires (Pauly), 433
Huckleberry (*Gaylussacia*), 10, 67, 68, 73, 81, 87
Hummingbirds, attracting, 158–59, 218, 355. *See also* Birds, attracting
Hydrology. *See* Water

Ice Age, 77
Illustrated Flora of the United States and Canada, An (Britton and Brown), 76, 77, 141
Indian grass. *See* Grasses
Insects
  ants, 5, 20, 26, 97, 159, 212, 214

beetles, 5, 21, 69, 248, 249
dragonflies, 21, 239, 240–41
grasshoppers, 156, 159
killed by burning, 435
ladybugs, 5–6, 248
pollinators lost, 280
skippers, 241
spiders (black and yellow argiopes), *154*, 156, 241
usefulness of larvae, 21, 241
See also Butterflies and moths
Interior, U.S. Department of the, 137, 139
Intrusive species. *See* Alien (invasive) species
Inventory of area, 274–77, 422–23
Iowa, loss of wetlands in, 24

Isle au Haut Mountain (Maine), 72, 78, 81
Ivy. *See* English ivy; Ground ivy

Japanese beetles, 69. *See also* Insects
Jerusalem artichoke, 25, 247. *See also* Sunflower
Joe Pye weed, *154*
Jordan, Marilyn, 227, 231, 232
Junipers, 53–54, *57*, 215

Kansas State University, 2
Kentucky Bluegrass Country, 12
Knezick, Don and Suzanne, 193–94, 195
Knotweed, Japanese (*Polygonum cuspidatum*), 237
Konza Prairie Research Natural Area, *2*
Kozlowski, Ted, 180
Krauss, Ruth, 89

Kress, Stephen, 355, 379
Kudzu, 170, 174, 178. *See also* Alien (invasive) species

Lacey, Louise, 242–43
Ladybugs, 5–6, 248. *See also* Insects
Land
  disconnection from, 68–70, 82
  "ownership" of, 16, 59
  "potentially" natural, 14
  See also Habitats, natural
Land abuse, 42, 43
Landscape plans. *See* Planning
Landscapers, professional, 23, 63, 114, 116, 417
Larner Seeds (California), 10, 242
Law, Polly, 33, 35–37, 40–47 *passim*, 82, 83, 84, 226, 257
Lawns, *18*, 19–31, 52, 237, 268–73
  deturfing, 75, 269–71
  difference between garden and, 30
  herbicide treatment of, 21
  housing development, 49, 50
  how to kill, 268–71
  "long-hair look," 20
  maintenance cost, 280
  "tree islands" in, *see* Tree islands
  See also Grasses; Mowing
Leather Man, 256
Leonard, A. M., 324, 376, 437
Leopold, Aldo, 243
Leucothoe 'Scarletta', 41
Levine, Carol, 348
Lewis and Clark expedition, 198, 199
Life of the Spider, The (Fabre), 69
Lolium multiflorum, L. perenne (ryegrass), 428*n*
Loosestrife, purple (*Lythrum salicaria*), 14, 237, 240
Loosestrife, yellow (*Lysimachia vulgaris*), 240
Lovegrass, purple (*Eragrostis spectabilis*), 76, 77–78, 81, 83, 85, 244
  germination of, 87, 91, 94, 101
Lowry, Judith, 10, 11, 242
Lupines (*Lupinus*), 245, 248
  taproots, 109–10

McKeag, Mike, 76, 183–88 *passim*, 196–98, 199, 210, 211, 249, 257
McRaven, Charles, 354

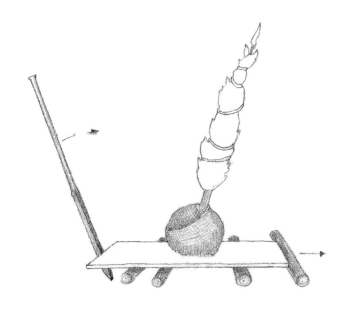

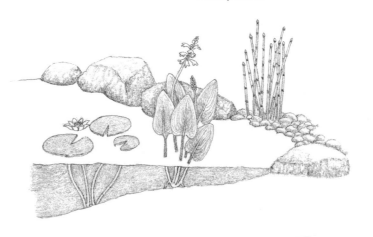